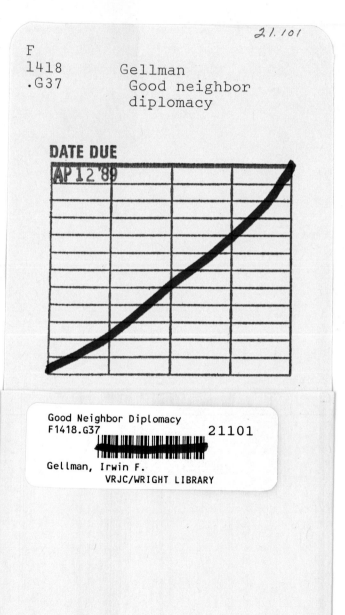

GOOD NEIGHBOR DIPLOMACY

THE JOHNS HOPKINS UNIVERSITY STUDIES IN
HISTORICAL AND POLITICAL SCIENCE

Ninety-Seventh Series (1979)

IRWIN F. GELLMAN

GOOD NEIGHBOR DIPLOMACY

United States Policies in Latin America, 1933-1945

THE JOHNS HOPKINS UNIVERSITY PRESS

Baltimore and London

Manufactured in the United States of America

The Johns Hopkins University Press, Baltimore, Maryland 21218
The Johns Hopkins Press Ltd., London

Library of Congress Catalog Number 79-7561
ISBN 0-8018-2250-5

Library of Congress Cataloging in Publication data
will be found on the last printed page of this book.

To honor my parents
    Albert and Mae Gellman
And those of my wife
    Horace and Lorraine Schwerin

CONTENTS

ACKNOWLEDGMENTS

During the decade in which I researched and wrote this book, many individuals assisted me. Without their assistance I am certain that my final product would have suffered. Thus, I wish to acknowledge the kindnesses that they provided. First, I would like to thank the library staffs that came to my aid. Patricia Dowling and Kathie Nicastro filled my almost endless requests. When I thought that I was finished, Mrs. Dowling provided me with additional matter until she, too, knew that I had exhausted her archives. Similar services were also given at the Library of Congress. Carolyn Sung and Charles Cooney suggested sources that I had not considered. "Chuck" especially wanted to be sure that I had examined even the most remote manuscript possibilities. Georgette Dorn of the Latin American, Portuguese, and Spanish Division cheerfully gave up her valuable time to locate material that I needed. Members of the staff at the Soper Library in Baltimore, Maryland, particularly Ms. Koyne and Mr. Padgett, filled my many inter-library loan requests for books and microfilm. To the archivists and librarians at the Franklin D. Roosevelt Library, Herbert Hoover Presidential Library, Hoover Institution of War, Revolution, and Peace, Harry S Truman Library, Columbus Memorial Library, Rockefeller Family Archives, Kansas Historical Society, Columbia University, Harvard University, Johns Hopkins University, Indiana University, Yale University, Princeton University, University of Delaware, University of Iowa, University of Virginia, and University of Vermont, thank you.

Various individuals read portions of this manuscript and provided useful information; they also prevented me from making errors. Ed Mishler shared his views on Herbert Hoover's foreign policy; James George, Jr., and Stephen Randall discussed economic issues with me; Wayne Rasmussen supplied material on Henry Wallace as did Sam Walker; Fred Ritter drew the no-transfer map; Leslie Rout, Jr., read and commented on Nazi penetration; Jonathan Utley confirmed my views on Japanese infiltration. Colonel John Child commented on inter-American military affairs and supplied additional material to support my conclusions. In regard to cultural matters, J. Manuel Espinosa and Frank Ninkovich shared their research with me. Finally Nelson Rockefeller and his staff, especially Hugh Morrow and Susan Herter, assisted me. Mr. Rockefeller held several extensive interviews with me on his role in government from 1940 to 1945, allowed me to use his oral history, and supplied me with documents from his private papers.

Others shared their thoughts with me and criticized portions of this manuscript. Willard Beaulac, who served in the diplomatic corps during the 1930s and 1940s, answered numerous inquiries on the personalities and policies of the era. James Roosevelt discussed his father's thoughts on foreign matters and the men who served in the administration. Wayne Cole allowed me the opportunity to hold wide-ranging discussions with him on a variety of topics in order to clarify my thinking by using him as a sounding board. John Finan and Donald Giffin also endured my questions and helped to shape my thoughts. Benjamin Quarles, Roger Trask, Martin Ridge, and Frank Freidel read sections of the manuscript and provided useful criticism. Finally, David Pletcher read and criticized parts of this book; his suggestions were greatly appreciated, for they surely aided in the improvement of my work's quality.

I would also like to acknowledge the professionalism shown by the staff at The Johns Hopkins University Press. Henry Y.K. Tom helped guide the manuscript through publication; Jacqueline Wehmueller saved me from making stylistic errors; and Mary Lou Kenney assisted in meeting the publication deadlines.

Lastly I want to extend my appreciation to my family. My wife, Barbara, and our children had to suffer through my moods and absences while I was writing and researching. I realize that I cannot pay them back for lost time; I only hope that they understand my idiosyncracies. I have dedicated this book to my parents and those of my wife. They deserve any recognition or value that comes from this effort. I alone, however, am responsible for the book's mistakes and errors of interpretation.

GOOD NEIGHBOR DIPLOMACY

PROLOGUE

O F ALL THE United States presidents in the twentieth century, none
has received as much attention as Franklin Delano Roosevelt. His
charismatic leadership and interaction with such epochal figures as
Winston Churchill, Joseph Stalin, Adolf Hitler, and Benito Mussolini have
produced a tremendous quantity of literature. William Shirer, reporter turned
historian, has written extensively on the rise and fall of the Third Reich and
the Third Republic in France. Popular author John Toland has carefully
detailed the military expansionism and ultimate collapse of the Rising Sun
and has examined the German dictator's life. Herbert Feis, economic adviser
to the State Department during the 1930s and early 1940s, retired to write a
series of books on the confrontations in Europe and Asia.

In comparison with the treatment given these titanic struggles, Latin
America has virtually been ignored. As a result, the concentration on the
movement leading to and the participation during World War II has distorted
the motivation of the United States, and needs correction. For the Roosevelt
administration's efforts in Latin America were intimately connected to international events elsewhere.

This hemispheric neglect is somewhat startling. Relatively few scholars
have written on the varied aspects of Roosevelt's Latin American emphasis.
Some have gone so far as to claim that earlier administrations had conceived
the Democratic policies, but this assertion is not substantiated by the record.
A few connections did apply, but this is valid for almost any cause and effect
relationship. Roosevelt's hemispheric diplomacy was a set of actions and reactions to unique circumstances. Accidentally labeled the "Good Neighbor"
at the start of the his first term, this simplistic phrase, in reality, covered the
complex totality of inter-American efforts from 1933 to 1945. The terminol-
ogy provided a convenient umbrella under which to lump various proposals.
The Good Neighbor did not have a precise definition in the public mind, but
this was inconsequential. It had enormous popular appeal and recognition.
The rhetoric created a positive atmosphere, and Roosevelt constantly alluded
to that spirit in order to accelerate momentum at home as well as in Latin
America.

When Good Neighbor diplomacy is separated into its components, sophisticated policies emerge. The United States ended many of its interventionist

1

practices in the Caribbean because their presence became a burden to American taxpayers and a convenient and legitimate target for critics. The government initiated economic measures during the depression that gradually merged, during wartime, into the first concerted foreign aid programs. Cultural and military contacts became major diplomatic considerations, and multilateral cooperation under the heading of the inter-American system received attention unheard of in earlier times.

The writers who relegate Latin American affairs to a secondary place— or completely ignore them—and devote their focus to the deepening European and Far Eastern crises have misconstrued Roosevelt's intentions. He knew that a skeptical Congress and public limited his diplomatic flexibility in regard to the Axis, while they concurrently accepted greater Latin American involvement. He accepted this political reality and used it in his crusade against Germany. He incorporated this regional base to influence other areas, and took advantage of support for inter-American defense and fear of Nazi hemispheric penetration to delineate a security zone and announce an explicit no-transfer statement.

The Good Neighbor was more than innovative projects and challenges from abroad; the driving ambitions of men to achieve their own personal goals were inseparable. The integral relationship between the president, Secretary of State Cordell Hull, and Undersecretary of State Sumner Welles was essential to the conduct of foreign affairs. The trio's association was a combination of respect and distrust, and when the latter triumphed in the summer of 1943, it helped destroy a decade's work. In the next two years the Good Neighbor began cracking, and victory over the enemy marked the end of the diplomatic triumvirate that enacted Latin American policy: Welles left first, in disgrace, followed by Hull's resignation because of poor health, and shortly afterward, Roosevelt died.

These human factors plus the critical nature of the Good Neighbor in world events graphically portrayed its vitality in Roosevelt's presidency. The steps taken in hemispheric matters also established models for postwar economic, military, and cultural legislation. These activities have not been systematically explored, and as a consequence the international picture painted during the Democratic rule is incomplete and needs significant revision.

1 ★ THE REPUBLICAN PRELUDE

T HE CONSENSUS of those who have written on United States-Latin American relations from the 1920s to the Great Depression is that the Good Neighbor had its antecedents in the administrations of the three preceding Republican presidents. Some continuity did exist, as it has throughout most of our history. This fact, however, did not guarantee consistent guidelines to follow. Just the opposite occurred. When the Democrats entered office, some steps had been taken, but they had not been woven into a sophisticated pattern.

The Republican predecessors had not plotted a careful hemispheric course, and without this clear direction, each president had emphasized his own individual causes. Secretaries of State Charles E. Hughes under Warren Harding and Frank Kellogg during Calvin Coolidge's administration generally relegated the Americas to an arena of secondary importance. Even Henry Stimson, who headed a special mission to Nicaragua in 1927, did not personally spend a great deal of energy on inter-American affairs after becoming secretary of state in Herbert Hoover's cabinet.[1]

Throughout most of this era the State Department leadership principally deferred to Francis White to handle Latin American issues. Born in 1892, White came from a patrician family in Baltimore, where he attended private schools; he then went on to graduate from Yale in 1913. Two years later he entered the foreign service as a career befitting his social class and appealing to his sense of patriotism. His first contact in the Americas started in 1920, when he was stationed in Cuba; the next year he was transferred to Buenos Aires. Returning to Washington in 1922, he became chief of the Latin American division and held that position for four years. After a short assignment in Spain, Kellogg chose him to serve as assistant secretary of state for Latin American affairs in 1927, a post he occupied until 1933.

White progressed rapidly within diplomatic ranks, becoming the department's leading Latin American expert. His primary purpose was to better what existed rather than strike out on bold initiatives. Using this philosophy, he closely scrutinized regional diplomatic appointments. Until his assistant secretaryship, most foreign service officers looked upon hemispheric positions as punishment duty; the bright career men were chosen for European or Far

Eastern service. As a result, ten of eighteen ambassadors and ministers in the Americas were political appointees in 1929; two years later, only three remained; the others were replaced by career officers. White was primarily responsible for this change.[2]

Along with upgrading personnel, White played a central role in terminating the military occupations in the Caribbean region. The United States had constructed these at the turn of the twentieth century to guarantee stability, secure the Panama Canal's defenses, and prevent the development of any European excuse to meddle in hemispheric matters. After World War I, with undisputed United States hegemony assured, the outside threat disappeared and so did the rationale for troop deployment. These soldiers, in addition, did not bring stability. Instead of winning Latin American gratitude, these armed forces caused critics throughout the Americas to cry out against United States imperialism. These adverse sentiments plus dwindling depression revenues stimulated the already existing undercurrent for military withdrawal.[3]

One example of this momentum came in Haiti. Woodrow Wilson originally sent troops into that nation to prevent a bloody confrontation. Once internal conditions improved, the United States pressed for local reforms and, at the same time, sought to reduce its military presence. Agitation to end the occupation gained support during the 1920s, and President Hoover added to this movement, when he publicly criticized the necessity of keeping soldiers in that nation. With this strong presidential position, the State Department succeeded in signing a treaty that granted the Haitians partial sovereignty, on September 3, 1932, but their congress wanted total independence. The Haitain president had underestimated this congressional sentiment; the treaty was rejected.[4]

Nicaraguan negotiations were far more fruitful. Marines had landed on several occasions since 1911 to restore order and maintain peace, but the desired results were not achieved. Stimson, who had directly witnessed that nation's difficulties, realized the futility in stationing troops there, for over the period of billeting, American personnel had become too closely involved with domestic decisions. Under the Hoover administration, the United States supervised national elections. The presidential victor ruled with the assistance of a national guard trained by United States Marines. Leaving behind this semblance of peace, the last soldiers departed for home at the beginning of 1933.[5]

Bargaining with Mexico was less rewarding. After the Mexican Revolution of 1910, Wilson sent troops across the border on two occasions. Mexican nationalists charged the United States with violating their sovereignty, and this conflict further deteriorated relations. Troubles also arose in the 1920s over debts owed to American citizens arising from the revolution's devastation, agrarian claims stemming out of expropriated lands, and oil disputes between foreign companies and the Mexican government concerning royalties and ownership rights. These three issues plagued both nations and were topics of frequent diplomatic exchanges. The Bucareli agreements in 1923 and Dwight Morrow's mission to Mexico six years later provided temporary solutions to these vexing problems. These short-lived answers did not satisfy either party. The United States insisted on the protection and sanctity of private property rights, while the Mexicans asserted that their national self-interest took precedence over foreign demands.[6]

The adherence to an outdated nonrecognition policy in Central America diminished the benefits derived from the efforts to end the armed presence in the Caribbean. Wilson had modified the traditional de facto policy by refusing to recognize the provisional Mexican government of Victoriano Huerta because it lacked "constitutional legitimacy." Harding went further by signing a nonrecognition treaty with the Central American republics in 1923, denying recognition to revolutionary regimes. This treaty temporarily preserved an uneasy status quo, for without normal United States relations, revolutionaries would have trouble maintaining control. Opponents to the treaty argued that it was a form of intervention, for many of the existing governments were repressive. The United States dismissed this reasoning as well as the fact that coups d'états were a traditional method for ousting unpopular rulers in the region.

Hoover honored this commitment. He refused to recognize a revolt in Guatemala during 1930, but his position did not end the disorder. Near the end of 1931 he followed a similar course in El Salvador. Despite the treaty's invocation, the new dictator maintained order and even broadened his base of support. A year later several European nations formalized relations. Some Central American nations intended to take the same action, which would have violated the 1923 treaty and made it obsolete. But Hoover held firm, maintaining an unenforceable policy and creating confusion in the area.[7]

The publication of the *Memorandum on the Monroe Doctrine* in 1930 also bewildered many observers. Written at the end of 1928 by Undersecretary of State J. Reuben Clark, it repudiated the Roosevelt Corollary of the Monroe Doctrine, asserting the United States' discretionary authority to intervene militarily in the Western Hemisphere if cases of wrongdoing arose. It did not reject the principle of intervention, only the use of the corollary as justification. Stimson gave the publication lukewarm approval, and its release generated only mild interest in Latin America. As for Hoover, he did not subscribe to all of it and did not want it printed.[8] Assistant Secretary White was far from enthusiastic. He did not contemplate renouncing for military option, and later defended intervention as called for "invariably to maintain order and protect the lives of foreigners and, in general, to oblige the countries concerned to meet certain minimum civilized standards of international relations and thereby to forestall intervention by European Nations."[9]

This lack of clarity also extended to the United States' role in solving Latin American boundary controversies. True to his paternalistic nature, White idealized the United States for assisting in these disputes: "If the United States was pursuing selfish motives it obviously would be to its interest to fish in troubled waters and to keep the waters troubled for the better fishing. Nevertheless, the United States Government has used its utmost endeavors to bring about a peaceful composition of these disputes."[10] He was able to help resolve the longstanding and bitter Tacna-Arica affair between Chile and Peru and a less volatile clash between Guatemala and Honduras.[11]

White also met with disappointments. The Chaco dispute between Bolivia and Paraguay defied solution. Dating back to the mid-nineteenth century, the question centered on a relatively worthless piece of border territory, largely desert, with little water and vegetation. Somehow ownership evolved into an emotional, nationalistic issue for both nations. In 1928 intermittent skirmishes flared up and steadily grew into a major war. Bolivia was larger, but Paraguay was better prepared militarily. More important, when war was officially declared in 1932, the combatants eagerly greeted it. Although neither could afford the devastation, bloody fighting lasted for three years.[12]

Another conflict emerged in the summer of 1932, between Colombia and Peru. The former controlled Leticia, a port at the headwaters of the Amazon River that had little value because of an overabundance of rainfall and vegetation. Like the Chaco dispute, this boundary disagreement was of long duration, but in this instance, the involved parties realized the price of the real estate was not worth a war. To remove Peruvian soliders who had precipitately seized the town, the League of Nations established a commission to supervise their departure and thus save as much face as possible for the Peruvian government, which was confronting chauvinists clamoring to fight.[13]

Closely associated with boundary conflicts and military intervention were economic problems. The United States had vastly expanded its trade with Latin America since the colonial era. By the end of the nineteenth century, the commercial interchange had greatly accelerated to the point where the United States sent 15 percent of its total exports to Latin America, and the other American republics sold 10 percent of their goods to the United States. By the beginning of World War I, the United States took approximately a quarter of the Latin American exports, concentrated mainly on raw materials and centered in the Caribbean region. American business followed a similar expansionist pattern. At the turn of the twentieth century, United States investment in Latin American reached $308,000,000; fourteen years later this figure had jumped to $1,650,000,000.[14]

By the end of the war the United States had dramatically altered its economic position in the Americas. It had moved from a debtor to the world's largest creditor, and New York City replaced London as the international financial capital. During this transition the United States' relationship to Latin America also underwent considerable changes. Without much planning the United States assumed the largest share of the market, filling the void created by European nations preoccupied with the struggle for survival. By 1929 United States exports to Latin America were a third of the United States total, and Latin American exports to the United States grew to 20 percent of their total. Investments showed an even sharper rise. By 1929 they reached $5,430,000,000, representing a third of all United States foreign investments, again principally confined to the Caribbean zone.[15]

A main source of this economic growth after World War I came as a result of United States investors buying large amounts of Latin American bonds yielding regular and often high interest, and dramatically expanded purchases during the prosperous 1920s. As secretary of commerce, Hoover had discouraged this type of speculation because United States bankers had not given most of the bonds scrupulous examination, but he refused to interfere in these private business transitions. After the depression struck, with the exception of Argentina, the Latin American governments defaulted on over four-fifths of their bond issues, making them practically worthless and sending investors to the State Department to demand payment on their bonds.[16]

The tremendous growth of United States exports and investments was not coupled with corresponding commercial policies that might help nations owing dollars to repay them. United States businessmen withdrew as much capital as possible from their Latin American operations, making debt payments extremely difficult. Americans also invested huge sums in highly speculative enterprises, most of which collapsed. Finally, while the United States pressed for open access to foreign markets, it restricted the flow of goods into the mainland. The Republicans were committed to high tariffs, and in 1930, over the strenuous objections of many financial leaders, Hoover signed the Smoot-Hawley Tariff, the highest in American history. When the depression broke, the lack of sound hemispheric economic planning helped to cause disaster—a precipitous decline in trade and an enormous loss for bondholders.[17]

These incoherent United States actions created deep resentment in Latin America. Hemispheric leaders accepted Washington's predominance by the end of World War I, but tried to find ways to limit its supremacy. Looking partly for collective security against the United States, many Latin American nations joined the League of Nations, but by the end of the 1920s they realized the futility of trying to build the League into a counterforce. In the midst of their frustration, Latin American leaders used the Fifth and Sixth International Conferences of American States held at Santiago de Chile in

1923 and Havana during 1928 to attack United States imperialism. The American delegations suffered through these assaults, and, placed on the defense, sought excuses to rationalize outdated practices.

Essayists from Latin America like Manuel Ugarte toured Latin America preaching solidarity in the face of Yankee expansion. In 1923 he expressed his fears:

In Latin America there has never been more than one influence, one force, and one tide: that which comes from the North. It has never been checked, either by an act of our will, absorbed in internal disputes, or by an effort from Europe, obsessed by bitter rivalries. Imperialist policy has always been able to proceed in the New World, without faltering or counterpoise, as if it were the master, multiplying strategic routes and advanced posts, without meeting any opposition or resistance. The growing domination of the United States, which has closed the epoch of Europe's world hegemony, has thus been favoured more by the dissensions of the Old World itself, which was unable to maintain its influence before the dominating advance of the Northern republic, than by the inefficacy of Latin American action.[18]

Notwithstanding such assaults and the economic chaos caused by the depression, Hoover had made some significant contributions during his governmental career. As commerce secretary he encouraged commercial opportunities and also called for greater understanding through movies portraying the realities of United States life and scientific cooperation. After his presidential victory, he dramatized his regional interest by taking an extended tour of nine Latin American republics, where he was warmly received. After his inauguration he criticized the Haitain and Nicaraguan interventions in his first annual message. While his administration worked toward ending these, Hoover tried to build hemispheric cordiality in 1930 by proclaiming April fourteenth Pan American Day and celebrating its first observance the following year.[19]

These limited steps did not offset the massive effects of the Great Depression. Having claimed much of the credit for the prosperity of the 1920s, Hoover now shouldered the blame for the nation's economic crisis. In the midst of his troubles, he stood before the electorate in the 1932 presidential contest promising to restore good times, but the voters overwhelmingly rejected him. At the end of his term, his popularity had plummeted and the optimistic business orientation that he symbolized has been discredited. The defeated incumbent only waited for his departure, a bitter and frustrated man.

Hoover left the White House in the depths of the depression. He and his two Republican predecessors willed a legacy of incomplete and often contradictory hemispheric actions. Besieged by his critics through much of his presidency, Hoover did not provide direction in regional matters. By inclination, neither did Stimson. White, almost by default, managed Latin American affairs from his narrow perspective without the benefit of encouragement or guidelines drawn by the chief executive or his principal foreign affairs adviser.

The assistant secretary consequently adopted piecemeal measures instead of mapping out broad strategies. Troops left the Caribbean, but the rationale for their presence, though clearly obsolete, was not repudiated. For example, the Republicans took bilateral actions to remove soldiers in Haiti and Nicaragua and mediated boundary controversies. During the same period the executive branch continued to enforce the discredited nonrecognition treaty of 1923 and could not even agree on the appropriateness of the Clark Memorandum. In commercial matters, inter-American interaction grew enormously but haphazardly, assuring harmful effects during the depression. The Republicans encouraged business expansion and concurrently raised tariff barriers, causing a tremendous financial imbalance. Symbolizing the dissatisfaction with these inconsistencies, inter-American gatherings were forums for assaults on United States imperialism instead of for building constructive regional policies. Under these circumstances, and given the uniqueness of the 1920s and the early depression years, claiming that the Good Neighbor policy's foundations evolved from Hoover and his contemporaries is not justified.[20]

2 ★ THE DEMOCRATIC TRANSITION

THE DIFFERENCES between the outgoing and incoming administrations did not appear immediately. Roosevelt did not treat foreign policy as a major issue during his presidential campaign, but after his victory he devoted considerable time to diplomatic problems. On several occasions Secretary Stimson briefed the president-elect. During their talks Roosevelt mentioned Hoover's Latin American record. He discounted the importance of his predecessor's preinauguration tour, but commended the troop withdrawals in the Caribbean and planned to accelerate them. The new president saw this activity as a part of his effort to remove legitimate causes of Latin American discontent aimed at the United States.[1]

Roosevelt's comments reflected his limited knowledge of hemispheric affairs. His firsthand contact with Latin America began casually in 1904 when his mother, Sara, took him on a six-week cruise of the Caribbean to see if she could dissuade him from marrying Eleanor. The trip failed equally to achieve its primary purpose or to awaken his interest in the other American republics. Eight years later he traveled to Panama, where he watched the last stages of the canal's construction.[2]

As Wilson's assistant secretary of the navy, Roosevelt exhibited many of his contemporaries' attitudes toward Latin America. He accepted the "white man's burden" and held that force was essential to bring civilization to developing regions. Without United States assurances of stability, American businessmen could not trade profitably, particularly in the Caribbean zone. Roosevelt further worried that chaos might invite European conquest, and to guard against this possibility he advocated more bases for the United States. Using this reasoning, he supported the Haitian intervention and visited the occupation forces on an inspection trip that included Cuba. When the United States landed marines at Veracruz in 1914, Roosevelt commended Wilson's decisive action and even suggested more force, possibly a formal declaration of war. During World War I his hostility toward German hemispheric penetration increased. In the summer of 1917 he told an audience about his Caribbean tours and claimed he had seen signs of German encroachment. To reduce the enemy's influence, he supported a continued United States military presence in the Caribbean and promoted the idea that the United States should restore order wherever anarchy existed. True independence for immature countries would not come for many years—perhaps never, he thought—unless the United States lent its assistance.[3]

His perceptions changed radically during the 1920s. Roosevelt came to oppose the Nicaraguan intervention and went so far to recommend that the United States request other Latin American nation's collaboration when intervention became necessary. An article in *Foreign Affairs* entitled "Our Foreign Policy," published during 1928, demonstrated how markedly his viewpoint had shifted. The Monroe Doctrine no longer was the aggressive declaration that his distant cousin Theodore proclaimed, but a cooperative effort directed at self-defense and the broader hope for continental peace. Surveying inter-American diplomacy since the Spanish-American War, he concluded that Latin Americans resented United States intervention. If the United States must dispatch military forces, it should do so in concert with other American nations, not alone.[4]

While governor of New York, Roosevelt spent most of his energies on state concerns, and paid scant attention to foreign affairs.[5] His presidential campaign and his inaugural address showed the same imbalance. The speech contained only a bit of vague optimism, a felicitously expressed cliché: "In the field of world policy I would dedicate this nation to the policy of the good neighbor—the neighbor who resolutely respects himself and, because he does so, respects the sanctity of his agreements in and with a world of neighbors."[6] Gaston Nerval, a journalist writing on hemispheric topics, felt that Latin Americans would welcome the "good neighbor" concept. He inquired of the State Department if this policy included the hemisphere; the reply was evasive. Obviously, at this early date, neither the president nor the State Department had given any serious thought to the practical meaning of "good neighbor" phraseology.[7]

While this policy remained vague, Roosevelt began placing his imprint on foreign policy. The chief of the European desk, J. Pierrepont Moffat, informed a colleague shortly after the inauguration:

You have no idea of the White House control over foreign affairs now. To do so you must go back to the regime of the great Theodore. Not only are the personal negotiations between the President and the Ambassadors, but telegrams go over by the score and return with notations in the President's handwriting. The system has its advantages and disadvantages. It gives a distinct finality and I think a degree of consistency to our policy that will bear fruit. On the other hand, it is extremely difficult to know what has gone before and this doubt of knowing the background extends even in high circles.[8]

Roosevelt hinted at his broad regional approach when he spoke for the first time before the Pan American Union on April 12. He placed his emphasis on cooperation by pledging to build regionalism based on a spirit of mutual respect; he repeated his interpretation of the Monroe Doctrine, that it was primarily designed as a defensive measure to keep non-American nations from invading the hemisphere. He added that boundary wars such as in the Chaco and Leticia were as harmful to the Americas as high tariff barriers.[9]

Latin America generally responded favorably to these statements and to Roosevelt's attempts at slowing down the pace of military rearmament. Throughout the spring of 1933, the new president tried to find a common basis for the Geneva Disarmament Conference to restrict military budgets. On May 16 he publicly appealed to world leaders for the elimination of all offensive weapons, but nations determined to rearm ignored his pleas.[10]

From this and other episodes, Roosevelt learned the limitations of his foreign policy options. Hitler and Mussolini began dominating European events, while Japanese expansionism preoccupied the Far East. United States public opinion abhorred evidence of belligerence but recoiled from any suggestions that might involve the nation in any action against a foreign war. While his constituency opposed commitments outside the Americas, the president understood that it would sanction measures to keep foreign aggression from the hemisphere. With this knowledge the president promoted inter-American solidarity against attacks from non-American powers. This support of a common stand—it could not yet be called an alliance—won Latin American support and at the same time provided a plausible explanation for drawing attention to European and Asian crises. Thus Pan American diplomacy became crucial to the Roosevelt administration, for the Good Neighbor served as both a regional bond and a platform from which the president reached across oceans to an international audience.

Before Roosevelt conducted his first diplomatic forays, he had to select a secretary of state, and by early January he decided on Cordell Hull. Lawyer, judge, congressman, and recently elected senator, this staunch Democrat from Tennessee had also been chairman of the national party. Widely respected by his fellow congressmen, Hull had the additional advantage of having been a loyal and effective southern associate of Roosevelt's during the 1920s. Roosevelt repaid this debt by advocating Hull's vice-presidential bid in 1928. Tall, handsome, elderly, with grey hair, he appeared as the ideal choice for the State Department. His appointment would please party regulars and bring their allegiance to the administration. Above all, this selection would publicly acknowledge the importance of southern Democrats in the New Deal coalition.[11]

Hull's lack of diplomatic experience did not disturb Roosevelt. On January 19, stopping briefly in Washington, he offered Hull the secretaryship; a month later, after much urging by his friends, Hull accepted. With this announcement, Hull began frequent meetings with Stimson, who foresaw certain problems before the new appointee even assumed his post. Hull told Stimson that he had acquiesced in Roosevelt's intention to act as his own secretary of state. In addition, he had never held any major administrative posts, and in many ways he was not tempermentally suited for his role. Hull demanded unquestioned devotion. If his all-too-ready suspicions were aroused, he brooded. Rather than calling for a direct resolution, he let a feud develop and waited until the proper moment to "get" his man. Hull was overly sensitive to congressional agitation, especially from former colleagues who vehemently objected to foreign entanglements.[12]

Roosevelt, not Hull, selected most of the major subordinates in the State Department and received their primary loyalty. The president brought a prominent Republican, William Phillips, into the administration as undersecretary of state, a post he had held under Harding. Roosevelt and Phillips became good friends during the Wilson presidency and in the presidential election of 1932, Phillips openly backed Roosevelt. The undersecretary complemented his superior. Hull disliked entertaining, while Phillips enjoyed it and filled many social responsibilities. Raymond Moley was another matter. His selection as an assistant secretary of state, solely responsible to the White House, irritated Hull and some of his associates. They were pleased when Moley resigned, and his successor, R. Walton Moore, Hull's close friend, fellow lawyer, and judge, who had represented Virginia in the House of Representatives, holding a membership on the Foreign Affairs Committee, came into the department. Southern Democratic congressmen respected Moore, and the diplomatic corps needed their votes. None of these individuals had any significant Latin American experience. Hull spent five months in Cuba during the Spanish-American War. When he returned home, any interest that he had had in the island quickly disappeared.[13]

Roosevelt was unperturbed, for he had already chosen Sumner Welles as assistant secretary of state for Latin American affairs. Raised in an aristocratic tradition of New York society, Welles followed Roosevelt's educational pattern, attending Groton and graduating from Harvard. Welles's mother and Eleanor's were close friends, and as a youngster, Welles had attended the wedding of Eleanor and Franklin. At college he and Eleanor's brother were classmates. After graduation from Harvard, Welles joined the foreign service in 1915 and was sent to Tokyo. Two years later he began his hemispheric career with a transfer to Buenos Aires. Returning to Washington toward the end of the Wilson era, he met Roosevelt. In 1921 he became chief of the Latin American division at twenty-eight years of age. He subsequently headed special presidential missions to the Caribbean, where he defused potentially explosive situations. Welles served in this capacity until his resignation in 1925.[14]

Welles retained his profound attachment for regional concerns as a private citizen, and, after 1927, frequently discussed these with Roosevelt. He also wrote a two-volume history of the Dominican Republic entitled *Naboth's Vineyard*, in which he praised Secretary Hughes for defining the

Monroe Doctrine as a defensive measure without aggressive designs. This did not mean that Welles repudiated military intervention. He foresaw the possibility of dispatching armed forces primarily to resolve crises—to protect lives, guarantee the Panama Canal's security, or deal with sudden emergencies. Even in these instances, the United States should consult Latin American nations instead of acting unilaterally. Deploying soldiers was not a permanent solution, for troops only assured temporary order. Long-term occupations would delay domestic settlements and raise cries against Yankee imperialism. Commercial policy might also damage Pan American cooperation, and Welles felt that the high protective tariff needed downward adjustments to stimulate hemispheric trade.[15]

Political cooperation and sound economic policies highlighted Welles's beliefs. At the end of his book, he urged the United States to recognize "that in the Western Hemisphere lies its strength and its support. In the identification of its interest both political and material, on a basis of absolute equality, with the interests of its sister republics of the continent, and in the rapid removal of the grounds for their distrust, lies it real advantage."[16]

As the depression worsened, Welles adjusted his views to meet the international predicament. He repeated his faith in the original, unadorned Monroe Doctrine and his conviction that the United States required Latin American support or at least neutrality to repel a possible canal attack. He added that close economic ties would come only with political stability, which would increase trade; finally, he favored ending military intervention without prior Latin American consultation. During Roosevelt's presidential campaign Welles endorsed the candidate and made a generous financial contribution. After the electoral victory Welles resumed his advisory role on inter-American diplomacy and the foreign service in general.[17]

Welles's appointment as an assistant secretary of state created a potentially dangerous situation in the State Department. He and Hull differed widely in background and personality. Welles's presidential access was well known, and Hull came to resent it. Welles aggravated the situation by giving loyalties entirely to the president, not to his direct superior. Fortunately for all three, Welles, with Roosevelt's confidence and Hull's grudging recognition of his abilities, formulated United States programs toward Latin America for the next decade—before the personal conflicts became irreconcilable.

Persistent rumors of drastic changes in the foreign service by the incoming administration proved unjustified. Stimson urged Roosevelt and Hull to carry out his commitments, and the new secretary frequently relaxed at Stimson's Washington estate, playing croquet. Many of Stimson's important advisers stayed in the department: Herbert Feis, economic adviser, Stanley Hornbeck in the Far Eastern Division, and Moffat in European affairs. Although still relatively small, the diplomatic bureaucracy had begun to grow, institutionalizing policy decisions and limiting alternatives.[18]

Francis White was the exception. Feeling that eighteen years in the diplomatic corps entitled him to special treatment, he asked for the vacated Cuban ambassadorial post, for which he considered himself the most qualified person available, and sought administration supporters. These included his old friend Welles, who had entered the foreign service along with White and had sailed to the Far East with him. With the announcement of Welles's selection to the post, White felt betrayed and asked Hull to relieve him from making any decisions regarding Cuban policies; the secretary agreed.[19]

White decided to resign when he did not receive any Latin American ambassadorship, but Hull convinced him to become minister to Czechoslovakia.[20] Bitter over his misfortune, he wrote on June 16: "My interests are entirely in Latin American affairs and it is with great reluctance that I go to another section of the world. My interest in Europe is merely as a vacation ground and, while I am looking forward with much pleasure to three or four months' complete rest after ten years of grind in the Department, my interests are still and will continue to be in Latin America."[21] White went to Prague, but his disappointment, coupled with family financial reversals, resulted in his resignation before the end of the year.

In contrast, Laurence Duggan experienced a rapid rise. Born in 1905, he attended Phillips Exeter Academy and graduated from Harvard in 1927. Two years later he took an extended trip to Latin America at the request of his father, Stephen Duggan, the director of the prestigious Institute of International Education. The son's report recommended professional exchanges, scholarships for graduate students studying hemispheric affairs, and increasing the number of United States books translated into Spanish and Portuguese. Duggan issued a note of caution. Any program must be taken in a cooperative spirit with stress on the mutual advantage of cultural understanding.

After entering the department in 1930 as a career officer, Duggan continued to work on regional affairs. By the time the Democrats assumed control he had made several specific proposals: the improvement of the peace machinery at the next inter-American conference; solution of the Dominican Republic's financial problems; renegotiation of the Panama treaty; reexamination of the United States position toward the nonrecognition treaty of 1923; and the development of a consistent policy to protect American businesses in Latin America.[22]

Welles shared many of Duggan's priorities and came to depend on his assistance. If anyone in the department knew Welles's thoughts, Duggan did. As a result he advanced quickly. In 1935 he received three promotions, ending as chief of the Latin American Division. Joseph Green, a career diplomat, commented on Duggan's ascendency late in the year: "His career has certainly been meteoric, but every one recognized the fact that he was the ablest officer in Latin America and that if the new Chief was to be drawn from the present personnel of that Division he was the obvious man for the position.

His appointment was generally approved, but I fear that it has created some jealousies which may make things difficult for him."[23]

Jefferson Caffery was destined to hold critical ambassadorial posts in Cuba and Brazil during Roosevelt's presidency. He had considerable experience in Latin America and exerted a good deal of influence at his station by an uncanny ability to win the confidence of the ruler.[24] On March 8, 1935, he offered a glimpse into his style: "The value of diplomacy, both tangible accomplishments and in good will, is very largely a matter of personal contact and human relationships, and results are obtained because of mutual understanding fostered by our officers in their out-of-office association with the citizens of the country wherein they are stationed. . . ."[25]

Men like Welles, White, Duggan, and Caffery were in the minority. Most foreign service personnel looked at a Latin American assignment as a demotion, and Hugh Gibson personified this sentiment. After he was moved from his European ambassadorship to South America, his friends flattered his ego by assuring him that this assignment to Rio de Janiero raised the significance of that post. When he arrived in the summer of 1933, he found the capital delightful and the Brazilians friendly.[26] By the new year the novelty had worn off, and he complained about his European exile. The embassy, for example, was "about the poorest dump I've ever seen, surrounded by nigger slums, warehouses, billboards and skyscrappers under construction, with pile drivers, electric riveting machines, and clouds of thick yellow smoke. We've fixed up a house in the hills above Rio, and I don't think we can be coaxed down until Uncle Sam finds a better place for us to live."[27] Until his transfer in 1937, Gibson's attitude retarded critical bilateral negotiations.

Career officers did not head every Latin American mission. Reversing Francis White's trend toward a professionalized corps, Roosevelt selected political appointees like Josephus Daniels to Mexico. Daniels requested this post because of his deep interest in that nation since his days as Wilson's secretary of the navy. Many worried that Daniels's association with the Veracruz incident would make his nomination unacceptable to the Mexican government, but this did not occur.[28] Shortly after his selection, Welles wrote him and predicted, "Your appointment to Mexico will be productive of the greatest benefit in promoting a good feeling towards the United States and a clear understanding of the continental policy of the Administration."[29] Daniels fulfilled Welles's optimism, becoming Roosevelt's principal good will ambassador to Latin America.

In all, Roosevelt appointed six men in 1933 for hemispheric posts. None had significant Latin American training. Four had some journalistic background; one was a lawyer and the other a politician. Four came from the South. Career diplomats had predominantly eastern backgrounds, Ivy League affiliations, and extensive Latin American field experience. Profiles of all mission heads showed that they were male, middle-aged, urbane, largely Protestant, and highly educated.[30]

The architects of the future Good Neighbor brought with them widely diverging quantities of knowledge about the Americas. Roosevelt's was superficial; Hull's almost nonexistent; and Welles's out of date. The career officers had the most current information, but they leaned heavily on Republican policies. The Democratic political selections were not influenced by the previous administration's decisions; however, these men lacked experience.

This mixture did not impede the formulation of the Good Neighbor policy. Roosevelt alone saw the totality of domestic and foreign interaction. From that vantage point, he realized his Latin American opportunity. Shut out of European deliberations by its governments and domestic opposition, and frustrated by Japanese ambitions in the Far East, the president moved toward internationalism through the only available opening. At first he did this casually, almost accidentally, but by the eve of the European war, Latin American actions played an integral part in shaping worldwide strategy. Hull made certain that Congress supported these initiatives by avoiding precipitate decisions. Welles incorporated the major guidelines into practical hemispheric programs. He promoted men like Duggan and Caffery, whom he perceived as sharing his ideas, and eliminated others like Gibson, who was disruptive and antagonistic.

Using these diverse individuals Roosevelt developed his hemispheric policy. He depended primarily on Hull and Welles, and the three of them produced the general policy directions. The president preferred Welles's brilliance, penetrating analysis, and quick reactions, but he also recognized the value of Hull's circumspection, which demanded patience and a complete examination of the issues in order to win the necessary congressional backing. This line of authority formed the basis for Democratic foreign policy decisions in the Americas over the next decade.

This new leadership did not work smoothly at the start of the New Deal. Two problems remaining from the Hoover administration dominated inter-American diplomacy during Roosevelt's first year. One deteriorating conditions in Cuba, was bilateral; the other, the upcoming inter-American conference, was multilateral. By the end of 1933 United States responses to these events helped to shape some of the Good Neighbor's major political and economic positions.

The United States had an enormous stake in Cuba. After the Spanish-American War, United States troops occupied the island. Before removing them, the American government insisted on a permanent treaty that included the Platt Amendment, empowering the United States to intervene militarily in the island's domestic affairs. Marines landed twice, once at the urgent request of the Cuban president; and in the early 1920s the American government sent a commission to supervise national elections. Economic connections, which had long antedated political involvement, sharply increased. In 1933 Cuba was the principal source of United States sugar imports; it received most of its imports from the mainland; and it contained a tremendous amount of American investments.

When Gerardo Machado won the Cuban presidency in the mid-1920s, he pledged stability and prosperity. While this situation prevailed, Machado had little difficulty amending his nation's constitution to allow for his reelection. When the depression struck, sugar prices plummeted and the veneer of stability cracked. The Cuban president had taken credit for most of the boom; his opponents, naturally blaming him for the succeeding misfortunes, attempted a coup d'état in 1931. After its failure, Machado adopted terrorism to squelch dissent; the opposition responded with its own form of brutality; and Cuba moved toward anarchy.[31]

Roosevelt and Stimson superficially discussed the island's problems toward the close of the Hoover era. The retiring secretary saw no justification for intervention, feeling that Cuba was more secure than most other Latin American nations, since Machado had the military's allegiance. With this assurance, Roosevelt adopted a relatively simple policy upon assuming office—negotiate a new commercial treaty to restore stability and eliminate political unrest. He failed to appreciate the intense Cuban hatred of Machado and anti-American nationalism.[32]

Even if Roosevelt or Hull had understood these factors, neither had time to seek solutions to the problem. When asked about the worsening predicament, both spoke in generalities. For answers they relied on Welles, the designated ambassador to Cuba. He publicly announced his intention to focus on economic troubles and refrain from any interference in domestic politics. Nevertheless, he privately acknowledged their close association. He wished to provide economic assistance to insure stability. With this accomplished, he would have the time to use constitutionally prescribed procedures for removing the present regime. He ruled out Machado's immediate resignation, since this would produce chaos and increase the possiblity of military intervention.[33]

Welles arrived in Cuba during early May. At his first interview with Machado, the ambassador outlined his goals. Economic recovery and political reform were interrelated. To achieve the latter, Welles asked the dictator to call national elections in 1934, a year before his term expired. Along with the political activity, the two nations would negotiate a new commercial treaty to improve the island's bleak economic picture.[34]

To guarantee the success of his program, the ambassador met with the regime's political opponents and induced many of them to accept his mediation. By early June he appeared optimistic, and within a month he opened talks between the government and some antagonists. While these groups jockeyed for position in the upcoming elections, many disapproved of the ambassador's activities as another form of intervention. They demanded Machado's immediate resignation.[35]

Even without political consensus on the island, the force of the ambassador's personality kept the talks going. Soon the ambassador noticed signs of discord. While Machado desperately clung to his presidency, he realized that Welles was eroding his authority. During early August a strike broke out in Havana that spread rapidly and immobilized the city. Machado sought to end this disturbance and neutralize or discredit the ambassador, whom he had come to loathe. His diplomatic representative in Washington complained to Roosevelt that Welles's activities were designed to upset Machado's government. The American president dismissed these charges and affirmed his confidence in Welles.

Machado had lost command, for, with Roosevelt's support, Welles had effectively compromised the dictator's authority. Unwisely, he chose to attack Welles while economic conditions on the island were growing worse and a strike gripped Havana. When the officer corps withdrew its support, Machado's last prop crumbled, and he fled the island in mid-August.[36]

Many Cubans had predicted the dictator's downfall, but his sudden departure shocked them. Victims of the regime's brutality immediately sought retribution by tracking down and killing the government's henchmen. Political factions fell apart, for the collapse of the Machado regime removed the bond of fear and hatred that had united them. The State Department did not accurately gauge this deep-seated antipathy, and impatiently waited for the restoration of order. Edwin Wilson of the Latin American Division expressed the general optimism: "The Cuban situation has . . . turned out wonderfully well. We are of course not out of the woods yet, but it looks much better than it did a few days ago."[37]

Dr. Carlos Manuel de Céspedes assumed the interim presidency and immediately faced charges that the United States embassy had chosen him for the post. Despite his denials, the accusations persisted. They might have disappeared had Céspedes proved an effective ruler, but he did not know how to use this time in consolidating his position. Welles lent his prestige and tried to provide tangible aid, but his requests for immediate economic assistance were fruitless. The Roosevelt administration had no agency for foreign aid. Despite these troubles, Welles believed that he had preserved constitutionality and that order would shortly return.[38]

Welles's optimism ended on the evening of September 4, when a group of sergeants revolted for higher pay and other reforms. These noncommissioned officers ran routine base operations while many superiors amused themselves in Havana. A political grouping at the University of Havana, the student directorate, soon convinced the sergeants to broaden their insurrection into a coup d'état that easily toppled the Céspedes regime, replacing it with a five-man junta. Twice on the following day, Welles, stunned and perplexed, specifically requested United States Marine landings to protect American lives and property. Both times Roosevelt refused. No soldiers came ashore, but reporters from both countries told their readers that Roosevelt had sent a large naval force to Cuban waters, indicating the likelihood of intervention.[39]

At a time when military occupation seemed likely, the Roosevelt administration found that a large portion of the American public opposed intervention. The State Department also consulted with several Latin American diplomats, who took the same position.[40] On September 6 Roosevelt tried to single out Cuba from other Latin American nations, telling reporters: "You can't say that the Cuban situation is the keynote of Latin American policy, because there is no other American nation that is in the same status as Cuba. In Cuba we have treaty obligations—in other nations we haven't."[41] This was not strictly accurate; the United States had treaty commitments and troops billeted in several other Caribbean nations.

The decision against military intervention did not stop Welles from recommending other coercive measures. He advised withholding diplomatic recognition to demonstrate United States displeasure with the current regime. To win recognition, the five-man junta dissolved in favor of a provisional president, Ramón Grau San Martín. Neither the Cuban revolutionaries nor officials in Washington realized the primary impediment to renewed relations— that the revolt had ruined Welles's plans. The ambassador was now using nonrecognition as a weapon to force the new government to compromise with him and the traditional politicians he represented. Welles seemed not to know or care that he had become the agent of the status quo while Grau had made himself the advocate of nationalistic reforms—the right of women to vote, advanced labor legislation, and hostility toward foreign ownership of basic industries. Under these circumstances, a stalemate was inevitable, for Welles denied normal United States relations so that Grau might legitimize his position and Grau's government condemned the ambassador for impeding nationalistic reforms. The rivalry between Grau and Welles was both personal and political.[42]

In October and November intermittent fighting disturbed but did not break the stalemate. In one incident an American citizen was accidently killed by a random bullet. In an earlier era such an event might have brought marines, but this time the death was officially ignored while Roosevelt and Hull tried vainly to find a recognition formula. Welles stood in the way, hoping to force Grau to form a coalition with his opposition. Cuban politicians frequently discussed a political solution, but no one found an acceptable compromise. By mid-October Welles understood the impossibility of his task.[43] Fatigued and frustrated, he wrote: "To be quite frank, for the past four weeks existence has been unmitigated hell. The complexities seem to increase rather than diminish, and all that I can say at the present time is that the main objective—namely, nonintervention—has not been impaired." He still wished "for a constructive program that will eventually get us out of the present unsavory mess into which Cuba has been plunged."[44]

For Welles, who came to symbolize hostility toward the Grau government, settlement was impossible. Nonrecognition encouraged traditional politicians to continue their opposition with hopes of recapturing the presidency. When Roosevelt considered recognition in mid-November, Welles returned to the United States and prevailed upon the president to release a statement on November 23, most of which Welles had drafted. In it Roosevelt declared that Grau would not be recognized since he represented a minority. The United States would not change its policy until the Cuban government had majority participation. However, once this happened, the United States would be willing to renegotiate the permanent treaty, including the Platt Amendment. With this statement in hand, Welles made a last desperate try at establishing a coalition government; failing, he left the island on December 13.[45]

The Cuban crisis confronted Roosevelt with his first highly complicated bilateral diplomatic problem just at the start of his domestic reform program. He had to consider not only what policy to follow in Cuba but also how he might hold the allegiance of both his secretary of state and his ambassador. To Hull he pledged his full support against military occupation; at the same time he professed his faith in Welles's abilities, and surrounded the island with warships. Neither Hull nor Welles was entirely satisfied, but each believed he had Roosevelt's support. Feelings were soothed; loyalty had been saved.

During the debate over Cuban policy, Roosevelt evolved a fundamental principle in his hemispheric commitment that he faithfully followed throughout his administration. The United States would not land troops to resolve the domestic affairs of Latin American nations. This decision won praise for the Roosevelt administration in the Americas. While military intervention was rejected in the Cuban case, nonrecognition had a crucial effect on the island's internal evolution. Instead of allowing the nation to determine its destiny, the Roosevelt administration, through its double-edged policy of not landing soldiers while surrounding the island with a cordon of warships, interfered with the resolution of the domestic political struggle. Some Cubans also argued that Welles retarded the revolution and conveniently ignored the fact that many traditionalist politicians maneuvered the ambassador for their own advantage. Welles could not have become so deeply engaged in local politics without this relationship.

In the midst of the Cuban upheaval, the State Department prepared for the Seventh International Conference of American States, meeting at Montevideo, Uruguay. Originally scheduled for early 1933, the conference was postponed until December 3 because of the depressing international situation. By the fall conditions had grown even worse. Latin American officials were agitating for a moratorium on their foreign debts, adversely affecting United States investors; the United States faced severe criticism for its Cuban policy; the Chaco and Leticia conflicts were not settled; and in Uruguay violence threatened to disrupt the presidential election and embarrass the government's preparations for the inter-American gathering.[46]

As Hull sat through the fiasco of the London Economic Conference, he must have realized the slim chances for success at the upcoming meeting. Argentina even attempted to get another delay, but Uruguay, with backing from other Latin American states, held to the December date. At first, Hull agreed with the majority, but by the end of October he changed his mind and advised Roosevelt to ask for a postponement. The president refused; the conference would be held on time. The State Department had one remaining hope—that an extremely limited agenda might prevent an open break and collapse.[47]

In the late summer, before hemispheric troubles grew worse, Hull decided to go to Montevideo, so as to meet with Latin American statesmen and improve commercial relations. By late September doubts replaced enthusiasm. Roosevelt ignored the secretary's misgivings, and on October 25 told reporters that Hull would go, the first secretary of state to participate at a Pan American meeting. Two days later Hull minimized any possible economic accomplishments, since lower tariffs depended on Congress, and the dismal experience at Geneva and London discouraged international reforms of any sort.[48]

The State Department personnel mirrored this negative attitude. Some diplomats looked for excuses not to attend. Welles was to have been senior delegate after Hull, but he refused to leave Havana. Caffery seemed the next logical choice, but he was passed over when Undersecretary Phillips objected to being left in the department without any experienced inter-American specialist. Finally Alexander Weddell, United States ambassador to Argentina, became senior delegate behind Hull. J. Butler Wright, minister to Uruguay, was another selection, and J. Reuben Clark, a diplomatic appointee under previous Republican administrations, represented the opposition. In addition, Spruille Braden went, in compensation for not receiving the Chilean embassy. Since he spoke fluent Spanish, he became the first truly bilingual United States delegate to attend an inter-American conference. Sophonisba Breckinridge, best known for her work in the field of social services, was the final appointee and the first woman in the United States to be sent as an official delegate to a foreign conference. She was a distinguished professor at the University of Chicago, and her family owned a powerful newspaper in Kentucky and was prominent in national Democratic politics.[49]

Many of the Latin American nations sent impressive delegations; among the leaders were seven foreign ministers, a president-elect, and two former presidents. For the first time at an international conference of American states, women served as delegates. The only unrepresented nation was Costa Rica, whose Congress refused to authorize funds for a meeting it expected to be unproductive.[50]

Of all the Latin American participants, Carlos Saavedra Lamas of Argentina was the most controversial. The son-in-law of a former president, he had recently been appointed minister of foreign affairs, and he stood for Argentina's supremacy in South America and its close ties with Europe. No one could mistake his high, stiffly starched collar—some critics sarcastically referred to him as "Juan Collar." His hair and mustache were dyed red, and he was a chain smoker who puffed a few times on a cigarette and cavalierly tossed it away without concern for where it landed. These idiosyncrasies identified him, but no one doubted his advocacy of Argentine foreign policy or his ability to carry his viewpoint at any gathering.[51]

On November 9, shortly before Hull left for the meeting, Roosevelt issued a press release that seemed to make travel the central theme of the conference. He offered to finance a scientific study of the Pan American Highway and provide funds for the installation of beacon lights at South American airports as safety equipment for night flying. Without mentioning the London Economic Conference, Roosevelt expressly opposed currency stabilization or tariff reforms. The press release displeased and discouraged the conference delegates, for in essence it told them not to expect any major achievements.[52]

Hull understood some of his problems in Washington and at Montevideo. Just before departing, he contradicted the president in the presence of reporters by emphasizing the importance of economic relations in the conference's agenda, and in particular, calling for a reciprocal trade program as part of the meeting's deliberations. Although privately he was not hopeful of any lasting accomplishments, he intended to attend a few sessions and use the trip to meet Latin American leaders, traveling down the east coast of South America and returning by the west coast.[53]

While steaming to Uruguay, Hull discussed his plans with his staff and also tried to cultivate the friendship of the Latin American delegates who happened to be on board. Samuel Inman, a Pan American specialist, talked with the secretary and was impressed by Hull's sincerity toward ending United States interventionism and his refusal to allow bondholders to use the State Department as a collection agency for their debts. These points made in private did not alter Hull's cautious nature. When stopping at Rio de Janeiro, he visited the president and the foreign minister and released a generally innocuous statement calling for economic cooperation and hemispheric peace.[54]

Arriving at Montevideo in late November, Hull reiterated his theme of peace and improved trade. While these declarations did not signify any dramatic policy change, the secretary began at once to break tradition. Instead of waiting for members of the smaller delegations to pay courtesy calls on him, he visited them first. This action flattered the Latin American diplomats, who decided that the secretary was a warm, sympathetic, understanding elderly statesman.[55]

While establishing his personal diplomatic style, Hull was simultaneously evolving his program. He feared that a Cuban demonstration against the United States nonrecognition policy would block his progress, and resented the Cuban delegation's tactic of bringing this issue to the forefront. The secretary had favored a grant of recognition, but Welles stopped it. In addition, Hull wanted to present his tariff reduction proposal. Needing Argentine support, he planned to win it by signing Saavedra Lamas's Anti-War Pact, which had gained acceptance throughout South America. Shortly after the Argentine foreign minister reached his hotel, Hull met with him and presented his ideas. Saavedra Lamas agreed to cooperate, and, at least temporarily, Argentina and the United States worked jointly to achieve their own goals.[56]

The Montevideo conference opened on a rainy Sunday at the beginning of summer. The sessions were held at the legislative palace, and the halls were equipped with earphones for simultaneous translation. President Gabriel Terra of Uruguay convened the meeting, calling for an end to the Chaco war and for economic reforms to stimulate trade.[57]

After these introductory remarks, the delegates began their working sessions. With minimal debate, Saavedra Lamas guided a resolution through committee, requesting the American republics to sign various peace treaties, including his Anti-War Pact.[58] True to his bargain, Hull seconded the resolution and associated peace with economic recovery. He unequivocally declared: "The people of my country strongly feel the so-called right of conquest must forever be banished from this hemisphere and, most of all, they shun and reject that so-called right for themselves. The new deal indeed would be an empty boast if it did not mean that."[59] Hull and the Latin Americans probably viewed this statement from different perspectives. The secretary spoke in generalities, expressing his lofty feelings, which opposed intervention in principle; his listeners took the statement literally to mean that the United States had renounced its practice of sending marines into the Caribbean region.

Hull next introduced his four-point economic resolution: reduction of high tariff barriers through negotiation of reciprocal trade treaties; abandonment of special trade preferences; abolition of import and export prohibitions; and lastly, equality of treatment based on the unconditional most-favored-nation clause. Latin American diplomats warmly supported these measures and were pleased that the secretary brought them up, since previous United States administrations had refused to consider economic problems at Pan American gatherings. Hull above all others was committed to this program, in many ways similar to the one outlined at the London Economic Conference. Even though he lacked presidential endorsement, he pushed independently for his free trade principle.[60]

Roosevelt's pessimism concerning any multilateral economic resolutions led him to defer accepting the Montevideo action until he was convinced that it would not interfere with any domestic recovery legislation. Although he permitted Hull to proceed, the day after the secretary's presentation, the president called in reporters to minimize the resolution's importance. Multilateral tariff agreements were unrealistic, he said; only bilateral bargaining was practical. The gulf between the president and the secretary was wide. Roosevelt kept his focus on the possible economic results at home. Hull undoubtedly knew of Roosevelt's objections but conveniently ignored them to pursue his cherished goal.[61]

While Saavedra Lamas and Hull joined forces, neither their cooperation nor their resolutions were the best remembered action of the conference. This was the declaration that read: "No state has the right to intervene in the internal or external affairs of another."[62] Latin American representatives had tried to have this issue debated at the two previous inter-American gatherings during the 1920s, much to the embarrassment of the United States. Now it was to be seriously considered. Early in the conference, Josephus Daniels vainly urged his government to issue its own self-denying declaration. Instead a committee of the conference drew up a draft and dramatically presented it to the plenary session. Delegates from the Dominican Republic, which had endured marine occupation, and El Salvador, which had experienced nonrecognition, emphatically denounced United States intervention. The Cuban delegate, whose nation was encircled by American warships, received a tremendous ovation for his statement opposing military intimidation. Representatives from Haiti and Nicaragua, which had both seen marine landings, continued the attack,[63] and finally Hull responded: "Every observing person must . . . thoroughly understand that under the Roosevelt Administration the United States Government is as much opposed as any other government to interference with the freedom, the sovereignty, or other international affairs or process of the governments of other nations." His government had already announced its willingness to renegotiate its Cuban treaty once the island achieved stability. Hull went even further by pledging that "no government need fear any intervention on the part of the United States under the Roosevelt Administration."[64] He received warm applause and signed the declaration but added a reservation that the United States had certain treaty and international obligations that still sanctioned military intervention.[65]

The Latin Americans ignored the supplement, which diluted the significance of the United States signature, and hailed the nonintervention declaration as the end of American military landings. Their viewpoints, however, differed from Hull's. He unquestionably believed in nonintervention and supported the declaration in principle. But his reservation reflected reality; the United States would not absolutely abrogate its military option. Little acquainted with Latin American affairs, Hull never understood the concrete problems of United States power in the Caribbean, but he was shrewd enough to avoid narrow commitments. Fortunately for him, Welles initiated programs that seemed to fulfill Hull's promises.

One other issue caused some difficulty for the United States delegation. Doris Stevens, a leader in the National Woman's Party, which championed sex equality, went to Montevideo as the accredited chairwoman of the inter-American commission on women established at the Havana conference in 1928. As a result of a resolution adopted at that meeting, she reported to the delegates at Montevideo on the inequality of women and the necessity for a convention guaranteeing equal citizenship rights in the American republics. Sophonisba Breckinridge, speaking for the United States delegation and the League of Women Voters, opposed this sweeping statement in favor of legislation that would protect women's rights. Stevens and Breckinridge would not compromise. In the midst of this conflict, some of Stevens's supporters approached Roosevelt and won his backing. The president wanted to please these women because the issue had aroused interest among women's groups.[66]

Becoming aware of Hull's favorable publicity, Roosevelt decided to attract his own. He wanted Hull to propose the immediate creation of an agency with United States funding to erect radio stations and landing fields on both coasts of South America, thus making night flying a reality. The secretary replied that while the idea was worthy, it had a tinge of "dollar diplomacy," anathema to the delegates. Nothing more was heard of it.[67]

The conference ended on December 26 after producing such items as Saavedra Lamas's peace package, Hull's economic resolution, and the non-intervention declaration. The delegates also got the combatants in the Chaco War to accept a temporary truce. The participants were elated over these achievements, and Hull reflected this enthusiasm in a radio broadcast, declaring that the Montevideo gathering marked a new era in hemispheric relations and the inauguration of the "good neighbor" policy. To increase his own prestige and reinforce this cooperative spirit, the secretary stopped in Argentina on his return trip to praise Saavedra Lamas's work. In Chile, Peru, Ecuador, Colombia, and Panama, he connected the conference's accomplishments and the close association between hemispheric peace and economic revival. When he resumed his office duties, his subordinates and his dutiful wife noted that the trip had improved his disposition.

Hull had scored a badly needed personal triumph. After his humiliation in London, the secretary received unaccustomed criticism from newspapers questioning his ability to manage the State Department as well as his worth to the president. In sharp contrast, the press following the Montevideo proceedings applauded his actions. Most of those who accompanied him, as well as other influential leaders, showered accolades.[68]

While the secretary publicly praised Roosevelt's cooperation, this did not extend to his private conversations. Shortly after his return, he told a confidant of the president's intransigence on economic reforms. In spite of this, Hull went on, he had moved forward with his own strategy, building trust by visits to the Latin American delegations and by working out a deal with Saavedra Lamas for his support. At first Roosevelt had rejected the economic resolution, and he only relented at Hull's insistence.[69]

Hull was accurate when he deprecated Roosevelt's actions. The president had undercut Hull's efforts in London with devastating consequences. The president also impaired the outlook for the Montevideo conference by releasing his statement emphasizing transportation topics and objecting to serious multilateral economic negotations. Immediately after Hull's presentation of his commercial resolutions, Roosevelt belittled them. When the president later brought forth his own proposal to make night flying possible, he did this at an inopportune moment, and Hull quickly shelved the idea. Hull conveniently forgot several items that illustrated his own uncertainty. When Hull tried to postpone the conference and attempted to cancel his own attendance, Roosevelt insisted on the original plan.

Even while Hull complained of being undermined, he and his chief were moving in the same direction. Throughout the year Roosevelt, like Hull, faced constant pressure to abandon interventionism. The president's refusal to send troops to Cuba and his approval of the nonintervention declaration were indications of growing acceptance. At the end of December the president was completely converted, telling an audience that "the definite policy of the United Sates from now on is one opposed to armed intervention."[70] Each American nation, he announced, should be responsible for its own stability. A few days later he moved closer to Hull's economic thinking by calling for an increase in inter-American commerce.[71]

Although Roosevelt changed his views, he did not generate any coherent Latin American program. Assessing his first year, the president felt that the United States should follow the "good neighbor" policy, but he did not give special attention to Latin American affairs. He had learned from the Geneva and London meetings of his limited influence on European diplomacy.[72] Herbert Feis best summarized Roosevelt's hesitancy in this area: "We remain half committed in a great number of directions and fully committed to none. Actions are in the main taken without too clear previous analysis of what future situations they will create, and as these situations arise, they are met by fresh actions, insufficiently analyzed in turn."[73] Feis was partially correct.

He should have added that unstable international conditions contributed largely to this doubt. Through little choice of its own, the United States' actions in Europe and Asia continued to be severely restricted.

Latin American affairs were an entirely different matter. Welles had failed in his quest for Cuban stability, but had returned to the State Department aware of his mistakes. Hull had turned the Montevideo conference from an expected failure into a personal victory and had laid the foundation for using inter-American conferences to support United States initiatives like his economic policies. Roosevelt, too, assisted by announcing his opposition to military occupations.

At the end of 1933 the Good Neighbor was still an abstract worldwide concept, for the president and the secretary had used the phrase in its broadest sense. Welles would restrict it to the Americas and give it concrete meaning, for he had the requisite specific knowledge that his superiors lacked. His return to Washington gave him the opportunity to terminate military occupations and expand commerce. Uncertainty plagued the first year, but emerging from this confusion was an outline of the Good Neighbor.

3 ★ NONINTERVENTION: REALITY AND ILLUSION

ROOSEVELT and Hull had made two noninterventionist promises before the end of their first year in office. The secretary accepted a broad pledge at Montevideo that a state had no "right to intervene in the internal or external affairs of another." Roosevelt added that the United States opposed military intervention. Both men acted without realizing the full implications of these statements, but in any event, they committed the administration to the principle. Others would have to try to reach this unobtainable goal.

Returning to the State Department in late December 1933 as assistant secretary of state for Latin American affairs, Welles had the responsibility for making nonintervention a reality. Relying on his diplomatic skills and learning from his mistakes in Cuba, he developed policies that helped make nonintervention become part of the Good Neighbor.[1]

In the case of Mexico, Welles's key was to establish cordial relations while carefully respecting the Mexican government's acute sensitivity over its ability to handle its internal affairs. Josephus Daniels assumed his ambassadorial assignment at Mexico City determined to win friendship by assisting in these efforts. He believed that Mexico had experienced a profound social revolution and was searching for its national identity. Welles's and Daniels's sympathetic approach succeeded in defusing several potentially explosive situations and at the same time continued the movement toward bilateral collaboration.[2]

For centuries Mexico had been embroiled in an internal dispute over the relations between the government and the Roman Catholic Church. Secular clerics, the religious orders, and some of the laity advocated close bonds, while opponents demanded a complete separation between church and state. American Catholics periodically joined in the effort to enhance the status of the Mexican Church, and at the start of Roosevelt's presidency, United States bishops lobbied the president to prevent alleged religious persecution in Mexico. Unaware of the church-state conflict, soon after taking up his duties, Daniels outraged the proclericals by a rash speech praising the Mexican government's efforts to improve education. Catholics on both sides of the border exaggerated Daniels's words, implying that he supported secular over parochial learning. Some United States Catholics became so distraught that they called for his removal.[3]

Throughout 1935 the embattled Catholics applied pressure on their congressmen, and found a powerful and unexpected ally in Senator William Borah, a prominent Republican from Idaho who formerly had chaired the Foreign Relations Committee. Erroneously informed that American lives were in jeopardy, he introduced a resolution on January 31 to investigate Mexican religious conditions. Despite persistent lobbying by Catholics, the resolution had no chance of being passed. Roosevelt minimized this agitation, refused to sanction an investigation, and expressed his confidence in Daniels's abilities. Some Catholics threatened to retaliate by working against Roosevelt's reelection, but by 1936 both the Mexican government and the Catholic Church realized the imprudence of their rigidity and moved toward moderation.[4]

While the large vocal Catholic minority made newspaper headlines, racial discrimination was quite another matter. Late in 1936 a Negro dean in Texas complained to the National Association for the Advancement of Colored People (NAACP) that several Mexican consuls in his state refused to issue him a tourist identification card for travel in Mexico until he posted a $150 bond, not required of whites. After several injuries, the NAACP learned the main issue was economic; the Mexican government wanted to keep penniless Negroes from the job market. Negroes protested vainly to the State Department. The replies varied, but the meaning was clear. Nothing was done until 1939, when Mexico abandoned this practice.[5]

Rather than considering Catholic and Negro complaints, Welles centered his attention on affirming his respect for Mexican sovereignty. Included in the Gadsden Purchase Treaty of 1853, for example, was an obscure provision that gave American troops and munitions transit rights across the Isthmus of Tehuantepec for faster lines of communications between the two coasts after the California gold rush. The article had never been invoked. In early 1937 the Mexican government asked for its abrogation, and the United States quickly agreed to its termination.[6]

Welles's diplomacy toward the Central American republics was highlighted by a similar refusal to become involved with their domestic politics. The Hoover administration had refused to normalize relations with El Salvador since 1931 or terminate the Central American nonrecognition treaty of 1923. On returning to Washington from Cuba, Welles immediately decided to reverse both policies. He knew the futility of nonrecognition from his Cuban experience. Central America, plagued by instability for a century, longed for order. If the United States wanted peace in that region, consistency was essential. On January 23, 1934, Welles wrote: "We are all delighted with the way in which our Central American negotiations are working out. I trust they will be concluded with complete success."[7] By the end of the month, El Salvador received United States recognition, and shortly afterwards the nonrecognition treaty of 1923 was cancelled. The United States no longer had any obligation to defend existing regimes from their opponents. To the assistant secretary, this meant that in the future the United States would follow a "hands-off" policy in the area.[8]

The first major test of Welles's determination came in Nicaragua. Hoover had withdrawn the last United States troops from that nation. When they left, the new President, Juan Sacasa, and the military leader, Anastasio Somoza, began competing for power. Augusto Sandino added to the political instability. Refusing to abide by a truce imposed by the United States in 1927, he took his forces to the mountains and became a folk hero by displaying his cunning and leadership in avoiding capture by United States soldiers.[9]

The Roosevelt administration took control in the midst of this explosive political situation and selected Arthur B. Lane to head the ministry in Managua. Coming from a wealthy background, Lane had attended private schools and graduated from Yale. In the summer of 1917 he officially entered the foreign service and spent eight years in Europe. He then went to Mexico and continued his association with that nation until his Nicaraguan appointment. Lane evolved a paternalistic attitude toward Latin America, accepting the Monroe Doctrine but rejecting the Roosevelt Corollary. He opposed intervention and sympathized with the Mexican Revolution's objective of raising living standards. At thirty-nine years of age, he was the youngest career minister in the diplomatic corps.[10]

Lane arrived at his post in the fall of 1933 and quickly realized Somoza's challenge to Sacasa's control. Under these circumstances, the minister urged Washington to take steps in behalf of the central government. Welles refused. The United States had to remain neutral. While these two argued over policy, Sacasa tried to increase his support by reaching an agreement with Sandino in early 1934. After Sandino surrendered his arms and disbanded his forces, the national guard arrested him as he was leaving the presidential palace and immediately assassinated him.[11]

To condemn Somoza's role in this murder and reduce his growing power, Lane wanted the United States to illustrate its displeasure by withdrawing recognition, but Welles denied the request. Placed in an impossible position, the minister wrote somewhat philosophically: "I have been . . . accused of the murder and even people who should have more sense indicate that they think I had some connection therewith. It is not very pleasant, but all in the day's work. The real trouble is that our intervention was greatly resented here and it will take many years before the antagonism which it created dies down. Consequently criticism of the United States or its representatives is a popular and legitimate sport!"[12]

Lane continued his vain efforts to thwart Somoza's emerging military dictatorship through subtle diplomatic maneuvers, and finished his tour of duty in Managua before his prediction came true. In the summer of 1936 Somoza ousted the president, gained prompt recognition for himself, and inaugurated his authoritarian rule, which lasted for two decades.[13] Toward the end of the year, Welles met with Sacasa, who still hoped for United States assistance. The assistant secretary put out any glimmer by promising "to cooperate with respect to economic and cultural matters, but the political cooperation would inevitably involve us in the internal affairs of Nicaragua."[14]

Welles offered further proof in 1937 to convince Central Americans of the United States' refusal to resolve political controversies. When a longstanding boundary dispute threatened war between Honduras and Nicaragua, the assistant secretary urged both nations to remove their forces from the common border, cancel accelerated armament purchases, and submit their grievances to arbitration. In any eventuality, Welles insisted that negotiations for a settlement must take place outside of the United States. Hitherto Central Americans had customarily let Washington settle their disputes, a procedure that easily led to American political involvement and enabled Central Americans to blame the United States for their troubles instead of solving their own problems. Although the disputants rejected arbitration, a mediation committee composed of the United States, Venezuela, and Costa Rica, meeting in San José, ultimately resolved the dispute. The State Department now abandoned its earlier practice of making decisions in local Central American politics, in addition to ending military involvement.[15]

Panamanian conditions provided their own unique problems for the State Department. The United States had actively assisted that country's successful revolt against Colombia in late 1903. To assure Panamanian independence, Theodore Roosevelt quickly made the tiny state a protectorate by signing a treaty guaranteeing its sovereignty, permitting United States troops on its territory, giving the United States control over a ten-mile zone for a canal, and paying the republic $10,000,000 at once, plus an annual zone rental fee of $250,000. American soldiers intervened in domestic affairs on several occasions. However, by the late 1920s Panamanian nationalists were condemning the occupation of the Canal Zone and demanding control for themselves. They vehemently resented the privileges given United States citizens living in the zone, especially their higher pay scale.[16]

When Roosevelt entered office, he faced a new Panamanian president, Harmodio Arias, who had won his election on a promise to gain greater authority over the canal's operations. As a result of this pledge, Arias journeyed to Washington in October 1933 to discuss with Roosevelt the rental fee and a variety of other common concerns. After the two presidents met, Roosevelt instructed Welles to begin talks with Panamanian diplomats. No previous United States president had been willing to conduct serious bilateral discussions, and the War Department held to that precedent, objecting to any changes. After almost two years of bargaining, a treaty was signed on March 2, 1936, and was later ratified by the Senate, acknowledging Panama's right to a large share of the canal's revenue and raising the annuity to $436,000. Perhaps more important, it ended the protectorate by stipulating joint responsibility for the canal's defense, upholding transit passage across the Canal Zone for Panamanian citizens, and abrogating the United States obligation of military intervention in Panama City and Colón. Other sections dealt with a transisthmian highway and greater freedom of radio transmission for Panamanians.[17]

Arias had carried out his campaign promise to renegotiate the treaty of 1903, thanks to the cooperation from the United States president and the State Department. Arias, not Roosevelt, had initiated these talks, but once they commenced, Welles took charge. In the case of the radio provisions, the War Department delayed ratification for eleven years on the grounds of defense considerations. In other matters, over the military's protests, Welles, with support from Hull and Roosevelt, allowed the Panamanian point of view to prevail.

Of course the treaty did not end Panamanian agitation, and nationalists were soon demanding more concessions. In August 1938, Duggan, who had participated in the negotiations, declared that the Panamanians wanted too much. He objected to any further changes because the United States had "stretched every point that we could to make it appear that the Panama Canal is a cooperative enterprise on the part of Panama and the United States."[18]

The truth of Duggan's observations became more cogent as the United States moved closer to war with the Axis. Military anxieties over the canal's security led to requests for additional bases. President Arnulfo Arias, elected in 1940, refused to discuss defense issues unless the United States made further treaty concessions, but he was driven from office before he could force a choice on Roosevelt. Shortly before Pearl Harbor the new regime solved the United States' dilemma by supporting hemispheric solidarity. Seeing this collaboration, some charged United States complicity in the overthrow, but no one could prove it. Indeed, administration spokesmen like Assistant Secretary of State Adolf Berle categorically denied the allegations. Panamanian agitation temporarily abated, but the fundamental conflict remained. The Panamanians wanted control over the canal, while United States opponents refused to alter the status quo.[19]

Welles faced different issues in the Caribbean Islands. Even though the proposed treaty between Haiti and the United States had been defeated at the end of Hoover's term, Stimson informed Roosevelt that the United States was reducing its military presence and making progress on other issues. To prominent Negro leaders like Walter White, executive secretary of the NAACP, this was not enough. Disapproving of imperialism in general, he stubbornly pushed to end the occupation of the only Negro republic in the Americas. White particularly objected to the American demand that this tiny, poverty-stricken nation honor its entire bond obligations at a time when the major European powers were defaulting with impunity on the payment of their war debts.[20]

The Roosevelt administration quickly moved toward terminating the American occupation by appointing as minister to Haiti Norman Armour, a highly respected career diplomat with wide Latin American experience. In early August 1933 he signed an executive agreement that was similar to the rejected Hoover treaty but did not require approval by the hostile Haitian Congress. The central provisions called for the Haitianization of the national guard by October 1, 1934, and the departure of the United States Marines within the next thirty days. Financial arrangements, however, were not significantly altered.[21]

The ease with which the agreement was concluded reflected the changing conditions in both countries and their attitudes toward intervention. From the United States perspective, the fear of European encroachment had vanished, and Haiti was no longer necessary for the defense of the canal's approaches. Since its government had imposed some degree of stability, occupation forces became unnecessary to assure peace. The Haitians accepted the agreement with some relief, for they knew of Roosevelt's boast about having written their constitution, and feared more intervention. Shortly after the signing, the Haitians asked for financial changes, which Roosevelt politely refused. Their delegation at Montevideo discussed the same subject with Hull. As a result of these efforts, the United States and Haiti made a new fiscal arrangement in early 1934 through the National City Bank of New York, but the basic terms were untouched. The United States hoped to find a way to end American financial responsibility, but not without protecting United States investments.[22]

President Stenio Vincent went to Washington in mid-April 1934 to gain more concessions from Roosevelt. These initial talks formed the basis for a joint statement made when Roosevelt journeyed to Haiti on July 5. The presidents declared that the national guard would take complete charge by August 1 and that the marines would leave a fortnight later, speeding up the American withdrawal by two months. The two nations would shortly begin discussions on a new trade treaty, but the existing customs arrangement remained in force until 1941, when the National Bank of Haiti took over the duties of the United States fiscal representative. All obligations were redeemed six years later, ending American responsibility for collecting the Haitian foreign debt. Although Roosevelt had grave misgivings about the Haitians' ability for self-government after the troops' departure, Armour did not share this pessimism. He regarded the visit as an unqualified success, for Roosevelt had treated Haiti as a sovereign state and thereby given its government a tremendous psychological stimulus.[23]

Soon after the occupation's end, some of the most vocal critics of the Haitian intervention reversed themselves. When Walter White learned that President Vincent had instituted censorship and terrorism against dissidents, he demanded an end to these practices. Others reported similar activities, but the State Department refused to investigate their allegations, for the United States had given up its duty to send troops, and interference in Haitian domestic problems was clearly outside American jurisdiction.[24]

The United States faced similar problems in the Dominican Republic. In 1905 the American government established a customs receivership to pay Dominican foreign debts, and eleven years later, troops landed to stabilize a potentially chaotic political situation. During the occupation, lasting until 1924, American marines trained a national constabulary. A member of this force, Rafael Trujillo, became president in 1930, maintaining order through the use of brutal repression. The United States ignored the dictatorship while continuing the receivership. Complications arose when the depression reduced government revenues. The regime defaulted on its foreign bonds that had come due but still paid interest on other ones. In order to adjust for the new conditions, the debt payment was renegotiated in 1934, and fiscal supervision ended before the United States' entrance into World War II.[25]

While this new arrangement solved the difficult economic problem, another depression-related issue caused an enormous loss of life. When the economic decline lowered the Dominican living standard, the government tried to halt the illegal migration of Haitian laborers seeking employment in the neighboring Dominican sugar cane fields. Overly zealous in its desire to stop these crossings, Dominican forces massacred between ten and twenty-five thousand Haitians on October 21, 1937. While seriously aggrieved, the Negro nation never considered war, for Trujillo had a far superior army. Instead, the two nations reached a settlement in early 1938, when the Dominican regime paid an indemnity of $750,000 to Haiti. Both sides acted reluctantly—Trujillo offered payment only because of widespread cititicism from abroad, and Haiti accepted the money since it had no alternative. The United States, as in the Nicaraguan-Honduran border conflict, played a minimal role, and Welles refused to dictate the outcome.[26]

To complete the United States removal from Dominican affairs, Welles moved to terminate the customs receivership. He was well acquainted with its operations since he had served as American commissioner in the Dominican Republic in the early 1920s and had subsequently written a detailed history of the republic. While wishing to end economic control, Welles waited until 1940 to accomplish this by sending a career diplomat, Hugh Wilson, to that nation. Arriving in August, Wilson found that the regime had already formulated an acceptable termination plan, allocating revenues to protect American interests, and servicing the loan. In less than a month the two parties reached an understanding, and the receivership stopped in 1941, with the final liquidation six years later. Here Welles followed his established pattern—as long as no crucial United States interests were involved, American intervention was to be abandoned or avoided. In the Dominican case, Trujillo provided political stability and guaranteed American investments. The United States needed nothing more.[27]

The issues presented by the Cuban Revolution of 1933 were much more difficult to resolve. Grau's supporters rejoiced at Welles's recall, assuming that this meant repudiation of his actions, but their elation was premature. Although Welles left the island, he continued to direct United States policy toward Cuba from Washington. His Cuban adversaries failed to comprehend that his return to the State Department made him more powerful than ever before, for his daily access to Hull and Roosevelt enabled him to present his case without letting his opponents answer.

Assisting Welles in his efforts was the new ambassador to Cuba, Jefferson Caffery, who arrived in Havana shortly after his predecessor's departure. Before taking up his duties, Caffery had directed Latin American affairs from Washington and was thoroughly familiar with Cuban conditions. He had demonstrated his ability to win the confidence of Latin American rulers at his previous posts, and Havana was no exception. Within a month of his arrival, local politicans knew that Caffery opposed Grau's recognition. The new ambassador abandoned Welles's plan for a coalition government and initiated his own scheme. He gained the confidence of the leader of Cuba's armed forces, Fulgencio Batista. With pressure from the United States embassy and the military leader's cooperation, Grau resigned in mid-January 1934.[28]

After several days of political negotiations, Carlos Mendieta, a traditional politician acceptable to the American embassy and Batista, took the presidency on January 18. Five days later Roosevelt recognized the new ruler, declaring that he had majority support and was maintaining order. Neither assumption was true. During his brief term, Mendieta suffered from his own inherent weaknesses, political bickering, outbreaks of strikes, and urban terrorism. Batista managed to provide a semblance of order, but in so doing he substituted military control for civilian rule.[29]

With the recognition of the Mendieta government, nonrecognition ceased to be a foreign policy option. The American failure to establish normal relations with Grau enabled Batista to rise; diplomatic ties consolidated his power. The recognition of Mendieta demonstrated the inconsistency of Welles's earlier refusal to establish relations with Grau. Mendieta did not win diplomatic approval for his personal popularity or claims of stability. He won support because Caffery recommended it, and in this Welles witnessed the futility of nonrecognition. The assistant secretary learned his lesson, and as long as he determined Latin American policy, nonrecognition was abandoned as a diplomatic weapon.

With formal relations restored, the United States and Cuba started negotiations in early April 1934 to change the permanent treaty of 1903. Welles opened the discussions in Washington, and two months later a new treaty was approved and ratified. Except for maintaining the naval station at Guantánamo Bay, United States troops no longer had the privilege to land on Cuban soil. The Platt Amendment, an emotional issue for three decades, had been abrogated without any serious opposition. Praising the new treaty, the Cuban regime saw in it the beginning of national independence, while the Roosevelt administration publicized it as a milestone in its nonintervention policy. Some Cuban critics still complained about the influence of the American ambassador and Batista's prestige. Their discontent was fully justified, for Caffery, with approval from both governments, kept warships in nearby waters for months after the end of the Platt Amendment to demonstrate continued American backing for the shaky Mendieta regime.[30]

Caffery gave another vivid illustration of his power to influence political decisions in 1936. For the first time in twelve years, Cubans conducted a presidential election, which Miguel M. Gómez won. Entering office in late May, he at once began a battle for control against Batista and his followers. Seeking an issue on which to base his campaign, the new president chose a piece of legislation for the funding of rural schools taught by the military. On the grounds that civilians and not the armed forces should direct education, he vetoed the bill. Agitated by Gómez's action, army officers called for his immediate ouster. When Caffery learned about a possible coup d'état, he informed Batista that the embassy would oppose it and support the preservation of the constitutional system. The military leader promised to respect Caffery's wishes. Using the legislative system, the military's congressional supporters and other presidential opponents overrode the veto, and then filed impeachment charges against Gómez. Since the constitution did not define impeachable crimes, the balloting represented a vote of no confidence. In late December, Congress formally removed Gómez from office. Batista had followed the letter of the law but not its spirit.[31]

No one staged demonstrations on the president's behalf, for he lacked broadbased support. Duggan dejectedly observed shortly after the removal: "Although the inauguration of the Gomez Government perhaps did not bring back democratic government in Cuba, it was at least a start in that direction. The Army is in complete ascendancy, which has given rise to considerable unfavorable publicity in this country. With regard to the specific point at issue, I can't imagine anything less likely to inculcate democratic ideals than education under the tutelage of the Army."[32]

Duggan's criticism indicated a dilemma that confronted the Roosevelt administration throughout Latin America. How should the United States react to the perversion of the democratic process? In this instance, Caffery had warned Batista to follow the constitutionally prescribed form in dealing with Gómez. Although Batista had violated the intent of Cuba's basic law, the ambassador continued his staunch support for the military. To be sure, American ambassadors were expected to proclaim democratic principles while at their stations, and Caffery was no exception. However, he knew that politics had dictated Gómez's fall and that nothing, not even the espousal of democratic precepts, would save him.

Roosevelt, unconcerned over such inconsistencies, popularized nonintervention as the hallmark of the Good Neighbor. In July 1934, for example, he visited three Caribbean nations for his initial voyage from the mainland as president. The trip attracted worldwide news coverage, and Roosevelt made the most of this exposure by accelerating the troop withdrawal from Haiti and announcing his willingness to discuss Panamanian concerns. At the same time he instituted a public relations campaign, in which he became the first American president to travel to a South American nation while in office. After his arrival at the ancient port city of Cartagena on July 10, he and the Colombian president, Enrique Olaya Herrera, toured the city and exchanged public compliments. Olaya's praise of American policies was significant, especially in view of Colombia's bitterness over the United States role in Panamanian independence.[33]

Through good will visits by prominent Democratic officials, specific bilateral agreements for withdrawing troops, and multilateral statements upholding sovereignty, nonintervention and the Good Neighbor became interchangeable. The Roosevelt administration spokesmen ignored or dismissed the fact that nonintervention had exceptions. Caffery continually influenced Cuban internal decisions, and Lane tried to prevent Somoza's rise. The United States kept its military forces in the Panama Canal Zone and at Guantánamo Bay. Roosevelt fulfilled his pledge by never landing troops to restore order, but he did station warships in Cuban waters, first at Welles's insistence and then as a sign of support for the Mendieta regime. In economic matters, the United States maintained its fiscal responsibilities in Haiti and the Dominican Republic until American investments were secure. In actuality, the United States abrogated what was obsolete and retained what it considered vital to the national interest.

The Caribbean rulers during the 1930s contributed to the Good Neighbor's exaggerated claims. Dictators like Trujillo and Somoza and others less despotic, such as Batista and Jorge Ubico of Guatemala, looked for United States approval. To identify themselves with the Roosevelt administration and curry its favor, they promoted the Good Neighbor. It meant something different to each of them, but all perceived United States support as enhancing their authority. Since they controlled or influenced much of their nations' news media, Roosevelt's Latin American diplomacy gained added credence.

The Roosevelt administration found the nonintervention principle appealing to the general public. The idea was easy to explain, and it was promoted simplistically. Nevertheless, few understood the complex nature of nonintervention. Previous Republican administrations had taken action that easily fell under the heading, like the withdrawal of marines from Nicaragua and similar attempts in Haiti. However, these independent actions were not woven into an overall concept. In the Roosevelt administration, Welles carefully coordinated and monitored complicated policies. Observers missed these subtle distinctions, and neither the Roosevelt government nor the authoritarian benefactors in the Caribbean were anxious to change the image. No intervention was never an absolute reality—only an illusion that was valuable in popularizing the Good Neighbor principle.

4 ★ DEPRESSION ECONOMICS

WHILE THE WITHDRAWAL of United States Marines from the Caribbean received most of the headlines, the Roosevelt administration moved unsurely into another equally vital area. The Americas had suffered a devastating depression, and the effects of the political actions would have been lessened without some corresponding attempts to develop proposals for economic recovery. Despite this realization, during the worst period of the depression the New Deal moved inconsistently in its efforts to expand hemispheric commerce. The conflict centered on antithetical viewpoints: some domestic groups wanted to protect and expand their share of the market, while at the same time, others called for increased foreign trade to resuscitate the United States economy. Both had the same goal—commercial revival—but their modi operandi were different. Each side placed enormous pressure on administration and congressional leaders to get its position adopted, but neither won a clearcut advantage. As a result, these warring factions caused confusion and limited the United States' ability to define its hemispheric commercial objectives during most of the 1930s.

American bondholders further clouded the economic forecast. They desperately turned to the government for collection of the debt owed on their bonds when most of the Latin American nations defaulted, but the Hoover administration rejected their pleas: the Latin American governments and private United States citizens had negotiated these loans, and the United States disclaimed any official responsibility for collection. Herbert Feis, the economic adviser in the State Department, objected to this rigid stand. He advocated the formation of an independent association that would try to salvage private investors' foreign bonds and receive assistance and encouragement from the foreign service. He advanced this plan under the Republican leadership and continued his efforts into the Democratic administration. Finally his activities led to the incorporation of the Foreign Bondholders Protective Council (FBPC) in December 1933.[1]

Feis's enthusiasm for the FBPC did not guarantee presidential backing. For example, Roosevelt declared in late 1933 that "the United States is not owed any money by any of the South American republics and it is therefore a matter between those republics and any of the bondholders . . . ."[2] Hull echoed similar sentiments, but unrealistically favored the formation of a bondholders' committee, somehow divorced from speculative banking interests, to collect small investors' debts.[3]

The president and secretary spoke in generalities and allowed their subordinates to fill in the essential details. For Latin America, that charge fell to Welles. Even before he entered the administration he consistently opposed general defaults, but could offer no solution to prevent them. In early 1934 he began working on revised payment schedules for Haiti and the Dominican Republic. The United States controlled both through treaty provisions, and Welles worked out plans for the former to continue paying its full indebtedness and the latter to pay at a renegotiated rate. The assistant secretary hesitated from taking vigorous action in most other nations during the depressed conditions, for those countries did not have the capability for payment.[4]

Welles's refusal to act aggressively, of course, did not inhibit FBPC activities. Its representatives exerted pressure on the diplomatic corps to support their cause. This was not unexpected, for the two leaders of the council were J. Reuben Clark, a former undersecretary of state, and Francis White, previously assistant secretary of state.[5]

While the FBPC met with little success in its campaign, the State Department turned to its own ineffective measures to improve the financial climate in the Americas. During the summer of 1934, for instance, the State Department sent a representative of the banking community to South America for two months to examine the growth of exchange controls that severely restricted United States trade. When he finished this trip, he concluded that only economic recovery would end those forms of protectionism.[6]

The United States also attended meetings like the Buenos Aires commercial conference in May and June of 1935. This dealt primarily with technical issues such as port facilities, customs duties, communications, and tourist traffic. American delegates also used this gathering to reiterate Hull's proposal for reducing tariff barriers. No concrete issues were resolved, but the United States representatives believed that this forum provided an opportunity to promote more cordial relations.[7]

One item on the conference agenda that Welles tried to further was the construction of an inter-American highway. Plans were begun under Coolidge, and his successor had routes surveyed in Central America. Roosevelt also approved of the project and ordered the continuation of the surveys, believing that a connecting roadway between North and South America would be a momentous accomplishment. Many proponents envisioned thousands of tourists traveling in both directions and increasing political, economic, and cultural exchange. These dreams remained unfulfilled throughout the Roosevelt years. During the 1930s Congress refused to appropriate adequate funding, and when money was available during World War II, technicians, equipment, and material were needed elsewhere.[8]

Another vital communication gap was in hemispheric shipping service. Assistant Secretary of State Breckinridge Long welcomed in a new inter-American maritime service in late 1938, but he feared that this new link did not necessarily mean increased trade. To assure success, Long recommended that the United States buy Latin American goods, not for import, but for resale elsewhere in order to provide the American republics with dollar exchange needed to purchase United States products.[9]

While the State Department vainly tried to improve Pan American economics ties, the Treasury Department naturally became involved. Hull would restrict the role of most government agencies in foreign affairs, but he continually complained about what he regarded as interference by Secretary of the Treasury Henry Morgenthau, Jr. One example of this so-called meddling was the silver issue. The United States and Mexico were the world's largest producers of the metal and American companies owned about half of the Mexican industry. By May 1933 both nations cooperated to bring some stability to the price of silver. Approximately a year later the United States passed the Silver Purchase Act, which gave the treasury secretary broad authority in buying and selling silver on the world market to bolster its price.[10]

For the rest of the decade Morgenthau used this power to help subsidize Latin American producers. When the Mexican industry needed support, the United States assisted by adjusting the international price of silver or buying Mexican surpluses. The Treasury Department also purchased Peruvian silver; almost two-thirds of the Peruvian silver industry was held by United States firms. Nine other Latin American nations benefited from the program. These purchases did not have a significant impact on the United States economy, but they had a major effect in the Americas, particularly in Mexico and Peru, which heavily depended on silver exports to obtain scarce foreign exchange.[11]

Morgenthau understood the political as well as the economic value of closer commercial interaction among the Americas and tried to encourage sound financial practices. In early 1937, for instance, Welles asked him to develop programs for currency stabilization and the establishment of a central bank in Brazil to serve as a hemispheric model. The Treasury Department held lengthy talks with Brazilian experts, and together they formulated proposals to obtain monetary stability, with technical aid and advice from the Treasury Department to draw the Brazilians closer toward United States commercial objectives.[12]

Toward the end of 1938 Roosevelt invited Oswaldo Aranha, Brazil's foreign minister and probably the strongest and most vocal Latin American advocate of the president's diplomacy, to visit the United States for bilateral discussions. In early 1939, shortly before his arrival, Welles wrote: "I am now trying to have formulated a definite policy with regard to commercial and financial cooperation in the other American republics which I am particularly desirous of having done before Aranha reaches Washington."[13] The foreign minister held talks from mid-February until mid-March on a wide range of topics. At the start of the discussions, Roosevelt talked to reporters about the South American giant's economic possibilities: "Brazil has one of the greatest futures for development in the world."[14] This flattering comment did not help in the conclusion of any major agreement, and the president acknowledged as much when he declared that the negotiations could increase trade and assist in stabilizing bilateral exchange rates. The Brazilians were even less enthusiastic.[15]

Most of the blame for the evaporation of the positive expectations can be placed on Roosevelt's cabinet members, who were unable to cooperate. The Treasury and State Departments simply could not agree on a united approach. Morgenthau had consented to assist Brazil in its foreign exchange problem and help establish a central bank and a stabilization fund. Before he had an opportunity to move forward on these ideas, Feis blocked any loans or credits until Brazil worked out a settlement with American bondholders. The treasury secretary argued that the State Department's insistence on a debt payment would prevent any meaningful agreement, but Feis's view prevailed, even though Morgenthau was right. The Brazilians half-heartedly committed themselves to negotiate with the bondholders and received a loan to assist in these efforts. This inflexible attitude, however, clouded the atmosphere of the entire discussions, and Aranha left the United States without any major commitment. The one trend that continued was the bickering between the state and treasury officials that strained their already unhealthy relations.[16]

Morgenthau, in spite of State Department hostility, continued to urge hemispheric financial order to offset the growing German penetration in the Americas. To cancel a serious Nazi threat, he wanted to study Latin American economic problems and find solutions to assure domestic peace. He tried to win Roosevelt's backing for his projects, but Hull jealously guarded his prerogatives in foreign affairs and vigorously fought against the treasury secretary's frequent intrusions.[17]

The State Department's refusal to follow Morgenthau's views elicited harsh criticism from Assistant Secretary of the Treasury Henry D. White. Devoted to enforcing his superior's beliefs, by late 1939 White concluded that the foreign service's efforts to improve Pan American economic relations had dismally failed and that the Axis had established a secure footing in the Americas. He condemned the diplomatic corps for ineptitude and urged the appointment of a cabinet member, presumably Morgenthau, to establish an inter-American bank that would make loans to stabilize economies and finance United States exports. He felt that Latin American entrepreneurs should direct industrial growth to avoid charges of American penetration. White hoped these proposals would prevent further Axis advances, but his suggestions were never carried out.[18]

As long as economic conditions remained generally depressed, the rivalry between the Treasury and the State Departments proved only a minor embarrassment. However, when the United States expanded its international financial commitments, this unwholesome relationship severely impaired inter-American economic diplomacy. The antagonism between the two departments also grew into personal resentment between Hull and Morgenthau over a wide variety of foreign policy recommendations. Roosevelt did little to end this discord, and may have encouraged it by allowing the two men to compete for his favor. Some of Morgenthau's ideas had considerable merit, but Hull refused to consider them because of animosity or anxiety lest treasury preempt a role in shaping large policy. By the outbreak of the European war this interdepartmental enmity was ingrained.

Henry Wallace also became interested in Pan American affairs, but without creating friction between the Agriculture and State Departments. Almost as soon as he assumed his secretaryship, he expressed his intention to cultivate better hemispheric relations. Under the Agricultural Adjustment Act and the Jones-Costigan Act, he allocated import quotas to Latin American nations for certain basic farm products such as sugar and tobacco. Wallace also illustrated his heightened interest in the Americas during 1935 by beginning Spanish lessons and learning Latin American customs. A year later he began to suggest improving inter-American trade by having Latin American countries ship tropical items that would not compete with the goods of domestic farmers. He avoided specific proposals during the mid 1930s, but as war drew nearer he became more vocal and definite in his declarations.[19]

One other agency slightly influenced Pan American financial matters in the 1930s. Early in Roosevelt's administration he issued an executive order creating the First Export-Import Bank, which had a five-member board headed by the secretary of commerce and significant State Department participation. The bank was originally established to stimulate trade between the United States and the Soviet Union, and when that failed to materialize, a Second Export-Import Bank was designed to assist any nation except Russia. Cuba received three silver loans designated to pay government employees' salaries, and a few other loans were concluded. Throughout the 1930s the bank operated under narrow commercial guidelines solely designed to increase United States foreign trade. Some called for the bank's expansion, but early in 1939 Hull answered them by urging the bank's continuation on the basis of its restricted confines. To his mind, freer trade, not government lending, was the solution to international financial problems.[20]

Democrats had traditionally opposed the Republican advocacy of the high protective tariff. During the presidential campaign of 1932, Roosevelt pleased party regulars by calling for lower tariff barriers to stimulate trade. After he entered office, his enthusiasm markedly declined. Hull, the leading administration exponent of lowering trade barriers, ignored the president's change of mood and urged him to ask Congress for new tariff legislation. Roosevelt rejected his advice, believing that congressional opposition was too adamant and that the time remaining before adjournment was too short for careful consideration. He would wait until the next session, in January 1934, to present this type of legislation.[21]

Hull learned about this decision while traveling to the London Economic Conference, and was disappointed. Later, during the conference, Roosevelt's refusal to cooperate with international currency stabilization raised another serious obstacle to his desire for reducing trade restrictions. During Hull's absence, the president, probably sympathizing with his secretary's commitment to this program, directed the State Department to open exploratory talks for bilateral trade treaties. Undersecretary Phillips warily took charge of these initial discussions with five nations. All treaties, he knew, would need approval by two-thirds of the Senate, and winning the necessary votes for significant tariff changes without arousing opposition from vested interests would take much careful maneuvering.[22]

These bilateral trade discussions failed to produce any treaties. One was signed wth Colombia but it never went to the Senate for ratification. Nevertheless, the negotiations helped evolve the State Department's foreign economics positions. Since the major exports of Colombia and the United States did not compete, both nations might hope to gain major advantages without injuring the other—Colombia for its coffee, the United States for a variety of products. The treaty also included an unconditional most-favored-nation clause, which meant that reductions in this agreement would also be extended to future trade treaties that either nation signed with any other countries. The announcement of the treaty shortly before the Montevideo conference assisted Hull in the passage of his economic resolution there, for during the debates, the Colombian delegate gave his unequivocal support to the United States position. With the passage of the economic resolution, Hull had not only the Colombian treaty but also an inter-American commitment to support his trade policies.[23]

Roosevelt knew that the secretary would resume lobbying for a still broader program on his return, and he remembered his own promise to ask Congress for tariff legislation during the next session. More realistically, he recognized the powerful sentiment for reducing trade barriers within his own party. During December 1933, still uncertain after considering alternatives, Roosevelt hesitantly allowed Hull to draft legislation, and on March 2, 1934, the reciprocal trade agreements bill went to Congress for debate. Hotly contested, its provisions delegated tariff regulation to the executive, permitting the president to negotiate agreements that raised or lowered tariff duties by as much as one-half. Congress also specified a three-year term for the law to gauge its effectiveness, giving Hull enough time to translate his ideas into a practical program. Using the primary argument that this act would provide new foreign markets, resulting in additional jobs, the Democratic majority passed the bill into law over vehement Republican congressional opposition.[24]

The secretary never relaxed his belief that somehow freer trade insured world peace. To translate this ideal into practice, the secretary brought Francis Sayre, Wilson's son-in-law and a Harvard law professor, into the State Department as an assistant secretary. Sayre shared the secretary's beliefs and worked to promote reciprocity. Others in the department were less enthusiastic, but Hull's determination demanded allegiance. There was no room for skeptics.[25]

Outside the State Department other influential Democrats promoted the program. Secretary of Commerce Daniel Roper favored reciprocity, especially in the Americas. Since the United States and many Latin American nations had noncompetitive exports, he reasoned that such negotiations would produce prompt and beneficial results. On this foundation, agreements with other countries with more complicated commercial policies might be erected. Albert Burleson, who was postmaster general under Wilson and active in Texas banking, was more doctrinaire. He held dogmatically to the principle that immediate free trade with all countries would end the depression. Employment must be stimulated, and trade expansion was the panacea. Burleson wanted to sign agreements with every western hemispheric nation,[26] for to him, "the day of the Protective Tariff is gone. It was not the tariff which made our country the richest and most powerful in the world, but the untrammeled free trade which has existed between the sovereign states making up this Union."[27]

Several powerful Republican spokesmen blunted their party's opposition. At the height of the congressional debate over the bill Henry Stimson spoke over the radio to a nationwide audience, supporting the proposed legislation and condemning congressional logrolling to determine tariff rates. His one-time undersecretary, William Castle, concurred but also implied that the Democrats would mismanage the program. William Culbertson, ambassador to Chile under Hoover, believed that artifically high tariff duties retarded recovery, and therefore he backed Hull's approach. Even the staunch Republican journalist from Emporia, Kansas, William Allen White, supported the measure as a means to provide more jobs for the unemployed.[28]

Hoover and many other Republicans opposed the act because it gave too much power to the president and infringed upon congressional prerogatives. Hull's most formidable threat, however, came from George Peek, whom Roosevelt had appointed foreign trade adviser in the State Department while Hull was at Montevideo. Peek advocated dumping United States surpluses on foreign markets, preferential treatment for farm commodities, and barter arrangements—all contrary to Hull's program. Because of these irreconcilable differences, Peek and Hull continually clashed. Nevertheless, Hull persevered, for Peek offered criticism but no workable alternative. Finally, toward the end of Roosevelt's first term, Peek resigned in disgust to conduct a futile public attack from the outside on the administration's foreign trade activities.[29]

Neither Peek nor any other critic shook Hull's determination to prove the program's merits. By the time of Roosevelt's reelection, the Democratic platform claimed that the act was assisting domestic recovery and helping to bring world peace. In 1937 Hull obtained the act's renewal without presidential endorsement, but in 1940 the secretary won Roosevelt's blessings. Even this belated White House support did not bring dramatic results. Too many international complications inhibited trading efforts. The Japanese developed their economic sphere of influence in the Far East; Germany relied heavily on barter arrangements; and the British had a system of commonwealth preference. These measure significantly restricted the flow of trade, and the outbreak of the European war destroyed any remaining possibility of success.[30]

While Hull set the general guidelines, Welles directed the reciprocity effort in Latin America. Less dogmatic than his chief, Welles was primarily concerned with constructing a firm hemispheric alliance, and regarded closer economic cooperation as merely one part of the desired whole. In practice the reciprocal trade agreements with many of the Latin American nations did not bring conclusive commercial expansion, but the agreements unquestionably moved the signatories toward greater understanding in other endeavors.

The first agreement was signed with Cuba in August 1934. Although Hull favored the unconditional most-favored-nation clause, this agreement omitted this provision and, indeed, stipulated exclusive preferential rate reductions. Cuba directly linked its sugar and tobacco exports to United States quotas, which guaranteed producers a portion of the market on the mainland. Once growers knew their allotment, uncertainty ended and economic conditions on the island improved. At the same time the United States received concessions on a tremendous variety of items that severely inhibited diversification efforts. Under the terms of the agreement the United States had bound the island's commercial activity closer than ever before to American-made decisions over which the Cubans had no control.[31]

Another country in which the United States did not reach its stated objectives was Brazil. While the two nations traditionally had close economic bonds, negotiations for a reciprocal trade agreement proved extremely difficult. Complicating the bargaining was the fact that Brazil and Germany signed a commercial agreement in late 1934 that included restrictive sections. Since Brazil had granted Germany special reductions, some in the State Department wanted to abandon the reciprocity principle and threaten to place duties on coffee imports if the Brazilians did not grant the United States the same concessions the Nazis had won. Hull refused to consider this alternative and instead tried to persuade the Brazilians to cancel their barter deal with the Germans in favor of his reciprocity concept. During these negotiations the Brazilians realized that the State Department would not retaliate commercially to win adherence to reduced tariffs, and as a result the United States lost a major bargaining point. In mid-1930s the Nazis provided the greatest incentives to the opportunistic Brazilians. The United States and Brazil did sign an agreement that did not substantially change trading patterns but drew the two nations toward closer cooperation.[32]

Other negotiations also illustrated how a variety of factors affected bargaining. The Colombian treaty was replaced by an executive agreement under the new act. Few provisions were changed, but internal Colombian politics delayed approval until 1936. An agreement of the same year with Guatemala provided minimal concessions, basically preserving the status quo. Problems over oil competition stalled Venezuelan talks, but with the outbreak of World War II, the insatiable demand for petroleum products ended the oil problems and made the signing of an agreement relatively easy. The bargaining with Argentina was another graphic example of competing goods. While the depression lasted, neither nation was able to export all of its farm surpluses. When the war increased demand, new markets emerged, and the two nations concluded an agreement in 1941.[33]

During the Latin American negotiations economic improvement was the major concern. However, in countries such as Brazil, Guatemala, and Argentina, an integral role went to political considerations—the desire to draw these nations closer to American international policies. The United States signed fifteen agreements with the Latin American nations from 1933 through 1945, eleven of them before 1940. The six mentioned above show that each situation contained a unique combination of commercial and noncommercial factors. At first Latin Americans welcomed Hull's initiative, but later some complained about their inability to develop diversified economies under the restrictions of the agreements. The act worked best where reductions were based on noncompetitive goods; it had to overcome serious obstacles from nations exporting products similar to those of the United States. Cuba won its quota over bitter opposition from United States sugar beet growers because of the island's strategic importance. Venezuela and the United States did not sign an agreement until oil consumption rose. To the end Argentina faced unyielding antagonism from American cattlemen.[34]

In spite of these troubles, Welles saw considerable merit in Hull's initiative, and praised his efforts: "The greatest positive achievement of the first Roosevelt Administration in the realm of international co-operation lay in the trade agreements policy [for] which Secretary of State Hull is wholly responsible, and which he has furthered with a single-minded and indefatigable devotion. . . . It greatly assisted in establishing the good neighbor policy in the Western Hemisphere."[35]

Welles later criticized Hull for insisting that the administration's influence plus a series of trade agreements would halt the Axis advance. The secretary advertised reciprocity as a measure to restore prosperity and later as a means to maintain international peace. Neither goal was reached. According to the undersecretary, Hull never understood the limited scope of his economic program.[36]

Certainly Hull was unrealistic and overzealous in his commitment to reciprocity. In the 1930s no trade program would have deterred the Axis. Yet he did succeed in removing tariff logrolling from the congressional arena. Since the New Deal, Congress has accepted Hull's legislation as the basis for its tariff policies.

Just as the reciprocal trade agreements program dwarfed the other economics initiatives taken toward Latin America in the 1930s, oil disputes were the most perplexing commercial dilemma to which the United States struggled to respond. The first dispute faced by the Roosevelt government arose in Bolivia over a Standard Oil of New Jersey subsidiary operating some Bolivian concessions since the early 1920s. Throughout their association, the company and the Bolivian government argued over production figures and royalties, and this disagreement was magnified in the Chaco War because of Bolivia's desperate need for revenue. The Bolivian officials, furthermore, requested a loan from the company on future production to help finance the war, but Standard Oil refused. It had decided that this business venture was unprofitable, intended to cancel its concession, and began shipping equipment to the company's Argentine oil fields.[37]

What the company had not anticipated was the government's reaction. On March 13, 1937, Bolivia annulled Standard Oil's contract and confiscated its holdings on the grounds that the company had avoided taxes and sent illegal oil shipments to Argentina. The government did not mention its bitterness over the scant oil production or the loan rebuff. Bolivian leaders hoped that they would gain political and economic advantages over Paraguay if the United States property was turned over to Argentina, a potentially powerful wartime ally. Standard Oil ignored these emotional and political considerations and focused on the purported charges. The company had already admitted to owing taxes and was awaiting a court decision to determine its penalty. As far as illegal transportation, Standard Oil denied that allegation. In any eventuality such protestations were inconsequential. Bolivians of all persuasions welcomed this action as a nationalistic triumph at a time of despair after a disastrous war.

No Latin American country had ever confiscated an American oil company's holdings. Since the seizure came as a result of illegal operations, the Bolivians asserted that Standard Oil was not entitled to compensation. The company refused to accept this judgment; it requested and received

State Department assistance in support of its case. At first Welles suggested exhausting local legal remedies, but Bolivian judges, coerced by threats of violence if they found for the company, could not fairly determine the merits of the case. Both sides then rejected arbitration. In the midst of these bargaining efforts, the State Department felt that Bolivia seemed inflexible. It had seized United States property and refused to pay for it. As a result the department decided to withhold any loans and financial aid until the issue was resolved. To Welles and his colleagues, Good Neighbor diplomacy required fair treatment on both sides.

The Roosevelt administration held to this policy until July 1941, when an allegedly Nazi-inspired coup d'état appeared to shake Bolivian domestic peace. Faced with the United States' policy of fair treatment and the necessity of hemispheric tranquility, Welles worked out an arrangement in early 1942 to achieve both goals. The Bolivians paid the company $1,500,000 for the sale of its property. At the same time Bolivian gained $25,000,000 in economic assistance from the United States. Each side was satisified and so was the State Department. The dispute had been localized and had not affected any other bilateral or multilateral relationships.[38]

While the relatively small-scale production in the Bolivian fields limited adverse repercussions, bilateral disagreements with Mexico seriously disturbed relations with the United States. The Roosevelt administration had avoided a potentially explosive situation when American Catholics tried to embroil Congress in Mexican religious policies, but the issue of land ownership touched on the much more basic conflict—private property rights versus Latin American nationalistic aspirations. Mexico suffered from insufficient arable land. Those few who had the money to purchase acreage naturally chose the best, and the remainder went to the poor. Lázaro Cárdenas pledged in his presidential campaign to redistribute the land to more Mexicans, and he began fulfilling this promise almost as soon as he entered office in 1934 by dividing large estates into smaller units. The government sometimes expropriated United States-owned property, and the titleholders demanded State Department protection.[39] By early 1937 these agrarian claims reached the White House, at which time Roosevelt issued a statement that if any government seized American-owned land, then the United States expected "prompt and effective compensation to be paid to the owners on not less than the same basis than payments are made to the nationals of the country making the expropriations."[40]

The president had taken an unrealistic position toward Mexico's land expropriation. Its government did not have the necessary funds to comply, and furthermore, Cárdenas had no intention of interrupting a nationally popular program to please the American president. The United States ambassador to Mexico, Josephus Daniels, realized that the agrarian expropriations would continue even without adequate capital for compensation. Under these circumstances he pressed for payment on what he considered especially valid claims. These usually involved smaller landholders, for more owners of large estates had vastly exaggerated their properties' worth, and this created unnecessary antagonism between themsevles and the Mexican officials.[41]

Welles sought to find grounds for compromise. In a letter to the Mexican ambassador to the United States, Francisco Castillo Nájera, Welles, on November 4, 1937, expressed his desire to assist Mexican aspirations, but added that Ameican residents must not suffer unduly in the land expropriations. Welles cautioned: "Unless we can show our own people that the good neighbor policy is responded to wholeheartedly by our neighbors, it can hardly be assumed that the people of the United States and the Congress which represents them will favor indefinitely a continuation by this Government of any policy which proves to be one-sided."[42]

While Welles mainly considered agrarian claims, he also mentioned the growing conflict between the oil companies and the Mexican government. At the turn of the twentieth century, foreign petroleum interests began developing concessions. However, after the Mexican Revolution, the nationalistic sentiment opposing foreign exploitation came out in an article of the Constitution of 1917, vesting subsoil rights to the state. The provision's enforcement caused bilateral troubles during the 1920s, but each time Republican administrations found ways to preserve the private companies' holdings. Thus, rather than addressing fundamental problems, these agreements maintained an uneasy status quo.

When Cárdenas assumed office, he advanced labor union organization and supported efforts to win higher wages and improved living standards for workers in the oil fields. The companies refused to discuss these issues, and as a consequence, the petroleum unions threatened to strike. Cárdenas decided to intervene in this labor-management struggle. After examining the existing conditions within the industry, the president sided with the workers and ordered salary increases and added fringe benefits. Rather than comply, the companies vainly sought court relief. After they exhausted their legal remedies, they still refused to accede to the president's directives. The companies began withdrawing large sums of money from Mexico in the hope that this form of economic coercion would force the government's capitulation.[43]

Instead of responding as desired, Cárdenas shocked the oil industry by unexpectedly expropriating their holdings on March 18, 1938. The British government, whose nationals owned 70 percent of the industry, quickly broke relations and enacted strong economic sanctions. The United States, whose citizens controlled most of the remaining fields, took a longer period to respond because of a split within the diplomatic corps. Many wanted to follow the English example, but Ambassador Daniels argued that such a harsh policy would destroy generally improving bilateral bonds. The United

States, he urged, must recognize the expropriation's legitimacy and insist on prompt, adequate, and effective compensation for its nationals.[44]

Daniels basically aligned himself with the Mexicans. The oil concerns had rejected the reasonable requests of Cárdenas, according to the ambassador, but he added that the companies were not totally at fault. Daniels admitted that the Mexican chief executive had acted imprudently and impetuously—a course of action to which the United States must not succumb.[45] He repeatedly wrote Roosevelt, urging patience and reminding the president that the Good Neighbor policy was "of the highest consideration in a mad world where Pan American solidarity may save democracy. Oil ought not smear it."[46]

Morgenthau supported Daniels by objecting to strong measures against the Mexican government. When the State Department considered using reduced purchases of Mexican silver as a diplomatic weapon, the Treasury Department tried to have to scheme aborted. The treasury secretary viewed such actions as antagonistic, further alienating the Mexicans and forcing them to trade with the Nazis. When Hull asked Morgenthau to lower the price of silver in treasury purchases, the latter not only refused but also bought Mexican silver on the world market, which helped Cárdenas in his efforts to obtain foreign exchange.[47]

State Department leaders in Washington preferred a much firmer approach. Assistant Secretary Berle thought that Daniels made his embassy reports reflect his own arguments instead of showing the actual situation. In early 1939 he confided to his diary: "Daniels is as bad an Ambassador as we have ever had. . . ."[48] Berle also blamed Cárdenas for precipitating the crisis; after all, he had expropriated and had an obligation to compensate. These hasty actions, according to Berle, had brought forth bitter resentment within the oil companies. When several of their representatives approached him with the idea of fomenting a revolution to topple the Mexican government, he tried to dissuade them.[49]

Counselor to the department Moore had other objections. He believed that Cárdenas was taking advantage of the Good Neighbor's overly ambitious declarations. Nonintervention, to Moore, was meant to cancel the Nicaraguan and the Haitian military occupations. The pledges at Montevideo against intervention were " a pretty unwise Christmas gift." As a result, "If Mexico. . . should take over American oil interests in that country, without being checked, the same can occur in Bolivia, where it has already occurred, and Columbia [sic], Argentina, Ecuador and Venezuela."[50] Assistant Secretary of State George Messersmith concurred. Expropriation must be stopped in Mexico to prevent its spread.[51]

Industrialist Bernard Baruch also feared the Mexican precedent. He acknowledged the right of expropriation and was not even overly alarmed at the loss of United States capital. What seriously troubled him was his trepidation that this action would concurrently jeopardize America's international trade and its national security. Baruch held that the original owners had explored, developed, and managed the properties. Since Latin American nations lacked managerial skills in petroleum production, the American oil companies should continue to be treated preferentially. If this did not happen, these developing nations might employ Nazi technicians, giving Germany control over critical supplies of raw materials, virtually assuring a lower United States trading volume, and ultimately decreasing the standard of living.[52]

Others, like William Borchard, an international lawyer who was teaching at Yale University, and John Moore, an international legal expert with a distinguished record in the diplomatic corps, aligned themselves with the oil companies because of their antipathy toward Roosevelt and their defense of property rights. Both men felt that the United States should refuse to recognize the expropriation's validity and deal firmly with Cárdenas. By rejecting this course, the oil companies lost their bargaining power to negotiate a favorable settlement.[53]

The Americans seemed split evenly over the oil controversy. In September 1939 an opinion poll asked, "Should the United States use force to protect American property if Mexico or any other Latin American nation seized it?" Approximately 39 percent responded both for and against, with the remainder undecided.[54]

Roosevelt listened to a variety of opinions, and in early 1939 offered his own solution. He reasoned that expropriation was justified only when accompanied by fair compensation. Since the Mexicans were unable to provide this, the president felt that the companies and the Cárdenas administration should sign a long-term contract to manage the oil properties. The two parties would share the profits until the business firms recouped their investment. Roosevelt naively believed that this was an equitable solution; he never perceived the deep animosity that existed between the opposing forces.[55]

When the oil firms did negotiate, they did so halfheartedly. In 1939 Standard Oil hired Donald Richberg, a well-known lawyer and prominent New Dealer, to reach an agreement with the Mexicans. Richberg tried to get both sides to compromise,[56] but by early 1941, he quit in disgust because of the firm's inflexibility: "The underlying policy of 'no compromise' was unwise in 1938 and has become abhorrent in 1941. Until recently I had assumed it was only supported by a small minority. Since it has now apparently obtained a majority sanction, I am glad to disassociate myself publicly from a policy which I have never been willing to support."[57]

The State Department throughout the crisis stood in favor of private property rights. Hull strongly supported this position and so did Welles, who felt that, once the oil companies decided to cooperate in reaching a settlement, Mexico must offer prompt, adequate, and effective compensation. This situation never arose; the firms remained intransigent during the entire affair.[58]

With the failure of this approach, other means were used to try to end the impasse. In early 1940 Hull unsucessfully called for arbitration. Later in the year, when Sinclair Oil broke the united front by signing a separate agreement with Mexico, the others held ranks. The Mexican presidential election was upcoming and the oil companies hoped that the victor would support them. This bitterly contested election matched the government candidate, Avila Camacho, against a determined opponent who allegedly had significant financial assistance from the oil companies. When Camacho was officially declared the winner, rumors of election fraud circulated and encouraged the opposition to make plans for a possible revolution to oust the incoming president.[59]

In the midst of this uncertainty, Roosevelt decided to demonstrate his support for the new Mexican administration. Shortly after winning his third term, he selected Vice President Henry Wallace to attend Camacho's inauguration. This was the first official vice-presidential trip to any Latin American nation, but, more critically, this overt symbol of backing pleased the Mexican leaders. Wallace left Texas on November 26, received a warm welcome in Monterrey, and next attended the inauguration at Mexico City. Afterwards, Camacho praised his guest before the chamber of deputies, and later, addressing the same body in Spanish, Wallace equalled his host's performance.[60]

The trip was much more than an excellent public relations campaign. Wallace personally heightened his own interest in Pan American affairs. He saw the need for industrialization to reduce the region's European dependence; he also wanted to find ways to diminish agricultural surpluses and raise living standards. Besides forming these general impressions, Wallace gained insight from a number of private talks he held with Camacho. After the vice-president returned to Washington, he reported that rather than settling just the oil dispute, the United States and Mexico could solve a broad range of problems. Roosevelt and Welles responded positively to this suggestion; they would try to use this new initiative in the ongoing bilateral discussions.[61]

While Welles worked on this idea, Daniels informed the president on October 31, 1941, that he was resigning because of his wife's poor health. He had gone to his post to incarnate the spirit of understanding and believed that he had accomplished that mission.[62] Roosevelt acknowledged that achievement and declared that Daniels "perhaps, more than anyone else, has exemplified the true spirit of the good neighbor in the foreign field."[63]

Before he retired, Daniels met with Hull at the State Department in mid-November and helped complete the final agreement. Within an hour after that meeting, the secretary decided to conclude the "global" agreement. Mexico agreed to pay $40,000,000 on general and agrarian claims to American nationals; a reciprocal trade agreement was signed; the dollar-peso rate was stabilized; and the United States pledged to purchase newly minted Mexican silver and finance Mexico's portion of the Pan American Highway. As for the oil controvery, Hull decided to act without the oil companies' consent. Each nation chose an expert to determine the compensation for the expropriation. The United States oil concerns had originally valued their properties at over $260,000,000, but after the experts evaluated the holdings, this figure was reduced to a little more than $29,000,000! Rather than compromise, the companies remained obstinate in their defense of property rights and grossly exaggerated the worth of their claims at a time of deteriorating world conditions and State Department pleas for cooperation.[64]

While this agreement effectively brought about wartime cooperation, the relationship between the Mexican oil industry and United States private business remained cloudy. During the war Mexico wanted economic assistance to expand its oil industry. A United States mission surveyed the petroleum industry's potential and recommended aid to build a high-octane gasoline factory and improve several existing refineries. Secretary Ickes, who directed the Petroleum Reserve Corporation, strongly supported the plans. Roosevelt concurred and even discussed oil development with the Mexicans through the use of intergovernmental loans. The State Department, led by United States ambassador to Mexico George Messersmith, objected and defeated the proposal. In spite of the oil companies' dismal performance during the 1938 crisis, the State Department never changed its basic position on private property rights, and placed continual pressure on the Mexican government to allow American companies to return to the oil fields.[65]

Other nations, like Colombia, had granted petroleum concessions to United States business during the 1930s. After the Mexican confrontation, the Colombian administration announced its opposition to expropriation, but at the same time insisted on a larger share of the petroleum revenues. In a cooperative atmosphere, the companies, the ruling oligarchy, and the American embassy worked to find a consensus—each, assuredly, for its own reasons. The firms wanted the oil, the government promoted foreign investment, and the embassy assisted in maintaining this working arrangement.[66]

Unlike its neighbor's minimal production, Venezuela had huge oil deposits. Juan Vicente Gómez gave foreign companies advantageous grants. In addition, the dictator supplied order, laborers, and favorable petroleum legislation; the companies brought capital and technical skills. After Gómez died in 1935, his successors proposed changes in the concessions. Venezuela did not follow the expropriation precedent because the government depended on oil exports for revenue and could not afford any interruption. However, it demanded increased profits, which the companies grudgingly surrendered.[67]

The State Department closely watched the Venezuelan situation to avoid a repetition of the Mexican conflict. American diplomats encouraged oil firm representatives to sign contracts more favorable to the Venezuelans. The companies complied; they had a substantial investment and realized the folly of intransigence. At the end of 1939 United States Ambassador to Venezuela Frank Corrigan evaluated petroleum trends. The companies believed that their investments brought prosperity to Venezuela. The businesses had also built schools and hospitals and conducted other public services. For these reasons, the oil interests believed that they deserved a continuation of the status quo in contractual rights and current tax levels. The Venezuelan administration did not have the same feelings. The government wanted a greater share of the profits, new public projects to keep pace with the peoples' needs, and assistance with agricultural diversification. The administration did not threaten seizure, for most officials deplored Mexico's action. Corrigan still warned: "There is, however, a nationalist element in the country which may in time gain sufficient force to make expropriation in some form a possibility. Attacking the oil companies is good popular politics in Venezuela."[68]

Welles recognized the chance of a confrontation and acted before any dispute arose. In early 1941, for instance, he personally helped to settle a controversy involving Gulf Oil. Two years later Venezuela drafted new oil legislation that gave the government higher royalties. The companies knew that the State Department participated in the drafting of the laws and did not object to them upon their passage.[69]

Throughout the period of oil confrontation, the United States government was unable to formulate any consistent policy. Events, rather than leadership, tended to dictate solutions. Roosevelt offered little direction. When he did get involved, he offered simplistic answers that were insensitive to the nationalistic forces that had created the expropriation mood. Secretaries Morgenthau and Ickes objected to diplomatic tactics for various reasons, while Ambassador Daniels bypassed superiors to present his opinions directly to the White House. Witnessing the struggles within government circles and between the companies' and Latin American desires, Welles ultimately resolved these issues during World War II. He prevented a repetition of the sudden and unexpected Bolivian and Mexican seizures by closely watching petroleum trends in Colombia and Venezuela. The State Department never abandoned its defense of private property. When settlements were reached, they resulted from the Roosevelt administration's commitment to hemispheric solidarity taking priority over the interests of the oil companies in a period of international tension. Even then, the United States tried to satisfy all parties. Bolivia paid off Standard Oil for a lucrative governmental assistance package, and Mexico followed a similar course on a grander scale.

These events, which ended in wartime cooperation, did not solve the problems of the late 1930s. The controversy generated by the oil disputes in Mexico and Bolivia merely added to the already perplexing confusion. An inability to determine direction seemed to grip the country.

Congress reflected the confusion over trading with Latin America; congressmen wanted more commercial interaction, but they differed on how best to achieve it. Representative John Murdock of Arizona in early 1938 called for expanded trade, but added that the Good Neighbor policy hurt domestic agriculture and industry. United States was paying for foreign labor, while domestic workers were unemployed.[70] By late 1939 other congressmen tried to find ways to help both local and Latin American economic growth. Resolutions in both Houses were introduced for a joint committee to improve commercial bonds. Since the war's outbreak, the United States had an unexpected opportunity to enlarge its trade. Democratic Congressman Joe Henricks from Florida wanted to exploit this advantage: "The future of the United States lies to the south, and if we bend our efforts to effecting closer relationship with Latin America we will never worry about getting entangled with the petty quarrels of old Europe."[71]

Outside of government circles, similar divergent viewpoints existed. Businessmen recognized the potential Latin American markets as the European war drew nearer. American financial leaders established committees in various American republics to promote commercial intercourse. Even while moving forward on these initiatives, some financial experts sounded a cautious note. William Culbertson, a prominent Republican interested in Latin America since his ambassadorship in Chile under Hoover, argued that the industrialized nations should only supply less-developed countries with capital if the latter guaranteed stability and security for foreign investment. Seizing private property, he asserted, retarded any cooperative ventures. Capital sent abroad would remain low unless the State Department took a firm stand in behalf of its nationals' rights.[72] An equitable agreement in the Mexican expropriation case, according to Culbertson, was "almost a prerequisite to the development of confidence in further Latin American investments."[73]

Not all internationally minded Republicans agreed with this position. By the end of 1939 William White editorialized in the *Emporia Gazette* that the United States needed to lead the Americas through the remainder of the century. Hull's reciprocity program was beneficial to the Democratic party. White reasoned that if his party were to win the presidency, it must provide bolder economic initiatives: "The United States can well afford to make concessions that will stimulate trade and industry in South America. We can well afford to take some risks. We can well afford to make heavy grants to put these South American countries on their feet. For a good neighbor is a customer. The industrial United States of the Western Hemisphere, may easily be a reality."[74]

Events, however, seemed to shape trading patterns instead of national politics. Trade statistics for 1939 illustrated trends that the threat of war and the actual fighting foreshadowed. United States exports to Latin America rose from an average of 18.3 percent from 1936 to 1938 to 19.9 percent in 1939, while imports moved from 23 to 23.7 percent. In the same time period, Latin American figures reflected a far greater dependence on United States markets. Latin American exports to the United States increased from 30.3 to 34.9 percent, while they dropped slightly to the United Kingdom and Germany. Latin American imports from the United States jumped from 32.8 to 40.5 percent and began to fall from the United Kingdom and Germany. These commercial movements clearly demonstrated that, while the United States was maintaining a slight rise in its Latin American trade, those nations saw their European markets shrinking, and this forced them to rely more on United States markets.[75]

The European war and the early Democratic efforts to promote inter-American commerce illustrated the lack of coordination and sophistication in the development of United States foreign economic policy. Hull's fixation on reciprocity forced the State Department to devote too much time to a program of limited value. To win a broader base of support, Hull naively claimed that acceptance of his trade program and world peace were synonymous.

Welles supported the reciprocal trade agreements program, but viewed it as part of a larger scheme. He understood the difficulties in translating broad concepts into specific proposals, but tried to bridge the gap, changing details to suit the case. As a result the agreements with the American republics did not follow a consistent pattern. Primary considerations were always bilateral; multilateralism played a secondary role.

The State Department never learned how to combine the talents of many agencies into a united foreign economic policy. Hull and Welles shared responsibility for this failure. The one jealously guarded his prerogatives and overemphasized the importance of reciprocity while the other, though less rigid, considered Latin American diplomacy his private domain that no one might enter without his leave. In spite of their shortsightedness, some outside departments had an impact on hemispheric financial affairs. In each case, however, the ability to influence came from special legislation, and even in these instances the State Department played a crucial role.

Internal rivalries and diversity of sources brought about the fragmentation of the United States' foreign economic policy during the 1930s. Hull's hopes came from his outdated Wilsonian free trade beliefs, but Welles's negotiations in the Americas significantly altered the secretary's original intent. Others, like Morgenthau and Wallace, offered suggestions for particular problems. Over them all Roosevelt devoted fitful attention to hemispheric commerce. The depression created most of this confusion and inconsistency. Only with its passing and the coming of World War II would the Americas establish comprehensive economic proposals.

5 ★ CONSOLIDATION BY THE FIRST TERM'S FINALE

EVEN THE ECONOMIC DOLDRUMS of the Great Depression did not dampen the growing enthusiasm for the Good Neighbor. The nonintervention declaration made at Montevideo, followed by the pledge at the Woodrow Wilson banquet, presented the public with the administration's commitment against the use of military force to carry out United States policies in Latin America. Since previous presidents had made similar promises, skeptics waited for concrete illustrations. After the Roosevelt government abrogated the Platt Amendment, withdrew its marines from Haiti, and concluded a more equitable canal treaty, many doubters were convinced. In addition, Hull's emphasis on reciprocity exaggerated the possibilities of improving hemispheric commerce. The Democratic party prominently featured these hemispheric initiatives in its 1936 platform, not only to win votes but also to further its Latin American objectives, especially peace and free trade.[1]

Gradually and with ever-increasing momentum and intensity, prominent leaders concerned about Pan American friendship embraced the Good Neighbor.[2] None was more delighted than John Barrett, a staunch Vermont Republican and former director of the Pan American Union. Shortly before the 1936 party conventions he declared: "I think I will be inclined to vote for President Roosevelt's reelection, solely because of his splendid Pan American policy, and his idea of the development of a good neighbor relationship between the United States and its sister American republics." He added that this chief executive had "done more than any other president of the United States to advance Pan Americanism, since the days of President James Monroe."[3]

Not everyone concurred. Some felt that once the United States had foresworn military intervention, Latin American governments would ignore the rights of American citizens and business interests. Arthur Krock, the Washington bureau chief for the *New York Times*, enumerated instances where inter-American diplomacy had failed: problems with Panama over the canal treaty, the United States' inability to enforce its embargo of munition shipments to the belligerents in the Chaco War, Welles's involvement during the

Cuban revolution, and American interference in the Mexican clerical controversy.[4]

William Castle, undersecretary of state during the Hoover government, raised somewhat more fundamental objections. He protested against the categorical nonintervention pledge, for American interests needed protection, and if necessary through the threat of force or even a troop landing. His main complaint, however, centered on what seemed to him excessive Democratic claims to innovation. While approving of the Good Neighbor's objectives, he insisted that Roosevelt was merely expanding earlier programs, especially those of the Hoover years. Castle was annoyed that the Democrats had appropriated these traditional commitments for their partisan ends.[5] In a speech delivered at the University of Virginia in the summer of 1934, he wished aloud that "there might have been a little less self-glorification, a little less strident assertion that the New Deal has changed the entire spirit of international relations because this is not true, in Latin America, or anywhere else."[6]

The attacks from Krock and Castle hardly dented public approval of Roosevelt's policies. Hugh Cummings, Jr., Hull's executive assistant, read Castle's address and wrote to him about the similarities between his and Hull's views. Cummings even acknowledged that the administration had purposefully exaggerated its Latin American contribution and that this partisan attachment might create political complications in future national elections. To be sure, Pan Americanism had deep historical underpinnings, but Roosevelt and his appointees would not gain any political advantage by discussing earlier contributions. Cummings recognized this and was trying to keep labels off foreign policy. He added that Hull shared these sentiments, but that his pride and pressure within the government forced him to advertise the Good Neighbor.[7] This did not help Castle or the Republican party to counter Democratic claims. Even though Castle's complaints had some validity, by the end of 1936 Good Neighbor diplomacy and the Roosevelt presidency had become synonymous.

Throughout the first term the principal hemispheric issue retarding peace in the Americas was the Chaco War. A truce signed at Montevideo was soon broken, and fighting resumed in early 1934. Many tried to end the conflict. In mid-1934 both the League of Nations and the United States imposed arms embargoes, with little effect. The League then gave up its efforts to resolve the controversy, leaving Argentina, the United States, and three other nations to work as a group, with Carlos Saavedra Lamas, as chairman, and Spruille Braden, the United States representative, playing the dominant roles. More from attrition and exhaustion than anything else, Bolivia and Paraguay signed a truce on June 12, 1935, after three years of bloody warfare with over 100,000 deaths and heavy financial losses. The fighting stopped; negotiations for an acceptable peace treaty commenced. For the next three years the intransigence of the two parties prevented Saavedra Lamas from directing the peace commission toward a successful conclusion and delayed a final settlement. This frustration lasted until the Argentine foreign minister relinquished his chairmanship, and Bolivia began to talk about mobilizing. These actions led to the ratification of a peace treaty on July 21, 1938, and ended one of the most tragic and costly South American wars.[8]

The Chaco War not only ruined Bolivia and Paraguay, it also interfered with Roosevelt's hopes for holding an inter-American peace conference. As soon as the Chaco truce was signed in 1935, the State Department began informal soundings throughout the Americas. The president was particularly concerned over the Spanish Civil War, German rearmament, the Italian conquest of Ethiopia, Japanese ambitions toward China, a dying League, and the indifference shown by most of his constituents to these grave threats to world stability. Rumors of Roosevelt's proposal rapidly spread throughout Latin America, and the president hoped that the hemispheric movement away from war would serve as an example to the rest of the world.[9]

When Paraguay and Bolivia signed a peace treaty on January 21, 1936, Roosevelt took the occasion to write to President Agustín Justo of Argentina, proposing a special gathering in Buenos Aires to consider means of preventing future conflicts. Justo accepted the proposal and expanded the agenda to include a wide variety of subjects. Nearly all Latin Americans applauded the initiative, and Roosevelt, too, was pleased, expecting the conference to attack practical problems and further encourage hemispheric friendship.[10]

Roosevelt had to wait almost a year for his proposed discussion of peace, for the American election campaign and the unstable international situation compelled the postponement of the conference to December 1. Even formulating an agreeable agenda took almost six months. Various suggestions were submitted to the governing board of the Pan American Union, discussed by committees, and approved or rejected. The agenda fell into six categories: organization of peace, neutrality, limitation of armaments, juridical questions, economic considerations, and intellectual cooperation. What had begun as a peace conference had turned into a general discussion of hemispheric concerns.[11]

An active advocate of the expanded agenda was Sumner Welles, the principal formulator. He retained the preservation of peace as the central topic and worked out a resolution with the Brazilians. They would present a hemispheric collective security proposal including sections condemning the possibility of non-American aggression in the Americas and creating a permanent committee of foreign ministers to convene quickly if a crisis arose.[12]

Hull was especially concerned about the protection of neutral rights. This question caused considerable debate within the State Department, for many influential officials believed that neither neutrality nor disarmament should be allowed to come before any multilateral body for consideration. Above all, Congress was particularly sensitive to both questions and would most likely resent Pan American interference.[13]

Another delicate question that surfaced in discussion of the agenda was the long-mooted American international association. Some Latin American countries were disappointed with the European orientation of the existing League of Nations. Guatemala had announced its plans to withdraw, and others were voicing similar intentions. Colombia, with considerable backing from a few other American republics, took the lead in trying to place an American league on the agenda, but Argentina had the plan rejected, fearing that this regional concept would diminish the prestige of the world League.[14]

As always, Hull closely equated peace with commerce. He hoped to introduce a resolution for a tariff truce, preventing signers from raising duties. Ironically, the strongest objection to this idea came from Hull's own creation, the reciprocal trade agreements division within the State Department. The reciprocity legislation was ready to come before Congress for renewal, and Hull's multilateral dreams might endanger the act's extension.[15]

Welles personally handled the subject of intellectual cooperation. He and Laurence Duggan proposed an exchange of graduate students and professors on government fellowships, of which each nation would receive two a year. The office of education wanted some flexibility in numbers, but the State Department felt that Congress would prefer definite figures. The latter view prevailed, and the delegation went to Buenos Aires with the first practical recommendation for cultural cooperation that the United States had ever introduced at a Pan American meeting.[16]

After the program had been arranged, the United States delegation was selected. Hull, as chairman, Welles, and Alexander Weddell, ambassador to Argentina, led the diplomatic contingent. The president also chose Adolf Berle, an original member of the Brains Trust, to assist them. Since this was a peace gathering, Roosevelt also sent representatives from peace groups, including Elise Musser, Democratic national committeewoman from Utah and a member of the state senate.[17]

On November 7 the delegation left New York harbor on the same ship that had taken the secretary to Montevideo. Once aboard, Hull reestablished his practice of meeting with his staff to develop the American positions. On his way he stopped in Brazil and Uruguay.[18] His statement at Rio typified his approach: "The prize for which we are all striving is the permanent peace, mutual understanding, and economic well-being of the peoples of all the Americas."[19] After a smooth trip in fine weather, Hull arrived in Buenos Aires—still optimistic—on November 25, the day that Germany and Japan concluded the anti-Comintern pact.[20]

While the delegation was heading for the conference, Roosevelt was contemplating making a personal appearance. His standing throughout the Americas had risen sharply during his first term. His speeches as well as his specific deeds had been widely hailed in Latin American newspapers, many of which had openly supported his reelection. Josephus Daniels urged him to attend the meeting to gain additional coverage for the Good Neighbor and greater acclaim for himself. After his stunning victory at the polls, he began seriously considering a visit to the Argentine capital for two purposes: to foster better regional relations and to use the Western Hemisphere forum as a vehicle to speak to the rest of the international community.[21]

When rumors of a possible trip reached Argentina, President Justo extended an official invitation to Roosevelt to participate at the gathering, and he accepted. On November 16 the president decided to take his first trip to southern South America and address the conference's opening session. The next day he left the White House, and on the following morning boarded the cruiser U.S.S. *Indianapolis* at Charleston, South Carolina. He enjoyed ocean voyages and welcomed what he considered relaxation after a strenuous campaign.[22]

Roosevelt devoted the first phase of his trip to strengthening the bonds of hemispheric friendship. He entered Rio harbor on the morning of November 27, which the Brazilian government had declared a national holiday. Thousands of school children greeted the president at the dock with red, white, and blue banners. Even though a slight rain fell throughout the day, Roosevelt insisted that his car remain uncovered so that he could return the salutations of the crowds that lined his route. He spoke to the Brazilian Congress, held a press conference, and went to a state banquet. During the entire day he avoided sensitive regional questions like the formation of an American league while emphasizing the Good Neighbor spirit and hemispheric peace.[23]

Three days later, Roosevelt arrived in Buenos Aires. When he came down the gangplank, he vigorously shook Justo's hand and called him "mi amigo"; in turn, the Argentine president warmly gave Roosevelt an "abrazo." The huge crowd, which was watching this meeting, responded wildly. Enthusiastic spectators lined the procession route, waved American flags, and showered the presidential car with flowers. When the presidents reached the executive's palace, both appeared on the balcony. Roosevelt dramatically wrung Justo's hand while a crowd of over 100,000 shouted its welcoming roars.[24]

The Inter-American Conference for the Maintenance of Peace convened on December 1. Roosevelt became the second American president to travel abroad to open a Pan American meeting. This was the last foreign policy statement of his first administration, and he clearly intended to use this hemispheric appearance to influence the Old World.[25]

He had given careful consideration to this idea and had tried to link his regional successes to a broader frame of reference during his first term. Besides reversing Yankeephobia in the Americas, Roosevelt wanted to use his Buenos Aires trip to speak out against warfare in all parts of the world.

Early in his administration he saw the deteriorating conditions in Europe and Asia moving toward confrontation. He also knew that prevailing domestic opinion opposed any active United States involvement to assure peace. By early 1935 he began considering ways to assist easing European tensions. Later in the year, the Neutrality Act passed, which seriously impaired his flexibility in the event of a foreign war. By connecting the legislation to both hemispheres, he illustrated how restricted he was if a hostile European power tried to develop some South American nation for a raw material source. To prevent this eventuality, he tried to win support for some discretionary power when applying embargoes. But a suspicious Congress refused to listen.[26]

The Ethiopian crisis reinvigorated Roosevelt's desire to find some means to avoid a potential world war. He warned his cabinet that after Germany and Italy divided other colonial areas, South America would follow. Some future American president might even face a European invasion of this hemisphere. To prevent it, he wanted to amend the Neutrality Act to give him the chance to assist American republics confronted by possible foreign encroachment. At Chautauqua in August 1936 he spoke to his audience about his efforts to achieve hemispheric peace and his hopes to find a way to extend this regional success to the rest of the globe. He also started to weigh the possibility of holding talks with the leaders of Germany, Great Britain, Japan, the Soviet Union, and France to find some pacific solution to disputes. Although he eventually discarded this idea, it illustrated Roosevelt's conception of tying hemispheric diplomacy with the rest of the international panorama.[27]

Before Roosevelt left for Buenos Aires, he wrote Ambassador William Dodd in Berlin about his intention to use his hemispheric policy to influence European leaders: "That visit will have little practical or immediate effect in Europe but at least the forces of example will help if the knowledge of it can be spread down to the masses of the people in Germany and Italy."[28] Others troubled by the emerging Nazi juggernaut hoped that the president's message from the Americas would reverberate in Europe.[29] Berle, who assisted in drafting the presidential speech, commented that it was "addressed to Europe more than the Americas, for this conference, if it succeeds, is plainly a threshold to the possibility of dealing in Europe with a conference looking toward peace, but we are working against horrible odds in point of time."[30]

Berle had overstated his case, but Roosevelt's address was designed to have some international implications. The president told the delegates that the Americas were at peace while others fought. Roosevelt committed his administration to maintaining hemispheric tranquility: "In this determination to live at peace among ourselves we in the Americas make it at the same time clear that we stand shoulder to shoulder in our final determination that others who, driven by war madness or land hunger, might seek to commit acts of aggression against us will find a Hemisphere wholly prepared to consult together for our mutual safety and our mutual good."[31]

Roosevelt's message received a mixed reaction in Europe. League proponents in Geneva perceived the president's statements as a regional threat to their universal organization. Some anticipated that Roosevelt might become an arbitrator for European quarrels. The Germans and Italians saw the conference as discrediting League actions, but once Roosevelt began attacking dictatorships, approval switched to antagonism. Dodd hoped that Roosevelt's efforts would lead to a world peace gathering, an idea the president was seriously considering.[32]

The president had tried to use the hemisphere to influence United States-European relations, but with little effect. Commentators seemed more attentive to the surrounding festivities of his trip, and with good reason. They made for interesting reading. Roosevelt, for example, left Buenos Aires on December 2. Rain was falling hard, but large crowds watched the departure. Almost as if he were on stage, the president pulled a handkerchief in Argentine colors from his pocket and waved it, to the audience's delight. The president arrived in Montevideo the following morning on his return home. He received another enthusiastic reception and reiterated his peace theme. This completed his tour, which not only provided excellent public relations for the United States but also reinforced Roosevelt's commitment to the Good Neighbor. He returned to the White House in early 1937 convinced that Latin Americans staunchly favored inter-American cooperation.[33]

He still dreamed about influencing the restoration of European security. At the height of his optimism, returning home, the president hoped that there would "be at least some *moral* repercussions in Europe."[34] But an economic slump and his battle with the Supreme Court took priority. He needed to solve domestic problems before moving toward a European peace meeting that would meet with severe criticism.[35]

Few, if any, understood Roosevelt's deep-seated motivation in going to the Buenos Aires conference. Reporters concentrated on the obvious: good will, festive atmosphere, and regional issues. These topics were clearly visible. The president's efforts to associate hemispheric events with a larger international picture were much more subtle and far less successful. His constituents were willing to accept the Good Neighbor in the Western Hemisphere but were not going to extend this diplomacy to worldwide involvement.

With Roosevelt's departure the meeting began focusing on agenda topics, but again Saavedra Lamas's presence dominated the proceedings. Long before Hull arrived, he received continual warnings about Argentina's hostile attitude.[36] Ambassador Weddell, for example, had predicted nearly a year before "that any conference entrusted to the guidance of Saavedra Lamas will be handled with a maximum of ineptitude and a minimum of hope."

Others also questioned the Argentine's competence, but too late to move the meeting to another site.[37]

Well before the meeting the foreign minister demonstrated his opposition to any new American organization and his strong attachment to Europe, which he had just visited. Even before returning home, he wrote Hull approving of economic cooperation but opposing any hemispheric collective security pact. During a discussion with Ambassador William Bullitt in Paris, Saavedra Lamas added that the American republics did not need any declaration concerning threats to the Western Hemisphere from non-American nations. Such a statement would be misconstrued in Europe as a movement toward hemispheric exclusiveness and away from universal cooperation. The reason for Saavedra Lamas's devotion to the League of Nations was readily apparent, for he had recently been elected president of the League Assembly and awarded the Nobel Peace Prize. At the pinnacle of his fame, the egotistical Argentine had somehow to reconcile his hopes for a hemisphere under his direction with his newly found allegiance to the League and Europe.[38]

Despite this opposition, Hull tried to win acceptance for his campaign to promote peace. On December 5 he addressed the delegates, listing his "eight pillars of enduring peace." Since international law and cooperation were at their nadir, they needed revitalization. Thus the peace pacts brought forth at Montevideo needed ratification and adherence. If war did erupt outside the Americas, a common neutrality policy was necessary. Within the hemisphere, each nation should educate its citizenry about how to prevent war. To encourage peace, the American republics must hold frequent conferences and communicate regularly. Finally, since order and prosperity were intimately connected, the secretary reiterated his hope for lower tariff barriers.[39]

The differences between the United States and Argentine delegations naturally led to conflict. The principal one centered on a permanent inter-American consultation committee to meet in the event of a war threat from outside the Americas. Saavedra Lamas rejected the proposal, for such a body would exclude the League and Europe. Hull tried vainly to appeal to the Argentine's pride, but flattery had no effect.[40] Samuel Inman, who attended the conference, reflected the bitterness within the United States delegation: "Everybody is disgusted with Lamas, but no one seems willing to tell him where he ought to go!"[41] Brazil offered a compromise that was adopted— in final form, a convention for the maintenance of peace that called for voluntary consultation in cases of threats to peace. The proposal for a standing committee was deleted.

Other items received less attention than the much-argued consultation proposal. The conference easily agreed to recommend ratification of the five peace treaties left over from Montevideo. Mexico introduced an additional protocol on nonintervention that was unanimously approved with applause. The neutrality issue was discussed but not resolved. Hull's desire to lower excessive trade barriers was reaffirmed in principle, but his proposal for a multilateral tariff truce was rejected. Welles obtained approval for a resolution to award two graduate students or teachers from each nation annual fellowships.[42]

The conference ended on December 23. It adopted two treaties, eight conventions, an additional protocol relative to nonintervention, and sixty-two resolutions, recommendations, and declarations. While Hull emphasized and probably overestimated the cooperative spirit, nevertheless the acts of the conference represented important advances in hemispheric relations. The delegates agreed to consult if their countries' security was endangered, reaffirmed a liberal trade policy, and arranged for cultural exchange. The conference, furthermore, had mobilized public opinion against war and charted a hemispheric path toward peace that served as a model to the rest of the international community.[43]

The president, eager to promote this attitude, complimented his secretary for a mission well done. Hull, for his own part, exaggerated the regional and international effects of the conference. He correctly gauged the Latin Americans' more cooperative sentiment, and through press, radio, and private conversations, capitalized this success once he returned to Washington.[44]

Hull never publicly alluded to the fact that Saavedra Lamas continually insulted him during the proceedings. The secretary, nevertheless, was visibly shaken and even considered asking Justo to replace his own foreign minister, but was dissuaded from making the request. When Hull left Argentina, Saavedra Lamas affronted him further by not coming to the ship to see his guest off. The secretary took these actions personally. He never appreciated Argentina's heritage of close European ties or that nation's desire to shape South American diplomacy. Instead, the secretary perceived the foreign minister's intransigence as a personal feud. This simplistic view reinforced Hull's antipathy for the Argentine foreign minister, which eventually extended to that nation's governmental system.[45]

Welles felt that the meeting marked a new epoch in Pan American relations by laying the foundation for consultation and cementing firm continental friendship. He and his chief assistant Duggan tirelessly publicized those two accomplishments. The spirit of cooperation the United States was constructing could not be quantified. However, the steps that the Roosevelt administration took before, during, and after the gathering depended on a cordial relationship to make the Latin Americans appreciate the State Department's concern about overseas aggression and its possible consequences on the Americas.[46]

Others apart from Roosevelt's spokesmen had their own perspectives concerning the conference. League proponents no longer feared a rival, for Pan Americanism was not yet strong enough by late 1936 to create a regional league. Within the Americas, many commentators expressed a variety of views. The American republics had pledged to consult in time of stress, which effectively meant that the United States would no longer need to make a unilateral decision on action to protect the continent under the Monroe Doctrine. Latin American delegates to the conference who were previously suspicious of the United States' motives overwhelmingly endorsed Good Neighbor diplomacy.[47] The Nicaraguan representative, who had personally witnessed direct American military intervention, spoke for many of his colleagues at the meeting when he proclaimed: "Franklin D. Roosevelt, Cordell Hull, Sumner Welles: a magnificent triumvirate, to whom all America . . . should offer a vote of admiration, of respect and of affection."[48]

Despite the positive results of the gathering, the central objective for peace was unfulfilled. During the first plenary session, Elise Musser of the United States delegation presented a petition of over 1 million signatures collected throughout the world calling for the repudiation of war. Female representatives demanded peaceful resolution to all conflicts, so their sons would not die in future wars. After the meeting's conclusion, one pacific feminist group, the People's Mandate to End War, sent a "flying caravan" to the principal Latin American countries to improve relations and encourage the governments to ratify the Buenos Aires peace treaties. This good will mission left Washington in early November 1937 and flew to most of the Latin American capitals, where it spent two months lobbying government officials. This hectic but well-intentioned effort proved futile; peace could not be won by any "flying caravan."[49]

By the end of Roosevelt's first term, the major characters who had evolved the Good Neighbor had also defined their roles. The president played a major part in determining foreign policy. He assembled the diplomatic staff and provided encouragement to foster improved relations. He focused public attention on Pan Americanism by his diplomatic initiatives and visits to Latin American countries. He not only moved to end past inequities, he also tried to broaden his hemispheric activities into wider international involvement. His actions within the Americas to build greater solidarity received widespread support, no doubt greater than he had originally envisioned. His subtle efforts to use this acceptance to influence European and Far Eastern affairs became more appearent as the world moved closer to another war.

Hull established his standing during the first four years in office. He made a fine appearance as secretary of state, and his old-fashioned southern sense of courtesy made a favorable first impression. Henry Stimson, for one, visualized him as the principal presidential adviser who opposed hasty and precipitous initiatives. Others held similar views. In fact, Hull ultimately became sort of a "father figure" to a public that needed a reassuring symbol of stability in a troubled world. He worked energetically. A man of strong opinions, he doggedly preached his reciprocity ideal and won its acceptance. He also adopted Pan American understanding as an example of how to achieve peace and tariff reform for the rest of the world.[50]

Hull had another side. In many ways, he was petty. Overly sensitive to press citicism concerning himself and the State Department, he brooded over its attacks. He demanded absolute loyalty and resented any suspected deviation. When he was angered, the coarsest and crudest Tennessee mountain language replaced his veneer of the southern gentleman. Hull also had a slight lisp, which changed *r* to *w*, resulting in the reciprocal trade agreements program sounding like "wecipwocal twade agweement pwogram." This impairment hampered his public speaking, but this was not his major problem. Both the White House and his own subordinates took advantage of his ineffectiveness as an administrator. Since he could not form clear organizational lines, Hull permitted his assistant secretaries to see the president without prior clearance from his office. Roosevelt magnified Hull's inadequacies by encouraging direct access.[51]

Toward the end of 1935 Hull contemplated resigning and again running for the Senate, but changed his mind. As secretary of state, he obtained the widest recognition of any cabinet member and relished that position. Unfortunately for both him and the administration, he found himself out of his depth in the diplomatic complications resulting from the rise of Hitler.[52]

After his Cuban assignment, Sumner Welles resumed his post as assistant secretary of state in charge of Latin American affairs. His mission in Havana had damaged his standing as a Pan American expert and problem-solver, and his personality created resentment. Formal and abrupt in manner, he seldom laughed or joked. He looked like a British foreign service officer, and, in fact, had his clothes made in London. Joseph Green, who was responsible for armament negotiations in the State Department, complained that Welles acted impetuously by appealing directly to the president. As a result, Green added, the department hierarchy rebuked him for acting independently. Ambassador Dodd in Germany, who never met Welles, grew to depise him as a symbol of the wealthy American who bought his government job. Francis White, who joined the diplomatic corps along with Welles and formed a cordial relationship, deplored the outcome of his Cuban endeavor—probably because he had wanted that ambassadorship for himself and believed that Welles had stolen it from him. Others just as staunchly defended his appointment, not only because of his training, experience, and diligence, but for his personality as well. After piercing the formal exterior, his friends found a charming host who entertained regally at his estate in suburban Maryland.[53]

As assistant secretary, Welles kept Hull informed concerning his negotiations. The secretary rarely interfered in these discussions, for he respected Welles's expertise. Both men shared many similar goals and complemented each other. Hull helped set the general guidelines, while Welles translated them into practical programs. The two men then worked together to win public and congressional approval. As long as this informal division of responsibility existed, their combination of mentality and temperament greatly enhanced the Good Neighbor's popularity.[54]

William Phillips's announcement in August 1936 that he planned to leave the undersecretaryship opened a breach that ultimately destroyed the working relationship between Welles and Hull. The choice for Phillips's replacement narrowed to either Welles or another assistant secreatary, R. Walton Moore. The maneuvering for the post created bitter animosities, and Roosevelt's tardiness in making the appointment added to the ill-feeling. Moore believed that he deserved the promotion and anticipated strong support from Hull because of their close friendship; he also felt that he had the president's endorsement. Another friend, Ambassador Bullitt, recently returned from the Soviet Union and a close presidential adviser, used his stay in Washington to advance Moore's candidacy. At the same time, Berle wrote Roosevelt that Welles was the best qualified, and several prominent diplomats expressed confidence in his brilliance and experience. Drew Pearson admired Welles and utilized his column not only to write about Welles's attributes but also to criticize Moore for making serious errors in judgment and being overly ambitious. Pearson also pointed to Moore's age (he was seventy-eight) and shrewdly reminded Roosevelt of his objections to the decisions of the elderly Supreme Court justices.[55]

Almost nine months lapsed before Roosevelt announced his decision in April 1937. As might have been expected, he tried to please both contenders. Welles became undersecretary, and Moore, counselor for the department. Moore reluctantly accepted his new post, but his bitterness found an outlet in a whispering campaign against Welles.[56]

Welles's promotion made him the second most powerful figure in the department. Retaining his dominant position in hemispheric policies, he now moved actively into European affairs. He also started a reorganization effort, principally by shifting personnel. Some approved, citing better coordination and efficiency. Others disapproved, especially officials who were demoted. Hull's reaction was ambivalent. He had complained about excessive work, for which Welles's appointment supplied some relief. Despite this assistance, the secretary resented Roosevelt's confidence in the new undersecretary and apparent lack of interest in his own projects and advice. Hull was annoyed about mounting rumors of discord between himself and Welles. The secretary, however, shared the blame, for he held regular Sunday staff meetings with his close associates that excluded Welles. The undersecretary's absence encouraged his opponents to assume that Hull disliked Welles, and they plotted to make that assumption a reality.[57]

Fortunately for the department, this intrigue did not interfere with Welles's conduct of the Good Neighbor. The undersecretary assumed his new duties on May 20. On the following day, a department order established the Division of American Republics, which combined the Mexican and Latin American sections. No one was assigned as assistant secretary to oversee these operations; instead, the president allowed the personnel to report directly to the undersecretary.[58] Emphasizing his control, Welles wrote, "My new duties will, of course, include continuing exactly as before in my relations with our inter-American affairs. To be quite frank with you, if they had not I would not have been interested in the position."[59] In actuality, Welles's advancement had further enhanced the status of hemispheric affairs within the department, for as undersecretary, Welles continued to see Latin American diplomats on a regular basis. Another by-product of his new standing was an ever-closer association between hemispheric and European matters. Roosevelt provided the general framework and impetus for this connection; the undersecretary had the delicate task of translating the president's ideas into workable programs.[60]

New personalities moved into powerful roles at the State Department. George Messersmith became an assistant secretary in 1937 and went to Cuba as ambassador three years later. Avidly anti-Nazi after leaving his previous posts in Vienna and Berlin, he adamantly held to that position in Washington and supported solidarity in the Americas. Tough, demanding, and intelligent, Messersmith was admired by many, and his supporters maximized those traits of his. His critics felt that his penchant for work personified his punctiliousness and egocentric nature. Berle, a friend of both Roosevelt and Welles, who likewise had won Hull's favor, took over an assistant secretaryship in 1938, handling many Latin American issues, especially economic ones. His admirers labeled him brilliant, able, and well organized, while detractors claimed that he was untrustworthy, devoid of common sense, and incapable of working with people.[61]

The diplomatic personnel in Latin America changed little in comparison to the Washington staff. Josephus Daniels stayed in Mexico City, Jefferson Caffery in Havana, Hugh Gibson in Rio, and Alexander Weddell in Buenos Aires. Diplomats continued to be mostly city-dwellers and Republicans; they also retained their dislike for hemispheric assignments.[62] When Minister Norman Armour invited a friend to visit, he sarcastically suggested that the friend "chuck a couple of burnt corks into you kit bag and come down to Haiti and go native with the rest of us."[63] Ellis Briggs in Havana deprecated Cuban politicians "for ineffective procrastination,—for fiddling while the ship of state runs down-wind for the reefs,—for prehensible incompetence generally . . . ."[64] Fred Dearing, minister to Peru since 1930, constantly grumbled about his plight: "To the newcomer the place seems like the Land of Gilead, but after six years of tropical air, artificially cooled but certainly not de-humidified by the Humboldt current, I am ready to go anywhere just so it is away and to a strong, dry and bracing climate."[65] Many restlessly longed for European posts; some with strong political support obtained them over better qualified candidates. Occasionally congressional animosity delayed appointments.[66]

A few selections were major blunders. Some incompetents were reassigned, but in one case, resignation was the only solution. Hal Sevier, a former member of the Texas legislature and an editor and publisher who backed Roosevelt in 1932, received the Chilean ambassadorship as a political reward. Unfortunately he was an alcoholic. After Sevier denied unsavory rumors that had filtered back to the department, Hull sent Robert Scotten to investigate.[67] Scotten confirmed the ambassador's illness: "He looks and acts more like a living corpse than a live man and although I still go through the motions of consulting him regarding the affairs of the chancery I found after a very few days that his mind was virtually dead and that he had only the haziest sort of idea what I was driving at."[68] Hull finally forced Sevier's resignation in May 1935, but not before he had impaired United States prestige in Chile.[69]

For a decade beginning in 1933, a triumvirate made the basic decisions in constructing the Good Neighbor. Roosevelt and Hull primarily built general guidelines and popularized the policy. Welles, with Duggan acting almost as his alter ego, added his ideas and more critically translated generalizations into specific measures. With few exceptions, diplomatic appointees played minor roles in formulating board policies.

The result was paradoxical: policy and personnel almost became separate entities. The public awareness and enthusiasm for the Good Neighbor was widespread. Yet within the administration, a surprisingly small group of individuals directed inter-American relations. This offered several advantages, like quick, decisive action and clear lines of authority. But this chain of command had serious flaws. Continuity depended on Roosevelt's ability to keep both Hull and Welles at their posts, for they supplied not only decisions and momentum but also many details of implementation ordinarily left to lower-ranking officials in Washington and abroad. More important, many in the diplomatic corps did not grasp the full significance of the Good Neighbor. Without this knowledge the Good Neighbor could not gain support within the department that was essential for its survival.

The Good Neighbor label applied solely to the other American republics by the first term's finale. While the president and the secretary of state spoke in generalities, Welles directed the practical application. Even though the resulting actions were hailed as a change in policy, they did not alter the fundamental relationship between the involved parties. The abrogation of the Platt Amendment, the withdrawal of troops from Haiti, and the updated canal treaty ended commitments that had forced American military intervention and sustained heavy financial burdens. The reciprocity agreements maintained, reinforced, and even exaggerated patterns of trade. In return for a variety of concessions, the United States granted preferences to agricultural products like sugar, bananas, and coffee. These reductions, if they did anything, strengthened the growth of monoculture at the expense of diversification.

Perhaps the most fundamental innovation that the Roosevelt administration introduced into hemispheric policy during its first term was its massive public relations effort. Multilateral conferences gave United States representatives an opportunity to meet, discuss, and debate with their Latin American counterparts in a more effective manner than they had been able to at earlier gatherings. Under Roosevelt, the United States aggressively solicited Pan American cooperation in order to formulate a continental consensus. Unlike their predecessors, Roosevelt and Hull traveled twice to South America and publicized the hemisphere's importance. After leaving Cuba, Welles returned to Washington, energetically seeking solutions to Pan American issues. When he was unavailable, Duggan competently took charge.

This leadership recognized the value of cooperation and moved to maximize it. Unable to play a significant role in European and Asian affairs, the president began developing a hemispheric position for its impact on international diplomacy. Shut off from negotiating trade agreements in much of the world, the secretary turned his attention toward Latin America. Welles and Duggan encouraged these activities and also stamped their own imprint by canceling military interventions, which proved unworkable, and substituting subtle diplomatic maneuvering to accomplish the desired ends. This concerted effort, more than anything else, made the Good Neighbor unique to the Roosevelt years.

6 ★ NEUTRALITY WITH AN ALLIED BIAS

THE DURABILITY of the Good Neighbor was severely tested in the six months following the Mexican oil expropriation. Petroleum companies across the United States exerted enormous pressure to abandon the nonintervention pledge and retaliate against the Cárdenas administration. As these demands slowly subsided, the preparations for the Eighth International Conference of American States at Lima were laying the foundations for further movement toward hemispheric unity and the use of this cooperative spirit to influence other international happenings.[1]

Although the meeting date was set for December 9, 1938, Argentina sought a postponement. José María Cantilo, the new Argentine foreign minister, who was returning from his ambassadorial post in Italy, believed in close European ties and feared that the upcoming meeting would revive the American league concept mentioned at Buenos Aires. The Peruvians dismissed his request, insisted on adhering to the schedule, and received widespread support throughout the Americas.[2]

Cantilo's expressed concern over the league topic also troubled the State Department. Welles hoped to eliminate potentially disruptive subjects like oil seizures and Nazi penetration by limiting the agenda to technical and scientific matters. He saw the possibility of coordinating the existing inter-American peace treaties, but the United States would not advance the American league idea. Less than a month before the conference convened, Assistant Secretary Berle added to this low profile by telling radio listeners not to expect any dramatic or spectacular results.[3]

The appeasement at Munich in late September 1938 changed the complexion of the conference. On November 6 Welles publicly called for hemispheric solidarity at Lima in the aftermath of the Czechoslavakian dismemberment. Until all peoples lived securely, the undersecretary pledged, "As a nation we will assure ourselves that we are in a position to defend ourselves from all aggression from whatever source it may arise, and to be prepared to join with our fellow democracies of the New World in preserving the Western Hemisphere safe from any threat of attack."[4]

Some interpreted this as an initiative for a common defense pact directed against totalitarian expansionism to be presented at the conference. At a press gathering nine days later, Roosevelt lent credibility to this assumption. The president warned reporters that modern aircraft technology provided the potential for an air attack from abroad on the Americas, and that if necessary he would ask Congresss for powers to guard the continent from this threat. Critics responded almost immediately that Roosevelt had exaggerated the possibility of an overseas air assault. This pressure forced the president to retract much of what he had implied the next day, but Latin American league proponents chose to use the original comments as a signal to bring their proposal to Lima.[5]

Cantilo also overreacted to the presidential statements, by announcing that Argentina would "continue its traditional policy of assisting the sister nations of the continent, but would find it difficult to subscribe to military pacts or engagements which might give the impression of drawing away from friendly European nations."[6] The foreign minister had misread the debate within the United States. Roosevelt had not proposed any military treaty, for he knew that neither the Congress nor the American public would consent to one.

In the midst of this uncertainty, Hull, for the third consecutive time, led the United States delegation to an inter-American conference. Stopping at Panama, Colombia, and Ecuador, he called for solidarity and firmer bilateral bonds. The delegation represented many constituencies. Assistant Secretary Berle and Minister R. Henry Norweb from the Dominican Republic led the diplomatic contingent. Others came from assorted backgrounds, like Kathryn Lewis, who was associated with the United Mine Workers of America, and Elise Musser, who spoke for women.[7]

While these individuals were well known in their fields, the most publicized selection was Alfred M. Landon, the defeated Republican presidential candidate in 1936. Roosevelt offered him a place on the delegation, and the former Kansas governor prompt accepted. He saw this trip as a patriotic duty in presenting a united bipartisan foreign policy, and this was his first visit to Latin America, which provided him with an opportunity to determine the extent of foreign ideological penetration in the Americas. Many friends applauded his decision, while others warned of possible Democratic manipulation.[8] He conceded as much: "But nevertheless, I think it is important that all parts of the world present a united front in South America right at this time. Then, too, I think everything that will divert our minds from our troubles and the hate and bitterness of the last few years, and help us get started pulling together, will be of direct benefit internationally, whether anything worthwhile comes out of the conference itself or not."[9]

As the opening date approached, State Department officials began to reflect the apprehensive public mood over the American league subject. A poll taken of United States citizens in February 1938 repeated a question asked in April 1936: "Should the Americas form their own league of nations?" Prior to the Buenos Aires meeting, 56 percent responded positively, but two years later the percentage had slipped by sixteen points. Brazil's opposition to the league further decreased its chances of acceptance. In its place the Brazilians offered a continental offensive and defensive alliance. Welles disapproved of both schemes; they went too far.[10]

Like the undersecretary, Cantilo rejected these suggestions, but was placed in a touchy position since he had already agreed to address the opening session. Staunchly opposed to regional exclusiveness, Cantilo decide to substitute the American league topic with the extension of the consultation principle established at Buenos Aires to include meetings of foreign ministers whenever necessary. Welles was delighted, for this was the suggestion that Saavedra Lamas had defeated two years earlier. Although the undersecretary wanted to improve the wording, he had not expected anything so far reaching coming from the Argentine minister.[11]

Cantilo opened the conference with a call for hemispheric solidarity, excluding regional defense pacts and reminding his audience of Argentina's close association with European states. During his stay in the Peruvian capital he spoke briefly with Hull about various proposals, but the two men did not reach any accord and the foreign minister left Lima for a vacation in the Chilean Andes.[12]

Cantilo's absence, coupled with the fact that the Brazilian and Mexican foreign ministers did not head their delegations, gave the United States center stage. However, the delegation did not capitalize on this situation. The staff occupied the entire sixth floor of the conference's hotel and had minimal social contact with the Latin Americans. Hull held delegation meetings each morning, attended few social functions, and went to bed promptly at 10:00 P.M. He did not understand Spanish and still sat through the sessions without earphones. When the secretary spoke publicly, he reiterated his trade philology. When he tried to negotiate privately, he was indecisive and ultimately relied on Berle and Norweb along with the Peruvian Foreign Minister Carlos Concha to finalize negotiations.[13]

The principal conflict centered on Hull's inability to convince Cantilo to support a resolution warning non-American countries about invading the hemisphere. Despite the foreign minster's rejection of this proposal, the secretary felt that many delegates wanted it. On the day following Cantilo's address, Hull warmly endorsed the improvement in the consultation machinery, linked the troubles outside of the Americas to the need for hemispheric cooperation, and added that the American republics had to announce their unequivocal opposition to any hemispheric attacks. He related peace to commerce by repeating his wish for reduced trade barriers and asked for greater understanding by enhancing cultural contacts.[14]

Besides following Hull's activities, the Latin Americans were equally interested in Landon's role. His participation assured United States bipartisanship in favor of Pan American cooperation. Landon spoke over the National

Broadcasting Company on December 18, declaring that propaganda aimed at creating dissension and barter arrangements would not destroy inter-American solidarity. No matter which party occupied the White House, the titular Republican leader said that the United States would enforce the Monroe Doctrine to prevent any foreign nation from gaining a foothold in the Americas.[15]

Many praised these statements, but Welles had misgivings. The former governor had resurrected the unilateral nature of the Monroe Doctrine and omitted any reference to the Good Neighbor. Overly sensitive to possible adverse reaction, the undersecretary publicly praised the speech with his own additions. The American people, Welles stressed, were committed to the continuation of Roosevelt's Latin American diplomacy based on nonintervention and the equality of all nations.[16]

While diplomats pressed for acceptance of their proposals, women's groups from the United States used the meeting for their own ends. Kathryn Lewis and Elise Musser officially represented the nation; Mabel Vernon, who had organized the "flying caravan," lobbied for peace organizations; and Doris Stevens, chairwoman of the Inter-American Commission of Women, addressed the delegations during a recess, advocating women's rights. These feminist groups also presented the gathering with a petition of 3 million signatures promoting the restoration of world peace.[17]

While these groups lobbied, Cantilo departed on December 11 without giving his delegation any flexibility to bargain on the resolution concerning hemispheric attacks by non-American powers. After nine days of futile discussion, Cantilo wired a new draft to his representatives, and on Christmas Eve the Declaration of Lima became a reality. It reaffirmed continental solidarity and the spirit of cooperation against foreign intervention without naming non-American nations. If regional peace were threatened, any American republic could call a meeting of foreign ministers to discuss the crisis.[18]

Latin American commentators generally regarded these results as another positive step in the evolution of Pan Americanism. In addition to the Declaration of Lima, Hull's trade policies won reaffirmation as well as encouragement for more cultural exchange programs. One gnawing problem persisted: the struggle between the United States and Argentina for diplomatic supremacy in the Americas. Some observers welcomed Cantilo's opposition to United States initiatives, while others berated the foreign minister for defeating a strong declaration directed against European totalitarianism.[19]

Overseas reaction was mixed. The French and Soviet presses concentrated on the ideological struggle between the democracies and the dictatorships. Fascists in Italy, Spain, and Portugal attacked the United States for trying to eliminate their influence from the Americas while perpetuating its own brand of imperialism. From the Far East, the Japanese carefully followed the proceedings and wondered how the Roosevelt administration had the right to keep some nations out of the Western Hemisphere while the United States pushed for the "open door" in China.[20]

The Third Reich, more than any other European nation, reacted to the veiled United States references concerning outside attacks by non-American countries. During the depression Germany won a certain measure of Latin American admiration by Hitler's charisma, the Nazi philosophy, and German militarism. Even before the Lima conference convened, the Reich's embassy staff was enlarged. Propaganda that it distributed emphasized the European heritage of the Americas. Scoffing at charges about Jewish persecution, the Nazis reminded their audience that the United States restricted Jewish immigration and regularly lynched Negroes. The Roosevelt administration wanted to remove Germany's hemispheric contacts, the Nazis argued, to promote its grand design of bringing the Americas under its tutelage.[21]

After the meeting ended, the German minister to Peru reported on the success of his embassy's activities: "Positive results could be registered in only a few fields of minor importance and with respect to the political resolutions directed against totalitarian states." The anticipated United States plan for a military and economic alliance dividing South American from Europe collapsed. As a poor substitute, Hull incited Latin American countries against dictatorships and took the Declaration of Lima home.[22]

Landon also questioned the gains at Lima. Speaking to the delegates at the end of the meeting, he emphasized the positive by stressing the need for peace and warning them to unite against any possible outside aggression. Major Democratic leaders thanked the ex-governor for his contribution;[23] however, he had ambivalent feelings concerning his role. Shortly after coming home, he confided to a friend that "I am . . . somewhat disappointed at the lack of concrete results from the Lima Conference. But the broad principles are there if we are willing to follow it up with a firm, vigorous and decisive policy. We are in one of those periods in the world's history where a bold and fearless statesmanship can save civilization you and I believe in. But I don't see such statesmanship anywhere."[24]

Two prominent United States citizens from different political persuasions minimized fears of Nazi penetration. William Borchard, professor at Yale, attended the meeting as a legal expert and did not see any evidence of German expansionism.[25] Norman Thomas, chairman of the Socialist party, complained about the hysteria over the influence of Hitler and Mussolini in South America: "Actually there is much crude and primitive fascism in Latin American countries, but most emphatically it is not pro Italian or pro German."[26]

The State Department disagreed. American diplomats reported on their opposition's enlarged Peruvian embassy staff and tried to sensitize Latin American delegates to the danger of growing Nazi organizations in the hemisphere. Hull especailly objected to the German barter arrangements, which were antithetical to his own trade dogma. Despite these efforts, Latin Americans remained skeptical about a serious threat from the Third Reich.[27]

After reaching Washington, the secretary summarized the achievements at Lima. Consultation and cooperation moved ahead and, equally critical, the Americas became more cognizant of the menace from abroad. The president and the undersecretary congratulated the secretary, and others also praised his leadership, which forged another step toward solidarity.[28]

Both Argentina and Germany claimed similar victories. Cantilo feared an American league because he misread American intentions. As a consequence, he introduced the basis for the Declaration of Lima and defeated an imaginary movement for some regional association. The Nazis worried about the United States negotiating hemispheric military and commercial alliances. In the anxiety to check these, the Reich's embassy increased its staff and propaganda efforts, which, according to United States observers, proved Nazi expansion.[29]

While Germany and Argentina focused on mythical dangers, the long-range advantage went to the United States. Solidarity held, and even inched forward. Since Cantilo presented the consultation draft, Argentina had to accept some modification. The Germans, trying to stymie United States hegemony, actually assisted Roosevelt's anti-Hitler crusade by the overt actions taken at the German embassy.

The results were not sharply defined at the meeting's conclusion or by the beginning of the new year. Shortly after the conference Samuel Inman, who unofficially assisted the American delegation, expressed his mixed feelings to a colleague:

It just wasn't in the cards—the present world situations being what it is—for anyone to be willing to take any long radical move for what you and I would like in Peace Machinery. Every one is too nervous, too apprehensive, too jittery . . . to do more than declare with thorough honesty that we do stand together on the American Continent for the principles of freedom and law and, while we refrain from calling names, if as and when our fundamental democratic life is challenged, we will lick the devil out of the interloper. To organize for the job, however—well, that might hasten rather than slow up the crisis, which, after all may not come. In the meantime, as a spiritually united America, let us go forward in solving a lot of problems which still devide [sic] the family.[30]

The year ended, filled with doubts. The international situation worsened, and the oil conflicts were unresolved. Despite these troubles, Pan Americanism was steadily gaining confidence and maturity. At this critical juncture the Roosevelt administration adapted multilateralism to fill two needs. First, these conferences provided dramatic resolutions, reaffirmed the Good Neighbor, and reinforced public approval for the policy. Second, Roosevelt used the inter-American system to address the world community in his battle against Hitler. As world war drew nearer, both themes were sharpened and used with considerable success.

Even during the unsettling international conditions at the start of 1939, critics who attacked the president's attempts to involve the United States in European and Asian affairs excluded hemispheric unity from their assaults. In a speech before the council on foreign relations early in the year, Herbert Hoover chided his successor for bias toward the democracies. They, the former chief executive believed, had adequate defense capabilities without United States assistance. Hoover objected to any American military partici- pation in a foreign war—except to repel a hemispheric invasion.[31]

Another Republican detractor, William Castle, specifically assailed current Latin American policies. While Good Neighbor proponents held the non- intervention doctrine as their exclusive contribution, Castle declared that this was a cardinal principle of American diplomacy and that Welles had violated noninterventionism during the Cuban crisis of 1933. The former under- secretary also did not understand why the Roosevelt government placed so much emphasis on the Western Hemispheric democracies, for many Latin American countries had regimes as repressive and authoritarian as those in Europe and Asia.

Castle's political critique meshed nicely with his assault on inter-American economic policies. Throughout 1939 he reflected his business orientation by hammering away on the theme that private enterprise suffered severely under the Democrats. Their handling of the Bolivian and Mexican oil seizures coupled with the neglect of bondholders' complaints resulted in decreasing hemispheric investments. German trade gains in Latin America, Castle held, demonstrated the failure of the reciprocity program.[32] In an address given on April 1, he mirrored many opponents' objections. The Roosevelt administration allowed Latin Americans to take advantage of the United States because "it did not want to disturb the harmony among the Ameri- can nations. But in the long run respect is more important than harmony and harmony which is not based on respect is only the prelude to discord."[33]

Some of these observations had considerable validity, but they did not dent the overwhelming support for the Good Neighbor. Advocates encouraged by closer Pan American ties believed that the United States had finally realized this continent far outweighed the importance of the others. As more Americans identified Europe and Asia with the devastation caused by warfare, calls for hemispheric solidarity grew louder. Raymond Clapper, a prominent syndicated columnist generally disinterested in Latin America, told his readers that the United States' first responsibility was continental defense. The defeated Republican vice-presidential candidate in 1936, Frank Knox, praised Roosevelt's Latin American policies in his paper, the *Chicago Daily News*.[34]

Of the State Department personalities concerned with hemispheric affairs, none held center stage like Welles. More than anyone else, he provided the guidance. As undersecretary he lent the prestige of his office to reassert United States adherence to the juridical equality of nations and nonintervention in Latin American nations' domestic matters. In early 1939 he categorically proclaimed the Good Neighbor's success and went even further that summer, when he spoke before an audience at Brown University. He unequivocally declared that the spirit of cooperation had replaced the fear of United States imperialism.[35]

Duggan reinforced these sentiments and added his own emphasis. Speaking in the spring of 1938, he enumerated the various inter-American programs. He not only listed them but also compared current actions against past ones. "In general," Duggan said, "the good neighbor policy does not enunciate any new concept for the conduct of our relations with the other American Republics. The principles of understanding, confidence, friendship, and respect, have been proclaimed by every President. What is new is a new and more far-reaching application of these principles."[36]

Others stressed more immediate concerns. Before the European war erupted, Assistant Secretary Berle and Ambassador Daniels called for New World security against the Old World's chaos. The administration instituted a futile campaign to ban foreign ideologies from the Americas. Since they felt these ideologies eroded democratic principles, the leaders of the United States wanted to protect their own citizens and defend the entire continent.[37] In May 1939 Berle concluded: "The Latin American policy is really the foundation of pretty much everything we are doing." If the turmoil in Europe did not spread to the Americas, the Good Neighbor had achieved a major goal.[38]

In addition to the promotions given inter-American cooperation by these leading spokesmen, statements regularly flowed from the State Department's American Republics Division emphasizing Latin American accomplishments. During 1939 the pace quickened and so did illustrations of how these efforts contributed to peace. Since Hull preached that trade and stability were interchangeable, the reciprocal trade agreements program not only brought greater prosperity but also contributed to pacific determinations of disagreements. The United States also relinquished its right to use military force in Latin America by abrogating this priviledge in bilateral treaties and signing the nonintervention declarations. In the multilateral arena, the unanimity exhibited at the inter-American conferences demonstrated solidarity.[39]

Individuals such as Welles, Duggan, and Berle had another tremendous advantage over their predecessors—presidential encouragement. Roosevelt had stamped the Good Neighbor label on his administration. By his second term Latin Americans generally applauded his diplomatic leadership and New Deal legislation. His affinity for personal involvement in foreign affairs quickly brought him into inter-American discussions. At first he dealt primarily with bilateral issues, but gradually he began using the Americas as an example to the rest of the world. The president declared that the Western Hemisphere faced the same problems that others had; yet, the American countries settled theirs by pacific methods.[40]

Roosevelt began denouncing the dictators who precipitated confrontations early in his second administration. Fearing the adverse effects of their aggression on the Americas in the event of a war, he promised an audience at the Pan American Union on April 14, 1939, that he intended to keep aggressors from the Western Hemisphere and pledged "that my country will also give economic support, so that no American Nation need surrender any fraction of its sovereign freedom to maintain its economic welfare."[41]

During press conferences in the first half of 1939, the president speculated on Hitler's plans for the Americas if the Reich won a European war. According to Roosevelt's scenario, Germany would next infiltrate Latin America. Since the Nazis would gain control of Europe's economy, Hitler would economically coerce the other American republics by buying or refusing to purchase certain exports. The president concluded that this indirect encroachment did not violate the Monroe Doctrine but warned that once Latin America fell under German tutelage, the United States would follow.[42]

As a partial answer to such hypothetical possibilities, Roosevelt considered practical measures to keep war from the Americas. As early as April 1939, he thought of ways to maintain the freedom-of-the-seas principle in the event of war. As assistant secretary of navy in World War I, he had firsthand knowledge of naval war zones and neutral shipping rights. One scheme he pondered would prohibit military action in the Americas by establishing a line somewhere in the middle of the Atlantic Ocean that the navy would patrol to keep belligerents from crossing. After the German invasion of Poland, he modified this course with a naval patrol. On September 15 he informed the press that this patrol extended 200 miles into the Atlantic to monitor belligerent activities. Roosevelt carefully watched the navy's deployment and complained about inadequate surveillance. To correct this, he ordered Welles to make certain that the liaison between the navy, coast guard, and State Department operated efficiently.[43]

The United States Navy faced an impossible task. The president had not consulted the navy in arriving at his patrol decision. Admiral Harold Stark interpreted the presidental directive to mean that belligerent vessels were to be reported and tracked to demonstrate the readiness of continental defenses. Organized on September 5, the patrol became operational a week later. At first the navy concentrated on looking for submarine bases and monitoring the combatants' activities within 200 miles of the Americas' coastline down to the Brazilian bulge. Despite the vast area of coverage, Stark recognized Roosevelt's desire to make the patrol effective.[44] On October 14 he commented on how closely the White House followed the patrol: "Every one of these the president follows from day to day or I might say in some cases several times each day. He realizes the problem with the lack in numbers of available vessels and is keenly interested in getting the recommissioned destroyers in the Atlantic at the earliest possible moment."[45] By the end of the month the patrol had flown over 100,000 miles and surface vessels had logged more than 120,000 miles.[46]

Hemispheric leaders wanted to keep the European war away from the Americas as much as most United States citizens. Using the Buenos Aires and Lima declarations for justification, nine American republics jointly sponsored a call for an emergency meeting. The State Department hurriedly drew up an agenda, which included items on neutrality, protection of hemispheric peace, and economic stability. Just as promptly, the Pan American Union's governing board approved of these topics, and Panama, as the gathering's host, chose September 23 as the opening date for the First Meeting of Consultation of Ministers of Foreign Affairs of the American Republics.[47]

Latin American diplomats almost unanimously gave their endorsement for the conference. Brazil and Mexico worked closely with the United States, and Argentine goals in many ways seemed to parallel those of the Roosevelt administration. Cantilo supported Argentina's traditional neutrality stand. In World War I, in fact, he even proposed a plan to establish an area around the Americas that banned belligerent actions. He also saw the necessity for economic cooperation, since the war disrupted normal trading patterns. The foreign minister had one brief reservation—he and several others resented the hasty preparations, but this disappeared as the European fighting intensified. In addition, Leopoldo Melo, the Argentine representative to the conference, worked harmoniously with Welles.[48]

For the first time, Welles led a delegation to a Pan American gathering, while Hull lobbied in Washington for new neutrality legislation to give the executive branch greater flexibility. When the undersecretary left from New York on September 15, he emphasized the conference's neutrality aspects. After a five-day ocean voyage, he arrived in Panama and held preliminary discussions with the Latin American representatives. His speech to the delegates on September 25 reflected the outcome of these talks. First, the Americas had to establish a common neutrality policy to keep hostilities from the hemisphere. Second, the American republics had to minimize economic dislocation caused by the war. The United States, the undersecretary assured his listeners, would financially assist those nations damaged by the loss of European markets through short- and long-term credits, cooperate in the development of new commercial ventures to encourage economic growth, and supply freighters for inter-American shipping.[49]

The meeting only lasted for eight days, but in that short time the delegates took decisive action in three areas: neutrality, the maintenance of peace, and economic cooperation. A neutrality committee to consider issues raised by the European war won immediate acceptance, while the economic resolutions were hotly debated. Latin Americans, led by the Mexicans, wanted a committee to discuss specific measures to relieve trade disruptions like commodity sales agreements, but the State Department did not want such specific guidelines. The impasse was broken with the formation of an economic committee composed of a member from each American republic that was a potentially powerful advisory body to recommend inter-American commercial initiatives.[50]

Even before the committee assembled, Roosevelt toyed with the idea of using this body for his own ends. He wanted to grant United States merchant vessels permission to register under the Panamanian flag to circumvent United States neutrality laws, which warned its nationals' vessels against traveling in European waters. Some shippers had already changed their registrations to Panama, and this idea on a larger scale appealed to the president. But first he decided to test the scheme's acceptability. Almost immediately after it leaked to the press, the reaction was extremely and violently negative. Most argued that any registration shift violated the neutrality laws' spirit and threatened to draw the United States into war by a need to defend the Panamanian flag in combat waters. The president quickly dropped the proposal and went so far as to disclaim any responsibility for initiating the idea. He had tested public opinion. It was not the first time or the last. In this particular case, Roosevelt moved against Hull's objections, only later to reverse his course.[51]

This did not destroy the economic committee's value. Approximately eighty belligerent merchant vessels lay idle in American harbors as a result of the fighting. The Latin Americans wanted to buy these ships and use them for coastal trading, but the Allies objected to giving the Germans any benefits from such possible sales. The status quo continued until late March 1941, when the United States seized all Axis-controlled ships in its ports because of attempted sabotage; shortly afterwards many Latin American countries followed a similar course. During the waiting period the economic committee kept abreast of the ships' locations, and when the United States acted, the committee readily endorsed the administration's action.[52]

While the steps in regard to shipping received scant attention, the Declaration of Panama had a profound impact. Roosevelt had already started the naval patrol, and before Welles left for the conference, he and the president had drawn a line around the Americas that no belligerent could cross (see map of Western Hemisphere). State Department personnel searched for precedents to support this concept and discovered that several Latin American nations, including Argentina, Brazil, Chile, and Peru, had advanced or promoted proposals in World War I to keep warring countries from committing hostile acts within a certain distance of their coastlines. Using these earlier Latin American recommendations and the president's map, Welles proposed the establishment of a security zone to the conferees and had it approved without any changes. As a consequence, the United States not only had its own patrol to watch belligerent movements, but it also gained hemispheric justification to keep combatants from engaging in warfare within a definite region. Welles hoped that both sides would respect the Declaration of Panama to free the Americas from the horrors of war. What remained unanswered was whether the belligerents would accept an unprecedented "do not enter" sign drawn approximately 300 miles around the Americas up to the Canadian borders.[53]

Welles enthusiastically affirmed the meeting's achievements. They demonstrated hemispheric unity and the value of consultations during a crisis. A day after the conference concluded, Hull wired his warm congratulations.[54] Drew Pearson seconded that sentiment in his column, but did not please the secretary: "For seven years he [Welles] has been doing the spade work for Pan-American conferences. He plowed the field where his chief, Cordell Hull, reaped. But previously Welles stayed in the background, and this was the first occasion on which he, himself, headed the American delegation to an important conference and steered the course single-handed."[55]

With few exceptions Latin Americans also reacted positively. Solidarity had been strengthened; a committee to solve economic problems had been formed; and neutrality was established. Besides taking these specific actions, the Latin American delegates had an opportunity to meet with Welles and discuss critical bilateral issues brought on by the war.[56]

In the midst of the movement toward greater hemispheric cooperation, the Germans miscalculated United States motives in the belief that Roosevelt would ask for military alliances. To thwart this, German agents, along with their Italian and Spanish associates, lobbied at Panama to defeat any treaties. These efforts, combined with promises of economic contracts after the war and thinly veiled threats suggesting reprisals for neutrality violations, comprised the counterattack. The Reich's representatives had inaccurately assessed United States intentions, and, by concentrating on erroneous assumptions, German diplomats had no chance of hindering Welles's mission.[57]

When no alliance materialized, the Reich failed to appreciate the meeting's significance. German spokesmen publicly voiced their approval for hemispheric neutrality and several other conference resolutions.[58] Privately the foreign ministry grudgingly acknowledged growing United States hegemony: "Roosevelt's influence on the Ibero-American republics has been further strengthened by the outcome of the Conference. Affirmation of the will to neutrality and of American solidarity, however, will compel Roosevelt to move cautiously as regards his well-known international position." In addition, the president established an economic committee to exert financial pressure in the Allies' behalf.[59]

German diplomats did not comprehend the zone's potential until the Nazi navy deployed some of its units. As part of this effort, the pocket battle-

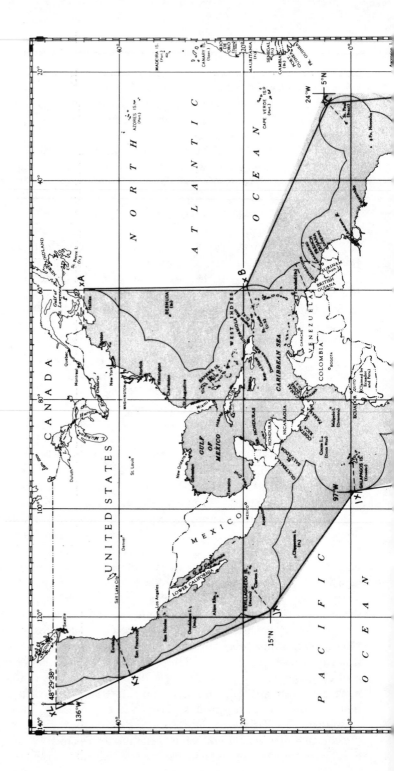

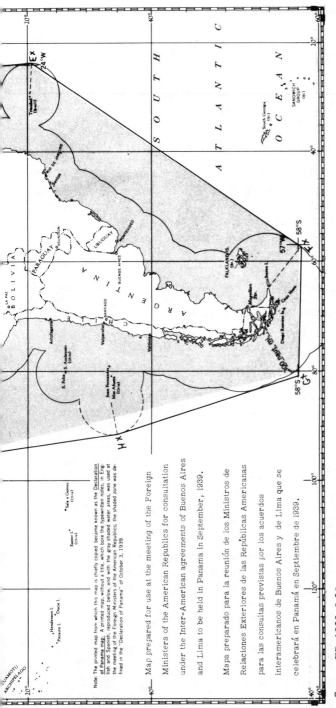

Note: The printed map from which this map is chiefly copied became known as the Declaration of Panama map. A printed map, without a title, which bore the typewritten notes, in English and Spanish, reproduced below, and with the gray shaded water areas, was used at the meeting of the Foreign Ministers of the American Republics; the shaded zone was defined in the "Declaration of Panama" of October 3, 1939.

Map prepared for use at the meeting of the Foreign Ministers of the American Republics for consultation under the Inter-American agreements of Buenos Aires and Lima to be held in Panama in September, 1939.

Mapa preparado para la reunión de los Ministros de Relaciones Exteriores de las Repúblicas Americanas para las consultas previstas por los acuerdos interamericanos de Buenos Aires y de Lima que se celebrará en Panamá en Septiembre de 1939.

Source: FR, 1939, 5:35.

ship, *Admiral Graf Spee*, was stationed in the Atlantic. By mid-December it had sunk nine British merchantmen and moved into the South Atlantic searching for more victims. On the morning of December 13 its lookout spotted three British warships. Mistaking three cruisers for a cruiser and two destroyers, Captain Hans Langsdorff engaged them between 150 and 200 miles off the Uruguayan coast, well within the security zone. During the initial encounter H.M.S. *Exeter* received extensive damage, but H.M.S. *Achilles* and H.M.S. *Ajax* continued the battle throughout the day. By evening the warships moved close enough to Montevideo for the city dwellers easily to hear the salvos. Then suddenly they stopped, and just before midnight the German vessel limped into port.[60]

The *Graf Spee*'s docking created a gigantic dilemma for tiny Uruguay. The Germans insisted on two weeks for repairs, while the British demanded that the warship leave within a day. Caught between the struggle of the two great powers, Uruguayan officials boarded the battleship, examined the damage, and decided that the *Graf Spee* had seventy-two hours for repairs. If it refused to abide by this decision, consultation with the other American republics was the next step, for Uruguay did not have the physical force necessary to intern a battleship.[61]

With a strict time limitation given by the Uruguayan government, Langsdorff realized his hopeless position. The ship had received several severe hits to its control tower, and its number one turret needed dockyard repairs. Besides the physical destruction, some of the crew had been injured for the first time in this battle. The sailors' morale had been shattered, for the crew had been indoctrinated to believe that the *Graf Spee* was invincible. Breakout was impossible, internment unthinkable. None of the spectators knew what Langsdorff would do. Near the appointed time of departure of 8:00 P.M. on December 17, the pocket battleship left its anchorage followed by the German merchant vessel *Tacoma*. About seven miles from the harbor the crew transferred to the freighter. Shortly after this both of the *Graf Spee*'s magazines exploded, creating a spectacular fire and intermittent explosions accompanied by huge columns of smoke outlined by blazing oil. Thousands lined the docks watching these convulsions for ten minutes, and then the pride of Hitler's navy listed sharply to starboard and settled to the bottom enveloped in smoke and flames.[62]

The scuttling did not end the saga. The *Tacoma* took the crew to Buenos Aires for internment. With his sailors' safety assured, on the evening of December 19, Langsdorff committed suicide with a single shot to his head. Both combatants received journalistic praise for their heroism.[63] Upset by Reich propaganda about the cowardness shown by British seamen, the Nazi minister in Montevideo cautioned his superiors in Berlin: "The attitude of the South American public toward those who died on *Spee* is so full of admiration and sympathy that such false reporting needlessly destroys this

popular sympathy for Germany once and for all and drives the public ir-
retrievably into the arms of the enemy propaganda. Up to now as a result
of counterpropaganda the man in the street was suspicious in the face of the
large-scale press propaganda of the enemy and had confidence in the German reports."[64]

Fragmentary reports of the first major sea battle during the European war
presented the State Department with a serious hemispheric predicament. The
American minister in Uruguay did not know where the initial encounter
commenced.[65] Welles insisted on ascertaining the facts "because if there has
been flagrant violation of the neutrality zone by the *Graf Von Spee* I think
that we cannot delay in taking up immediately with the other American
Republics the desirability of making joint representations. If we do not take
action quickly the whole thing is going up in smoke and we are all of us going
to be subjected to very serious danger."[66] Battle accounts confirmed that the
fighting had begun well with the zone, and hemispheric diplomats began discussing the most effective response.[67]

Assistant Secretary Berle understood the complications of the *Graf Spee*
incident: the violation of the zone, the action taken by the Uruguayan government, and the question of the appropriate reply.[68] He felt relieved after
the battleship's destruction "because it saves us the embarrassment of having
to argue out a violation of our neutrality zone, or perhaps send a fleet to try
to stop somebody's else's fight . . . ."[69]

Argentine diplomats had a far different reaction. The interment of almost
1,000 German seamen created internal difficulties because of hostility shown
by its large Allied population against these new Nazi residents. To prevent
any repetition, the government wanted a strong protest, but did not win
enough support for vigorous action by the other American republics. On
December 23 the Panamanian government released a mild hemispheric protest and informed the British and the Germans of their zone violations. To
halt any recurrence, hemispheric diplomats threatened to strengthen neutrality rules to refuse warring vessels supplies and repairs in American harbors
as a result of a battle within the zone.[70]

When compared to the demands for prompt and specific sanctions, this
diplomatic note merely admonished the belligerents and lent credence to
criticism of the zone's ineffectiveness. Some who had skeptically greeted
the concept sarcastically referred to it as the "chastity belt." They had
prematurely judged it as useless and saw the results of a single, dramatic sea
battle as conclusive proof.[71]

Hull, who remained silent while Roosevelt and Welles championed the
zone, harbored deep resentment. The idea, he was firmly convinced, violated
international law, for nothing justified a restrictive belt on the high seas. The
secretary also reasoned that the United States might be drawn into the war
if the combatants violated the zone. When the press mirrored this anxiety,

Hull momentarily considered filing a formal protest over the zone with the president, but chose to modify the zone's intent through his public explanations. Stressing the pacific nature of the zone, he stated that if violations occurred, consultations would follow. When Hull defended the zone, he did so in the cause of strict neutrality. The primary objective was to stop interference with neutral rights on the high seas and to stop warfare from coming to the Western Hemisphere. State Department press releases reinforced the zone's defensive character—the goal was to keep belligerents out of American waters. Although the navy gathered information, no provision in the Declaration of Panama forced the United States to guard any Latin American coastline or exercise military power.[72]

Others criticized the zone. David Walsh, Democratic senator from Massachusetts and chairman of the committee on naval affairs, believed that the Panama resolutions favored the Allied powers because of their naval superiority. Neutrality, he held, called for equal treatment toward both sides if the United States were to avoid entanglement. William Borchard and John Moore, both experts on international law and anti-Roosevelt in temperment, feared that the security zone might draw the United States into the European imbroglio. They wondered if Roosevelt would protect the French and British colonial possessions within the zone. This would certainly compromise hemispheric neutrality.[73]

Alfred Landon expressed other worries. He wanted to maintain the geographical insulation that the United States had through its natural water boundaries and did not want to extend continental defense to the entire Western Hemisphere. Latin American nations, he knew, did not have the capabilities to assist the patrol, and the United States alone did not have sufficient forces to defend the Americas. Lacking adequate surveillance within such a vast territory, Landon thought that the United States might be drawn into war instead of the reverse.[74]

The British, speaking for the Allies, presented problems by objecting to the zone as a possible haven for German raiders. After diplomatic consultation, the United States agreed to English requests for rights of "hot pursuit" and access to territorial possessions. The State Department, however, would not guarantee that Nazi warships would not use the zone or that the United States would provide information on German shipping. These answers did not satisfy the Allies, who thusly rejected the Graf Spee protest and declared the zone inoperative. Privately, however, Prime Minister Winston Churchill confided to Roosevelt that as long as raiders did not enter the zone, neither would the British.[75]

While the Allies relied heavily on sea power, Hitler relegated his navy to a low priority. When war began, the Reich's sea forces were inferior to those of their enemies. To compensate for some of this disadvantage, Admiral Erich Raeder argued for unrestricted submarine warfare when attacking Allied shipping. The Fuhrer rejected this advice. Hitler reasoned that the kaiser had made a serious blunder in World War I by sinking United States vessels, which resulted in Wilson's declaration of war. Although Germany publicly rejected the zone concept, it, like the Allies, privately respected it. The admiralty consistently objected to this decision, because by limiting the war theaters, the Allies gained a tactical advantage of being able to concentrate their fleets in a smaller area. Hitler still would not budge in his desire of not provoking the United States.[76]

Amidst charges of its weakness, the security zone was doing even more than the president had anticipated. It gave the Allies a distinct advantage over the enemies. Critics dwelt on exceptions like the *Graf Spee* incident and minimized the total effectiveness, for the zone proved an extremely potent weapon in Roosevelt's diplomatic arsenal.

Even before the events off the Uruguayan coast, the American navy allowed the British to capture Axis merchantmen within the zone. On October 24, for example, the German tanker *Emmy Friedrich* left Tampico, Mexico, and the British intercepted her the next day. Other ships were captured or scuttled, which led to accusations in the German press that the American navy radioed ship locations to the enemy. The Nazis had no concrete proof to substantiate these allegations, but too many coincidences occurred. The German minister in Mexico, for instance, requested and received an escort from the heavy cruiser U.S.S. *Tuscaloosa* for its cargo ship *Columbus* when it left Vera Cruz. By December 14, after steaming to a point between 320 and 480 miles off Cape Cod, a British destroyer appeared. Rather than risk casualties, the Germans scuttled the ship, while the *Tuscaloosa* watched and took the crew aboard. Many other similar incidents happened, yet the Reich refrained from filing any protests until late 1941.[77]

Besides assisting the Allies in this regard, Roosevelt further helped them by actively and arbitrarily extending the zone's size. The president knew the limits established at Panama, for he drew the map. Without consultations or formal hemispheric approval, Roosevelt included Greenland within the patrol area and sent coast guard cutters to find Nazi weather stations. Such an initiative did not comply with the Panamanian resolutions, nor was anything like it even tangentially discussed. The action clearly benefited the Allies, but for public consumption the president said that Greenland's inclusion inside the zone was a measure taken for hemispheric defense.[78]

Roosevelt stretched the safety belt to convoy Allied shipping. By April 1941 American naval units protected British shipping upon entrance into the neutrality zone. In addition, whenever American warships spotted a German presence, they notified the English. Secretary Ickes did not believe that the deception fooled a public that knew the difference between convoying and patrolling.[79]

Secretary of War Henry Stimson urged the president to tell the public the truth, but he refused—opposition to overt Allied assistance was too powerful. Roosevelt doggedly held to his masquerade; the patrol was defensive, purely to keep belligerents out. On April 25, 1941, he told reporters that the patrol reached sometimes up to 1,000 miles: "Now this is a patrol," the president lectured, "and has been a patrol for a year and a half, still is, and from time to time it has been extended, and is being extended, and will be extended—the patrol—for the safety of the western hemisphere." He went even further by enlarging the patrol's scope to "as far on the waters of the seven seas as may be necessary for the defense of the American hemisphere."[80]

More Allied aid came in the spring of 1941. After the Germans invaded Russia, the United States sent troops to Iceland. The president retained his hemispheric orientation.[81] He admitted the island lay outside the Americas, but added that it was "terribly important to Hemispheric defense."[82] By fall Roosevelt declared that Axis vessels entering the zone did so at their own peril. All of this was done under the guise of inter-American defense.[83]

Vast distances separated the North Atlantic from the Americas, but this did not trouble Roosevelt. He protested the sinking of the American freighter *Robin Moor* in that region as a zone violation. On September 11 he labeled a submarine attack on the destroyer U.S.S. *Greer* a week earlier as an act of piracy and threatened to fire first if a similar situation arose. He neglected to mention that the *Greer* had radioed the U-boat's position to a British aircraft, which proceeded on a depth-charge run. During October Roosevelt used the torpedoing of the destroyers U.S.S. *Kearney* and U.S.S. *Reuben James* as examples of Nazi aggression and zone violations. Despite such provocations by the United States president, Hitler held firm. Until after Pearl Harbor, American shipping within the zone was not molested. That fact assumed added proportions when the success of the U-boat in American waters from 1942 until mid-1943 was examined. In spite of heavy losses, the submarine never had the initiative. It had been confined too long, and though inflicting grievous losses, this was a prime example of too little, too late.[84]

Roosevelt had established an intimate connection between the Good Neighbor and Allied aid. Hull, not cognizant of this fact, fought a losing campaign for strict neutrality. Welles stood somewhere between the president and the secretary. The policies that he adopted as the war drew nearer illustrated his bias toward defending the Americas, and yet he also recognized the need to assist the democracies in order to contain Hitler's aggression.

No matter how diligently Hull and Welles pressed their points, Roosevelt steadily moved toward his appointed end. He publicly held to hemispheric defense rhetoric but privately pointed the nation in the British direction. After the Panama conference the president used his power to change the intent of the security patrol from neutrality to Allied assistance. He turned the safety zone from a defensive measure to keep combatants from the hemisphere into a Allied sanctuary. Roosevelt probably rationalized these decisions as political maneuvers. The public, in large part, agreed; only a few saw the duplicity.

7 ★ NO TRANSFER

T THE START of 1940 Roosevelt continued to focus his attention on
strengthening Allied resistance and cementing hemispheric bonds. He
claimed that the Good Neighbor, based on peace and built on mutual
respect, was universally accepted throughout the Americas, while elsewhere
brutal force determined peoples' fates. After the German invasion of the Low
Countries, the president reiterated his opposition to military conquest and
began to prepare the continent for the possibility of becoming the sole
defender of Western civilization. The collapse of France brought even more
antagonistic statements aimed at the Third Reich and greater efforts to aid
the English.[1]

As Hitler's military forces marched across Europe, the president's appre-
hension concerning hemispheric economic vulnerability mounted. He speculated that the German population in Argentina might be receptive to Nazi
propaganda. This combined with that nation's heavy reliance on European
markets might enable the Reich to coerce the Buenos Aires government into
signing a restrictive trade pact and placing its military under German direction.[2]

Roosevelt feared that the Nazis might form a continental trading union to
negotiate with Latin America. He reasoned that this type of commercial
enterprise did not violate the sovereignty of the American republics but
would be the first step toward complete domination. To remove that danger,
Roosevelt formulated a general outline for his own hemispheric cartel proposal by the end of May, and on June 21 issued a statement recommending
the creation of an inter-American trade organization to supervise joint marketing of significant Latin American exports in order to supplement defense
efforts and safeguard hemispheric peace by protecting the American republics
from outside economic intimidation.[3]

Inadequate planning and insufficient preparation, however, assured failure.
Berle, placed in charge of winning the cartel's acceptance, faced even Hull's
opposition. The reciprocity program came up for congressional renewal
later in the year, and the secretary had no intention of abandoning his creation for an untested cartel. Treasury officials also reacted lukewarmly. They
were committed to help bolster monetary supplies and stabilize currencies

in the other American republics, but not on the level of the cartel's grandiose design.[4]

Adverse criticism outside government circles also contributed to the cartel's rejection. During the height of the debate over the proposal, William Culbertson, a Republican supporter of Hull's trade principles, acknowledged the opposition against the cartel scheme, for as he observed, it "outhitlers Hitler." William Borchard, an avid Democratic critic, doubted if Latin America would accept the proposal and predicted that passage would start an international trade rivalry. The Nazis, with promises of expanded markets after the war, encouraged various American republics to oppose the idea. To illustrate its impracticality, the Germans pointed out that the United States did not have enough markets for its own surpluses let alone Latin American exports, and added that if the other American republics accepted Roosevelt's suggestion, they would fall under total Yankee domination.[5]

While the administration vainly pushed the cartel, others tried to mobilize public opinion behind the British cause. By the end of May, William A. White, editor of the *Emporia Gazette*, called for a united foreign policy at the Republican party's 1940 presidential convention and formed the Committee for the Defense of America by Aiding the Allies to provide planes to the English, food for French refugees, and if necessary, defense of the Americas.[6]

To assist White's efforts and split his political opposition, Roosevelt brought two Republican internationalists into his cabinet that summer. Frank Knox became secretary of navy. "If we can bottle Hitler up on the Continent," he wrote on May 22, "that will give England a chance, and on our part, make our defense problem a great deal simpler. Instead of having to fear continually, an attack somewhere in this Hemisphere, we could make our defense far from our own shores across the Atlantic with ships and planes and as much mechanized equipment as the situation in England might require."[7] Henry Stimson, who joined the cabinet as secretary of war, expressed similar feelings. In addition, he advocated maximum assistance to the Churchill cabinet and dismissed rumors of any American fifth-column movement as a German diversionary tactic.[8]

The imminent fall of France intensified resentment against the dictatorships, encouraging the president to take a bolder Allied position during an address at the University of Virginia on June 10. He called for accelerated aid to the democracies and condemned Italy's stab-in-the-back of its neighbor. On the next day Getulio Vargas gave a speech designed for internal consumption to maintain the allegiance of his nation's large Italian and German populations. While adding Italy to Brazil's neutrality proclamation, he seemed to condone the dictators' victories as a sign of vitality. Some hemispheric observers mistakenly linked both presidential pronouncements, diminishing the effectiveness of Roosevelt's attack on the totalitarian powers.[9]

In these bleak days of the European war the United States never relented in its determination to prevent German hemispheric penetration. During the early months of 1940 Welles traveled to Europe to make his own evaluation of the conflict. In Berlin, Foreign Minister Joachim von Ribbentrop told his guest that Germany wanted the same security on the continent that the United States had gained under the Monroe Doctrine. Welles resented his host coupling inter-American and Nazi diplomacy. The doctrine, the undersecretary contended, did not imply United States hegemony over the Americas or coercive trading practices, but merely prevented non-American nations from exercising political or military might in the Western Hemisphere. Ribbentrop ignored Welles's distinction. On June 14, as Hitler's armies pushed toward Paris, the Fuhrer echoed his foreign minister's interpretation in a widely circulated press interview. The dictator asserted that he had no aggressive designs on the Americas. What he wished was the original intent behind the Monroe Doctrine, which meant Europe and the Americas would stay out of each other's affairs.[10]

The fall of France brought the Monroe Doctrine to even greater prominence. Under it, the United States had implicitly held that European colonies in the Americas were not transferable to any other continental powers. The United States traditionally had objected to any potential European antagonist gaining a possible base of operation in the Western Hemisphere. To stop Hitler from doing just this, the State Department hurriedly drafted a no-transfer resolution for congressional consent, and on June 17 the Senate unanimously passed it and the House quickly followed, with an overwhelming vote of 380 to 8.[11]

Even before receiving this vote of confidence, Hull notified Berlin that "the United States would not recognize any transfer, and would not acquiesce in any attempt to transfer, any geographic region of the Western Hemisphere from one non-American power to another non-American power."[12] Ribbentrop's answer continued to link the Monroe Doctrine with the sphere of influence concept. He mimicked Hitler's press declarations and added that his nation owned no American territories or wished to acquire any. France and England, he stressed, had colonies and received preferential treatment with security zone protection. This was prejudicial; the Monroe Doctrine only had validity if all European nations received equal treatment.[13]

Hull publicly rejected Germany's reply on July 5. He traced the doctrine's origins, which made allowances for existing European possessions but implied opposition to future transfers. The doctrine also rested on the right of self-defense and the maintenance of the status quo. Since the United States opposed any European ownership changes, it did not display any preference under the current situation. Germany took what it wanted through conquest; the Monroe Doctrine did not condone United States domination, but instead provided for hemispheric defense against any non-American nation's aggressive intent.[14]

While the Roosevelt administration chose the Monroe Doctrine as a means to shut off foreign expansion in the Americas, some suggested other options. Before the war erupted, those who opposed foreign involvement wanted to buy European hemispheric territories. Various individuals recommended canceling World War I debts in return for these colonies. American military planners urged preclusive occupation to assure United States defenses. What these suggestions ignored was the expected stiff resistance from both Europe and Latin America.[15]

Many Latin Americanists also had their views of the Monroe Doctrine. By 1940 some claimed that the principle was being continentalized, but they were mistaken. Until Hitler's spring offensive, few even mentioned the doctrine, especially within the diplomatic corps. Subtle changes had occurred since 1933, with the growing acceptance of Latin American nations following Roosevelt's leadership. By the time the Nazi blitzkrieg swept across Europe, the State Department, with a hemispheric consensus, held similar policies of not questioning the existence of present European possessions and restricting future colonization, the extension of any outside influence, or the use of military force by any European nations in the Americas.[16]

Several Latin American countries affirmed the State Department's position through a number of declarations and treaties. However, the United States used these actions as complements to its existing policies. As Duggan stressed, these supplementary resolutions did not "alter the existence of the Monroe Doctrine as a fundamental part of the policy of the United States nevertheless [they] are important and significant since they represent parallel action on the part of all of the republics of this hemisphere."[17] The Monroe Doctrine remained a unilateral tenet of United States foreign policy. What had changed was the Latin American perception of its enforcement. Before the Roosevelt administration came into office, the other American republics believed that the United States would use the doctrine against them. Under the current conditions, the opposite was true.

Earlier presidential decisions helped to create this positive attitude. In early 1935 Roosevelt began discussing the purchase of the Galapagos Island, located approximately 300 miles off Ecuador's coast (see Map of No-Transfer Concept), but ended the talks because of unfavorable hemispheric reaction. As an alternative the president considered a Pan American Union (PAU) acquisition for an international park financed by the United States. Although this was not carried out, Roosevelt consistently advanced this type of recommendation as the best assurance against enemy occupation. Using similar logic in early 1939, he included the Easter Islands, about 1,750 miles from Chilean shores, under this umbrella. That summer he proposed that Antarctica fall under a Pan American trusteeship where the United States would

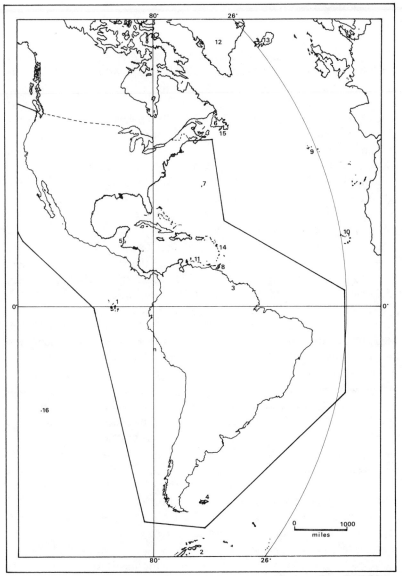

Cartographer: Fred Ritter

KEY

1. Galapagos Islands
2. Antarctica
3. Guianas
4. Falkland Islands
5. Belize
6. Newfoundland
7. Bermuda
8. Trinidad
9. Azores
10. Cape Verde Islands
11. Aruba and Curacao
12. Greenland
13. Iceland
14. Martinique
15. St. Pierre and Miquelon
16. Easter Islands

undertake the initial exploration and then an inter-American governing board would supervise settlement. Growing concerns over possible German claims forced the administration to abandon this project in favor of its own expedition that winter.[18]

The Allied defeats in the spring of 1940 convinced Roosevelt of the trusteeship's merits. When his wife suggested the Guianas as a possible re-settlement haven for refugees, he confidentially informed her on May 4 that he was "considering the broad thought of creating a form of Pan American trusteeship for situations of this kind. It is a new idea in international or Pan American relationships but it is worth studying—especially if there is a remote possibility that the American Republics may be forced to do something about European possessions in this Hemisphere."[19]

The president's plan called for inter-American collaboration. A conference had been tentatively scheduled for October, but the fall of France provided an urgent need for prompt discussions. A Panama resolution stated that any possible change of ownership of American territory held by any non-American state that might precipitate a danger to hemispheric peace justified a consultative conference. Havana was chosen for the gathering, and the Cuban foreign office along with Ambassador Messersmith energetically made prep-arations. In fact, the Cubans acted overzealously by recommending an extremely ambitious agenda and an opening date that many delegates found impossible to meet. The State Department changed the starting time and drafted an agenda that the PAU governing board easily approved in late June. The preparations for the Second Meeting of Consultation of Ministers of Foreign Affairs of the American Republics were confirmed.[20]

Neutrality, the no-transfer principle, and economic issues were the main agenda topics. Some vigorously argued for concerted action on the last, but the no-transfer item dominated the discussions. Hull had sent the proposal to several Latin American capitals for comment. The resolution included a general statement, a trusteeship format, and the administration of the ter-ritories. All the nations except Argentina agreed with the concept. At first Cantilo even opposed the entire meeting because the United States had already made its unilateral no-transfer pronouncement. Only after Welles assured him that the agenda was far broader did the foreign minister agree to send a representative. A serious illness of Argentine President Roberto Ortiz further clouded his nation's foreign policy. When he relinguished his powers on July 3, Vice President Ramón Castillo took charge, and the American embassy in Buenos Aires predicted that he would not be as cooper-ative as his predecessor. Ambassador Norman Armour quickly learned that Castillo did not regard any transfer to be inimical to the Americas and would not risk war to maintain the status quo of certain European colonies. Any trusteeship plan, furthermore, involved possible military occupation, vio-lating neutrality and making the American republics the guardians for Euro-pean possessions. Argentina would not sanction such an arrangement and would recommend that these territories become sovereign or incorporated into Latin American countries that had claims on these colonies.[21]

Germany also acted to defeat United States proposals by increasing its embassy staff in Havana to accelerate its propaganda campaign against Yankee imperialism. Besides relying on Argentine intransigence, Nazi diplomats tried to intimidate several Latin American nations. If they maintained their neutrality, they would benefit after the war through the expansion of German trade. If they refused, then they would suffer the consequences. Most of Berlin's efforts concentrated on these economic concerns and defeating a cartel scheme that was already dying. The Reich had miscalculated badly; the Democratic leaders primarily focused on winning approval for the no-transfer resolution.[22]

In the middle of the summer Hull led a delegation to an inter-American conference for the fourth time. On July 18, shortly after Roosevelt accepted his third term nomination, the secretary left for Havana, taking along diplomats like Berle and Duggan. According to his custom, he worked on the agenda aboard ship and arrived in Cuba two days later. He was returning to Cuba for the first time since his tour of duty there in the Spanish-American War.[23]

The meeting opened on July 21 in an uncertain atmosphere. On the eve of the conference Roosevelt requested expansion of the Export-Import Bank's lending capacity to assist Latin American economies, but new loans depended on congressional action. Welles, furthermore, relegated commercial issues at Havana to a minor role since he directed those efforts from Washington. His principal interest at the meeting was the extension of hemispheric solidarity by the American republics announcing their confidence in Roosevelt's diplomacy. Berle, who accompanied the secretary on the trip, expressed his anxieities: Hull really did not want to attend; many foreign ministers was absent due to German pressure; and Argentina opposed the no-transfer proposal.[24]

Hull addressed the delegates on the second day of the conference emphasizing the no-transfer principle and the trusteeship concept. He had already held private talks with the Argentine representative Leopoldo Melo, who declared that his nation favored a general statement supporting the United States proposals. The Argentine people, however, refused to defend European possessions in the Caribbean so far from the Rio de la Plata region. Hull assured Melo that the United States had no intention of protecting any warring nation's colonies against another's and that the United States had no imperialistic designs toward these territories. The Roosevelt administration's single concern was to provide a contingency plan in the event of possible foreign invasion.[25]

Hull chaired the committee considering the no-transfer resolution and received widespread Latin American backing. Since Havana was the gathering place, Cuban leaders wanted a landmark Pan American declaration to bring prestige to their nation and therefore became the secretary's most enthusiastic ally. Panamanian and Brazilian delegates also served on the committee and promoted the United States draft. In this cooperative atmosphere, the representatives finalized a proposal by July 26, calling for the application of the no-transfer plan except in areas under dispute between European and Latin American nations, like the Falkland Islands and Belize. If aggression appeared imminent, the committee had the authority to recommend emergency measures under the Act of Havana. This act allowed any American republic to move unilaterally if there were a threatened attack by seizing the colony and establishing a temporary trusteeship to run routine affairs. The Convention on the Provisional Administration of European Colonies and Possessions in the Americas would supersede the emergency act after two-thirds of the American republics approved the convention. Under its provisions, the American republics would form a joint trusteeship to govern these territories. The Argentine delegation found these declarations too far-reaching and refused to accept them. To reverse this decision, Hull appealed directly to the Argentine president, who gave his consent, ending opposition and guaranteeing unanimity.[26]

These activities received most of the headlines; another resolution passed without being recognized as a major inter-American step against overseas aggression since the birth of Pan Americanism. The Declaration of Reciprocal Assistance and Cooperation for the Defense of the Nations of the Americas stated that any attempt by a non-American power to interfere with the sovereignty of an American nation would be considered an attack against all. Consultation would follow and the American countries would discuss defensive measures to stop any potential threat. The reciprocal assistance declaration thereby became the first inter-American security statement directed at non-American powers and served as the foundation for many wartime military agreements.[27]

Many praised the conference results. Roosevelt told reporters that "the unity of the Americas is more nearly a fact that ever before in history, without any question."[28] Latin Americans echoed these sentiments, and this outward display of solidarity materially benefited United States diplomacy. With the results at Havana, the Democratic administration had won blanket permission, without defining precise guidelines, to seize European possessions in the Americas threatened by a real or imagined foreign invasion. To make certain that the Act of Havana properly followed the State Department interpretation, Welles became the United States delegate to the emergency committee.[29]

The spirit on Pan American unity was not immediately translated into concrete actions. Hull and his subordinates, much to the chagrin of army leaders, wanted to proceed cautiously, while the military wished to act quickly, before the Latin Americans decided to negotiate with Hitler. Economic considerations followed a similar pattern. Secretary Morgenthau promised to help solve inter-American financial problems, but his constant bickering with Hull over foreign economic policy retarded effective collaboration. United States defense capabilities were untested, and economic assistance programs lacked direction. Time, however, remained an American ally. As long as the British navy controlled the seas, the Western Hemisphere was secure.[30]

The Germans seemed more concerned about maintaining economic access to a blocked market than the adverse consequences of the political declarations. Instead of looking at the totality, the foreign ministry compartmentalized issues. The meeting did not hamper fifth-column activities; the delegates rejected the cartel; the no-transfer resolutions were meaningless since the Third Reich had no hemispheric possessions. Just as the Germans never fully appreciated the importance of the neutrality zone and patrol, they did not understand how Roosevelt would tie the Havana resolutions directly to the European war.[31]

The fact that the Act and Convention of Havana were never enforced did not impair their usefulness to the United States. Even before the Havana meeting, Roosevelt and Churchill started negotiations to bolster the British navy. When the president announced in mid-August that he was leasing British bases in the Americas for overaged United States destroyers, he claimed that he had made the deal for hemispheric defense. In fact, the United States already had their use. What happened was that Britain wanted warships, and the United States needed a way to justify that request and simultaneously maintain public approval. Bases for destroyers accomplished both missions. The agreement appeared in accord with the no-transfer resolutions by offering Latin American nations use of these bases in British territories such as Newfoundland, Bermuda, and Trinidad. Roosevelt once more succeeded in attaching aid to the Allies and the Good Neighbor.[32]

The president even thought about deploying Latin American troops to occupy European colonies. In the spring of 1941, for example, fearful of a Nazi invasion of the Iberian Peninsula, he briefly considered sending a token Brazilian task force to the Azores and Cape Verde Islands until Portugal regained its independence. This never happened, but it did show that Roosevelt was ready to mobilize Latin American military forces to keep German troops from strategic Atlantic islands.[33]

Other incidents involving the victims of Nazi conquest illustrated how the president distorted Pan American actions to suit his own ends. The collapse of the Netherlands in April 1940, for instance, worried the United States. Rumors spread that a German filibustering expedition from Venezuela might try to seize the Dutch West Indies and sabotage the large oil refineries at Aruba and Curaçao. Recognizing their vulnerability, the Allies secretly detached troops to those islands on May 10, but the United States called for their removal because the Japanese might use the same pretext to occupy the

Dutch East Indies. To minimize that possibility, the Allies belatedly announced that their forces were under Netherlands command. By frequently
consulting the Venezuelan government over the status of these islands and
avoiding widespread publicity, the State Department avoided Latin American
hostility. The Roosevelt administration, after all, directed the Havana declarations against the Axis, not the Allies.[34]

Denmark's territories stirred up considerable controversy. Even though
Roosevelt had not included them in the neutrality zone, he declared on
April 12, 1940, that Greenland belonged more to the Americas than to
Europe. After the Havana meeting, Berle, with the president's blessings, announced that Greenland fell under the jurisdiction of the Monroe Doctrine and
the Havana decisions. During April 1941 Roosevelt signed an agreement with
the exiled Danish government that placed the island under United States
protection. In his statement for justifying this action, the president said that
the American republics knew about this decision. They may have been
informally notified about this unilateral step, but they were never given any
opportunity to discuss its hemispheric implications.[35]

After the administration established the Greenland precedent, Iceland
quickly came under the same heading. In early 1941 Welles determined that
both islands had the same standing, and on July 7 United States soldiers
landed in Iceland. Secretary Stimson urged Roosevelt to admit openly that he
had taken this step to protect the North American trade route to embattled
Britain. The president refused. Instead he informed the public that while the
island lay outside the Americas, it was crucial to inter-American defense. By
using this rationale, he stuck to his strategy of linking hemispheric security
with acts designed to assist the English. This explanation was palatable to
Americans and less exposed to severe criticism by his adversaries.[36]

Opponents like Charles Lindbergh spoke out against the president's lack
of candor. The world-famous aviator knew that Iceland clearly lay in the
European sphere, but the president had convinced the people through his
Pan American rhetoric that the island belonged to the Americas. The United
States, Lindbergh recorded in his diary, sided with the English, and the occupations of the islands presented the Germans with an affront. He wondered: "It is now Hitler's move—or will he pass? In one sense, the most
serious part about this occupation of Iceland lies in Roosevelt's making such
a move without consulting Congress. I am not sure which is worse—the
danger of being thrown into the war or the internal implications of such
dictatorial procedure."[37]

Another problem was created when the Vichy government took control
of French possessions, since some French colonies fell within the Americas.
Martinique, for instance, had the best harbor in the Lesser Antilles, and,
even more bothersome, a French aircraft carrier, cruiser, gunboat, and six
tankers sat in port. The United States decided not to disturb the existing

situation as long as Marshall Henri Pétain kept his territories neutralized. Since the United States maintained surveillance through its security patrol and consular observers on the French islands, this gave adequate protection. However, the State Department insisted that Vichy withhold any assistance to the Germans in the Caribbean. The French resented this ultimatum but had to consent. In this situation the Roosevelt administration did not enforce the Havana declarations, but they certainly provided strong political leverage in discussions with Vichy officials.[38]

While the foreign service carefully watched Vichy activities in the West Indies, it ignored St. Pierre and Miquelon, two tiny island territories off the southern tip of Newfoundland. Shortly after the Pearl Harbor assault, the Free French under Charles de Gaulle sent naval units to Canada with a plan to occupy these possessions. The State Department, however, favored the continuation of the status quo and believed its objections effectively scrubbed the operation. Defying this opposition, DeGaulle ordered the attack early on the morning of December 24. His troops seized the islands without incident and held a plebiscite on Christmas Day in which the local inhabitants gave the Free French an overwhelming plurality.

Diplomatic reaction came swiftly. Vichy demanded restoration. The British and Canadians, publicly embarrassed, privately rejoiced. Roosevelt and Churchill, who were in Washington planning military strategy, minimized the incident's importance, while the American press hailed the landing as the first allied triumph. The State Department was far from elated. Occupying these islands was inconsequential compared to the negative precedent being set. To Hull, DeGaulle's defiant and foolish occupation had violated the Monroe Doctrine and the Havana resolutions. As a result the irate secretary insisted that the "so-called Free French" withdraw and restore Vichy rule, but DeGaulle refused. Adding to the secretary's anger, the press and radio took Hull's disparaging remarks about the Free French and poked fun at him by referring to him as the "so-called secretary of state" leading the "so-called State Department." Not accustomed to such jibes, Hull sought presidential backing, but Roosevelt rebuffed him, maintaining that since the islands stayed under French authority, no one had violated any Pan American principles. The immediate question was settled; however, this incident haunted the Allies throughout the war. Hull exaggerated the episode's signifi-cance, while Roosevelt and Churchill underrated the possible impact. Policy disagreements and personality conflicts surfaced over two tiny islands. Hull's suspicions of Churchill's motives turned to open distrust, and both Roose-velt and his secretary of state developed an unrelenting antipathy toward DeGaulle.[39]

Excluding the St. Pierre-Miquelon operation, Roosevelt successfully fit inter-American diplomacy into his broader international strategy. Finessing his opposition through Pan American rhetoric about continental defense, the president directed the public mood toward Allied objectives. Critics like Lindbergh saw the movement to aid the democracies and tried to warn the country of the dire consequences, but he did not win a large enough following. As long as the president manipulated protection of the Americas into a positive British commitment and avoided the advice of advocates like Stimson who called for a frank admission of the government's real purpose, administration antagonists could not cut into Roosevelt's broadbased support.

The Germans also confronted a problem they did not even begin to comprehend. They consistently underestimated the effects of inter-American policies on the war. Tacitly accepting United States hegemony in the Americas, the Nazis unrealistically concentrated on maintaining potential commercial markets in Latin America, which British sea power effectively canceled.

At the same time, Roosevelt used the no-transfer declarations to end any enemy operations in Greenland and Iceland and to neutralize Vichy possessions. In its entire effort the Roosevelt administration imperceptibly changed its Good Neighbor emphasis. The Americas served as an example to world peace before the war's outbreak. After the fighting commenced, the president directed inter-American diplomacy to support British goals by pursuing policies that relieved the English from defending their hemispheric colonies and by extending the no-transfer principle beyond its traditional meaning in order to patrol much of the North Atlantic shipping routes.

8 ★ THE SPECTER OF
NAZI PENETRATION

LTHOUGH THE UNITED STATES concentrated its attention on the fear of Nazi penetration in the Americas, the diplomatic corps also watched other foreign influences. While the Union of Soviet Socialist Republics had minimal political and economic connections in the Western Hemisphere, the Soviets' avowed purpose of spreading communism internationally worried the State Department and especially disturbed Latin American Catholics, who vehemently opposed Russia's atheistic practices. Axis supporters capitalized on these criticisms during the 1930s by suggesting that nazism formed a bulwark against the Bolsheviks. The signing of the Russo-German nonaggression pact in the summer of 1939 temporarily halted this type of propaganda, but it resurfaced approximately two years later, when Hitler's troops attacked Stalin's forces. Some foreign service officials at that time argued against giving the Russians any assistance, but their views represented the minority. Roosevelt and a powerful backing considered the Nazis the principal threat. Using this rationale, the administration established an alliance of convenience with the Soviet Union to defeat the common foe.[1]

At the other end of the political spectrum stood the fascists in Spain and Italy. Some Latin Americans felt a strong cultural bond with their former mother country and closely watched the events of the Spanish Civil War. Although Francisco Franco triumphed after three years of exhausting warfare, his nation was too weak internally to export his brand of fascism to Spain's former colonies. Italy held out a far greater potential challenge. Over 6 million of its citizens immigrated to South America, with a particularly large concentration in Argentina. Despite the size of their group, these Italians assimilated rapidly into their adopted homeland, diluting whatever enthusiasm local fascists tried to generate. Further decreasing Spanish and Italian influence, both nations accounted for less than 5 percent of Latin America's total imports and exports during the 1930s.[2]

Japan also caused some anxiety. With the exceptions of settlements in southern Brazil and coastal Peru, few Japanese lived in South America. Some

United States observers worried about Japanese commercial expansionism, especially the purchase of Peruvian minerals and Mexican oil. On May 7, 1941, Herbert Feis complained about possible Japaneses purchases: "The Lord knows," he claimed, "I have bestirred myself to try to get the buying branches of our Government to be there first. But they apparently again failed somewhat."[3] Feis was overly pessimistic, for nothing came of the Japanese negotiations. The Rising Sun was far too busy in the Far East to threaten United States predominance in the Americas.[4]

While the foreign service reported on the activities of the above-mentioned nations, few doubted that the greatest peril came from Germany. By the depression an estimated one-half to one million of its colonists inhabited Latin America, most of them in southern South America. Not following the Italian pattern of acculturation, German immigrants maintained their identity with the Fatherland through schools, newspapers, radio broadcasts, and social organizations.

As early as 1932 the Nazis demonstrated their appeal in the Americas when Paraguayan adherents organized the first Nazi party in Latin America. As Hitler gained power and prestige, the Reich's overseas organization grew. The Reichsdeutsch, citizens born in Germany or possessors of passports, could join Gau Ausland, the Nazi party outside of the Reich. Individuals of German blood born abroad, called the Volksdeutsch, were barred from entering the party, but this did not dampen their ardor for the Nazi cause. These individuals sometimes embarrassed Wilhelmstrasse by their vitriolic Yankeephobia. Although German diplomats tried to discourage and disassociate themselves from the Volksdeutsch, its members played a major role in the sophisticated German espionage network throughout Latin America by providing valuable information on military operations and ship movements throughout the war.[5]

Political motivation, however, was not the primary interest of Berlin in the Americas. The Nazis' main drive centered on commercial expansionism. Like many nations during the depression, Germany looked for external markets to improve internal economic conditions. To win new customers, Hitler's foreign financial advisers turned to barter agreements where the Reich and another country exchanged goods under quota arrangements using special German currency. To begin this program in Latin America, the Reich sent a trade mission to South America from July 1934 to January 1935 promoting the sale of German industrial products in exchange for raw materials. The initial reception exceeded expectations. Before the depression Germany had negligible commercial dealings with Latin America. From 1936 to 1939 Reich exports jumped to over 14 percent of Latin America's total, and imports from Latin America climbed to slightly over 7 percent. The European war effectively stopped this commercial traffic because of the

British naval blockade, but this did not halt Nazi promises of huge commodity deals between Europe and the Americas after the fighting ended.[6]

Long before the British cut off German trade, the State Department complained bitterly about the barter system as antithetical to Hull's reciprocity program.[7] Reflecting this position, Assistant Secretary Sayre, in charge of the Trade Agreement Division, flatly rejected any bilateral pact with Germany in May 1935: "Unless and until she abandons her present economic program and offers to give us genuine most-favored-nation treatment with respect to exchange allotments, quota regulations, et cetera, we can not find any way of reconciling our fundamental differences and therefore see no room for a trade agreement."[8] Each nation had its own distinctive commercial philosophy, and even an astute diplomat like Duggan never questioned the underlining assumptions of Hull's policy and its benefits. Writing on July 16, 1938, he fully accepted the United States' international economic direction and hoped that the administration could "impress Germany with our sincerity in having no desire whatever to restrict German trade with the other American countries on a fair and aboveboard basis."[9]

The conflict between the two great powers was especially apparent in Brazil. From 1935 through most of 1939 Vargas played off Germany against the United States in gaining trading advantages for his nation. The Brazilians first signed a reciprocity agreement with the Roosevelt administration, pledging freer world commerce; next they negotiated a barter arrangement with the Nazis, reducing American manufacturing exports in favor of German goods. Whenever one government complained to the crafty dictator about the other's negotiations, Vargas placed the blame for his predicament on the opposite nation. Even after the Germans lost their South American markets, the Brazilians continued to bargain with the Nazis (in the event of their victory) and used these discussions to win additional concessions from the Americans.[10]

Several prominent American spokesmen recognized that the United States was losing customers to the Reich and openly advocated commercial Germanphobia. Leading this effort throughout 1937, Ambassador Dodd in Berlin warned the administration about a Nazi campaign to negotiate more barter arrangements with Latin American nations at the expense of United States business.[11] Mayor Fiorello La Guardia of New York City told a nationwide radio audience in the spring of 1938 that the Nazi system resulted in layoffs of American workers. To reverse the trend, he called for the creation of a government agency to subsidize American exporters, which would allow them to compete favorably against foreign rivals. He warned his listeners: "For the maintenance of our economic well-being, for the preservation of peace, it is vital that we take immediate steps to eliminate this new growing sore on the soil of the Western Hemisphere. In this way, we may lay the foundation of peace and security for our world of the future. A united people in the Western Hemisphere, without invasion of the sovereign rights of any government. The Americas for the Americans."[12]

Others expressed similar concerns. Secretary Morgenthau argued that unless the Treasury Department supplied capital and credits to Latin American countries through gold and silver loans that would stabilize their currencies, those nations might turn to the dictators for aid. Industrialist Bernard Baruch recommended increasing exports, even including armaments. Such unrestricted sales would reduce German foreign markets and correspondingly decrease purchases of raw materials. If war came, the Nazis would lose these customers in any event since the Allies would halt German shipping. This would end the barter agreements, but Baruch cautioned that if the Nazis defeated their adversaries, Latin America would desert the United States and rush to Hitler's banner.[13]

The British fulfilled Baruch's expectations by blockading Europe, but many government officials pessimistically foresaw the eventual victory of the Reich over the Allies and an assault on the Americas. Prophesies of when this would happen differed, but few doubted the likelihood that the United States and Germany would battle over control of the Western Hemisphere. Before the actual fighting, many predicted that the Nazis would economically absorb Latin America, and the French armistice heightened these convictions.[14]   At the end of 1940 a United States businessman well acquainted with German commercial practices forecast that the Nazi-dominated continent would buy over half of Latin America's exports. During the commercial negotiations Berlin officials would make other demands adversely affecting the United States: "Markets would be closed to our exporters. Political, naval and aviation concessions would be linked to commerce. We should soon find a European 'sphere of influence' creeping up toward us from the south, and outposts of the Empire appearing closer and closer to the Panama Canal."[15]

The fear of German commercial penetration sometimes proved extremely advantageous to private United States corporations operating in the Americas. This applied particularly to the competition for air service. After World War I, German companies established airlines in several South American nations: Scadta in Colombia, followed by Lloyd Aereo Boliviano, and Varg coupled with Condor in Brazil. Pan American Airways (PAA), a United States corporation, inaugurated a business rivalry for air routes throughout Latin America in 1927 when the company flew its maiden flight to Havana. Four years later PAA quietly purchased majority control of Scadta, expanded passenger and mail service to the principal American republics, and received federal subsidies through postal contracts to Cuba and Mexico.

By the onset of the depression United States and German firms dominated Latin American air traffic. Shortly after Hitler entered the chancellory, the competition intensified. Deutsch Lufthansa began service between Europe and South America in 1934, increasing the Reich's commitment to support its private citizens and also providing pilots with long-distance flying experience. Other German-supervised airlines started with Vasp in Brazil and Sedta in Ecuador. From 1934 to 1938 German airlines doubled their service, while PAA correspondingly lost business. By 1934 PAA had 54.5 percent of the total market; four years hence, while retaining its status as the single largest carrier, its overall share slipped to 42.5 percent.

Fortunately for PAA, its decline coincided with the War Department's rising anxieties toward Nazi hemispheric intentions. In order to assure continental security, the United States military clandestinely began supplying PAA with funds to eliminate foreign competitors and construct auxiliary airfields with usage potential for military aircraft. While the start of the European war ended Reich operations, the Italians founded Lati for service from Rome to southern South America. Even after this link ceased, the Roosevelt government wanted more—total elimination of German personnel. Unaware that PAA controlled Scadta and could summarily dismiss its foreign staff, the United States pressured the Colombian administration to nationalize the industry. This occurred in the summer of 1940 with the establishment of Avianca. German employees were promptly replaced, something PAA had avoided doing.

From this episode to the beginning of 1942, the United States effectively crushed any vestige of Axis influence in Latin American airlines. Despite the fact that PAA had not cooperated in ridding its subsidiaries of German staff, the corporation still gained an unquestionable monopoly throughout the Americas. Fears of Nazi ownership and the value of auxiliary airfields to repulse a potential invasion guaranteed the outcome, even though the Nazis never contemplated an assault on the Americas and did not have any plans for military operations in the area. The practical result was that what had begun at the conclusion of the first war as a commercial rivalry ended at the start of the second with PAA holding the Americas as its exclusive territory.[16]

Some United States citizens felt that the issue of Nazi penetration in the Americas had been grossly overstated, especially before the European war commenced. From Berlin, Prentiss Gilbert, counselor at the American embassy, wrote, "All sorts of ideas are floating around about Germany and Latin-America, and I cannot but feel that some of these are exaggerated."[17] J. Fred Rippy, a well-known Latin American historian at the University of Chicago, conceded that many dictators headed hemispheric governments, but added that totalitarianism had existed in the region long before the rise of nazism. These rulers, according to Rippy, did not mimic Hitler, for they were nationalists and strongly attached to the Allies through traditional political, economic, and cultural bonds. Others reached similar conclusions, adding that newspapers sensationalized the fifth-column menace to increase readership.[18]

Josephus Daniels in Mexico offered a little different approach. Recalling his career as secretary of navy during World War I, he advocated letting the Europeans solve their own dilemma. Throughout his ambassadorship he promoted hemispheric solidarity and advised against foreign involvement. He wanted no repetition of the disillusionment that followed the first war.[19] Even after the Nazi spring offensive of 1940, he called for neutrality. "Our true course," he warned, "is to keep aloof and have no entangling alliances with a Europe whose roots of hatred and suspicion are as deep as the centuries."[20]

These opinions became less vocal as many powerful United States officials began to express their disdain toward Hitler. As early as April 1939 Secretary Wallace wrote a friend, mirroring many of his colleagues' beliefs: "Hitler is a mad man and will not be diverted by anything but a full appreciation of force."[21] Secretaries Ickes and Morgenthau joined in this chorus and continually cautioned their constituents about the Nazis' aggressive nature and the need to deter their advances. Stimson and Knox, both ardent Anglophiles, directed the military departments and moved openly to assist the Allies and antagonize the Germans.[22]

Outside official government circles, many prominent citizens took similar positions. Alfred Landon had pledged his support at the Lima conference to keep foreign ideologies from the Americas. After the European conflict broke out, others joined this cause and advocated British assistance as a deterrent to Nazi infiltration in the Americas. The Committee to Defend America by Aiding the Allies led this refrain. Adlai Stevenson, president of its Chicago chapter, felt that the United States remained at peace because the British formed a barrier between the Americas and the Germans. If the island kingdom fell, Hitler would ultimately conquer Latin America and then turn to the United States.[23]

Journalists capitalized on this topic, oftentimes exaggerating their stories. Popular writer Carleton Beals, who frequently wrote about Latin America, warned his readers to watch out for German hemispheric infiltration and its potentially disastrous consequences. Syndicated columnist Raymond Clapper demanded military preparedness for the defense of the Americas. Historian Samuel Flagg Bemis demanded adequate hemispheric security.[24]

Welles encouraged John Gunther to write a book on Latin America and solicited Roosevelt's support for the project by having him and the well-known author discuss the subject. When *Inside Latin America* came off the press in the summer of 1941, predictable themes emerged: (1) "Latin America is our exposed frontier, the vulnerable back door to our continent"; (2) "If we declare war on Germany, most will probably follow us. But the first line of defense of Latin America remains the British fleet"; and (3) "The living future of Latin America is bound to that of the United States. What is more of the United States is indissolubly bound to that of Latin America. We need Latin America just as much as it needs us."[25]

Public-opinion polls reflected many of Gunther's conclusions. Shortly after the Polish invasion, a Gallup survey found that a little over half of its sample favored the United States fighting to keep European powers away from South America. Just before the Germans marched into Paris, *Fortune* reported that two-thirds of those interviewed wanted to supply the Allies; almost four-fifths believed that if Hitler won he would try to penetrate the Americas; and about half believed that the Reich would attack the United States as soon as possible. By the end of the year a Hadley Cantril study revealed that approximately half of its respondents wished to aid the British while simultaneously avoiding the risk of war; however, almost two-thirds would fight to prevent Germany's absorption of the Americas. Various polls throughout 1941 underscored the public's overwhelming support for this latter point. Gallup, for example, asked: "If a European power attacked Latin America, should the United States fight?" Eighty-six percent answered affirmatively, and that high percentage remained constant until Pearl Harbor.[26]

While the American public steadily moved toward Allied support and the defense of the Americas, the State Department presented a more cautious and less unified position. Secretary Hull clung to strict neutrality in the hope of avoiding a war. His two principal advisers, Counselor Moore and Assistant Secretary Long, subscribed to the secretary's general outline, but gradually began urging assistance to the British as the best way to keep the Nazis from the Western Hemisphere. Welles also wanted to avoid armed conflict, but at the same time he loyally enacted the president's pro-Allied initiatives and fervently acted to strengthen hemispheric defenses. Others within the Washington diplomatic corps, like Herbert Feis, deplored nazism. Berle argued that hemispheric unity was essential to halt Hitlerism in Latin America. If German expansionism were allowed to continue unchecked and the Allies lost the war, he predicted that the United States would eventually fight the Reich for control of the New World. Messersmith was even more gloomy. He personally watched the Fuehrer's rise and concluded from his observations of the dictator's aggressive designs that Berlin already had planned the conquest of the Americas. Unless the administration moved immediately, the enemy would take over Latin America and then attack the United States.[27]

Many diplomats in the field reflected this antipathy toward Germany. Shortly after the appeasement at Munich, United States minister in Haiti, Fred Mayer, expressed the disappointment and disgust of many colleagues: "Hitler is an international highwayman and held the boys up at the point of a gun when asked to stand and deliver, they delivered." When the European war erupted, he privately called for a war declaration against the Nazis, but knew that the American public would not sanction such a drastic step.[28] Ambassador Joseph Davies, writing en route to Rotterdam after the commencement of the warfare, predicted: "It will take 'all we've got' to prevent the free world and ourselves from being enslaved by the Nazi 'Superman'—

who believed that it is their divine destiny and duty to rule over all of us 'inferiors' on the rest of the earth."[29]

The most vocal and influential critic of nazism in South America throughout the war was Claude Bowers. Born in Indiana and trained as a reporter, he won national recognition as a columnist for the New York *World*. He also became a powerful figure in the Democratic party, chaired the 1928 national convention and presented its keynote address. As a reward for his activities, Roosevelt made him ambassador to Spain, where he served throughout the Spanish Civil War and formed an intense hatred of the Nazis. In 1939 he left Madrid and assumed a new ambassadorial post in Santiago at the onset of the European war. Though he was thousands of miles from the battlefields, he quickly decided that the Reich's blueprint for conquest included South America. Since Chile had a large German population along with support from sympathetic political groups and a Nazi-oriented military, the German assault, Bowers reasoned, would naturally commence at his station.[30] Once the swastika flew over Europe, Bowers wrote Roosevelt, "the German Nazis are more likely to strike here than in any other South American republic."[31] The president assured his appointee that he would act before allowing the establishment of any puppet regime in the Western Hemisphere.[32]

Some allegations about the Nazi menace boarded on the absurd. Senator Joseph O'Mahoney, a Democrat from Wyoming, recklessly charged at the start of 1941 that Haiti was the headquarters for Nazi spying in the Americas. He later amended his complaint to imply that German agents used the tiny Negro republic for smuggling operatives to the mainland. A prominent Haitian businessman read O'Mahoney's statements and admitted that some of his countrymen and a local newspaper admired Hitler. The German legation also distributed propaganda and supported its citizens working in Haiti. These activities, the businessman claimed, should not worry the senator. The government backed the State Department's policies, and if the Germans became belligerent, Haitian officials would act swiftly against them.[33]

Another senator embarrassed the Roosevelt administration far more with his imprudent remarks. On July 29, 1941, D. Worth Clark, the Democrat from Idaho who adamantly objected to the president's Allied position, proclaimed the Good Neighbor's failure. In its place the United States "should take over control" of the Americas. "It probably would not be necessary to fire a single shot. . . . We could make some kind of arrangement to set up puppet governments which we could trust to American interests ahead of those of Germany or any other nation in the world."[34] When the president learned of this statement, he expressed the wish that no one should pay any attention to it. Few, if any, did, not even O'Mahoney.[35]

Roosevelt led the anti-Hitler campaign. During his 1936 trip to Buenos Aires, he praised the Pan American resolve to settle disputes through pacific means as an example for the rest of the world to emulate. He called for an end to warfare and initiated futile diplomatic feelers for an international peace gathering. In his quarantine message in late 1937, he repeated his peace theme. During early 1939 he sent requests to Hitler and Mussolini for assurance that they would not attack certain countries.[36]

The president slowly discarded the image of peacemaker to take a more belligerent stand against the dictators. Following the Munich agreement he warned the nation of a potential air invasion and called for vigorous defense measures to protect the Americas. He also declared that the Nazis would use economic coercion in the Western Hemisphere before politically dominating the other American republics. To counteract this possibility, Roosevelt inaugurated additional programs for economic growth and political stability of the Americas.[37]

The allegations that German subversion would overthrow Latin American governments fit remarkably well with Roosevelt's Allied assistance efforts. The security zone, for instance, not only protected the Americas from belligerent activities, but it also decreased the vast expanses of oceans for British patrol. The no-transfer position had similar results. The United States directed its prohibition against the Reich; existing British possessions were not endangered. After the Anglo-American destroyers-for-bases deal reached the press, Roosevelt emphasized its contribution to hemispheric security, while minimizing the military assistance to the Churchill government. Despite this inherent bias, the president still feigned neutrality.[38]

Throughout 1941 the president moved more openly and boldly in support of the Allied cause. On February 27 he lectured an audience: "Implicit in our plans for national defense, is a natural outgrowth of our good neighbor policy in our relations with the other American Republics. Happily for democracy, the Americas stand forth today as a notable example of international solidarity in a world in which freedom and human liberty are threatened with extinction."[39] Naturally, aid to the British contributed to hemispheric defense efforts.

The links between British assistance and hemispheric security allowed Roosevelt flexibility to send supplies to the Allies, but he was unable to convince the public that the Nazis seriously threatened its freedom and survival. The president sought evidence to prove that Hitler planned to attack the Americas.[40] After Rudolf Hess, a Reich cabinet minister, had flown to Scotland and was taken into custody, Roosevelt wrote Churchill on May 14, requesting information on "what Germany's plans really are in relation to the United States or to other parts of the Western Hemisphere, including commerce, infiltration, military domination, encirclement of the United States. . . . If he says anything about the Americas in the course of telling his story, it should be kept separate from other parts and featured by itself."[41]

Hess's capture quickly faded from the headlines when the German pocket battleship *Bismarck* broke out of the British blockade into the Atlantic

Ocean. Some feared that she would steer a course for the Americas, but His Majesty's Navy quickly located her position and sunk her on May 27. That evening Roosevelt gave his annual Pan American Day address. Before hemispheric diplomats in the East Room of the White House, he surprised his guests by declaring an unlimited national emergency. He called for solidarity and proclaimed: "Adolf Hitler never considered the domination of Europe as an end in itself. European conquest was but a step toward ultimate goals in all the other continents. It is unmistakenly apparent to all of us that, unless the advance of Hitlerism is forcibly checked now, the Western Hemisphere will be within range of the Nazi weapons of destruction."[42] Roosevelt pledged that Germany would not invade the Americas. A stunned audience politely applauded and newmen rushed to file their stories. Admiral William Leahy felt that the speech perilously bordered on a war declaration; Secretary Ickes, on the other hand, correctly understood that the nation still remained ambivalent about a real Nazi threat. The day following the address, the public outcry against the implication of possible warfare forced Roosevelt to declare that he did not intend to lead the nation into any armed conflict.[43]

The president's retraction did not change his private beliefs; it did, however, caution him to move more circumspectly. Instead of making such bellicose statements against the Reich, he returned to his themes of hemispheric defense, Allied support, and German aggression. When a U-boat sank the American merchantman *Robin Moor* in mid-June 700 miles off the Brazilian coast, Roosevelt implied that the submarine had violated American waters and therefore had committed an act of piracy by the sinking. At the start of July, United States troops occupied Iceland, supposedly to defend the Americas, but at the same time the navy began escorting Allied shipping to the island. During the same period the president sent a request to Congress for an extension of the Selective Service Act. Roosevelt tied it directly to hemispheric security, declaring that the army needed greater manpower to fulfill its traditional continental defense mission. Without additional troop strength, the president foresaw Nazi penetration weakening hemispheric bonds.[44]

In a fireside chat on September 11, Roosevelt tried to promote Naziphobia by disclosing that a U-boat had unsuccessfuly fired twice at the United States destroyer *Greer*. He failed to mention that the warship was relaying the submarine's position to British aircraft for depth-charge runs. Relying on this incident and others equally tenuous, Roosevelt told his audience that the Nazis were attempting to restrict freedom of the seas. The United States would not tolerate this, for American commerce depended on open sea lanes. To end this alleged menace, the United States would protect any merchant vessel within its patrol area from submarines and merchant raiders. The president also informed his listeners that besides its attempts to confine shipping, Hitler's espionage network unsuccessfully conspired to overthrow the governments in Argentina, Bolivia, and Uruguay. In addition, Nazi agents had constructed secret airfields within easy striking range of the Panama Canal.[45]

Roosevelt's allegations against the Nazis demonstrated not only his own personal prejudices toward Hitler but also his lack of candor with his constituents. First, both combatants violated the neutrality zone at some time, and in reality the British were the worst offenders. While His Majesty's vessels moved undisturbed, Hitler, over the strenuous objections of his admiralty, refused to enter the neutrality zone. Second, Reich diplomats did not encourage Latin American coup d'etats. Quite to the contrary, the plots that did unfold stemmed from local agitators who acted independently. Despite this fact Berlin received the blame. Finally, the secret air bases near the canal were a myth. The Luftwaffe had enough trouble with the Royal Air Force. It did not have the capability of flying planes to the Americas or supplying existing squadrons for a strike on the canal.

These contradictions did not disturb the president. In an address on October 27 he became even more irresponsible by telling his listeners that he personally had a secret Nazi map for the conquest of certain Latin American countries. Instead of fourteen separate states, the Germans planned five vassal countries. When a reporter asked him the next day to produce the map, Roosevelt refused because its notations might divulge his source's identity. Berlin immediately, categorically, and truthfully denied these allegations. Some Nazi sympathizers had indeed drawn several maps of conquest, but Hitler never encouraged this activity.[46] Even with the wild presidential accusations and the public's growing aversion to Nazi tyranny, the American people remained adamantly in opposition to entering the war. They simply did not wish to become entangled in the European fighting.

Though clearly and vividly cast as villains, the Nazis avoided any major confrontatation with the United States over Latin America. The Roosevelt administration never obtained evidence to prove that Germany was trying to foment revolution in the Americas. If anything, Wilhelmstrasse attempted to restrain local enthusiasts who became overly zealous in their crusade for the establishment of nazism in the Americas. Instead of responding positively to those political initiatives, the Reich's diplomatic corps focused on increasing foreign trade, and in the end lost both commerce and a powerful political base.

Rather than acknowledge the limited scope of the Nazi movement in the Americas, Roosevelt exaggerated its potential in order to aid the Allies. He excited peoples' emotions by warning of invasions, surprise attacks, and fifth-column revolts in Latin America. He neglected to point out, as foreign service officers did throughout the war, that the United States was not receiving complete cooperation from the other American republics in ending subversion. Because of insufficient surveillance, the Germans developed a powerful espionage network in the Americas, but the public never learned of this fact. Instead the American people was conditioned to the premise that Hitler menaced the Americas. Since the Allies prevented the Nazis from crossing the Atlantic, aid to the British was a logical consequence. That was the limit. Roosevelt and his supporters failed to persuade the country to declare war on anyone—unless someone invaded the Americas.

9 ★ TO WAR

W HEN ROOSEVELT received the Democratic presidential nomination in 1940 for an unprecedented third term, many Republicans saw
the upcoming campaign as an opportunity to present the electorate
with a referendum against the administration's pro-Allied policies. This wish,
however, went unfulfilled, for as Frank Knox observed a month before the
voting, "The policies of both President Roosevelt and Wendell Willkie so
parallel each other that it is hard to distinguish them."[1] The president's reelection pleased not only the British; Latin Americans also viewed the Democratic triumph as a vindication of Good Neighbor diplomacy and four more
years of hemispheric solidarity.[2]

While Roosevelt steered a steady course toward England, the State Department zigzagged on the same heading. After the initial flurry of activity
created by the European war had subsided, the foreign service seemingly
reverted to prewar patterns. The country desks made most of the routine
decisions, while diplomats in the field emphasized daily events, overlooking
or dismissing major trends.[3] Dean Acheson recalled a staff "without direction, composed of a lot of busy people working hard and usefully but as a
whole not functioning as a foreign office. It did not chart a course to be
furthered by the success of our aims, or to aid or guide our arms. Rather it
seems to have been adrift, carried hither and yon by the currents of war or
pushed about by collision with more purposeful craft."[4]

Powerful personalities like Secretary Ickes, an early admirer of Hull,
openly attacked his inability to formulate foreign policies. Morgenthau, in
treasury, criticized the State Department for improperly gauging the Nazi
menace, concentrating on a worthless reciprocity program, and listening to
the misguided opinions of career diplomats affected by Anglophilism. Political appointees like Dodd and Bowers assailed the wealthy aristocrats who
pledged the diplomatic fraternity and gave lip service to the New Deal,
while in reality they sabotaged Roosevelt's programs.[5] "As a matter of fact,"
Josephus Daniels asserted, "the philosophy of the New Deal and the Good
Neighbor policy are dispised [sic.] by most of the career men in the diplomatic corps. . . ."[6]

The attacks did not cause any major changes in Washington. Hull maintained overall authority. However, by the late 1930s poor health reduced the

time that he spent at his desk. The American people, unaware of this problem, still held the secretary in the highest esteem and trusted him above any other cabinet member. The public approved of his battle to lower trade barriers, his advocacy of the Good Neighbor and search for peace in the Far East.[7]

As the 1940 presidential contest approached, prominent Democrats began mentioning Hull as a candidate. Encouraged by these feelers, the secretary recognized the desirability of Roosevelt's support and tried to maintain cordial relations with the White House. By the end of 1939 Hull must have been heartened when the president nominated him for the Nobel Peace Prize. Yet, once the secretary learned about the third-term bid, he knew that at seventy years of age his presidential aspirations had ended.[8]

After the reelection Roosevelt gave no thought to replacing Hull. He wielded enormous power and the president relied on his cautious nature to reflect the public's mood. Hull's continued presence reassured the public, but at the same time certain negative aspects of his secretaryship became more pronounced. Unable to assert firm control over his staff or restrict the president's independent forays into international relations, Hull grew frustrated and disillusioned. His style demanded time for study and contemplation, but his health was progressively deteriorating, forcing him to take protracted leaves of absence.[9]

When Roosevelt needed an immediate response to Nazi advances, he increasingly turned to Welles. The undersecretary assumed command of the State Department during Hull's absences, and furthermore, Roosevelt personally found the undersecretary's temperament more compatible with his own.[10] Besides directing inter-American operations, Welles began to give more attention to European matters. During his trip to Europe in early 1940 he met with the principal leaders and gained a deeper appreciation of the conflict. Welles, in some instances, made poor character judgment—like his admiration for Mussolini. This did not trouble the president; Welles filled a crucial spot in the administration.[11]

Hull acknowledged the undersecretary's supervision of Latin American affairs, but slowly began to resent his growing responsibilities in other regions. Berle commented on this friction as early as the start of 1939, believing Hull's objections centered on Welles's frequent trips to the White House. Later in the year Drew Pearson, whom the secretary hated, contributed to the secretary's jealousies by forecasting Hull's retirement because of ill health and Welles's assumption of the top position. Hull resented this rumor and believed that the undersecretary leaked confidential diplomatic information to the muckraking columnist. The secretary became even more distraught when he was excluded from the plans for Welles's European mission. Faced with a fait accompli the secretary remained silent, but these happenings almost imperceptibly, moved the two men toward confrontation.[12]

Roosevelt did not foresee the evolving Hull-Welles conflict. He needed the secretary to reassure the general public of the administration's peaceful intentions and to cater to his former congressional colleagues in order to win passage for vital legislation. The undersecretary worked energetically on a multitude of tasks and translated vague presidential ideas into precise proposals. The president used the talents of both men. He did not notice Hull's growing irritation, for the secretary did not press Roosevelt to end Welles's White House visits.

This unwholesome situation did not disturb Welles's almost absolute hold over hemispheric appointments and transfers. He placed key personnel at strategic stations and rid the foreign service of those who could not handle their jobs. Career officers with wide experience held several critical posts. Jefferson Caffery, for example, remained in Rio for seven years, exceeding the normal tour of duty. Norman Armour moved to Chile before the European conflict and, in recognition of his abilities to direct delicate negotiations, went to Buenos Aires after the fighting started. George Messersmith, a seasoned career diplomat, left his assistant secretaryship for the Havana ambassadorship and later replaced Daniels in Mexico. Spruille Braden, after serving as a delegate to the Montevideo conference and assisting in the resolution of the Chaco War, became ambassador to Colombia and afterwards was transferred to Cuba.[13]

Ambassador Bowers in Chile reflected the spirit of these diplomats who sought to build stronger inter-American ties shortly before the Germans marched into Paris:

We may as well get down to brass tacks and admit to ourselves that our interest in South America MUST be lasting and not merely the gesture of the moment. Were it to develop otherwise we would lost the confidence of South America which we have gained through the policy of the "good neighbor." In view of the slaughter and destruction in the Old World I think there can be no doubt that domination is passing to the New and that makes South America more important to us. I hope that even the press will conclude that news from South America is as important to us as gossip from Roumania or politics from Bulgaria.[14]

The general public increasingly appeared to accept Bowers's evaluation. During December 1940 an opinion poll found 84 percent of its sample wanted to know more about Latin America. Seventy-five percent called for more articles on the Americas and favored closer contacts, even at the cost of greater governmental expenditures. Over 50 percent advocated loans for Latin American industrial development, railroads, and defense and were willing to pay higher taxes to support them. Stories alleging German infiltration and sabotage along with the pleas for hemispheric security heightened regional awareness. With European vacation resorts closed, many tourists traveled within the Americas. Spanish and Portuguese language classes' attendance rose sharply; in 1941 *Reader's Digest* and *Time* inaugurated Spanish editions, and the two largest United States radio networks started weekly broadcasts to and from Latin America. The Copacabana and Latin Quarter opened in New York City, where performers like Carmen Miranda from Brazil popularized songs like "South of the Border" and "The South American Way," while patrons danced to the conga and rumba.[15]

Some worried that the Latin American upsurge was a craze. Once the Axis threat disappeared, some felt, the enthusiasm for continental solidarity would fade. Pan American proponents wondered if Roosevelt had institutionalized Pan Americanism, or if the termination of his presidency likewise would signal the collapse of the Good Neighbor.[16] Philip Jessup, a professor from Columbia University, reflected upon these concerns after a tour of fifteen American republics in the summer of 1941 and optimistically predicted: "A decade of the good neighbor policy has helped enormously to overcome the results of mistaken policies of the past but the postwar situation will be a great challenge to our intelligent self-restraint. We shall meet that challenge successfully because the government and the people of the U.S. are irrevocably committed to the sound conclusion that the old stupid type of imperialist policy can never be used again."[17]

A boundary controversy between Peru and Ecuador temporarily shattered hemispheric peace. Beginning over disputed border claims dating back to the colonial era, the argument between these two nations flared periodically over which one owned certain lands. The Peruvians actively settled what they considered to be their northern provinces, while Ecuador claimed the territory as its southern frontier. Both nations at various times threatened war. When Roosevelt took office, some hoped that his mediation would settle the dispute, but this did not happen. Instead, border incidents increased, and Peruvian nationalists agitated for war. Ecuador, realizing its inferior military position, worked for a diplomatic solution. Peru refused to bargain, and on July 5, 1941, its troops and planes crossed into the frontier. The fighting lasted for less than a month with superior Peruvian might overwhelming its weaker opponent. As Ecuador's situation worsened, its government desperately pleaded for assistance to end the combat, but only after Peru had occupied its objectives and agreed to a truce did the bloodshed stop.[18]

While this conflict created a deep bilateral rift between the combatants and openly displayed the fragile nature of the Pan American system to end warfare, these issues were temporarily submerged when the Japanese attacked Pearl Harbor and the rest of the Axis declared war on the United States. During the World War I, eight Latin American states, most of them considered United States protectorates, declared war. The majority, however, clung to neutrality, and some even sympathized with the Central Powers. At the end of 1941 the United States no longer maintained its protectorates. The question was: How would the Americas respond? All nine

Central American and Caribbean republics answered by declaring war on Japan by December 12; by the new year they had signed the United Nations Declaration and considered Germany and Italy enemies. In the same period Colombia, Venezuela, and Mexico further contributed to hemispheric solidarity by severing diplomatic relations with the Axis.[19] Berle reflected the department's elation on December 10: "The heartening thing in all this is the swift and virtually unanimous support from all the republics of this hemisphere. If ever a policy paid dividends, the Good Neighbor policy has. So far, they are sticking to us with scarely a break and you will have a united hemisphere. . . ." A week later he recorded: "Even the doubting Thomases in the United States are beginning to see what the Good Neighbor policy was all about. . . ."[20]

The outpouring of bilateral support received a multilateral boost on December 9, when the United States and Chile cosponsored a meeting under a resolution at the Havana conference that stated that an act of aggression on any American national by any non-American power constituted grounds for consultation. The American republics agreed to the request and set a January meeting date to gather in Rio de Janeiro. This display of solidarity came during the bleakest moment of the war for the Allies. Spain flirted with the idea of joining the Axis, while the Russians and British desperately fought for survival. The Japanese had inflicted a stunning defeat to the United States fleet and landed soldiers in the Pacific, demonstrating American military unpreparedness.[21] Assistant Secretary Long was distressed: "The result is loss of prestige on our part. The invincibility of the United States is being questioned by the world. The effect of that on the coming Rio Conference may be of the first importance. We *have* to be impressive there."[22]

Internal uncertainties plagued the Americas. The sudden death of the Chilean president forced an election in early 1942; in the meantime the nation was left without firm executive guidance in foreign affairs. Because of a terminal illness President Ortiz of Argentina, sympathetic to Allied goals, surrendered his authority to Vice President Castillo, who depended on politicians and military leaders with Axis proclivities. In addition, even though the fighting between Peru and Ecuador had ceased, the antipathy on both sides had not diminished.

These troubles did not interrupt United States plans for the meeting. Hull, exhausted from his futile talks meant to avoid war with Japan, decided to remain in Washington and in his place sent Welles. Both men worked on the agenda, which featured a resolution requiring the American republics to sever all relations with the Axis in order to limit any subversive activities. United States planners ruled out a hemispheric declaration of war, especially since American armed forces were incapable of protecting the entire hemisphere.[23] The undersecretary knew that the proposal would meet stiff opposition from two nations. Chile feared Japanese hit-and-run attacks on its long, exposed coastline if the nation signed the suggested resolution. Large segments of the Argentine population sympathized with the Axis or wished to retain the nation's historic commitment to neutrality. These serious problems did not discourage Welles. He first intended to overcome Chilean trepidation over cutting relations with the Axis, and win its approval. After he accomplished that goal, Welles felt "that Argentina will not permit herself to be placed in a minority of one at the meeting, even on an issue of this fundamental character."[24]

Welles left for Rio on January 10, 1942, in a confident mood. Nine nations had already declared war, and the Dominican Republic announced its intention to present a hemispheric declaration of war. Three other countries had severed relations, and Peru, Bolivia, and Paraguay were leaning in that direction. When the undersecretary arrived at the Rio airport, thousands of enthusiastic Brazilians led by the cabinet warmly welcomed him. He quickly gained an audience with Vargas, who pledged his support and hoped for Argentine cooperation.[25] Amidst this positive atmosphere, Welles wired Washington: "The Foreign Ministers of all the Caribbean, Central American and northern South American Republics are vehemently of the opinion that the destiny of the hemisphere should not be determined by the veto power which the Argentine Government apparently desires to exercise. This tendency . . . is stronger today and is I think uncontrollable."[26]

Welles also had a major tactical edge, the full cooperation of Brazilian Foreign Minister Oswaldo Aranha. The two had developed a warm friendship when Aranha was Vargas's ambassador in Washington. As chairman of the meeting, Aranha exercised considerable power by exchanging information on the positions of the various delegations and working closely with the undersecretary. To aid the United States even further, the foreign minister intended to announce his country's break with the Axis at an appropriate moment.

Brazilian support depended in large part on winning Chilean cooperation. Juan Rossetti, politician and newspaper editor, had been foreign minister for only six months and impulsively cosponsored the meeting as a way to enhance his own presidential ambitions, but he had miscalculated. Chilean voters wanted to remain neutral because of their vulnerable coastline. Caught between domestic politics and inter-American solidarity, Rossetti knew that he did not have any mandate to bind his nation to strong commitments at Rio.[27]

Argentina presented a far different picture. At every major inter-American gathering since 1933, the United States had made major concessions to the Buenos Aires governments. Welles understood that Argentina considered itself the diplomatic spokesman of South America, for he had begun his hemispheric training in the Argentine capital. He hoped to use his experience and his relationship with Foreign Minister Enrique Ruiz Guiñazú, who would attend the gathering, to negotiate an agreement. The undersecretary had already held two rather lengthy conversations with the foreign minister in the spring of 1941, and characterized him as "a man of considerable background, well-educated, measured and moderate in his views and in his decisions." Wells detected no hostility toward the United States, but Ruiz Guiñazú did concede that he was "very conscious of the fact that his many years in Europe have left him very much out of touch with the problem of inter-American relations."[28] The undersecretary had inaccurately judged the foreign minister's sentiments. Ambassador Armour in Buenos Aires later presented a far more pessimistic picture: "Stupidity and vanity are a bad enough combination in any individual, but when they are found in a Foreign Minister with pro-Axis leanings they become positively dangerous."[29]

Welles also seemed to ignore Argentina's public refusal to cut its ties with the Axis. Castillo went so far as to decree a state of siege, which prohibited potentially embarrassing public demonstrations favoring the Allies. In the face of these internal restraints, the foreign minister tried to form a South American bloc to oppose the rupture resolution and make economics the paramount issue. When these tactics failed, Ruiz Guiñazú searched for other ways to defeat the proposal, such as declaring that the American republics who had signed the United Nations Declarations had violated the principles of consultation and prejudiced the Rio agenda.[30] These obstructionist maneuvers brought a firm and inflexible response from Washington: "The feeling in the Department from Secretary Hull down is in accord, believing that a breach in unanimity would be preferable to a compromise formula. This is a situation in which the Argentines must accept the situation or go their own way, in which case the overwhelming public feeling in Argentina may be relied on to supply the corrective."[31]

In the middle of an oppressively hot summer, the Third Meeting of Ministers of Foreign Affairs of the American Republics opened on January 15. After Welles received warm ovations from large crowds outside and the delegates within the halls, he outlined the United States position at the first plenary session. The Japanese attack on Hawaii followed by German and Italian declarations of war, according to the undersecretary, were parts of the plan for Axis worldwide conquest. The dictatorships, however, had miscalculated in their dreams of world domination, for the United States entrance into the conflict marked the beginning of the enemy's inevitable decline. To quicken this, the Roosevelt administration needed hemispheric cooperation to halt Axis penetration in their nations, while the United States supplied economic assistance to insure domestic tranquility.[32]

The acceptance of Welles's offer depended on the decisions made in three South American countries. Aranha, fully committed to the United States, required Vargas's authorization to break with the Axis, but the Brazilian military feared that any pro-Allied action might provoke an Argentine invasion of Brazil's southern provinces. Before Vargas would publicly cut ties with the Axis, Aranha had to eliminate this possibility. Chile also needed incentives to break relations. Despite local problems created by the presidential campaign and fears of Japanese reprisals, Chile had traditionally aligned itself with Brazil as a balance to Argentine military superiority. The Chileans, furthermore, desired United States trade and economic assistance. With these latter considerations in the forefront, Rossetti asked his government for permission to sever relations if the Roosevelt government guaranteed to provide financial and military aid. With these two countries committed to breaking relations, Welles convinced Ruiz Guiñazú that his nation would be the lone nonsignatory, and he, too, agreed to the break on January 21. The undersecretary seemed to have won unanimity according to his preconference strategy. For the first time since his arrival he went to bed early, after cabling the State Department about his apparent success.[33]

The severance accord lasted only a day, for President Castillo in Buenos Aires ordered his foreign minister not to cut relations. Unless some wording could be arranged that would allow Argentina time to sever ties at a later date, Argentina would not sign the resolution.[34] With a January 23 deadline for proposals, Castillo's decision caused a great deal of confusion and anguish over how to proceed. Welles worked frantically to find a compromise, and after a full day of heated debate, he arrived at a new draft. The crucial section read: "The American Republics . . . recommend the rupture of their diplomatic relations with Japan, Germany, and Italy, since the first of these states has attacked and the other two have declared war upon an American country."[35] Instead of requiring a break, the article recommended one. This provision permitted Argentina the leeway to move at a pace dictated by domestic events. Argentina agreed to this draft and so did Chile. Other countries, like Brazil, also accepted the changes because they could safety cut ties with the Axis and not worry about Argentine military retaliation.

Welles believed that he had adhered to State Department guidelines. He had directed United States negotiations from Rio without gaining prior clearance from Washington; the procedures established at earlier meetings did not demand concurrence as long as the general outline was followed. He felt that the severance resolution met his interpretation of departmental instructions, which, in reality, he had helped formulate. Hull did not concur with his subordinate's understanding. The secretary had closely scrutinized past Argentine intransigence and demanded the requirement for the rupture. He learned of the recommendation wording from a radio commentator, who editorialized that this resolution meant that Argentina had defeated the United States' main objective. In no mood to challenge the broadcaster's viewpoint or make his own careful evaluation of the conference proceedings, Hull phoned Welles, gave him a profane tongue-lashing, accused him of undermining departmental policy, and predicted widespread criticism because of his folly. Hull ended his assault by insisting that the undersecretary reinsert *require* in the place of *recommend* and force Argentina and Chile to decide whether or not to sign. When Welles refused to comply with the secretary's ultimatum, Roosevelt came onto the line and listened to both arguments. To Hull's displeasure, the president sided with Welles, ending the heated exchange. The undersecretary had won his point, but an irreparable breach between Hull and Welles had been opened.[36]

Hull was incorrect in thinking that the change in the severance resolution diminished solidarity at Rio. In fact, just the opposite occurred. With the draft's acceptance, Peru and Uruguay announced that they had immediately complied with the recommendation; Bolivia and Paraguay acted next; Aranha made Brazil's rupture known at a dramatic closing session, for Vargas, over military objections, acceded to his foreign minister's arguments. Almost anticlimactically, Ecuador became the eighteenth republic to break rela- tions.[37] As a United States observer in South America happily concluded: "Vargas turned what threatened to be a River Plate victory into a Washington triumph. It was excellent statesmanship—and damned fine showmanship, too."[38]

As a result of Argentina's actions at the meeting, its diplomatic prestige plummeted. Ruiz Guiñazú's vacillation lowered his standing; Castillo's failure to honor the original draft weakened his internal and external authority. Argentine esteem slipped even more when, shortly after takeoff for Buenos Aires, the plane carrying Ruiz Guiñazú had to force-land in Rio harbor. Once all were rescued, the emergency lent itself to many jokes. Aranha, for example, jested: "The plane was not overloaded. . . . It was simply Ruiz Guiñazú's conscious that was heavy."[39]

The Rio conference had achieved much more than the severance resolu- tion. While all of the measures were not effectively enforced throughout the war, the results were impressive. The conferees worked on mutual economic problems like shipping, production of strategic materials, price controls, and a stabilization fund. Actions to limit subversive activities were also put into effect. Several wartime bodies were established: the Inter-American Jurid- ical Committee, to discuss legal issues of the war and postwar periods, an Inter-American Defense Board comprised of a representative from each republic and located in Washington, to discuss war strategy, and an Emer- gency Advisory Committee for Political Defense meeting in Montevideo, to publicize fifth-column activities and investigate subversion. Finally, the dele- gates had Ecuador and Peru sign a protocol ending their border war.[40]

Welles returned to the United States by the end of January and announced the conference a triumph for hemispheric solidarity. Roosevelt reinforced this sentiment by stating that Pan American unanimity and actions taken against Axis subversion markedly enhanced the Allied cause. Hull also grudgingly admitted to some of the meeting's accomplishments and congratulated the delegation upon its return. Some did express criticism, but it was nothing like the adversity that the secretary had envisioned.[41]

The Rio meeting marked the pinnacle of inter-American multilateral cooperation—a new dimension that the Roosevelt administration introduced to inter-American affairs. From 1910 until 1923 the United States did not participate in any major hemispheric meetings; from 1933 to 1942 the Democrats attended six. This United States participation at these regional conferences flattered Latin Americans, and they responded in turn by cooperating with the United States. These frequent gatherings brought diplomats into closer contact, and they became better acquainted. The meetings also provided a forum for the American republics to debate a variety of issues and evolve a hemispheric consensus. The practical benefits of these interchanges were clear at Rio, where the Roosevelt administration won a critical vote of confidence at a time when the United States desperately needed a morale boost.

This multilateral victory did not extend to the personal relations between Hull and Welles. Since the late 1930s the secretary's resentment toward his subordinate had steadily grown. His suspicious nature coupled with deteriorating health aggravated the situation. The secretary's failure to prevent the war with Japan and Roosevelt's rebuff over the St. Pierre-Miquelon incident lowered Hull's spirits so much that he penciled out his resignation in mid-Janaury 1942. The phone conversation between Hull and Welles during the Rio conference allowed the secretary an opportunity to release his long-contained anger and frustration, which sealed Welles's fate. The secretary was raised in the Tennessee feuding tradition. Hull would wait for the right moment "to get his man," for he intended to rid his department of a man he considered to be a disloyal subordinate.[42]

10 ★ SOLIDIFYING
INTER-AMERICAN DEFENSES

T HE OUTPOURING of Latin American support for hemispheric solidarity displayed at the Rio conference resulted from much more than the Roosevelt administration's political efforts. Military collaboration grew from infancy into a major inter-American commitment. At first the State Department took the initiative, trying to encourage armed forces' interest, but the military leaders did not respond until they saw German and Japanese expansion as possible menaces to American security. Even with this recognition, the United States government never developed a clearly defined military strategy for the Western Hemisphere.

Most military forces in the other American republics, in fact, had long associations with European officer corps. Besides training Latin American military leaders, several European nations subsidized arms sales and maintained extensive military missions in the Americas. German advisers, for example, held instructorships in over half of the Latin American countries in 1939. Of the seven officer groups sent out from Latin America before the invasion of Poland, all went to Europe; and of the 184 Latin American officers and cadets studying abroad, only fourteen came to the United States.[1]

The United States military, on the other hand, virtually ignored Pan American cooperation. During the late nineteenth and early twentieth centuries, military leaders made unilateral decisions in regard to the Americas. They considered the Caribbean Sea an "American Lake" and the nations that bordered it as part of the United States defense perimeter. The Caribbean republics had to remain stable to prevent European intervention that might threaten the security of the Panama Canal. When American presidents believed that it was endangered, they ordered marines into the region to restore domestic order. By the end of World War I, the possibility of any European invasion had vanished, and along with it, the urge to land troops. By the mid-1930s most United States soldiers had left Latin America, and with their departure, military planners discounted any major hemispheric role in their tactics or strategies.[2]

From the outset of his term as assistant secretary, Welles worked for military cooperation, especially with respect to Brazil. That South American giant had established friendly relations with the United States during the nineteenth century and had been the sole South American nation to declare war against the Central Powers in World War I. After the fighting, the United States maintained its military contacts in Rio through small army and naval missions. The Brazilian officer corps welcomed this assistance because they needed a powerful ally in the face of superior Argentine military strength.[3]

To improve bilateral military contacts, Welles went directly to Roosevelt in early 1936 to convince him that the Brazilian navy should become an auxiliary force to the United States in any potential confrontation between the Old and New Worlds. He gained presidential approval, Hull's acquiescence, and the navy's permission to sell ten cruisers to Brazil. Several State Department officials, however, actively opposed this initiative. Welles had gone straight to the White House before full discussions within the diplomatic corps. Some career men feared that in addition to violating normal procedures, this sale would alter the balance of naval power in Latin America and encourage an armaments race, which could only lead to a series of costly wars. Once the purchase proposal was publicized, these criticisms appeared valid. Argentina not only immediately expressed its objections but also took the precaution of ordering five cruisers to maintain its supremacy. This kind of agitation prompted Hull to cancel the project.[4]

Welles refused to accept defeat. Early in 1937 he tried another approach to achieve the same goal. Instead of selling warships to Brazil, the administration would lease them. This would allow United States personnel to train Brazilian sailors and provide the United States Navy with a legitimate pretext to survey the Brazilian coastline. Again armed with presidential approval, the State Department submitted a resolution to Congress in early August to lease six outdated destroyers to Brazil for training purposes. Hull saw two principal benefits for the proposal: Brazil would receive American rather than European warships and the Vargas government instead of the United States would pay the normal repairs on the vessels.[5] Opposition quickly surfaced; Pan American specialist Samuel Inman reflected some of the anxiety for Hull's consideration: "Liberal Brazilians will feel you are seeing the fastening of a dictatorial government on them. Argentina will feel that you are aiding, unfairly, a potential rival. Every Latin American, who ever objected to United States dominance, will interpret this as a return to the old program."[6] These kinds of objections were sufficient to have the resolution shelved.

Even this reversal did not deter Welles. Growing Nazi might had led to speculation that if Hitler fought and won a European war, he would control France's African colonies, including Dakar, which was approximately 1,500 miles from vulnerable Natal on the Brazilian bulge. In early 1939 Welles held private talks on military assistance with Brazilian Foreign Minister

Oswaldo Aranha. Later in the year military leaders from both nations ex-changed visits to discuss topics of mutual concern. Despite these moves toward closer collaboration, no specific agreement was signed.[7]

Without any accord, Brazil was virtually defenseless. Only one of fifteen admirals was at sea; the rest stayed in their armchairs. Obsolete, Brazil's largest warships were approximately thirty years old, slow and lacking in cruising range. Ammunition for their guns was in such short supply that target practice was almost nonexistent. Under these conditions the United States embassy predicted that "the best the Brazilian Navy can hope to do is to defend Rio de Janiero until help arrives. From the American point of view this defense is a defense of the navy yard. In a sudden emergency the radius of action of the Brazilian Navy would be only a few miles from Rio."[8]

Welles's seemingly losing battle to improve Brazil's military capabilities demonstrated not only opposition to his ideas in the State Department but also the armed forces' lack of concern and even open bias against Latin Americans. The diplomatic corps did win some token concessions in the sum-mer of 1938. Latin Americans received presidential permission to attend the military service academies. Since most of the republics did not allocate funds to send their officers to the United States, few nations benefited from this gesture. Some United States officers who began to understand Latin Amer-ica's strategic value started studying Spanish, but their enthusiasm was not contagious.[9] Army officers generally felt that any hemispheric assignment would damage their advancement. To combat that sentiment, Welles wanted a presidential directive sent to the military departments requiring officers with "superior" or above ratings sent to Latin American posts, for "so long as the officers in the Army and Navy believe that service in such capacity is prejudicial to their promotion," he argued, "it is clearly very difficult to persuade really first class men to accept these positions." Another diplomat went even further: "As in the body of our citizenry, there are certain ele-ments in the American Army and Navy who are inclined to be prejudicial against foreigners in general, including those of Latin origin."[10]

Naval leaders especially fit into this mold. By the end of the 1930s the few naval missions were slightly enlarged, the attaché program was expanded, and twenty Latin Americans began attending the Naval Academy. The State Department tried to encourage various admirals to take a greater interest in hemispheric defense. William Leahy, for instance, confirmed that diplomats applied pressure on him to send warships on tours of South American ports.[11] On April 12, 1938, Claude Bloch, commander-in-chief of the United States fleet, wrote: "Several times I have been on the point of recommending the sending of one division of cruisers to Panama with a periodical trip around South America in order to cultivate good feeling and to show the people down there what our flag looks like." Later that summer he thought about annual cruises by a division for three or four months to demonstrate the United States' commercial and military sea power.[12] The establishment and extension of the neutrality zone prompted Admiral Ernest King to consider having destroyers from several Latin American countries join the Atlantic fleet to study and learn United States operations, but this idea, too, was discarded. The navy did not want to attach any Latin Americans to its operations.[13]

The army air corps viewed Latin America differently. On February 15, 1938, six B-17 bombers flew from Langley Field, Virginia, to participate in the inauguration of the Argentine president, and twelve days later returned via the canal to an enthusiastic welcome from over 5,000 aviation supporters. The crews had logged more than 12,000 miles without any serious mishap and demonstrated their aircrafts' range. A week later seven Flying Fortresses traveled to Rio for the republic's fiftieth anniversary. They returned after a smooth flight, again displaying the capabilities of the airplanes for hemispheric defense. After the fall of Poland the army quietly tried to obtain permission to construct airfields in Mexico and Brazil. When the governments rejected these overtures, the army secretly supplied funds to Pan American Airways for auxiliary air fields. The company started work in the autumn of 1940, and in spite of engineering, climatic, and political complications, by the end of the war, the army had built over forty landing fields and eventually won unrestricted flying permission in most of Latin America.[14]

Although the War Department echoed many of its naval colleagues' sentiments toward the other American republics, the army's mission forced movement for greater hemispheric contacts. The repercussions of Munich started military planners to revise their thinking about continental defense. The army neglected Latin America in the post-World War I era in favor of concentrating on Japanese aggression in the Far East. By the spring of 1939 world conditions necessitated a reevaluation. German and Italian expansion preempted Japanese aspirations. If Hitler and Mussolini were victorious in a war against Great Britain and France, then the United States would have the sole responsibility for hemispheric defense. Under these conditions the War Department designed five Rainbow plans to prevent any belligerent from invading the Americas: (1) the military's first option would be to protect the Peruvian and Brazilian bulges; (2) the army would concentrate its forces in the Far East rather than the Atlantic; (3) troops would secure the Americas from attack before moving against the Japanese; (4) the War Department would guarantee the safety of its Atlantic front before turning to the Pacific; and (5) the United States would ally itself with the English and French, assure hemispheric security, and defeat the Germans first and then turn to the Far East. Realizing that these plans called for Latin American assistance, the War Department began several exploratory bilateral military soundings by the summer of 1939.[15]

These talks were not coordinated with other related activities. The armament issue was an excellent example of inept handling. Although United States manufacturers had never seriously competed against European suppliers for Latin American orders, the question of arm sales became a highly volatile and emotional issue during the mid-1930s. The Special Committee Investigating the Munitions Industry, better known as the Nye Committee, began its hearings in the spring of 1934 to determine the extent of the involvement of the "merchants of death" who allegedly caused World War I. That fall investigators briefly turned their attention to United States firms selling their wares in the hemisphere.The inquiry exposed unsavory and unethical business practices like bribing Latin American officials to obtain orders. Armament companies also sold to both sides in the Leticia and Chaco disputes and to the government and various revolutionary factions during the Cuban crisis of 1933 and 1934. Businessmen dismissed moral aspects like the destructive nature of the weaponry and armament races; their primary purpose was to increase profits in a depressed economy. Several Latin American nations threatened to lodge protests over these revelations, which embarrassed their administrations. To stop these adverse repercussions, Hull asked the committee to abandon its hemispheric focus, and since the committee had exhausted this avenue of investigations, the request was honored.[16]

The hostility engendered toward the armaments industry plagued the State Department throughout the remainder of the decade. Although the administration did not officially discourage arms sales, diplomats were forbidden to assist any sellers. Some in the foreign service applauded this policy, for they hoped for an inter-American disarmament gathering. Toward the end of the 1930s a career officer on the Latin American desk, Ellis Briggs, challenged this position. He understood the reasoning behind the government's opposition to arms proliferation, but in order for United States advisers to train Latin American forces, these instructors needed to use their own materials.[17]

Welles agreed with this rationale. After the European war began, Chile asked for military supplies. Since Chile had traditionally depended on European weaponry, this request was unique. That South American nation's armed forces were woefully unprepared, and their value to continental defense was nonexistent. The undersecretary wanted to seize this opportunity as a way to strengthen ties: "This is really the last link in our South American chain. If we can get Chile in cooperation with us—both the army and the navy—the chain is complete."[18] The chain remained broken because no immediate assistance was forthcoming.

While Welles worked on the specific Chilean request, he also recognized the fundamental dilemma. In early 1939 he helped to draft a joint congressional resolution that would allow the government to furnish Latin America with military equipment.[19] To the undersecretary, the resolution's "enactment would foster the growing spirit of American solidarity and would constitute a further and a necessary step in the interests of the national defense."[20] He hoped to sell outdated American armaments in order to reduce German and Italian markets, but skeptical congressmen revised the legislation to restrict purchases to include solely defensive weapons like coastal artillery and antiaircraft guns. Additionally, the United States would not actively solicit any sales and would only accept cash payment for goods. With these severe limitations attached, the Pittman Resolution became law on June 15, 1940. It brought the government into the military armament business, but the conditions were so restrictive that the resolution's practical value was negligible.

In spite of this reality, the precedent bringing the United States government into the munitions business was established. In early 1941 the Roosevelt administration used this approach to help the Allies with the introduction of the lend-lease legislation. Patterned in many ways on the Pittman Resolution, the new bill avoided the resolution's pitfalls. The president had the authority to provide a wide range of goods to assist any nation vital to the United States without a cash payment requirement. Latin American governments carefully followed the debate and welcomed the passage of the legislation.[21]

Just as critical as the change in government armament policy was the development of the coordination of the hemispheric defense effort. Here again the State Department provided the impetus. The first major breakthrough in this direction came with the formation of the Standing Liaison Committee (SLC) in early 1938. With Hull's full knowledge and approval, Welles established this body composed of the second ranking officials in the State, War, and Navy departments to coordinate inter-American security measures. In the committee's early stages, the undersecretary used the group to win greater backing for hemispheric solidarity. After the military officers realized the value of the SLC, they depended on Welles to win Latin American acceptance for their proposals. The committee's workload expanded so rapidly that by 1940 a foreign service official worked full time to handle SLC activities.[22]

Secretary of War Stimson opposed the SLC. As secretary of state under Hoover, Stimson had objected to his undersecretary's influence on the president, and he carried over that disapproval to Welles's relationship with Roosevelt. As for Latin America, Stimson viewed the region in a patronizing manner. The area was incapable of laying the foundations for democratic institutions. Rumors of fifth-column movements in South America, the secretary of war contended, were mythical, only a ruse to divert attention from the real battlefronts. A man of firm convictions, Stimson tried to limit the SLC's prerogatives by forming by his own planning group composed of the secretaries of war, navy, and state. They did not meet as regularly as Stimson wished, but their discussions during the war reduced misunderstandings and allowed the secretaries to present a unified position to the president.[23]

More than Stimson's resentment toward the SLC, the events in Europe and diplomatic reaction forced the military to seek greater hemispheric collaboration. The rapid collapse of Polish resistance followed by the "phony war" temporarily slowed down American defense preparations with the exception of the neutrality zone and patrol. Since the Allies controlled the Atlantic Ocean, speculation of a Nazi hemispheric invasion appeared remote. The blitzkrieg through the Low Countries brought forth an abrupt awakening that the Americas were vulnerable to attack.[24] Ambassador Hugh Wilson confided to his diary on May 20, 1940, the dilemma the United States faced:

We have assumed defense of the hemisphere and at the same time we have nothing south of the Caribbean Sea which will aid us in making such an assumption definitive. We have neither landing fields nor sea bases, nor have we any such control of policy of the individual states which would prevent them from inviting trouble. Our underwriting of the defense of the hemisphere, while, I think, an indispensable step in the defense of this nation, is nevertheless a blank check for bad behavior or irresponsible action on the part of the States of South America. How can we find an answer to this difficulty which is compatible with the Good Neighbor Policy?[25]

The swift disintegration of Allied resistance in France vividly reinforced the concern that the Nazis might next turn on the Americas. Congress dramatically increased the armed forces' budget. The navy sent warships to Latin American ports to give a graphic demonstration of United States might. Military staff conversations intensified to find acceptable agreements on land, sea, and air bases to secure transit rights for troops, planes, and naval vessels, and to fulfill Latin American requests for supplies to ward off foreign-inspired coup d'états or invasions. The military wanted long-term leases for bases with full jurisdiction. While such arrangements seemed apropos to staff officers, they did not understand the Latin American antipathy to any surrendering of sovereignty, particularly when this concerned the stationing of Yankee soldiers on their soil. After protracted negotiations with several nations, military leaders accepted less than their original expectations. The agreements allowed for army and navy installations constructed by the United States and manned by a limited number of unarmed technicians in civilian clothes. The host country retained sovereignty at the installations and furnished its own security forces. Once the war ended, the United States presence would promptly be withdrawn.[26]

These steps did not comfort Ambassador Messersmith. On the day France signed its armistice, he pessimistically concluded: "The news from Europe this morning is so devastating that I think we must now seriously face practically complete collapse and we simply cannot permit the British and French fleets to fall into the hands of the Germans. If we do that we will put our defense program two years back and will open the way to almost immediate developments among the other American Republics where our second line of defense now lies, with the first one gone or almost gone."[27]

Such ominous warnings prompted the public to support greater hemispheric defense measures, while they still desperately clung to their opposition of any military involvement in Europe or the Far East. Americans appeared unimpressed by international events like the signing of the tripartite pact in late September of 1940 between Germany, Italy, and Japan. Instead the United States public focused on the presidential campaign, in which both candidates unrealistically pledged to keep the nation from war. With victory assured, Roosevelt openly preached peace and hemispheric defense, while he privately used his authority to expand Allied assistance. Recognizing this direction, War Department strategists moved to enact the fifth option of the Rainbow plan of protecting the Americas, concentrating on defeating the Nazis by aiding the English and slowing Japanese expansionism.[28] In early 1941 United States experts predicted that, if the British surrendered, Hitler would then penetrate the Americas: "In the kind of world the totalitarians have now brought into being, only full assurance of the impregnable strength of the United States and of our ability to defend the hemisphere could effectively prevent appeasement and other dangers from threatening the integrity of inter-American relations."[29]

The German invasion of the Soviet Union provided welcome relief. The attack allowed additional time to build hemispheric defense, for military leaders expected the Russians to fall quickly under the Nazi onslaught. In the interim the United States tried to consolidate its hemispheric gains. The navy extended its patrols to provide greater coverage in the Atlantic; the army better defined its inter-American goals; and lend-lease talks expanded. Senior Latin American military leaders began touring United States facilities in large numbers, and service academies increased their admissions of junior officers from the other American republics.[30]

The diplomatic commitment to inter-American military solidarity was reinforced, over the military's strenuous objections, after the Pearl Harbor attack. At the Rio conference the delegates established the Inter-American Defense Board (IADB). Stimson and his associates argued that the IADB would be too large, unwieldy, and diversive. After all, many Latin American states had traditional rivalries that would prevent meaningful cooperation. Besides, the War Department preferred bilateral negotiations as the best way to resolve Pan American military questions. Despite these arguments, Welles's intentions of making the IABD the multilateral symbol of inter-American military unity prevailed.[31]

The War Department as yet did not understand the intimate association between multilateral and bilateral contacts. After the United States entered the war Stimson was principally concerned with the Panama Canal's security. The fleet needed the canal for transit, and army detachments guaranteed passage and supplied the force to repel any attacker. While the military considered sabotage or naval bombardment on the locks and dams extremely unlikely, the advent of air power created new anxieties. The War Department felt that the canal's aircraft defense needed additional fortifications outside of the zone. The Panamanians, on the other hand, hoped to use the American military requests to gain additional concessions in the treaty with the United States before granting any new defense sights. Although the army reinforced the Canal Zone, instituted antisabotage improvements, and sharpened its air-alert procedures with the advent of the European war, the requests for additional bases failed to win Panamanian approval, as did pleas for local laborers to help with new construction. After the United States refused to make any treaty concessions, the army imported Jamaican workers—to the chagrin of the Panamanians. Although the bilateral negotiations dragged on and antagonisms on both sides intensified, American personnel began occupying defense sights outside of the Canal Zone by the spring of 1941. When Stimson took his sole wartime trip to Latin America to inspect the canal shortly after the United States' entrance into the war, he concluded that any land assault was remote. A surprise attack, however, launched from two or three aircraft carriers, might inflict extensive damage. To prevent this slim possibility, the secretary initiated a long-range air patrol to assure the canal's safety.[32]

The Caribbean served as the security perimeter for the canal. Guantánamo Bay in Cuba had already gained the status as the major United States naval base in the region. Puerto Rico and the Virgin Islands, both American possessions, had small troop detachments that were enlarged in late 1939. Puerto Rico became a strategic post for short- and long-range air surveillance in the entire region. A year later the armed forces officially recognized the Caribbean's importance by organizing the area into a threater of operations for the purposes of defending the canal, patrolling the neutrality zone, and, in late 1941, administering European hemispheric colonies like the Dutch West Indies.[33]

When Hitler declared war on the United States, he removed the U-boats' restrictions that prohibited them from entering the neutrality zone, and Nazi submarines quickly demonstrated the region's vulnerability to attack. Assistant Secretary Long recorded in his diary: "All this is having a distinct political effect in South America. Venezuela is querulous. Brazil is experiencing a resurgence of the opposition Nazi party. Bolivia even is backing away from its ejection of Nazi diplomats. Ecuador and Peru are hesitant. It means that all of Latin America is weighing in the balance their ideas of United States invincibility against these challenges to our authority in our own yard. . . ."[34]

Conditions temporarily deteriorated before permanent solutions were found. On February 16, 1942, a submarine moved into Aruba's harbor and lobbed a few shells at the oil refinery to announce the enemy's presence. The incident created dramatic headlines but did little material damage. The real danger came from the enormous loss of Allied shipping by torpedoes that disrupted the normal channels of commerce. By the end of 1942 the navy instituted a convoy system and deployed sub-killer groups. These steps significantly reduced U-boat operations by mid-1943, and the elimination of this threat freed many of the forces defending the Caribbean for more critical assignments.[35]

Mexican assistance was also essential for the region's safety. Despite the acrimonious oil controversy, secret bilateral military discussions started in the summer of 1940. The War Department, believing that Mexican troops were unable to withstand an invasion, wanted permission to station United States soldiers on Mexican territory, but the Mexicans rejected any proposal that would violate their sovereignty. President Camacho made an exception on March 26, 1941. He allowed the United States the privilege of using Mexican airfields to service aircraft en route to Panama. Other discussions, such as those concerning naval base arrangements, were futile, but these obstacles did not impede the steady trend toward fuller cooperation.[36]

After the United States began fighting, thousands of Mexicans voluntarily enlisted in the American armed services to battle the Axis. The two countries signed a joint defense pact, and in May 1942, Camacho declared war on the enemy. This decision created complications, for once the Mexicans entered the conflict, they wanted to send soldiers to war theaters. Over the vehement objections of the War Department, Roosevelt supported Ambassador Messersmith's recommendation to form a Mexican air squadron, and thus, the 201st Fighter Squadron was born. Mexico already had experienced pilots, and after additional training in the United States, the 201st's 300 officers and enlisted men, along with 35 pilots, left for the Philippines in mid-March 1945. The flyers saw relatively little combat, but when they went into action, the squadron compiled an excellent record.[37]

Brazil played a crucial role in hemispheric defense. When German occupation in Africa or the nearby Spanish and Portuguese islands became more plausible, the War Department increased its efforts to guard against a surprise assault on Natal. During the autumn of 1940, the United States and Brazil signed a bilateral military agreement. The Brazilians promptly presented a long list of military requirements, but only token deliveries arrived. In the meantime the United States tried to convince Vargas that marines should be stationed at strategic locations. He rejected this suggestion, but did let the navy patrol his nation's territorial waters, and in April 1941, he granted American warships access at two ports in the northeast.[38] By the time of the

Rio conference, Welles demanded a significant commitment: "Like all armies, the Brazilian high command is not inclined to be enthusiastic about getting into war if they have none of the basic elements for defense. If they are not promptly given the necessary assurances and if they are not able to see with their own eyes before long some concrete evidences of help coming, exactly that kind of a situation which the Nazis could use to their best advantage will be created."[39]

Assistance did increase, and the Brazilian declaration of war in the summer of 1942 against Germany and Italy further cemented the alliance. The need for bases in Natal to fend off surprise attacks faded away by 1943; these installations, instead, became a principal funnel for ferrying supplies to the international battlefronts. Disenchanted with this transportation function and patrol duties, the Brazilians asked to send troops into combat. Once again the War Department objected, but Welles overrode this with presidential intervention. Preparations to outfit an expeditionary force commenced, and after several delays, it left for Italy on July 2, 1944, to become the only force from a Latin American nation to see a European front. While the troops had training, personnel, and liaison difficulties, they fought well and returned to a heroes' reception. Few failed to note Brazil's new military strength. It had moved ahead of Argentina as the number-one military power in South America as a direct consequence of its alliance with the United States.[40]

Whether or not a Latin American country sent troops to fight the Axis, it still probably received lend-lease assistance. Stimson had hoped this legislation had come in time to save the Allies and never dreamed that equipment would be shipped to the other American republics. He argued: "If and when they get into danger, we shall in all probability have to do their fighting."[41] Because of the secretary's blatant hostility, Welles had the lead-lease administration process Latin American requests where the undersecretary felt that the American republics would receive more sympathetic treatment. He also had the State Department negotiate these agreements with most of the Latin American states, but their requests far exceeded actual shipments until 1942.[42]

Lend-lease aid to the Americas became a difficult problem in the midst of the fighting. When the threat to the hemisphere vanished, many called for an end to arms shipments except to those nations actually engaged in the conflict. Welles hoped that this policy would stop arms races, and although it was adopted, some charged that the cut-off came too late. Lend-lease supplies had already helped dictators hold power by the sheer weight of their armies over democratic rivals. This criticism persisted through the remainder of the war, yet the claims were exaggerated. Of the total lend-lease disbursement, a mere 1.1 percent went to Latin America, with Brazil obtaining over 75 percent of the hemispheric allotment and Mexico a distant second. Long before World War II, hemispheric despots had learned how to maintain their control.[43]

Despite this type of criticism, military cooperation gained momentum. Even the IADB, over the War Department's initial opposition, grew in its importance. The board held its first session on March 30, 1942, and met regularly throughout the war. By the summer, Welles stated: "I wish to do everything that is possible in order to maintain its full effect and maintain its prestige. I don't want anything to happen which would give the American governments the impression that we are taking this superficially and that we are not interested."[44]

The War Department by 1943 began to see the value of IADB and became its most avid supporter by the end of the war. Military leaders believed that the contact with their Latin American counterparts engendered good will and friendship. The board provided sort of a hemispheric war college where the host nation instructed its guests on the benefits of receiving United States training and equipment rather than relying on European rivals. American officers also arranged inspection tours of bases and held social functions. United States military leaders hoped that their Latin American equivalents would be favorably impressed by these efforts. The Latin Americans were, and this resulted in greater wartime collaboration. Since the army knew that it would lose many of its hemispheric bases shortly after the end of hostilities, the War Department intended to extend inter-American comradeship into the postwar era. This change in attitude by the military toward greater cooperation not only illustrated an abrupt shift, but it also closely paralleled an emerging conflict between the armed forces and the State Department over which agency would establish inter-American defense policy.[45]

One specific postwar military question centered on air power. Latin America, Roosevelt insisted, was vulnerable to an air attack; this theme persisted during the war. Various American republics also realized that those countries with powerful air corps would have an enormous advantage over their opponents, and they requested lead-lease assistant for airplanes. Of the number promised in 1941, half were ultimately delivered, 60 percent of which reached the Mexican contingent, but most were designated for long-range reconaissance, surveillance, and transportation. In the final stages of the war, the army began exploratory talks to provide the Latin American military with surplus training planes. Such sales would reduce the stockpile and also help extend United States military influence in the hemisphere.[46]

General Henry "Hap" Arnold of the army air corps backed these proposals and briefly flirted with the idea of an inter-American air force. Impressed by his inspections of Mexican and Brazilian forces during the war, he reinforced his favorable opinions by traveling to Rio in late April 1945. After meeting with Vargas, he visited several major cities and inspected some aviation facilities.[47] Upon returning to the United States, he wrote the Brazilian air minister: "The progress that Brazil has made in aviation under your leadership is remarkable. Brazil is an ally of whom we live in the United States of America are exceedingly proud and is a worthy partner for the future."[48]

Like many of his colleagues, Arnold severely criticized the diplomatic corps at the war's termination. He believed that timid, unduly cautious, and egocentric foreign service officers impeded greater military collaboration: "The State Department apparently does not realize the fact that this has been a world-wide war, that Americans have been in almost all parts of the world, and that no longer can their foreign policies be obscure, indefinite, and vague." The foreign service should pattern their programs, according to the general, after those of the armed services, "instead of assuming an antimilitary position." With the exception of aircraft allocations to Mexico and Brazil, diplomats objected to further wartime sales; and they stymied postwar negotiations. Arnold attributed those actions to self-servicing motives: "It is somewhat apparent that the State Department may have as their objective to take credit for themselves for every item transferred to Latin America. This selfishness on their part is costing the nation as a whole considerable prestige. Because of the paramount interest in Latin America and because of the desire to prevent other nations from securing influences in Latin America that would jeopardize our security, the Army has served as a spearhead."[49]

While the War Department eventually benefited from Latin American collaboration, naval leaders generally downgraded its importance. They believed that the defense of hemispheric waters was solely their responsibility, and blatant prejudice appeared prevalent in the navy's inter-American dealings. Secretary Knox, for example, told Henry Wallace that Latin Americans were genetically inferior.[50] Speaking on August 31, 1942, Admiral Frederick Horne, responding to the suggestion of enlisting Latin Americans, snapped: "I think that as far as the Navy is concerned I can give you a flat 'no.' We will fight that as long as we can." Only direct presidential orders would change that position. Admiral William Spears supported his colleague by declaring that Latin American enlistments primarily were for propaganda since "their actual value is nothing compared to what we can train our own people to do."[51]

In early 1943 Adlai Stevenson, an assistant to the navy secretary, illustrated his department's growing suspicion of the diplomatic corps. He proposed a study that was intended to show the State Department's refusal to supply critical information to the navy prior to Pearl Harbor. After documenting that the navy might have used this information to prevent the surprise attack, the navy would make a case to devote more time to foreign policy issues in order to guarantee its future interests. These concerns, however, did not involve Latin America.[52] Late in 1945 Admiral Ernest King reiterated his disinterest: "There is little that they [Latin Americans] can contribute to the enforcement of peace under the United Nations charter. The possession of armament and equipment by those countries tends toward two undesirable situations: first, use of force in internal (domestic) affairs; secondly, the threat to use force in relations between states themselves."[53] Except for those used in essential policing, King wanted to reduce armament sales in the Americas. The secretary of navy agreed; he did not want the United States accused of fostering South American wars.[54]

Toward the end of the war, diplomats began to look as warily at the military establishment as it viewed them. Some feared that the armed forces overemphasized sales of surplus arms, which could have two adverse consequences: these goods might keep unpopular dictators in power or revolutionaries might steal the weapons and initiate a civil war. Ambassador Messersmith called for civilian authority to halt the military's role in foreign affairs as soon as possible after the warfare had ceased.[55]

John Dreier in the State Department was more specific in allegations about the growing military presence during the closing stages of the war. He argued that Latin Americans needed a minimal amount of armaments for hemispheric defense. Instead of contributing to an arms race, the United States had to support democratic groups who wanted to raise living standards. If the administration rejected this social and economic emphasis while distributing military hardware, some Latin American reformers might turn to the Soviet Union for aid. To Dreier the choice was clear:

The thesis implicit in the approach of many of the military and naval people, that we should assiduously cultivate the military groups in the other American republics, involves a certain conflict with our foreign policy in that by and large military groups in the other American republics represent reactionary elements standing in the way of the world-wide trend toward greater political and economic democracy. While we should not willingly antagonize or neglect any important elements in the other republics, our efforts to cultivate the military groups should in no way be permitted to prejudice our basic aim of developing a closer and more effective collaboration, and moral support, amongst the pro-democratic forces.[56]

Dreier's sentiments reflected the diplomatic corps' concern over the growth of the War Department's attention to Pan American affairs—which, ironically, had been stimulated by State Department prodding. The change in viewpoints within both the military and foreign service had emerged over a relatively short period and demonstrated a significant about-face. Military planners virtually ignored hemispheric considerations until the late 1930s, but once inter-American collaboration proved beneficial, the War Department actively sought postwar continuity.

The bureaucratic struggle over leadership within the administration grew steadily. At first the SLC, chaired by the State Department, coordinated hemispheric defense. By the close of the hostilities, IADB, directed by the military, dominated the arena. While the navy retained its aloofness, the army and air corps became deeply involved in Pan American affairs. The latter two branches hoped to replace the European military tradition through extended postwar involvement. With the termination of lend-lease, the military pressed for assistance pacts as a replacement. Foreign service officers feared that this emphasis would trigger armament races and reinforce authoritarianism. Funds needed for social and economic improvements would be diverted to military budgets. The War Department vigorously objected to this hypothesis. If the United States did not work with the Latin American armed forces, previous European suppliers would fill the void.

As a result of this conflict, a confrontation within the United States government, which began during wartime, continued into the postwar period. The immediate battle centered on the amount of military aid for Latin America, but that only masked the much deeper struggle. Until the late 1930s the State Department held unquestioned supremacy in building Pan Americanism. During the war the military began challenging the diplomats' dominance. The postwar issue was relatively simple to pose and extraordinarily complicated to resolve. How much influence would the armed forces have in shaping foreign policy?

11 ★ THE EMERGENCE OF CULTURAL COOPERATION

T HE MILITARY had ignored the necessity of building an inter-American defense network until the 1930s; a similar pattern of neglect applied in the development of cultural cooperation. Unwholesome stereotypes of lifestyles prevailed throughout the hemisphere. Latin American critics portrayed Yankees as aggressive, militaristic imperialists who were obsessed with the accumulation of weath. Many United States journalists depicted Latin Americans as shiftless daydreamers, who lacked intelligence and took siestas under huge sombreros or who were preoccupied with emulating the sexual conquests of the lengendary Don Juan. These characterizations were seriously challenged during Roosevelt's presidency for the first time in a systematic fashion. The United States awoke to realize that fighting the Axis in hand-to-hand combat was not enough; the battle extended to winning the allegiance of mens' minds.

While the United States had dismissed this problem until World War II, Europeans living in Latin America had not. They established local businesses, married into prominent families, and formed cultural associations. European governments allocated funds to subsidize some of their citizens' efforts and brought Latin American leaders to the continent for a variety of reasons, including good will tours as well as military and university training.

The United States' initial activities in this direction were meager. During the nineteenth century, Protestant missionaries set up schools to spread American democratic ideals and teach English. Horace Mann's educational techniques influenced Argentine President Domingo Sarmiento in the 1870s; the Appleton publishing firm printed textbooks for Latin American consumption during the same period. Some Latin American revolutionaries studied the writings of leading American independence figures like Benjamin Franklin and Thomas Jefferson and also came to the United States in order to observe the workings of the new democracy. Brazilian Emperor Pedro II toured the United States in 1876. But these contacts were undertaken by individual initiatives and were not planned to instill a Pan American spirit.[1]

The foundation of the Bureau of American Republics in 1890 by the State Department was a quasi-governmental effort designed to foster greater hemispheric commercial intercourse, but many Latin Americans disapproved of this undisguised materialistic motivation. The organizational framework further damaged credibility. The headquarters were in Washington; the director was a United States citizen and the chairman of the governing board was the secretary of state. Early in the twentieth century, the bureau changed its name—to the Pan American Union (PAU)—and, to some extent, its mission. Along with trying to increase commercial contacts, the PAU moved into cultural affairs. The union encouraged educational exchanges of students and teachers and also conducted meetings to bring hemisphereic intellectual and scientific leaders into direct relationships. Late in World War I a division of intellectual cooperation was founded to promote hemispheric art, literature, and scientific collaboration.[2]

In addition to the PAU, several major United States foundations began financing Latin American projects in the twentieth century. The Rockefeller Foundation focused its attention on eliminating tropical diseases, enlarging public health facilities, training nurses, and searching for medical cures. The Carnegie Endowment for International Peace granted fellowships for student and professorial exchanges and sponsored trips to the United States for editors, journalists, and agricultural leaders. The Institute of International Education (IIE), directed by Laurence's father, Stephen Duggan, energetically lobbied within higher education circles for scholarships to bring Latin American students to the United States. The Guggenheim Fellowships, started in 1925, allocated 1 million dollars by 1930 for Latin American proposals.[3]

The enthusiasm generated by the Good Neighbor also stimulated university interest in Latin American studies. Although Latin American students still preferred studying in Europe, more began entering American universities to pursue their educational opportunities, which were enhanced by a growing number of scholarships provided by universities to meet their needs. An accelerating demand for Latin American courses provided further impetus. Offerings on hemispheric topics increased dramatically, especially the study of the Spanish and Portuguese languages.[4]

Other actions within the academic community to encourage inter-American cultural cooperation evolved from individual efforts. In the summer of 1936 Laurence Duggan asked Dean Carl Ackerman of the graduate school of journalism at Columbia University to explore ways to increase hemispheric journalistic contacts. The dean traveled to Latin American the following year and perceived an alarming acceptance of European totalitarianism.[5] In September 1937 he reasoned:

The nations of South America are endangered both from within and without by the philosophy of dictatorships with the result that we are witnessing today the test of Pan American solidarity. We must devise a broad program of activities, outside of the government, in education, literature and journalism for mature men and women, not students. The scientific world of the US must be made aware of opportunities in Latin America. College graduates must realize that they may look to the East and West to see the past but to the South to see the future. The next few years will determine whether South America is to remain American or become Italo-Germanized. We must provide recognition for South America in the news, in education, in science and in literature.[6]

To encourage greater Pan American interaction, Ackerman solicited a donor to establish the Maria Moors Cabot Gold Medals for Latin American journalists who preached the democratic faith. The first recipients of the Cabot Prize flew to New York City in late 1939 to accept their gold medals and honorariums.[7] The following year President Nicholas Murray Butler of Columbia University told the winners that the award was "evidence of our determination as Americans to turn the good neighbor policy from a declaration of words into deeds and policies of understanding and cooperation."[8] Ackerman hoped that the prize would become a permanent legacy in the cause of Pan American understanding, and his wish was fulfilled. The Cabot Prize has become one of the major academic and professional honors for excellence in Latin American journalism.

By the late 1930s private and governmental agencies began to cooperate in their efforts to promote inter-American cultural affairs and simultaneously drive the totalitarian menace from the hemisphere. American diplomats assisted in exchange initiatives. The PAU, largely ignored by previous administrations, gained a larger role in reaching these objectives. In the spring of 1938 hemispheric intellectual leaders held a meeting designed to advance Pan American cultural cooperation. Other conferences followed, like that of the Inter-American Bar Association, which convened in 1941 for the first time at Havana. The gathering served as a forum for jurists to announce their support for peace and to attack the destruction and chaos caused by the dictators. Other similar conventions echoed these sentiments, and at the same time brought influential members of their respective fields together to discuss their areas of specialization and form friendships.[9]

While these private activities increased, the State Department began to consider its own internal role in cultural diplomacy. Several members of the diplomatic corps, led by Duggan and shaped by his earlier association at IIE, called for exchange programs in the early 1930s. The United States supported this concept at the Montevideo conference, and during the spring of 1935 Welles considered a proposal for awarding twenty annual fellowships to Latin American graduate students after they went through rigorous screening. From his vantage point, the main concern was to provide a conducive learning environment. He did not envision government funding for this project, but instead hoped to find foundation support and tuition fee waivers from universities and colleges.[10]

While trying to win adoption for these ideas in the United States, the State Department also wanted Latin American concurrence. To assure this, the United States delegation at the Buenos Aires conference drafted a student and faculty exchange resolution. The measure was introduced and unanimously passed as the Convention for the Promotion of Inter-American Cultural Relations. Under its provisions each nation would annually select and finance two graduate students and one or more professors for the exchange program. With the passage of the convention, Hull and Welles returned to the United States and began publicizing the need not only to enact the proposal but also to stimulate a broader cultural effort. They asserted that the United States had neglected this type of enterprise, which impaired the movement toward hemispheric understanding.[11]

The Buenos Aires convention did, in fact, much more than generate Pan American educational opportunities; it provided a take-off point to pursue a number of other cultural initiatives. On May 26, 1938, the Interdepartmental Committee on Scientific and Cultural Cooperation, directed by the State Department and chaired by Welles, met to recommend inter-American technical and scientific proposals. The committee's job was to coordinate the propaganda effort against the Nazis and act as a clearing house for various suggestions. Activities were divided into three general topics: (1) the exchange of hemispheric leaders, professors, and graduate students, the establishment of fellowships and grants to finance lectures, research, or study under the terms of the Buenos Aires convention or of scholarships to Latin Americans to train at United States agencies; (2) the exchange of specialized information like scholarly journals, library holdings, and laboratory equipment; and (3) arrangements for United States experts to be temporarily detailed to Latin American assignments in need of specific skills.[12]

Besides this indepartmental committee, the State Department moved to create a Cultural Relations Division (RC). In the summer of 1938 Secretary Hull announced the division's establishment to meet the challenge of Nazi infiltration in the Americas. Once RC was approved, Welles hoped to designate a foreign service officer to direct these matters, including the administration of the exchange program and the coordination of other projects inside and outside of the government.[13] The undersecretary wanted to proceed quickly, but he understood that this effort needed Latin American adherence. "We can do our part," he claimed, "but that is only half of this picture. The peoples of the other Americas must reciprocate and demonstrate a willingness and a desire to understand and appreciate the ideals and life of this country."[14]

The mission of RC, at first, caused some confusion. Hull maximized its propaganda value, while Welles and Duggan saw its origins as a natural outgrowth of the inter-American effort. Congress was dubious of its worth, which was reflected in its appropriation of only $25,000 to fund the division.[15]

In the midst of these varying views, Hull appointed Professor Ben Cherrington at the University of Denver to direct RC in June 1938. After he accepted the post, Cherrington spent his first year developing guidelines for the office by touring Latin America, speaking to individuals interested in the division's development, and studying various cultural proposals. When he completed his analysis, he decided on certain ground rules. The exchange component would be channeled through the Office of Education. He would establish an advisory committee from government and private sources to initiate new programs; he would establish other contacts for additional advice; and his division would establish other contacts for additional advice; and his division would serve a clearinghouse and coordinating function for other United States agencies and with Latin American governments. By 1939 Cherrington had drawn up a broad program for cultural exchange activities, travel to and from the United States, Latin American studies projects, and translation efforts. Turning these proposals into actual programs was quite another matter. Congress provided him with an initial operating budget of only $75,000 and restricted spending to the exchange program. The war greatly restricted the original intent of providing a flow to and from Latin America. Manpower requirements and travel restrictions severely inhibited the movement of United States citizens by late 1942, but many Latin Americans, particularly those studying dentistry, medicine, and engineering, took advantage of the opportunity. In all, approximately seven hundred and fifty Latin Americans came to the United States from 1940 to 1945 as part of the Buenos Aires convention.[16]

The rest of RC's proposals, such as appointing cultural attachés at American posts in Latin America, were gradually funded. When this idea was first seriously taken up, in the late 1930s, both Welles and Messersmith opposed it as being too much like the system of European attachés who specialized in propaganda; the department also feared that a new staff would disrupt a unified foreign service. However, as various cultural projects expanded, the need for trained personnel in this field mounted. As a result several attachés received embassy appointments in 1941 to supervise cultural affairs, and two years later, all of the legations had attachés drawn from a middle-aged, highly educated group of men who served as liaison in a variety of activities.[17]

One problem these men confronted was counteracting the influence of the well-financed European communities in the Americas. Before the war eight United States-oriented cultural societies, without any government support, had established operations in Latin America. After the United States joined the Allies, the number of societies grew to over twenty and received some indirect federal assistance to combat Axis propaganda. Meetingplaces called cultural institutes were opened to disseminate Allied viewpoints, but the institutes did not always operate smoothly.[18] One example of discord came to the surface in 1941, when Ambassador Messersmith reported that Havana's cultural center had many supporters, "but, unfortunately, a good many of them are 'prima donnas' and find it very difficult to work with each other."[19] Personality clashes and other disagreements created some anxieties, and yet, the cultural institutes accomplished a great deal by presenting a favorable image of United States intentions.

Congressional authorizations in 1939 also enabled RC to provide funds outside of the Buenos Aires exchange program to bring influential Latin American leaders, like novelist Erico Verissimo from Brazil and Argentine historian Enrique M. Gandía, to the United States on tours, lectures, and study. A number of professors came upon invitation; some Latin Americans received training in businesses, government agencies, or at universities and colleges. Some difficulties arose over developing impartial selection standards, but even the controversial appointees did not damage the overall value of the operation. Problems concerning hospitality toward foreign guests also emerged in growing numbers, and by the spring of 1942 a conference was held to discuss the question of how to prepare Latin American students coming to the United States and how to treat them once they arrived. The issues presented and discussed at this meeting helped to lay the foundation for the National Association for Foreign Student Advisers in the postwar period.[20]

While personal contacts enlarged, the United States also considered the power of the printed word. Europeans had translated far more of their literature for Latin Americans to consume than the United States. When spurred by the war, the Roosevelt administration encouraged Spanish translations of North American publications to compete against foreign ideologies. The RC established libraries in Latin America to lend books, offer lectures, and hold art exhibitions. The first important United States library, the Benjamin Franklin Library, opened in Mexico City during April 1942, and several more followed in other American republics. When fire destroyed the National Library of Peru, the State Department helped the next year in its reconstruction by providing materials and lending library experts. False statements in textbooks throughout the Americas had generated enough adverse reactions to place this topic on the agendas at the Montevideo, Buenos Aires, and Lima conferences. Conventions were passed to eliminate errors, and during the war, real efforts were undertaken to carry out these pledges. Finally, the cultural division encouraged English language classes in Latin America, and several republics responded by making the study of English compulsory at primary or secondary educational levels.[21]

The growth of RC and its successor organizations in the State Department was continually plagued by budgetary restrictions. Funding this newest division of the State Department proved to be extremely difficult. Congress was not convinced that the division's primary role was to spur private initiative, and reflected this view by cutting its monetary requests. This difficulty, in many respects, reflected the uncertainty over the original concept of RC's foundations. The State Department's efforts to establish the division grew from private momentum; foundation leaders spearheaded the drive for an international perspective and accepted the Buenos Aires student exchange convention as a part of the global effort. Duggan served as a coordinator to bring the private and governmental sectors into a joint enterprise, and the burning desire to find innovative ways to deter Nazi penetrations provided additional stimulation to the evolving cultural program. These limitations caused later stress, for when RC started, the State Department promised Congress to keep the cultural budget small. RC was to serve merely as a clearinghouse for private groups.

Lack of funding and sometimes overly cautious planning for RC retarded its program, but Nelson Rockefeller ultimately became the catalyst of an agency that vastly expanded cultural diplomacy. In the spring of 1940 he and a group of his business associates traveled extensively through the Americas and returned filled with trepidation over the extent of Nazi infiltration. To impress the administration with the danger involved and the necessity to reduce the impact of German penetration, Rockefeller went to the White House and presented his friend and presidential confidante Harry Hopkins with a memorandum on June 14, 1940, calling for an agency to provide greater economic cooperation and closer cultural, scientific, and educational ties. Hopkins read the document and then had the president examine it. Roosevelt saw enough merit in the recommendations to ask Hull to prepare a response to the proposals by the next week's cabinet meeting. The secretary did not attend, but Welles did, and he argued adamantly against any new agency outside of the State Department's control.

Roosevelt rejected this argument, and by the end of the month, he appointed James Forrestal, an administrative assistant on inter-American affairs, to formulate a program based on Rockefeller's recommendations. By early July, Forrestal proposed the establishment of a committee to supervise hemispheric economic matters and cultual projects. Movement toward the formation of the committee was temporarily delayed when Roosevelt selected Forrestal to become undersecretary of navy. Someone else would have to undertake the hemispheric assignment. Shortly after Forrestal received his naval appointment, he called Rockefeller to Washington and asked him if he wanted to direct this effort.[22]

Rockefeller did, but briefly hesitated because of the hotly contested presidential campaign of 1940. Coming from a famous Republican family, he wanted to be certain that accepting a government position would not jeopardize Wendell Willkie's chances. Rockefeller flew to Salt Lake City, met privately with the nominee, and received his permission to accept the post. With

that obstacle hurdled, Rockefeller looked forward to assuming his government duties as a "dollar-a-year man." He had met Roosevelt in March 1939 to
invite him to speak at dedication ceremonies for the Museum of Modern
Art. The president agreed and spoke to a nationwide radio audience on the
need of promoting art in a free society. Rockefeller felt that he and president had formed a cordial relationship. Besides this, Rockefeller had established warm friendships with powerful Democratic figures like Hopkins
and Forrestal.[23]

Roosevelt was also delighted to bring a Rockefeller into his administration, but in all likelihood for political purposes. During the 1940 campaign
Roosevelt hoped to split the Republican party by having Stimson and Knox
join the cabinet. The addition of a Rockefeller to the list would add to the
rumors in some circles that influential Republicans were deserting their
party for the Democratic nominee.

By an order of the Council of National Defense, the Office for Coordination of Commercial and Cultural Relations between the American Republics
was created on August 16, 1940. The name was changed to the Office of the
Coordinator of Inter-American Affairs in 1941, and, toward the end of the
war, to the Office of Inter-American Affairs (OIAA). Throughout most of
this emergency agency's existence, Rockefeller served as coordinator with the
mission of curtailing Nazi penetration and increasing Pan American solidarity. The OIAA duplicated many of RC's functions by acting as a liaison
with groups interested in Latin American matters, reviewing existing legislation and recommending new initiatives that affected the Americas, coordinating governmental and private hemispheric efforts, and directing projects outside of other agencies' prerogatives. The OIAA mandate led to activities in
three fields: economic cooperation (discussed in the chapter 12), cultural
matters, and information. OIAA was liberally allocated monies from the President's Emergency Fund to finance the coordinator's enterprises, which came
to $3,500,000 during the first year's operations and reached $45,000,000 by
the war's end.[24]

Rockefeller began his government career at the age of thirty-two, an unknown factor in administration circles. Many officials were wealthy and came
from well-established families, but none matched Rockefeller. These aristocrats had other misgivings. Instead of attending traditional private academies
like Philip Exeter and Groton, the youthful multimillionaire had gone to the
experimental Lincoln School in New York City. Dyslexia, a reading dys-
function, almost caused him to fail the ninth grade, and because of his medio-
cre academic record he entered the Ivy League through Dartmouth rather
than Harvard, Yale, or Princeton. Upon graduation he moved into his family's
business ventures and philanthropic concerns.[25]

His interest in Latin America developed after leaving college. He briefly
visited Mexico in 1933, but his real Pan American focus did not sharpen until

he became a minority stockholder in Standard Oil Company's Venezuelan susidiary called the Creole Petroleum Corporation. As he became more active on Creole's board of directors, his involvement deepened. A three-month trip to Latin America in 1937 led to a realization that United States businessmen in the Americas were generally detached from community participation. Not enough American citizens spoke Spanish or became engrossed in local matters. Impressed with the region's potential, he returned to the United States, learned to speak Spanish, and participated more intimately in Creole's activities. Throughout this period of growing interest in the Americas, he met periodically with a group of associates in New York City to discuss hemispheric events. By the time he became coordinator, he was commited to building firmer hemispheric ties.[26]

State Department officials, led by Welles, were unaware of Rockefeller's sentiments; their central fear was that he challenged diplomatic prerogatives. In mid-September 1940 Assistant Secretary Berle had a long dinner conversation with the newly appointed coordinator. The diplomat concluded that OIAA had a large budget, but pessimistically commented that Rockefeller had "boundless strategy and good will, and only the slimmest notion of what it is all about except in the limited field of commerce—which does not take anyone very far." Berle also knew that OIAA staff came primarily from private enterprise. "The trouble with these people," Berle noted, "is that they merely see redemption by a mildly benevolent capitalist process. Perhaps they are right; but I fear that there will be more needed besides that."[27] This viewpoint did not take the reality of the agency's potential and power into account. Duggan gave Welles a far more accurate assessment by the end of the month: "Since it is Nelson Rockefeller and not we who have the three and a half million dollars, the responsibility for initiating action in the cultural field rests with him."[28]

This fact did not inhibit the State Department from fighting to protect its vested interests. Hull guarded against any encroachment into his department and saw OIAA as an adversary of RC. Welles held like opinions and felt that anyone who decided inter-American matters without his expressed permission violated his domain. As a result Welles did not hide his displeasure. When the undersecretary and the coordinator met, Welles, standing behind his desk, would stiffly greet Rockefeller, bow, sit, conduct business, and end the conversation. In such an unreceptive atmosphere, Duggan quickly assumed a liaison role between the State Department and OIAA. He worked to develop effective programs and gradually became attuned to and even favored the coordinator's efforts and the positive functions of OIAA.

This type of relationship did not satisfy the State Department. Rockefeller acted directly through the White House for clearance; he did not require diplomatic approval for his hemispheric actions. Although OIAA regularly consulted foreign service personnel, Hull demanded greater control, and by late April 1941 the secretary had Roosevelt order Rockefeller to clear his projects through diplomatic channels. In the area of cultural relations, this meant that OIAA handled short-range cultural initiatives and RC assumed charge of long-range projects.

The undercurrent of suspicion in Washington extended to field operations. Powerful ambassadors like Braden, Caffery, and Messersmith objected to sharing their authority with OIAA staff members, but no matter how much they tried to take command of the coordinator's projects, their attempts failed. Rockefeller knew that with his budget, which eventually reached ten times that of the RC, the State Department had to have his cooperation and consent.[29]

While the State Department battled OIAA over lines of authority, Rockefeller managed to become the almost absolute master of the United States information network in the Americas. Before the coordinator's office took form, the administration had no concerted effort to advertise its positive accomplishments, while European governments actively sought hemispheric support through a multitude of media devices. The coordinator's office promptly set up radio, motion picture, and press divisions to combat their opponents, but even this thrust did not go unchallenged within the Washington bureaucracy. William Donovan, Coordinator of Information, tried to gain control over radio broadcasts. A well-known New Deal intellectual with warm presidential support who was deeply concerned about Latin America, Archibald MacLeish headed the Office of Facts and Figures and attempted to supersede the coordinator's media programs. Later the novelist and playwright Robert Sherwood, in charge of the Coordinator of Information, tried a similar maneuver. All of these efforts failed because Rockefeller retained his presidential backing.[30]

Roosevelt understood the need for hemispheric coordination in this vital area. He received constant objections throughout the 1930s from diplomats and other sources who protested distorted articles published in Latin America with European news services' by-lines. These news bureaus received government subsidies, and France's Havas News Agency, the worst offender, frequently informed its hemispheric readership of the unsavory character of life in the United States. The White House asked Associated Press and United Press to increase their Latin American coverage, but they declined on the grounds that their clients and readership were not interested in hemispheric news. When headliners like Hitler and Mussolini captured the front page, crucial State Department policy statements received little if any space. The advantages of more positive United States exposure was evident, yet little was done to correct the situation.[31]

Rockefeller quickly acted by opening a press section, which became one of OIAA's largest programs. Rather than supplying total coverage, its news department provided supplementary services like writing features for Latin American newspapers and sending out photographs and cartoons. *En Guardia*, a magazine patterned on the format of *Life*, reached a wide literate audience. The "American Newsletter," carrying hemispheric news, went out to 13,000 specially selected individuals. Welles realized the value of this press campaign. In late June 1942, when shipping losses dramatically increased, he tried to allocate sufficient newsprint to papers with pro-Allied biases to assure their uninterrupted publication. OIAA subsidized growing shipping costs for newsprint, and when United States advertisers reduced their ads because of decreasing sales, Rockefeller encouraged them to continue their activities to keep up the circulation of friendly newspapers.[32]

As in the case of the press, the United States badly trailed Europe in providing radio transmissions to Latin America. The Nazis exploited this medium; before the European war the Germans supplied seven hours of broadcasts per week. To answer Hitler's propaganda and build a greater following for hemispheric understanding, in early 1938 Democratic Senators Dennis Chavez of New Mexico and William McAdoo from California introduced a bill to erect a Pan American broadcasting station under State Department control. Secretary Ickes also favored government broadcasting for similar reasons. Roosevelt, acutely aware of radio's value, ordered action. Welles's solution was a government-owned and controlled wireless broadcasting system to beam important official speeches and educational programs in concert with private commercial programs like opera presentations. The undersecretary hoped to provide a feasible format by 1940 to compete against Axis stations, but this was not accomplished.[33]

OIAA promptly established a radio section, which worked closely with the commercial radio networks. Before Pearl Harbor this combined effort significantly expanded United States shortwave broadcasts throughout the Americas. After the United States joined the fighting, programming accelerated even further, almost doubling the peak output of Nazi broadcasts. OIAA produced everything from news to popular music, all to enhance the spirit of inter-American solidarity.[34]

Movies had another audience. Until the establishment of the coordinator's office, United States films sent to the other Americas presented a wide variety of images, including negative ones, which distorted life in the United States by portraying gangsterism, corruption, and incompetence. To limit the effects of these harmful films, OIAA formed a movie section in the winter of 1940. Private motion-picture studios staged most of the government-financed productions, glorifying the Allies and vilifying the Axis. Starting with a film depicting the events at the Rio conference, the coordinator began circulating newsreels in Spanish for Latin American matinee audiences. After this initial offering, the United States rapidly increased this service. Viewers, however, preferred commercial entertainment like Walt Disney's

Saludos Amigos, which described the adventures of Donald Duck and his cartoon friends as they traveled throughout the Americas. By the end of the war millions of Americans had attended these features, which not only had amusing plots but also plugged the Allied cause. OIAA, in effect, became a watchdog for films going to Latin America by suggesting deletions as well as inclusions. If not a censor, the coordinator's office had certainly assumed a clearinghouse function.[35]

Other related activities contributed to the encouragement of greater Pan American understanding. The coordinator financed art displays. During 1942, for example, New York museums sent three exhibitions that covered over 50,000 miles across Latin America and were viewed by some 218,000 people. South American artists and art students won grants to study in the United States. Besides visual art, OIAA sent glee clubs, ballet groups, and opera companies to the other Americas to give Latin American audiences a new perspective of North American cultural diversity.[36]

This media saturation reached *almost* every Latin American segment. Printed material called for reading skills; radio required a receiver; movies needed theaters. Some adverse opinions toward Yankees never changed, but at least this was the first major attempt to offer audiences an in-depth view of life in the United States.

Some questioned the worth of various projects. The consult from El Salvador in Miami complained about OIAA special missions: "They send 18 or 20 men down in a group for three weeks. These men talk to desk clerks in their hotels, to stewards on their boats, pick up Chamber of Commerce pamphlets—and come back with definite ideas what's wrong with South America and what the United States can do to fix it!" Speaking in March 1942, Dean Ackerman found shortcomings. He argued that sending movie stars like Douglas Fairbanks to Latin America wasted taxpayers' funds. Diplomats performed well in establishing cordial relations. He concluded: "Latin America does not need and does not want more propaganda, does not need or desire more cultural missions." Another critic believed that the coordinator published exaggerated profiles, like the one depicting the Guatemalan dictator Jorge Ubico as a democratic ruler. Samuel Inman went even further. He was upset over the selection of some personalities who had come to the United States on travel grants. "It is a strange thing," he unhappily observed, "that some of the officers in that section on cultural relations of the Department of State and in the Coordinator's Office should spend the money of our hard pressed Democracy to approve Fascist thinking."[37]

Critics argued that once the war emergency ceased so should the agency. By late 1943 curtailment of the coordinator's activities commenced. The State Department began to gain control of most cultural projects. Rockefeller's persistence and Roosevelt's support delayed the inevitable, but on May 20, 1946, OIAA was terminated.[38]

The dismemberment of OIAA had been planned from its inception; the coordinator's office was a wartime agency. It differed substantially in its purpose and operating style from RC. Rockefeller, although he participated in his family's varied philanthropic foundations, conceived of OIAA as an instrument for national defense. He therefore used cultural diplomacy as an aggressive weapon to defeat the Axis in the Americas. With this purpose in the forefront, OIAA preached and won converts for its widely diversified cultural interchanges with large-scale federal fundings.

Although OIAA and RC had deep philosophical differences in addition to their bureaucratic rivalry for supremacy in cultural diplomacy, both agencies by the closing stages of the fighting began moving toward a merger. Recognition of this fact came grudgingly from the State Department's reorganization in late 1944. The change called for six assistant secretaries of state, including one to handle public and cultural relations. Thus, what had started as a small program to enact the Buenos Aires exchange convention had grown into RC and OIAA and in principle had attained equal rank with the regional divisions. An important status distinction prevailed—most of the staff were not members of the foreign service. With the elevation of cultural affairs to the assistant secretary level, Archibald MacLeish was named to fill the post. Welles wished him success in presenting the State Department's policies more vigorously and openly to the public. Inman hoped MacLeish would lead in spreading democratic ideals and associate himself with Latin Americans who shared these beliefs.[39] Finally, Ambassador Bowers declared that the new post placed the recent appointee "in the front line trenches in the battle which will be prolonged to wipe out on this Continent the ancient prejudices against the United States. . . . Your reputation here as one intelligently interested in the culture of this region will stand you in good stead and make a fine impression. I have felt for some time that we needed a more militant policy in the cultural field."[40]

MacLeish relinquished his position before the end of 1945, but even during that short span, he demonstrated the heritage of the regional groundbreaking. New legislation was presented to Congress to expand the inter-American student-professor exchange into a global framework.[41] That June, MacLeish announced that the bill was offered "to extend to the rest of the world its cultural activities as developed over some years past in South America and to adopt those activities to the needs of the postwar situation in Asia."[42] The bill had a difficult time in Congress and did not pass until the start of 1948. Still, from a Pan American embryo, cultural affairs had matured.

Shortly before the war ended, Laurence Duggan left the diplomatic corps and assumed his father's role as director of IIE. He closely followed the United States' educational efforts in the Americas and warned against reducing hemispheric cultural relations projects: "If we throw them all overboard, junk the good with the bad, our Latin American neighbors will be convinced of what they always suspected was true, namely, that our 'cultural' programs were only bait dangled to win their support."[43] His hemispheric orientation blurred his reasoning. Inter-American efforts were reduced because postwar involvement took on a global mission. The United States committed itself to ambitious campaigns in Europe and Asia and relegated Latin America to secondary standing. The demand for funds exceeded supply, and as a direct consequence, Pan American cultural contacts suffered in the wake of expansion in other parts of the world.

12 ★ WARTIME ECONOMICS

T O SOLIDIFY inter-American political, military, and cultural cooperation into a complete program of hemispheric security, the United States
needed to develop extensive economic programs. The Roosevelt administration had groped for programs to accelerate commercial intercourse during
most of the 1930s, but the government's actions, torn by the uncertainty of
the Great Depression and internal bureaucratic bickering, did not significantly
enlarge the trading volume. Bilateral efforts like the reciprocity agreements
and limited Export-Import Bank loans coupled with minor agriculture and
treasury actions were insufficient in stimulating significant commercial
expansion.

The Nazi attack on Poland further contributed to the atmosphere of inter-
American economic bewilderment. The reduction of Allied purchases to
absolute necessities along with the German blockade meant that European
trade, which traditionally accounted for over one-third of Latin America's
foreign commerce, was seriously jeopardized. The United States took approximately one-third of the other American republics' exports, but if this
figure did not increase sizably, Latin America confronted severe economic
dislocation. Hemispheric leaders desperately looked to the United States for
a solution to this pressing financial quandary.

The first chance to discuss inter-American economic anxieties came at the
Panama meeting, where Latin American delegates expressed their troubled
feelings to Welles. More than any member of the administration, he understood the close connection between prosperity and political stability, but his
options were extremely restricted. Latin American nations had defaulted on
over a half billion dollars in bonds, many of which United States citizens
held. The oil seizures caused added friction. While businessmen clamored for
the return of their properties, they concurrently showed their hostility by
reducing hemispheric investments. Lobbyists warned the administration
against advancing any economic assistance to Latin America until investors
received compensation for their loans.[1]

Citizen complaints and the lack of any real foreign economic policy limited
administration commercial initiatives at the Panama conference. Indeed,
Welles had not formulated any far-reaching economic proposals, but the
Latin Americans, remembering the economic dislocation in World War I,

emphasized the critical nature of the trade problem and energetically pressed for the creation of an economic advisory committee. After Welles won approval from Washington, he agreed to the establishment of the Inter-American Financial and Economic Advisory Committee (FEAC) to discuss financial problems along with urgent economic and commercial questions. Welles realized its potential importance and decided to chair the committee. To emphasize the urgency of the FEAC, its enabling resolution set the inaugural session for no later than November 15, 1939.[2]

On that date Welles addressed the assembled representatives in Washington and called for a two-pronged hemispheric economic approach. First, the committee would attack immediate wartime dislocations. If conditions warranted aid, the United States would respond favorably. Second, the FEAC would explore long-term solutions to increase inter-American trade and seek ways to stimulate Latin American economic growth. Reciprocal trade agreements would help by ending tariff discrimination; monetary and banking negotiations would attempt to slow down currency fluctuations in exchange rates. These actions, Welles optimistically predicted, would halt any trends toward depression while his government searched for specific ways to achieve hemispheric economic stability.[3]

Roosevelt lent his personal support to this effort. On January 12, 1940, he lectured reporters to learn more about Latin Americans because "they are human beings and consider themselves just as good as we are." Businessmen needed to assist them by building and managing basic utilities. Combining these skills with technological advice and sophisticated equipment, "that is a new approach that I am talking about to these South American things." Emphasizing the spirit of joint cooperative ventures, the president asserted: "Give them a share. They think they are just as good as we are and many of them are."[4]

Secretary of Agriculture Wallace also encouraged strengthening hemispheric economic bonds and offered his own ideas to enlarge inter-American commerce. More than any of his predecessors, Wallace showed a genuine concern in Latin America. He studied the Spanish language, Latin American customs, and hemispheric agricultural conditions. He found that from 1930 to 1940 80 percent of Latin America's exports came from farming, and that half of the these competed against United States products; furthermore, the other American republics sent most of their surpluses to Europe and bought large quantities of its manufactured goods.[5]

Under these circumstances Wallace recommended measures of changing this pattern of hemispheric trading. Since only half of Latin America's imports to the United States consisted of tropical or semitropical items, he reasoned that the administration should help hemispheric countries develop more complementary crops. He showed that Latin America supplied less than $16,000,000 worth of tropical and semitropical goods, while the

United States' total imports reached $236,000,000. His studies indicated that Latin America had suitable climatic and soil conditions to raise many of these crops. Rubber, for example, was indigenous to South America, yet its production was negligible, while the United States imported approximately $250,000,000 worth of rubber from the East Indies. His argument in this case resulted in a hemispheric rubber project, when in the summer of 1940 Congress authorized $500,000 for research. A year later several Latin American nations signed agreements with the United States to cultivate rubber trees, but since they took five years to mature and needed intensive care, wartime labor shortages assured the project's failure.[6]

Wallace also tried to improve cooperation through his departmental administrative reforms. In the spring of 1939 he gained congressional authorization to lend agricultural experts to the other American republics, and four quickly took advantage of this legislation. During the summer of 1940 he established the Office of Foreign Agricultural Relations to boost foreign agricultural trading; the new division was comprised of three sections, one of which handled Latin American matters. On May 11, 1940, before the Eighth Pan American Scientific Congress, the secretary proposed an institute of tropical agriculture to improve hemispheric farming by finding cures for diseases and pests, experimenting with cattle raising and diary production, adapting new crops, training agricultural students, offering fellowships, and providing a meetingplace for experts. Two years later, the secretary's vision was rewarded with the foundation of the Inter-American Institute of Agricultural Science.[7]

To alleviate some food shortages created as early as 1940, Wallace promoted crop diversification. However, this effort met with mixed success. As demands for major cash crops expanded, producers stuck to their principal sources of revenue, canceling or retarding many diversification programs. Some United States officials were relieved by this trend. They advocated perpetuating Latin American monocultures for fear that food development efforts might adversely affect domestic growers in the postwar period. Some planners warned of enormous surpluses after the fighting and tired to limit production. Their failure to predict accurately the tremendous foodstuff shortages in the postwar era assured sales for farmers and also caused starvation once the fighting ceased. These internal disagreements over international agricultural policies for the postwar era made logical planning for inter-American commodity cooperation virtually impossible.[8]

Even with these troubles, Wallace believed that he had bettered hemispheric agricultural relations. When he was asked about the major accomplishments of his secretaryship, he replied that he took "considerable pride in making the Department more conscious than it had been before of the problems of Latin America and the way in which we could help the farmers of Latin America."[9]

The State Department tolerated Wallace's role because it never impinged on the overall formulation of foreign economic diplomacy. Hull and Welles insisted on supervising this operation. By the advent of war Hull unrealistically clung to his reciprocity program as the major vehicle to expanded trade. Welles was less dogmatic; he supported reciprocity, the FEAC, and other endeavors as long as he directed them.

Other administration financial leaders strenuously objected to the State Department's supremacy in foreign commercial transactions. Every affected cabinet officer tried to bypass Hull by going directly to the White House, but Roosevelt seldom took decisive action in the his area, deferring to State Department guidelines. Secretary of Commerce Jesse Jones, as head of the Reconstruction Finance Corporation and chairman of the Export-Import Bank's executive committee, closely guarded his prerogatives and made certain that his department participated in any decision affecting his charge. Secretary of Interior Harold Ickes, although only marginally involved in Pan American economic policies, loudly complained about the diplomatic corps' inefficiency. Secretary of Treasury Morgenthau was directly concerned about financial matters and offered suggestions to assist hemispheric economic stability, but his ideas often clashed with Hull's positions, and as a result, both secretaries and their assistants continually fought over policy. While each cabinet member had access to the executive office, Hull managed to keep control over foreign economic matters. In late 1939 he won presidential backing for a committee composed of the secretaries of state, commerce, and treasury to resolve any hemispheric disputes. Explicit in the committee's operations was the understanding that neither Morgenthau nor Jones could act unless Hull first agreed. Since both the commerce and treasury officers objected to following State Department orders, the committee's mission failed before even the committee met.[10]

Morgenthau was Hull's constant nemesis. Subjects of disagreements ranged from minor to major points. The State Department, for instance, supported resolutions at the Buenos Aires and Lima conferences to hold an informal meeting of treasury officials. While Welles warmly backed the idea, Morgenthau flatly rejected it. To him, the best way to negotiate was bilaterally. Over the treasury secretary's objections, Welles gained Roosevelt's approval to hold the First Meeting of Finance Ministers of the American Republics in Guatemala from November 14 through 21, 1939, to draw hemispheric treasury officials into closer and more cordial contact. Assistant Secretary of Treasury Herbert Gaston attended the gathering and was favorably impressed by the outcome. He even recommended future meetings to discuss specific issues, but treasury ministers did not meet again during Roosevelt's presidency. With the foundation of the FEAC, Welles decided to solve financial troubles through that committee and no longer wanted a potential rival from treasury gatherings. Their actions might interfere with his plans.[11]

A proposal to establish an inter-American bank created another controversy between the two departments. Assistant Secretary Berle vigorously pushed this project during talks at the FEAC. He saw the bank as a sound mechanism for assuring stable rates of exchange by guaranteeing dollar-to-peso ratios. After Berle gained presidential support, he temporarily forced the Treasury Department's acquiescence, and in early 1940 the United States along with nine American republics signed the bank's charter.

With the public announcement, opposition immediately surfaced. Morgenthau led administration forces who objected to the multilateral financial institution. Private bankers voiced their antagonism to the scheme through the Federal Reserve System, and Carter Glass, Democratic senator from Virginia who headed the powerful banking and currency committee, balked at replacing private capital with government funding. Some Latin Americans further hurt the bank's chances for approval by rejecting Berle's assumptions; they wanted the bank to make loans for public works projects during depressions to stimulate recovery. With the confusion over the bank's purpose and the hostility from banking circles, the inter-American bank legislation never came out of the Senate committee for floor consideration.[12]

Morgenthau's battle against the State Department's handling of the bondholder conflict created even greater ill will. By 1939 Welles began calling for payment by Latin American governments who had defaulted on their private debts. If their leaders refused, he threatened to withhold any possible economic assistance. This policy forced many countries to negotiate, and by 1940 settlements were being arranged. Diplomatic pressure sometimes failed, and various foreign service officials urged blunt ultimatums, as in the Peruvian case.[13] Laurence Steinhardt, former ambassador stationed in Lima, declared that he would not mince words with the Peruvian president, "but would tell him quite frankly that neither the American Government nor American private investors were prepared to play the role of Santa Claus, and that, he himself having admitted that the proposed debt settlement was fair and within the capacity of Peru to pay, there was not the slightest excuse for asking assistance until payment . . . [had] been resumed on the old debt, and that the prospects of future loans or credits was nil until he put the agreement already arrived at . . . into effect."[14]

The Treasury and Interior Departments resented this approach. In late 1937 Secretary Ickes complained that "there is no compulsion to invest money in foreign enterprises and it ought to be at the risk of the investor. Certainly we oughn't to be expected to go to war . . . to protect people who are doing something they want to do and are doing voluntarily."[15] By the summer of 1939 Morgenthau used this argument and added his own—that the United States had to stabilize Latin American economies as a precautionary measure against possible Nazi hemispheric penetration. The State Department and bondholder groups blocked treasury efforts in this direction;

both wanted settlements as a prerequisite for financial help. Frustrated by this sentiment, Morgenthau rhetorically asked the president "whether it is the policy of your Administration that we can't do business with a country that owes our private citizens money."[16]

Morgenthau already knew that Roosevelt had voiced his opposition to governmental support for the bondholders. When the treasury secretary pointed out that the State Department was enforcing a contrary policy, the president publicly criticized the bondholders' organizations for failing to negotiate satisfactory agreements and privately instructed Welles to break impasse. These presidential actions intensified negotiations, and by the end of 1940 most disagreements had been settled. In the remaining cases the bondholders lost diplomatic leverage, for the State Department subordinated the collection of private debts to promoting financial stability, vital for hemispheric security.[17]

The conflict within the administration reflected a far more significant dilemma. As long as the "phony war" in Europe continued, domestic considerations took precedence over international crises. American farmers still produced unsold surpluses; industrialists complained about property seizures; and bondholders agitated for payment. The uncertainty in the war theaters coupled with domestic unrest stalled economic assistance proposals. Hull had his Reciprocal Trade Agreements Act renewed in 1940 and even negotiated several new pacts, but these served to strengthen political bonds as much as commercial ties. The Treasury and Agriculture Departments continued their existing programs, but they did not generate large-scale trade expansion.[18]

The collapse of France reversed priorities. Hemispheric security took first place while domestic opposition to aid slowly and steadily started to slip to secondary importance. Hasty and ill-conceived schemes like Roosevelt's cartel plan were discarded while the administration looked for more effective ways to assist Latin American economies.[19]

The Export-Import Bank emerged as the most convenient vehicle for quickly enlarging inter-American commerce. During the 1930s the bank operated within narrow guidelines. Its loaning practices did not give any indication that the bank would ever become a major factor in Pan American commercial expansion. In fact, the opposite seemed to occur. Private business loudly objected to the bank as an alternative to private capital, feeling that the government should not supply funds to countries seizing United States property. Toward the end of 1939 proposed loans received careful scrutiny, and Hull saw no reason to change the bank's limited role. Some American republics asked for military credits, but Congress specifically forbade them. In early March 1940 Secretary Jones frankly informed the president that the bank lacked sufficient capital to assist Latin America to any meaningful extent, and therefore the bank granted few requests. El

Salvador's loan for an aerial survey as well as Colombia's proposal for currency stabilization were denied. The bank maintained that its charter only permitted appropriations to help finance United States exports.[20]

The Nazi conquest of Europe called for drastic changes. With the presumption that Hitler threatened hemispheric security, the administration made defense considerations paramount; Latin America needed economic assistance to ward off fifth-column infiltration. To meet this challenge, Roosevelt asked Congress on July 22, 1940, to increase the bank's lending capacity from $200,000,000 to $700,000,000 in order to halt any possible disruption of hemispheric trade. Private business still opposed governmental foreign aid, and the bill was hotly debated throughout the summer months. When the legislation finally passed on September 26, the administration had to accept provisions prohibiting loans for war material and to any nation that owed money to the United States government.[21] These restrictions did not diminish Jesse Jones's elation: "We shall thus have for the first time ammunition to deal with South America. . . ."[22]

The financing of the Brazilian steel mill illustrated the policy shift. Vargas and his fellow countrymen pressed diligently for the loan, but Jones and others originally denied it[23] James Forrestal sarcastically commented that the mill was "just as practical as a proposal to grow cotton in Montreal."[24] Bernard Baruch wondered: "After the property is developed, will they [the Brazilians] turn a Mexican stunt on us?"[25] United States Steel as well as other companies considered the project, but finally rejected it. Without any source of private capital available and the vast expansion of the bank's funding, Brazil received a total of $45,000,000 not only to construct the plant but also to bind the Brazilians closer to the Roosevelt administration.[26]

Throughout the war period grants went for a multitude of proposals, but the underlying motivation was similar. Economic security and political solidarity were synonymous. Chile received $5,000,000 for currency exchange. Uruguay accepted the same sum to purchase vital United States supplies and obtained an additional $2,500,000 "for useful public works projects." Paraguay acquired $400,000 to expand agricultural production. Nicaragua borrowed $2,000,000 for highway building.[27] William Culbertson, formerly ambassador to Chile under Hoover, observed by late 1940 that the United States was embarking on a new form of diplomacy "to use Federal funds in order to conserve and develop the economic life of the Latin American countries, I presume with the idea in mind that we are to keep them lined up politically for the purpose of economic defense of the hemisphere. You are really witnessing the entrance of the American Government into the field of political loans."[28]

Other economic programs, like preclusive buying, were also undertaken. Insufficient supplies in certain raw materials prompted the administration in the summer of 1939 to have an appropriation bill of $100,000,000 passed to stockpile strategic and critical materials. This action had a profound effect on Latin Americans because they exported many of these products. In order to coordinate these purchases, the Reconstruction Finance Corporation in the summer of 1940 created subsidiaries. The Rubber Reserve Corporation, for instance, bought all available hemispheric surpluses; the Metal Reserve Corporation established virtual mineral monopolies; and the Commodity Credit Corporation obtained Cuba's entire exportable sugar crop. The president lent the weight of his office to this effort on Septebmer 27, 1940, by calling on his administrators to give Latin American goods priority for strategic and critical material procurement to assure political security in the Americas. In mid-June 1941 the government went further by stockpiling additional stores to prevent Axis purchases.[29]

Besides buying from Latin Americans, the United States had to fill their normal orders and also those from Europe. Export controls commenced in 1940, creating sets of regulations oftentimes confusing to exporters. In spite of these troubles, manufacturers were able to supply essential hemispheric needs. The administration aided this flow by decreeing that as long as sending goods did not damage the defense effort, the United States would continue to supply Latin America. Throughout the war the administration tried to live up to its pledge, and the Office of Price Management made special allocations to Latin America for its transportation and power requirements.[30]

This commitment did not prevent inflation and speculation. Vastly expanding exports along with reduced imports resulted in huge surpluses of unspent dollars in the Americas. Prices for United States products soared. During the war the Office of Price Administration tried to stabilize costs on United States exports by setting price ceilings, but complaints over inflation and imposed rationing in Latin America persisted.[31]

Shipping shortages caused more disruptions. Latin America had traditionally sent more goods and tourists to Europe than to the United States. The attack on Poland reduced this normal traffic pattern, and at the same time, American vessels normally used for regional needs were transferred to aid the Allies. To maintain the hemisphere's transportation network, Admiral Emory Land, head of the War Shipping Administration and the United States Maritime Commission, in early 1941 established a committee on inter-American shipping to assure minimum tonnage requirements to maintain Latin American economies.[32]

This committee did an effective job until the Pearl Harbor attack. Shipping services thereafter decreased because of U-boat strikes and the transference of vessels to vital war fronts. During this critical period from 1942 to mid-1943, the United States continued its Latin American purchases and stored them in local warehouses until transportation was available. Shipments to the other American republics were a more difficult problem. At the peak period of submarine sinkings, the administration still provided enough

deliveries to maintain minimum needs in the Americas. Through this concerted effort, Latin American nations retained their economic stability. At
the end of 1942 the shipping crisis had almost peaked, and commercial
disruptions abated by the middle of the following year.[33]

While the administration used public works projects and expanded commodity and mineral purchases as the primary means to stabilize Latin American economies, the coordinator's office (OIAA) contributed by allocating
funds for numerous programs and helping to focus attention on the crucial
nature of hemispheric solidarity. Rockefeller originally wanted to devote his
main attention to Pan American economic activities, but quickly found that
the powerful cabinet members assumed control of the major economic
thrusts and resented his intrusion. Despite this limitation and coordinator
avidly pushed for preclusive buying, strategic loans, and price stability to
ward off rampant inflation. OIAA also studied financial problems, recommended solutions, and cooperated in funding other agencies' projects when
their budgets were inadequate to meet the demand.[34]

Rockefeller accepted these constraints and moved into areas not explored
by other agencies. The coordinator was extremely active, for example, in
obtaining cooperation from United States corporations that conducted
business in the Americas. An early OIAA study concluded that many United
States firms employed representatives who damaged the Allied cause by
advertising in pro-Axis publications, hiring workers hostile to United States
interests, channeling profits to Axis concerns, and supplying vital and confidential commercial information to the enemy. The coordinator's office wrote
thousands of letters to United States firms asking for their support in eliminating these harmful practices, and over 85 percent of them voluntarily compiled by ridding their companies of suspected Axis agents or sympathizers.
In the case of General Motors, the individual directing Latin American
operations admired Hitler and used Nazis for agents. When he was asked to
replace them he refused, and remained intransigent until Rockefeller threatened to publicize his unpatriotic attitude.[35]

The coordinator's office also established the "blacklist." When Rockefeller took charge of the OIAA, Harry Hopkins asked him to eliminate Nazi
financial backing in the Americas. As a consequence, OIAA constructed a
list of those firms connected to Axis interests. These activities became more
pronounced in July 1941 when the president ordered the publication of "The
Proclaimed List of Certain Blocked Nationals" to monitor compliance with
the "blacklist." After the declaration of war against the Axis, the State Department assumed authority in this pursuit, and the transition from OIAA
was smooth. Its personnel was merely placed under the jurisdiction of the
diplomatic corps, and "blacklist" adherence became mandatory.

Some Latin Americans strenuously objected to this action. During World
War I a "blacklist" was unpopular, and those memories extended to the next

war. In many instances the "blacklist" came periously close to direct intervention in hemispheric domestic decisions. Because of the power exerted by influential German, Italian, and Japanese groups in various American republics, some refused to freeze certain companies' assets, totally ignored the list, or only partially complied. The controversy over the "blacklist" lasted throughout the war, and United States embassy staffs frequently reported on their unrelenting struggle to force Latin American governments to take firmer actions against Axis businesses. [36]

The coordinator's office also inherited the Inter-American Development Commission (IADC) established by the FEAC, which was designed to build closer inter-American business and financial cooperation along with studying short- and long-term economic questions. Rockefeller took charge of the IADC in late 1940 and helped conclude the Inter-American Coffee Agreement, which allocated coffee quotas for Latin American countries sending this commodity to the United States market and allowed the participating nations to plan crop production more realistically. Since United States farmers did not cultivate coffee, domestic opposition was nonexistent. In the war years the IADC studied other possible commodity agreements like those for wheat and cotton. However, no pacts were signed since these were basic United States cash crops and their growers had powerful lobbyists in Congress to protect their interests against any conceivable outside competition.

IADC took over multilateral actions to improve hemispheric economic conditions. The commission, depending on Export-Import Bank funding, established small development corporations in Bolivia, Ecuador, and Haiti to assist these financailly troubled countries in diversification projects. The intentions were positive, but the results were meager because wartime conditions impeded careful planning. In the spring of 1944 IADC took a step in multilateral diplomacy, when the commission sponsored a conference to discuss the transition from wartime to peacetime economies. This was the first hemispheric gathering that talked about this pressing issue, but unfortunately for all concerned nations, the discussions did not lead to concrete actions. [37]

While the early OIAA activities were undertaken at the beginning of the agency's existence without the benefit of careful planning, the coordinator's most meaningful economic contribution came after the Pearl Harbor assault and had the advantage of considerable thought. Rockefeller recognized that United States lend-lease sales not only improved hemispheric military defense but also brought forth charges that the administration was overemphasizing the armed forces' role in Latin America. He, therefore, recommended spending an equal sum on assisting civilians to demonstrate the United States commitment to enhancing democratic elements in the Americas. To achieve this goal, the coordinator's office, with Welles's encouragement and active support, drafted a resolution for the Rio conference in 1942 to better public health and welfare. The delegates enthusiastically passed this resolution, and it was promptly labeled the Basic Economy project. One startling fact immediately arose—no machinery existed to put these lofty ideals into practice. Rockefeller tried to obtain loans from the Commerce Department, but Secretary Jones refused. He only lent funds; he did not make outright grants. Jones, however, suggested the answer to the coordinator's dilemma. Since the president had the authority to establish governmental corporations to fund projects, OIAA should have Roosevelt approve one for the improvement of hemispheric sanitation and health. The secretary even helped Rockefeller win congressional consent for this legislation, and on March 24, 1942, the Institute of Inter-American Affairs (IIAA) was formed to provide technical aid and advice in health services.

Many of the IIAA activities followed Rockefeller Foundation work in combatting tropical diseases. The coordinator's office worked through a government ministry that established a special division known as a *servicio*. Under its guidance the United States supplied a director and the technical personnel to carry out a wide variety of operations. By the end of the war, over fifty *servicios* in eighteen countries with approximately $18,000,000 in grants carried out worthwhile projects.[38]

These activities were not entirely altruistic. Curing tropical diseases and improving health and sanitary conditions increased workers' productivity at strategic hemispheric installations. United States soldiers, suffering from malaria, veneral diseases, and other maladies caused by inadequate water purification and sewerage treatment, benefited as much as local inhabitants. Emphasizing this point, the United States army medical corps considered the effort significant enough to send more than seventy health and sanitary engineering officers to over 2,000 projects in a four-year period. The outcome of their efforts resulted in the construction and improvement of clinics and hospitals where United States personnel trained Latin Americans to teach health education, treat diseases, and train nurses. These actions not only bettered the troops' living conditions, they also enhanced the general welfare of the region.

Several other corporations modeled on the IIAA were formed. In September 1943, for example, the coordinator established the Inter-American Education Foundation, Inc., to stimulate vocational and health education. Grants lasted three years, during which time the United States lent experts, instructed Latin American teachers in specific skills, and helped develop learning aids. The host nation was obligated to make its own contribution, and the involved ministry had to increase its budget over the previous year to carry on the work. By the expiration of the grant, the United States expected to reach certain goals and hoped that the participating countries would make these projects part of their permanent programs.[39]

The coordinator's office also initiated other projects to meet emergency situations. Yet, the pattern remained constant. Cash and technicians were furnished until local management took control of the operations. OIAA stimulated food production for domestic consumption, especially in the Caribbean region, where critical shortages arose. By increasing yields, these small islands offered a better diet to their inhabitants, freed vital shipping for other requirements, and provided small surpluses to soldiers in the Canal Zone. Funds for rehabilitation went to the El Oro Province in Ecuador, devastated by the border war with Peru. Another allocation went to Honduras to construct its section of the Pan American Highway; the country, disrupted by wartime economic dislocation, needed jobs for its workers. Through these activities, the coordinator's office not only filled gaps left open by other agencies, it also anticipated the postwar Point Four Program by using American dollars and technical assistance to raise living standards through food, sanitation, and health projects.[40]

The Roosevelt administration's economic initiatives significantly accelerated Inter-American commercial interaction. By 1940 the United States took 43.7 percent of Latin American exports and provided 54.6 percent of Latin American imports. This jumped even more in the first six months of 1941, when the United States bought 54.3 percent of Latin America's output, and the other American republics purchased 60.5 percent of their goods from the United States. By the end of the year United States commerce with Latin America reached its predepression levels, and this figure rose higher throughout the war years.[41]

Latin America responded favorably to this stimulation. During 1942 most of these countries experienced good harvests, increased mineral production, expanded manufacturing, and witnessed banking growth.[42] In the bleakest days of the fighting, these trends prompted the chief of the American republic section in the Commerce Department to conclude: "I believe that the Good Neighbor Policy in the hemisphere has been the laboratory in which have been distilled the essences from which a post-war plan can be realistically brewed for the entire world."[43] This view, however, distorted the reality. The Roosevelt administration ably met Latin America's wartime needs by reacting to existing pressures. Welles coordinated much of this effort from the State Department with assistance from other agencies. They worked together to find solutions to emergency situations, but the government did not look to the future. No long-term planning was given serious consideration.

The scope of this indecision came to the forefront with the establishment of the Economic Defense Board in the summer of 1941. By executive order the board's mission was to strengthen economic security and curb Axis purchases in the Americas. Vice President Wallace chaired the board and vigorously tried to expand its role. Given his Pan American sympathies, he urged sharing domestic production with the Latin Americans, supported preclusive buying, and favored cooperative ventures to stabilize trading in primary agricultural crops, all of which hemispheric spokesmen warmly endorsed.[44]

With the United States entrance into the war, a name change to the Board of Economic Warfare (BEW) placed added stress on expanding Latin American production of strategic and critical materials. The board acted as the chief procurement agency for these goods, and Wallace, with constant reinforcement from Milo Perkins, director of BEW, also tried to impose a social philosophy on the Latin Americans by doing such things as inserting labor clauses into their contracts to improve working conditions, wages, hours, sanitation, and safety.[45]

BEW's activities overlapped into diplomatic prerogatives, a fact that deeply disturbed the State Department. Wallace grew progressively more independent in his foreign negotiations and attempted to bypass diplomatic channels by using BEW personnel in direct bargaining. Hull reacted forcibly, for he had no intention of allowing Wallace to act without prior approval. The secretary argued that BEW set procurement policy, but the State Department supervised bilateral discussions. As usual Hull won his point; BEW had to follow traditional guidelines.[46]

Wallace's struggle with the State Department revolved around proper procedure; his battle with the Commerce Department involved much more fundamental and emotional issues. Whereas the vice-president admired Hull, both Wallace and Perkins detested Secretary Jones and his chief procurement official, William Clayton, who adamantly defended the private enterprise system. The commerce secretary was prominent in Texas banking circles and reflected his business orientation by his cautious financial nature and commitment to maintaining fiscal integrity. Clayton also came from Texas and was well known as an international cotton exporter. Since the Commerce Department distributed procurement funding, Jones and Clayton insisted on keeping costs down and carefully bargaining for the best possible price.[47]

Jones also chaired the executive committee of the Export-Import Bank. Since it had authority to stockpile critical and strategic materials, the secretary became deeply involved in purchasing several Latin American basic exports like copper and tungsten. The bank loaned money for numerous other projects, such as waterworks, highway construction, dollar exchange, and agricultural diversification. In 1941 the bank lent almost $52,000,000, with undistributed commitments of over $262,500,000; the next year more than $83,000,000 went out while just under $350,000,000 remained unspent. These careful allocations of funds illustrated Jones's first concern; in every transaction he demanded that the bank demonstrate its fiscal soundness.[48]

Wallace's and Perkin's insistence on promptly distributing funds and placing labor clauses in their contracts precipitated an acrimonious bureaucratic confrontation. BEW tried to obtain presidential authorization to order Jones to make purchases under its guidelines, but the commerce secretary fought BEW's recommendations as being fiscally unsound. This maneuvering for supremacy in procurement policy had disastrous consequences. The vice-president's commitment to BEW's expansion and Jones's refusal to surrender any of his authority led to personal attacks. Wallace complained that the commerce secretary's overly cautious nature retarded BEW progress. Jones retorted that the vice-president acted irresponsibly and interfered with his department's operations. Each side charged the other with damaging the war effort and leveled accusations of incompetence. The controversy reached the press, and what had been an internal dispute surfaced and grew more vicious. By the summer of 1943 Roosevelt admonished both parties for their imprudent behavior and abolished BEW. Without it, Wallace lost his specific planning role for the Americas and precluded a firm advocate of inter-American economic cooperation from influencing the administration's outlook. The president established a new agency to coordinate foreign procurement efforts, but its director showed no particular hemispheric inclination.[49]

The dismemberment of BEW meant more than just the end of another wartime agency; it also showed how fragile inter-American economic planning was. During the 1930s the United States tried to expand its hemispheric commercial dealings principally by increasing trade and removing the barriers to freer commerce through the reciprocity agreements. With the European war, Latin Americans, recalling the dislocations from World War I, called for stronger measures, but at first all they received was the FEAC and pledges of financial cooperation. The Roosevelt administration did not conscientiously seek to dominate regional markets and never did offer any long-range commercial programs for the postwar era.

United States responses for closer inter-American commercial ties came as reactions to deteriorating Allied prospects. Instead of concentrating on winning long-term trading concessions, the administration focused on assuring economic tranquility for the present to relieve any pressure that would disturb the political order. Export-Import Bank loans, stockpiling, and the funds distributed from the coordinator's office were not molded into any grand design. Some officials, of course, did hope that the United States would retain its overwhelming hold on inter-American commerce, but the Roosevelt government basically concerned itself with the wartime emergency. Men like Hull, Wallace, Morgenthau, and Jones were too busy resolving immediate questions and protecting their vested interests to consider the economic transition from war to peace. Neither the president nor his chief advisers gave serious thought to this basic issue, and by the end of the fighting the commercial advantages gained during the conflict slowly started to erode.[50]

13 ★ AT AND OVER THE SUMMIT

PLANNING viable postwar economic strategy did not interfere with the daily job of maintaining the spirit of inter-American solidarity during the fighting. Never before had a United States government enacted such ambitious, sophisticated, and inclusive Latin American programs, and the results clearly benefited the Roosevelt administration. All but two of the other American republics rushed to join the United Nations' cause by the end of the Rio conference, which was a vivid demonstration of the Good Neighbor policy's value.

Because of the expanded Pan American emphasis, a larger United States audience became aware of regionalism. Sometimes fads resulted; the Brazilian samba, for example, became the biggest dance craze of 1942. Other trends showed signs of more permanence, like the mass media's greater detailed coverage of hemispheric events.[1] Prominent leaders pressed to sustain this interest and urged inter-American activists to capitalize on this sentiment: "To permit the attention of the citizens of the United States to be diverted to the Far East and the Pacific now, overlooking our Western Hemisphere relations, would be to give Hitler the opportunity in the Western Hemisphere he seeks."[2]

These anxieties were justified, for the growing Latin American interest did not shake the general public's traditional European and Far Eastern orientation. The majority associated the Good Neighbor with the Americas and understood some of the hemispheric operations, but only a small number comprehended the broad scope of the administration's entire Pan American effort.[3] The syndicated columnist Raymond Clapper illustrated his prejudices: "There is a lot of talk about Latin pride and so on, but personally I have felt, without knowing them, unfortunately, that they are a pretty cheap sleezy kind of people and are pretty much [ready] to set the money price on anything."[4]

While this kind of undercurrent persisted throughout the war, Roosevelt stressed the Good Neighbor's value. In the spring of 1942 the president listed several reasons for his inter-American programs: earlier practices had seriously damaged hemispheric relations; he preferred to negotiate rather than land marines; he objected to bankers making unscrupulous loans at exorbitant interest rates with outrageous commission fees for promoters;

he denounced these methods and sought ways to change them.[5] No wonder the Mexican chargé d'affaires in the United States, Luis Quintanilla, in the widely read *A Latin American Speaks*, published in 1943, proclaimed: "Today, for the first time in the history of the Western Hemisphere, we of Latin America may confidently clasp the open hand extended to us by a President of the United States."[6]

Quintanilla spoke for most Latin Americans, and Roosevelt did not disappoint them. Even in the midst of his hectic wartime scheduled, the president plugged the Good Neighbor. He told reporters in late 1942 that the administration's Latin American policies were "part of the national policy here, regardless of what the political complexion of the Administration is here. Same way down there. In all the other Republics, whoever is the government in different places, they will go along with the idea of 'Democracia', and the thought of the Good Neighbor."[7] He entertained Latin American leaders at the White House and used these occasions to reiterate his inter-American commitments to solidarity, continental defense, and economic collaboration.[8]

The president took these messages to Latin America audiences. Returning from North Africa in early 1943, he met with Vargas in Brazil to discuss South American defenses. While the fear of an assault on Natal had vanished, Roosevelt pledged to eliminate any future attack by demilitarizing Western Africa and establishing United States bases there. In April he met with President Camacho and became the first United States president to greet his counterpart on Mexican soil. At least for the moment, the heritage of Yankee imperialism disappeared while both leaders preached bilateral cooperation.[9]

Eleanor Roosevelt helped to advertise the administration's hemispheric commitment. In early 1944 she spent almost a month flying to many Caribbean island and two Central American and three South American republics to talk with United States troops and effectively serve as a good will ambassador. Though the stops were brief, the first lady directed public attention to the Americas.[10]

Vice President Wallace also followed the president's example. He enthusiastically endorsed the Good Neighbor and worked to encourage democratic institutions within the hemisphere. Although he believed that some dictators were moving in this direction, he felt that too many political dissidents fled their homelands or languished in prisons. Recognizing that strong authoritarian tradition in Latin America, he reasoned that the United States had to work with hemispheric strongmen to prepare their countries for wider citizen participation in government by decreasing illiteracy, improving nutrition, and expanding industrialization.[11]

To gain a greater appreciation of current Latin American conditions, Wallace accepted an invitation to visit Chile and then broadened his itinerary to include seven Central and South American states. His trip lasted from mid-March to late April 1943, and at each stop he received a warm reception.[12] Ambassador Bowers in Santiago on March 29 declared that the mission was "one of the best things in Chilean-American relations that happened since the 'good neighbor' policy was enunciated." A few days later he added that "never in Chilean history has any foreigner been received with such extravagant and evidently sincere enthusiasm."[13] Besides generating favorable publicity, Wallace returned to Washington more committed to strengthening inter-American relations. He deplored a commonly held notion that Latin Americans were of genetically inferior races. He affirmed that they sincerely advanced the Allied cause, but that poor health and inadequate sanitation conditions limited their direct participation in the war effort.[14]

While the Roosevelts and Wallace publicized the Good Neighbor, routine affairs fell principally to Welles. He directed the inter-American policies that resulted in the overwhelming acceptance of the United States' wartime diplomacy. At the center of this strategy was Welles's cogent assessment of the South American political situation. He knew that in order to gain the greatest degree of cooperation, Argentine influence had to be minimized; to accomplish this goal, the undersecretary worked to align its traditional allies with the United States.

Welles was extremely successful in this effort, with the notable exception of Chile. During the 1930s it had been severely shaken economically because of sharply declining export markets. To recover its commercial health, Chile attempted to obtain United States economic assistance through loans, credits, or a favorable reciprocal trade agreement—none of which materialized.[15]

In addition to financial weakness, Chile faced a political crisis when the sudden death of its president in late 1941 forced an election. Powerful Allied and Axis factions within the country exerted pressure in behalf of their causes, which clouded the political climate. Even more worrisome to voters, rumors circulated that if they took a pro-Allied stand, the Japanese would attack their long-exposed coastline. The candidates for the presidency reflected these concerns by refusing to take a strong stand for or against any of the belligerents. As a result the foreign ministry acted cautiously and clung to neutrality.

Before this consensus emerged, the Chilean Foreign Minister Juan Rossetti tried to promote his presidential aspirations by cosponsoring the Rio meeting, but instead committed a political blunder. His countrymen preferred neutrality in the hope that it would allow them to export to both sides and thus capitalize on an expected wartime economic boom. This expectation coupled with the nation's military unpreparedness influenced the Chilean delegation at the Rio conference to join with Argentina in opposing the severance of relations with the Axis. After Rossetti returned from the meeting, he pressed for the break, but the interim government decided to leave this explosive issue to the incoming administration.[16]

Rather than choosing sides, the new President Juan Antonio Rios followed public pressure to remain neutral. Welles understood the reasons for this decision but felt Chile's adherence to the Rio gathering's political resolution had a higher priority. On February 7, 1942, he expressed his deep concern:

The dangers inherent in the situation developing in Chile and in Argentina are so great as to make it . . . of the greatest importance that the Axis agents be forced to leave Chile at the earliest possible date. More than that, the relations between Argentina and Brazil will, at least for a while, become extremely strained. If Chile wavers and fails to support the position taken by Brazil, the situation—fantastic as it seems—may really become highly critical. If Chile supports Brazil, Argentina will not be able to create any open trouble.[17]

Under these circumstances the United States maintained its existing economic assistance programs to Chile and concurrently exerted discreet diplomatic pressure for the break.[18] By the summer of 1942 Welles changed his position and bluntly informed the Chileans "that they couldn't expect any assistance, either military, naval, or financial, until and unless their policies change. . . ."[19] Roosevelt applied additional pressure on August 12 by pledging that "if Chile should be attacked by an Axis power or if real trouble should be created in Chile by Axis nationals or by elements instigated and dominated by Axis agents after Chile has broken relations with the Axis, President Rios may of course count on the support of the United States to the extent that the Chilean Government may request such support and to the full extent of the ability of the United States."[20]

When these measures failed to produce the desired results, Welles addressed an audience on October 8, 1942, and condemned Argentina and Chile for allowing Axis forces to operate in their territories. The undersecretary could not "believe that these two republics will continue long to permit their brothers and neighbors of the Americas, engaged as they are in a life and death struggle to preserve the liberties and the integrity of the New World, to be stabbed in the back by Axis emissaries."[21]

The Chileans publicly reacted indignantly to the undersecretary's rebuke, but privately knew that the Roosevelt administration would withhold assistance until the break came. In December Rios called on Congress to debate the topic, and by the new year he had decided to sever diplomatic relations. While political opponents employed parliamentary tactics to delay the break, the government arrested Axis agents and sympathizers who were engaged in espionage or who might conduct sabotage. With their incarceration, on January 23, 1943, Rios issued a carefully worded statement to please both the Allied and Axis sides. The severance of relations, according to the president, had not come sooner so that his countrymen could arrive at a national consensus. The majority now desired this measure, but the opposition, too, had rights. Rios then praised those Chileans who favored the Axis and promised to continue friendly bonds with Argentina, even though Chile had adopted a pro-Allied posture. In this delicate balancing act, the president hoped to satisfy both parties.[22] Duggan, for one, dismissed the hedging: "All is well that ends well. The break has occurred and Chile is once more a 100% member of the American community of nations."[23]

Chile's break with the Axis further isolated Argentina and fit neatly into Welles's Brazilian strategy. Throughout his career in the Roosevelt administration, the undersecretary had steadily moved to make Brazil the United States' principal ally in South America. The depression initially interrupted this goal, but as war grew closer to the Americas, his ideas crystalized. Economic aid, like the steel mill's construction, bound the two nations more firmly; Brazil received more military assistance than the rest of the other American republics combined; and Welles considered Foreign Minister Oswaldo Aranha his primary confidant in hemispheric affairs. The Brazilian diplomat repaid Welles's trust by advocating the strongest possible ties with the United States, which led to severing relations with the Axis and, before the end of the year, a declaration of war. This unofficial alliance between the two nations changed the traditional power alignment in South America. The resolve to follow the United States resulted in the modernization of Brazil's armed forces and sustained economic growth. These changes gradually took form, and by the end of the war Brazil emerged as the first power in South America, while Argentina faded to second place.[24]

Mexico also altered its status. Even before the oil settlement, the Camacho government began to cooperate with the United States. As this interaction increased, the Mexicans allied themselves with the Roosevelt administration at the Rio meeting and, before the year was over, had declared war on the Axis. Besides regular economic and military aid programs, the two nations added other projects because of the common border. Over a long period, *braceros* Mexicans who worked seasonally in the United States for extraordinarily low wages crossed the border. In 1942 the two countries arranged for these laborers to fill agricultural and railroad jobs because of United States manpower shortages. After two years the program reached its peak when 62,000 Mexicans held farming positions and 80,000 more were employed by the railroad industry.[25]

The United States' rehabilitation of the National Railways of Mexico was another unique enterprise. The submarine menace drastically reduced shipping traffic, which caused a greater reliance on land transportation. The abysmal condition of the Mexican rail system retarded this effort; to reverse this, the coordinator's office dispatched railroad experts in early 1942 to examine the problem and make recommendations. The specialists quickly reported that Mexico's antiquated network faced total collapse without immediate repairs. If the collapse occurred the United States would have to supply additional vessels from war theaters to meet Mexican requirements. To prevent this crisis, a bilateral rehabilitation pact was signed before the end of the year, and the coordinator's office sent a mission of United States experts to keep the trains running and the tracks open.[26] The specialists did not provide solutions to all of the industry's troubles, but the mission did win the praise of Ambassador Messersmith, who originally had objected to the entire scheme. Writing in the mid-1950s, he forgot his initial hostility: "Today when we are talking about the Point Four program it is well to recall the work which was done by the United States Railway Mission in Mexico. I doubt if anything more constructive or helpful has been done at less cost and with more effect under the Point Four program than what was done by the U.S. Railway Mission in Mexico during the period of the war."[27]

By the end of 1943 the United States appeared to have forged an almost solid inter-American front against the Axis. Thirteen Latin American nations had declared war; six others had severed diplomatic relations; Argentina maintained its solitary dissent. Mexico and Brazil contributed combat troops, and others might have been encouraged to do so had the United States military been less vociferous in its opposition. The State Department expended considerable time and effort in crushing Axis subversion in the hemisphere with admittedly less than wholehearted compliance. Some Latin Americans continued their apathetic or even hostile United States attitudes, and a few opponents sent critical information to the enemy. But in general the push for hemispheric solidarity was remarkably effective.

To some extent the neutral or pro-Axis sentiment came from the many Latin Americans who despised the Soviet Union. The Catholic Church and its supporters throughout Latin America found communism an anathema. Besides deploring the atheistic doctrine, many oligarchs opposed Russia's call for the proletariat to overthrow them. Finally, some condemned Stalin's opportunism. During the Russo-German Nonaggression Pact, he aligned himself with Hitler and abruptly reversed this policy with the Nazi invasion of the Soviet Union.

United States spokesmen had widely divergent opinions concerning Russia, but Roosevelt ignored these and welcomed the Communists as an ally against the common foe. Wallace and other leaders in the administration felt that a lasting peace required Soviet-American friendship and applauded the president's decision. During 1942 the Russians decided to test American cooperation by expanding their Latin American contacts. Some Soviet leaders felt that the United States objected to these efforts—an accusation that had some validity. Welles promoted greater Allied interaction, including support for diplomatic relations between the Soviet Union and the other American republics—under certain conditions. If the Russians agreed not to intervene in Latin American domestic affairs, the undersecretary promised to advance the Soviet initiative.

Although the State Department's approval was a qualified one, Latin American Communists and other impressed by the heroic Russian resistance against the Nazi onslaught called for direct relations. In October 1942 Cuba became the first to grant recognition to the Soviet Union, and Batista subsequently brought two local Communists into his cabinet as ministers without portfolio. Mexico acted a month later, and in June 1943 Constantine Oumansky went to the capital as ambassador. Assistant Secretary Berle feared that this appointment marked the beginning of a Communist political campaign in the Americas, but Ambassador Messersmith disagreed. Soviet hemispheric intentions, according to the ambassador, had been grossly exaggerated. The administration had to accept possible Russian economic expansion in the Americas, but Communist political success depended on instability. If the United States intended to maintain its hemispheric hegemony, it was imperative that the administration sustain economic growth.[28]

The debate over Soviet intentions in Latin America was insignificant compared to the worsening relationship between Hull and Welles in the State Department. By the start of Roosevelt's third term, the secretary's physical condition was deteriorating, and personal diplomatic reversals compounded his problems. He took direct charge of the negotiations with the Japanese, and after the Pearl Harbor fiasco, some reporters intimated that he had refused to provide the military with certain Hawaiian intelligence, which led to the attack. Late in December 1941 he exploded over the St. Pierre-Miquelon episode, and less than a month later Hull accused Welles of disloyalty at the Rio conference. In both cases Hull sought presidential support, and he was twice rebuffed. Exhausted and depressed, the secretary took an extended leave in early February 1942 to regain his health, and resumed his duties in late April looking well rested. Since Hull commanded a large national following, the president had no intention of removing him and tried to squelch any resignation gossip. When Hull returned to Washington, he had two major objectives—to take firm control over his department and remove Welles from office.[29]

To achieve the latter, Hull employed a seemingly unrelated event that made the undersecretary a political liability. On September 15, 1940, Speaker of the House of Representatives William Bankhead, Democrat from Alabama, died of a heart attack. After a state ceremony, a special train carried the coffin and the funeral party to Bankhead's hometown of Jasper, Alabama. Roosevelt went, and he ordered full cabinet attendance. Although Hull and Bankhead had been House colleagues and friends, the secretary stayed in the capital to monitor foreign affairs and sent Welles to represent the State Department.

Shortly after the services were completed in Jasper on September 17, the train carrying the president and his staff started back to Washington. That evening Welles became intoxicated, retired to his sleeping compartment and began ringing his service bell. Several Negro male porters answered the calls, and to their dismay, the drunken undersecretary greeted them with homosexual advances. None accepted. The train pulled into Washington the next afternoon, and Welles resumed his daily schedule as if nothing had happened.[30]

Unfortunately for the undersecretary, rumors about the episode spread rapidly. In order to ascertain the facts, on January 3, 1941, General Edwin "Pa" Watson, the presidential appointment secretary, directed J. Edgar Hoover of the Federal Bureau of Investigation (FBI) to make a thorough and discreet inquiry. Within a month two special agents conducted an investigation and Hoover went straight to the president with the findings that confirmed the allegations. Despite the episode's potential explosiveness and embarrassment to the administration, Roosevelt decided to retain Welles and prevent any recurrence by assigning him a bodyguard who had orders to stop the undersecretary from displaying any deviant behavior. This closed the affair—or so thought the president.[31]

Even before Roosevelt heard the FBI report, Ambassador William Bullitt learned about the incident and obtained an affidavit from a porter outlining the events on the train. Bullitt's dislike of Welles dated to the contest for the undersecretaryship in 1936. The ambassador had unsuccessfully lobbied for R. Walton Moore and then returned to his post in Paris and asserted that he, above anyone else, spoke for the president in European matters. When Bullitt learned of Welles's European mission in early 1940, he told various officials that had he been informed about it early enough, he would have had it aborted. The undersecretary confirmed some of Bullitt's fears by making some intemperate remarks about his admiration for Mussolini. This error in judgment combined with Welles's growing responsibilities in European matters and Moore's hatred of the undersecretary reinforced Bullitt's antipathy toward Welles.[32]

As long as Bullitt held the French ambassadorship, his criticism of the undersecretary was limited to long-distance gibes. However, after France fell to the Nazis, he returned to the United States without any diplomatic assignment. When his friend Moore died in early February 1941, Bullitt seized the occasion to approach the president in April with his evidence against Welles and explained that he had made Moore a deathbed promise to expose the undersecretary's criminal conduct. Bullitt then handed his evidence to Roosevelt and urged immediate dismissal, for Welles had committed an offense that, if made public, would seriously demoralize the foreign service. The president readily verified the charge's validity, but rejected Bullitt's conclusions. No one, according to the president, would publish an account of the train ride, nor would anyone file a criminal complaint. Only a few knew of the affair, and Roosevelt had taken suitable precautions to prevent any recurrence.[33]

Shaken by the president's attitude, Bullitt issued an unwise ultimatum. He would not accept any diplomatic assignment until after Welles's removal. To achieve that goal, Bullitt sought administration supporters to put pressure on the president. These lobbying activities quickly reached the White House, and Roosevelt decided to stop Bullitt's campaign by giving him a special assignment to Africa and the Near and Middle East in late 1941. At least temporarily, Bullitt's anti-Welles crusade halted, while he directed his energies toward more productive enterprises.[34]

This trip delayed the inevitable alliance between Bullitt and Hull. The ambassador returned from his mission just after the confrontation between Hull and Welles over the Rio resolution in early 1942. After the secretary had rested and resumed his duties, he and Bullitt combined forces to plot Welles's ouster by spreading stories of the undersecretary's immoral conduct. On October 24, 1942, the secretary held a secret meeting with J. Edgar Hoover where he accused Welles of "headline hunting" and asked to evaluate the FBI report on the train incident. The director refused; he would not provide a copy without presidential consent.[35]

Since Roosevelt would surely deny permission to use the investigation's conclusions to remove Welles, the plotters sought another route to their destination. They selected congressional pressure as the best avenue and enlisted the assistance of Senator Ralph Brewster, Republican from Maine. On April 27, 1943, the senator, using information supplied by Bullitt, saw Hoover about the shocking allegations against the undersecretary and demanded to see the report. The director declined, but admitted making an inquiry and recommended that the senator see Hull, who knew some of the facts. Brewster did not know about the secretary's efforts to oust his subordinate when the senator proceeded to the State Department where he asked the secretary why Welles remained at his desk. Hull replied that Roosevelt refused to fire the undersecretary. The senator's next stop was the Justice Department, where he threatened Attorney General Francis Biddle with a Senate probe of the sordid matter. Biddle promptly informed the president of the conversation and its potential repercussions. If hearings were held, how would Roosevelt explain keeping Welles in office for three years after learning about his homosexuality?[36]

The train episode had finally made Welles a political liability, and Roosevelt had to relieve him. The president, still hoping to keep Welles in the administration, offered him a roving ambassadorship, but Welles rejected the idea and sent his letter of resignation to the White House on August 16, 1943. Since Hull had wanted his removal, any new assignment would only aggravate the situation. Welles cleared out his office and then retreated to Bar Harbor, Maine, to escape his humiliation and Washington's hot, humid summer.[37]

Shortly before Welles's departure, rumors of discord between Hull and him leaked to the press. Reporters speculated that the two men had policy disagreements and arguments over Welles trying to usurp the secretary's prerogatives. Columnists also learned that the undersecretary might take a special mission to Moscow to hold crucial talks with the Russians. None of the stories hinted of the homosexuality issue.[38]

Roosevelt tried to change Welles's decision by inviting him to go to Hyde Park and accept the Soviet mission.[39] Welles considered the offer, but on September 21 he wrote the president that his decision was firm because "Hull's feelings with regard to myself—unjustified as they are—would make any such relationship impossible. He would be constantly imagining that I was threatening his legitimate jurisdiction, or undermining his authority, and possibility for the success of what you desire accomplished would be seriously jeopardized."[40] Five days later Roosevelt announced that Welles had left the foreign service and claimed that the resignation came as a result of his wife's poor health.[41]

The Hull-Welles conflict had a devastating effect on the State Department. The diplomatic careers of both Welles and Bullitt were destroyed, and neither man ever again served in any major government position. Hull, weakened by poor health, age, and departmental bickering was unable to fill the void created by the undersecretary's departure. Although the secretary minimized Welles's importance to State Department operations, Hull needed him for his managerial skills. Roosevelt further eroded the secretary's authority by looking more frequently outside of the diplomatic corps for advice in making critical foreign policy decisions. The president knew that Hull had engineered Welles's dismissal, and this plotting, to the president's way of thinking, made the secretary of state an unwelcome, though powerful, cabinet personality. Roosevelt's sentiments became clear throughout the remainder of Hull's tenure. The president acted without consulting the secretary or even informing him of many momentous wartime decisions.

When translated to Latin American affairs, this tragedy marked the beginning of the disintegration in Pan American solidarity. The president was preoccupied with the war and holding shaky domestic and Allied wartime coalitions together. Vice President Wallace had lost his hemispheric influence with the Board of Economic Warfare's dismantling. These problems did not damage the overall conduct of hemispheric diplomacy because Welles maintained continuity as well as handling routine events. Hull acknowledged the undersecretary's experience by giving him wide latitude in the conduct of inter-American affairs. Latin American leaders also realized Welles's central role in solving their troubles. Shortly after the undersecretary left office, Ambassador Bowers reflected the Latin American anxiety over Welles's departure: "There is a general fear through South America that the passing of Welles from the Department means less interest in South America in Washington, and even a change, if not abandonment of our 'good neighbor policy.' "[42]

Welles also contributed to the crumbling of the Good Neighbor. His principal strength was also his major weakness. The undersecretary prided himself on being the most knowledgeable official on hemispheric matters.

Because Welles viewed Latin America as his private preserve, his resignation eliminated the individual who coordinated and personified the entire regional effort. Unfortunately for his successors, none had worked closely with him or had his training, and the undersecretary seldom wrote memoranda outlining his trend of thought. The pieces of the Good Neighbor fit neatly in his well-ordered mind. Without him, no one had the background or the presidential mandate to maintain current operations or construct a new frame of reference. The inter-American system that Welles had worked so hard to build began breaking apart, at least partially, because of his egocentric nature and inability to institutionalize his programs within the diplomatic corps.

14 ★ THE DISINTEGRATING ALLIANCE

WELLES'S DEPARTURE destroyed the unofficial division of diplomatic functions that had grown within the administration since 1933. Continuity was shattered, and as a result the United States started to lose its leadership role in shaping inter-American diplomacy. Roosevelt had supplied the generalship, encouragement, and many of the Good Neighbor concepts. Hull had added his commitments to lower tariff duties and peaceful resolution to disputes. He sometimes had served as the cautious voice of a skeptical public or Congress, which made Roosevelt and Welles temper some of their more ambitious schemes. The secretary also had become deeply involved in specific controversies like the Cuban revolution of 1933 and the Mexican oil expropriation, but once the crises peaked, he had expected Welles to find the long-term correctives.

Besides ending this triumvirate, the undersecretary's resignation added to the bureaucratic intrigue inside the foreign service. Some diplomats were labeled "Welles men" and now were vulnerable to attack. No longer confined by the secretary's authority, the former undersecretary used the media to criticize Hull's actions, and the secretary overreacted. Supersensitive to any type of attack on him or his department, Hull exaggerated the negative consequences of Welles's comments and accused the undersecretary's past close associates of divulging diplomatic secrets to their former superior. Duggan in particular was suspected of revealing information to Welles, and because of his questionable loyalty, Hull ignored Duggan's suggestions. Placed in this untenable position, this experienced foreign service officer resigned in the summer of 1944, and several others connected with Latin American affairs also left their posts, which further contributed to a breakdown in formulating consistent hemispheric programs.[1]

The selection of Edward Stettinius, Jr., to succeed Welles as undersecretary further weakened inter-American collaboration. Trained as a corporate executive, he became vice-president at General Motors by the age of thirty-one and seven years later chaired the board at United States Steel. As a reward for supporting Roosevelt's second-term bid, he was appointed chairman of the War Resources Board in 1939 and after two years was placed in charge of the lend-lease program. On September 25, 1943, he came into the

181

State Department without the benefit of significant diplomatic experience and with almost no contact in hemispheric matters.[2]

His rapid rise in business circles had not prepared him for his new role. Stettinius was unaccustomed to shaping independent policies. He preferred to discuss problems with his associates and arrive at a consensus. Shortly after Stettinius assumed his duties, Philip Bonsal, chief of the American Republics Division, urged him to put forth a positive hemispheric image by assuring Latin American diplomats in Washington that he embraced the Good Neighbor policy. His influence, according to Bonsal, depended on his personality: "Practically all of these representatives were and are close personal friends and admirers of Mr. Welles. All of them feel a definite sense of personal loss at his removal from the work which he contributed so much for so many years."[3] Unfortunately for Stettinius, he did not inspire the same confidence as his predecessor.

The major personnel changes at the State Department did not extend to field assignments. Jefferson Caffery at Rio, George Messersmith in Mexico City, and Norman Armour in Buenos Aires held their critical posts. Spruille Braden went to Havana from his station in Bogotá, and the career diplomat Arthur Bliss Lane assumed the embassy in Colombia and William Dawson went to Uruguay. These men directed vastly enlarged wartime staffs to handle the purchase of strategic material as well as maintain political stability. Critical bilateral decisions continued to be carried out, but the overall supervision, which connected the separate parts of the Good Neighbor whole, was severely impaired.[4]

The inability of the State Department leadership to formulate broad policies encouraged criticism. Some accused Hull and his subordinates of inaction when movement was essential. Others disapproved of the high percentage of wealthy men who received foreign service appointments. A few opposed the diplomatic corps as an elitist club and called for a thorough reorganization.[5]

The State Department faced an additional handicap in its congressional liaison. The administration had to rely on members of the Senate like Key Pittman, Democrat from Nevada and chairman of the Foreign Relations Committee, to defend the foreign service. Although he held that post from 1933 until his death in 1940, Pittman had no real international interest unless the silver industry of his home state was involved. His unfortunate weakness was alcoholism, and he was so intoxicated at times that he could not carry out speaking engagements. In August 1933 he talked with reporters about Latin America, proposing better hemispheric cooperation by scrapping the Monroe Doctrine and thus demonstrating the resolve to end military intervention. Even though the administration was moving in that direction, Pittman's counsel was seldom sought.[6]

His successor was Thomas Connally, Democrat from Texas, and he was not much of an improvement. Henry Wallace characterized him as "in some respects . . . the lowest type of senator we have. He loves to get at cross purposes with the White House and bluster around. He is essentially a demagogue with no depths of perception, no sense of the general welfare, and no interest in it. He has a high sense of personal dignity and is likeable personally. . . ."[7] He showed some of these traits in the midst of the Rio conference by predicting the fall of the Argentine president unless he adhered to the meeting's resolutions. To negate any retaliation caused by the widespread press coverage of Connally's remarks, which might damage Welles's negotiations, Hull promptly informed reporters that the senator did not speak for the administration. The senator, angered by this disclaimer, phoned the secretary and voiced his displeasure. He did not understand why Hull had issued an official repudiation.[8]

Other senators periodically criticized the State Department. Theodore Green, Democrat from Rhode Island, who served on the Foreign Relations Committee, visited Argentina in the summer of 1938. During his discussions with Ambassador Alexander Weddell, the diplomat disconcertingly reported that Senator Green lacked any strong commitment to the foreign service and even spoke of its abolishment. Joseph Guffey, Democrat from Pennsylvania, wrote Hull in early 1939 that he took an assignment on the Foreign Relations Committee because the diplomatic corps was profascist and anti-New Deal.[9]

These hostile congressional opinions of the diplomatic corps seldom extended to inter-American policies. Even at the height of the heated debate over Allied assistance, hemispheric security measures easily passed.[10] When Representative Louis Ludlow, Republican from Indiana, introduced a bill giving the people a right to vote on participation in foreign wars, he made an exception: "The proposal would not in any way interfere with our national defense, for if the United States or any other country in the Western Hemisphere is attacked or invaded the referendum would not apply."[11]

Congressmen frequently traveled to Latin America during the New Deal era to gain firsthand knowledge of the region. On August 9, 1941, one congressional group began a fifty-eight-day tour. At its completion the members noted certain specific problems, but optimistically concluded: "There was a sincere demonstration of real feeling toward the good neighbor policy. In no place, was the United States criticized or its general diplomatic policy toward South America."[12]

The aviation subcommittee of the House military affairs committee, led by Representative Matthew Merritt, Democrat from New York, took a 15,000-mile inspection tour throughout the Caribbean islands, Central America, and Brazil lasting from November 3 to November 20, 1943. When the committee published its findings on December 13, the members, while including some

criticism of current activities, generally favored a strong hemispheric commitment. A controversy arose over some of the committee's recommendations, which contradicted the administration's pledge to return air bases in
Latin America after the war. The Ecuadoreans immediately objected to the
report's suggestion "for the continued utilization by this [United States]
country of its Galapagos base after the war in the interest of hemispheric
defense." Other American republics wondered about the status of their
bases, for the report concluded that "the unsettled questions about the future
utilization of American-built bases are vital and pressing ones whose disposition should not longer be delayed." Did this mean that the State Department
would reverse its announced promise in the face of House pressure? This
question remained unanswered while diplomatic and armed forces leaders
fought over their roles in Latin America during the postwar period.[13]

The issues raised by the Merritt report were minor compared to the
charges that Senator Hugh Butler, Republican from Nebraska, made. He
had traveled through Latin America for fifty-five days during the summer of
1943, had talked to embassy officials and briefly discussed international
problems with local politicians. After Butler returned from his journey, the
State Department learned that the senator intended to launch a campaign
against the administration for trying to buy Latin American friendship, but
those forebodings were ignored.

Late in November 1943, Butler's attack, alleging that the government
had allocated over 6 billion dollars to win inter-American allies, appeared in
Reader's Digest. The administration, the senator charged, had doled out much
of this huge sum to worthless, duplicative projects, while bureaucrats argued
over who had the responsibility for these wasteful pursuits. Some of his
statements had considerable validity, but Butler had overdramatized the
abuses and exaggerated the costs.

At first the State Department did not know how to respond to this attack.
When the administration did reply, key Democratic and Republican leaders
accused Butler of acting irresponsibly and jeopardizing the Good Neighbor
spirit. The senator retorted that he, too, approved of the policy's intent but
objected to the economic wastefulness. This complaint found sympathetic
listeners; however, his initial foray was so extreme that his more moderate
criticisms were ignored.

Although Butler was forced to discontinue his unpopular cause, he re-
kindled Latin American skepticism about United States postwar intentions
and simultaneously sparked an outpouring of support favorable to the Good
Neighbor. The Latin American press aggressively attacked Nebraska's junior
senator for his inexperience in hemispheric relations. His allegations that the
United States had purchased Latin American allegiance was condemned, for
Latin Americans loudly proclaimed that no nation could buy their cooperation. Finally, commentators affirmed their belief in the Good Neighbor and
their backing for Roosevelt's wartime objectives.[14]

The State Department's inept responses to the Merritt report and Butler's claims demonstrated much deeper problems than poor public relations. By the end of 1943, the departure of Welles and the demotion or resignation of his close associates stalled inter-American operations. When Stettinius was unable to assume his predecessor's responsibilities, Hull took personal charge for shaping hemispheric strategy without having the necessary skills or the energy. His decision not only was a major personal blunder, but it also led to serious policy mistakes that shook the foundations of Latin American solidarity.

The first critical mistake came in Bolivian relations. On the morning of December 20, 1943, some disenchanted military officers along with the politicians from the Movimiento Nacionalista Revolucionario (MNR) quickly and bloodlessly overthrew the government of President Enri Peñaranda. By afternoon the new junta established order and publicly pledged it would cooperate in the Allied war effort by supplying strategic materials and crushing Axis subversion within the country.[15]

Neither the junta's unquestioned authority nor its pronouncement in favor of the United Nations satisfied the State Department. Hull, along with supporters like Berle, believed that the junta was pro-Axis and that Argentine fascists had inspired the revolt. The secretary accepted these allegations at face value and as a result refused to recognize the new regime. Duggan and Bonsal futilely argued for restraint until the La Paz embassy sent more detailed information, but Hull brushed aside the advice of two former Welles counselors. Instead, without substantiating the charges against the new leadership, the secretary hastily and unilaterally adopted a nonrecognition policy.[16]

Hull based his decision on two assumptions: the junta had assumed authority as the result of a pro-Axis plot and Argentina had encouraged this movement. The State Department decided that Axis sympathizers dominated the MNR using three factors: some party members met with Nazi officials, the MNR preached anti-Semitism; and the MNR used Yankeephobic slogans. These claims were vastly distorted. Some MNR officials had talked with German embassy personnel; a few even favored the Axis cause. This, however, was not unusual in a nation where the Reich had a prominent and influential following. The MNR did not subscribe to Hitler's beliefs in the inferiority of non-Aryan races; this would be political suicide given Bolivia's racial composition. Nor did the MNR follow the Nazi form of anti-Semitism. The party did claim that Jewish refugees took jobs from Bolivians, and opposed Jewish immigration for this reason. Other Latin Americans expressed similar opinions. The most dramatic incident came with the refusal by the Cubans to let almost 1,000 refugees aboard the *St. Louis* land in Havana during the summer of 1939. The MNR, like many hemispheric nationalists, also objected to foreign exploitation, and their attacks included United States firms operating in Bolivia.[17]

The coup d'état was not a Nazi-MNR conspiracy. Had Hull carefully examined Bolivian conditions in late 1943, he would have discovered that the revolt evolved from the political fragmentation since the Chaco War. That conflict depleted the nation's human and economic resources. Stability collapsed and coups d'états occurred in 1935, 1936, and 1937. After this three-year period of turmoil, Peñaranda, a popular general during the Chaco fighting, assumed the presidency. His military reputation, however, did not guarantee strong domestic leadership. Corrupt officials exploited laborers, especially in regard to the country's main export, tin. Late in 1942 a clash between miners and soldiers at the Cataci mines ended with a brutal massacre of workers. Political dissidents as well as military opponents used this incident to topple the government. When junior officers combined forces with the MNR, they easily overthrew the existing order.[18]

Hull, unaware of Bolivia's heritage, accepted simplistic notions of Argentine intervention and Nazi subversion as the rationale for nonrecognition. He ignored United States embassy reports from La Paz that showed minimal Axis and Argentine influence in the revolt and preferred to select those events which sustained his prejudicial beliefs. When the Buenos Aires government granted recognition to Bolivia on January 3, 1944, Hull's suspicions of Argentine complicity were confirmed. The Emergency and Advisory Committee for Political Defense meeting in Montevideo came to the secretary's assistance by calling for consultation of those nations participating in the war effort before recognition was accorded. Hull agreed to this recommendation, not to exchange information but to persuade Latin Americans to follow his nonrecognition lead.[19]

State Department hostility did not deter the Bolivian junta from trying to assure the American nations that it warranted normal diplomatic ties. The government continued its supply of raw materials to the Allies and also prepared for local elections.[20] Washington did not know how to respond to these steps, and this indecision bothered Bonsal, who warned on March 14, 1944, "that nonrecognition and economic pressure . . . are wholly unsuitable tools to combat nationalism, non-cooperation and Axis espionage activities in the other American Republics. Not only do they fail to secure the immediate results but they produce situations which are destroying the confidence and good-will which we have built up in South America during the past decade."[21]

Hull persisted in a nonrecognition policy without any criteria to normalize relations. Although the secretary denied that his actions strained hemispheric friendship, dissatisfaction began to emerge. Latin American leaders started to grumble, and rumors began to circulate that some of the American republics would defy the United States and shortly recognize the junta. Under these circumstances the State Department needed to find a solution to the Bolivian impasse in order to maintain hemispheric unity.[22]

The State Department tried to solve its Bolivian dilemma by sending Avra Warren, a career diplomat, to La Paz in May to examine the political situation, report his findings, and determine if a policy change was indicated. The action, rather than winning hemispheric applause, created additional suspicions. Hull had not consulted any Latin American governments before making his decision, and Brazilian Foreign Minister Oswaldo Aranha was especially upset by this omission.[23]

Hull's error in not holding consultations did not stop Warren from carrying out his assignment. He flew to Bolivia, met with government officials, and worked out a plan to restore normal relations. The junta would demonstrate its Allied loyalties by expelling about eighty agents and sympathizers. These measures would lay the foundation for recognition. After Warren returned to Washington, he argued that since the junta was fulfilling its promise the United States should resume normal relations. Prefunctory consultations followed, for the Latin American republics already favored the policy change, and on June 23 Bolivia gained hemispheric recognition.[24]

The Bolivians held national elections that July, where the MNR confirmed its popularity by winning a sweeping victory at the polls. The party's triumph surprised the embassy, but it stressed that the MNR had eliminated most of any Nazi influence and predicted that the new administration would fully cooperate with the Allies. Bolivia, however, would still be strongly affected by political activities in Buenos Aires because of heavy reliance on Argentine foodstuffs. Hull had tried to rid Bolivia of both the MNR and Argentine influence—he failed in both pursuits.[25]

The nonrecognition policy toward Bolivia was as unsuccessful as Welles's battle against Grau in Cuba. The undersecretary learned from his mistaken judgment and never again employed nonrecognition as a weapon in his diplomatic arsenal. Hull, who played a prominent role in the Cuban crisis of 1933 and who tried to reverse Welles's policy, insisted on exerting pressure for hemispheric adherence to recognition ten years later. Yet, after Hull enacted his policy, he did not know how to proceed. When the State Department finally moved, it did so initially without hemispheric consultation, which further weakened inter-American cooperation.[26]

Hull did not learn from his Bolivian errors; indeed, he compounded them in Argentina. That South American country's diplomacy called for its supremacy in the Americas. Oftentimes this position placed Argentina and the United States in conflict. Along with this political rivalry, both states exported many of the same agricultural products, which stimulated trade competition. Despite these problems the Roosevelt administration seemed to open the way for closer contacts when Hull and Saavedra Lamas combined their talents at the Montevideo conference to assure a productive meeting.

The secretary placed too much emphasis on this contact. The peace negotiations during the Chaco War settlement demonstrated how Saavedra Lamas dominated the proceedings. When he and Hull met at the Buenos Aires peace meeting, the secretary found Saavedra Lamas hostile to his proposals. He perceived this intransigence as a personal affront—something that he would never forgive or forget.

Welles viewed Argentina from a different perspective. The Buenos Aires embassy was his first Latin American post, where he spent the closing years of World War I observing Argentine reaction to the global conflict and its insistence on strict neutrality. Welles gained a firsthand appreciation of the Argentine national character and knew that the Argentine government had to be approached cautiously. His key to unlock the door to Argentine cooperation were prudence and patience.[27]

American-Argentine collaboration received additional support when Roberto Ortiz entered the presidential palace in 1938 to serve a six-year term. He wanted to strengthen relations with the Roosevelt administration and advance Pan American cooperation. At the outbreak of World War II his nation announced a neutrality policy, but at the same time Ortiz accepted the measures taken at the Panama gathering. His government urged a strong protest in regard to the *Graf Spee* incident, and the Russian invasion of Finland and the German occupations in Norway and Denmark prompted a bolder initiative. On April 19, 1940, Foreign Minister José Cantilo reasoned that, since the common hemispheric neutrality policy had failed to gain acceptance from the combatants, each American republic should protect its own best interests through nonbelligerency. This proposal would allow each American nation to treat the warring countries as separate entities. The State Department, surprised by this suggestion, rejected it without careful consideration. Nonbelligerency might involve altering current neutrality legislation, and Congress, reflecting the public's opposition to European entanglement, would balk at any kind of commitment. Probably just as critical, United States diplomats wanted to lead, not follow, Argentine proposals. Upset by the rebuff and intense domestic pressure, the foreign minister shelved the plan. The scheme demonstrated an unexpected willingness by Argentina to side with the Allies and illustrated the United States' inability to seize a favorable opening. Rather than move vigorously, the Roosevelt administration hesitated in the midst of domestic uncertainty, and after the Nazis invaded the Low Countries, the State Department supported only a weak hemispheric protest against Hitler's aggression. While the Reich disapproved of the declaration, German diplomats assumed that this measure was another indication of how Roosevelt, checked by internal pressure, turned to inter-American diplomacy to manifest his Anglophilism.[28]

The failure to win approval for nonbelligerency did not stop Argentina from acting in behalf of the Allies. One example was allowing congressional investigations of local fifth-column activities, which unduly worried the Reich ambassador, for the Nazi victories were impressing Argentine political and military leaders to become more receptive to German's interests. Buenos Aires steadily grew as the center for pro-Axis activities, at least partially because of United States unwillingness to take a more open pro-Allied stand.[29]

President Ortiz's terminal illness ended his government's Allied bias. An advanced case of diabetes left him almost totally blind by the summer of 1940, which forced him to relinquish his duties to Vice President Ramón Castillo, who had markedly different feelings than those of his predecessor. Since Castillo had not been elected to the presidency, he had to establish his own base of power. In order to achieve this political end, he tried appealling to the widest following by clinging to neutrality, opposing any move to severe Axis relations, and assisting the Allies with huge sales of raw materials to the British.[30]

The State Department concentrated its attention on Argentina's Axis leanings and ignored United States shortcomings like the cattle dispute. In 1926 the United States halted Argentine beef imports on the pretext that its cattle had hoof-and-mouth disease. The real issue, however, was not hygienics. American cattlemen wanted to limit foreign competition, and the congressmen from the cattle-raising states voted for the prohibition. This action caused great consternation in Buenos Aires and effectively reduced United States economic interaction. During the depression Argentine beef exports slipped by 25 percent, and United States markets also suffered a significant decline.[31]

In an effort to enlarge Argentine-American trade, the two countries signed a sanitary convention in May 1935 to allow for the importation of Argentine beef that was not contaminated by hoof-and-mouth disease into the United States. While United States cattlemen mounted a vigorous campaign against its passage, the administration thought that the measure would be approved. At the Buenos Aires conference Roosevelt confidently told an audience that the convention would go into effect, and the State Department pressed to make those assurances a reality. This lobbying proved fruitless, and by the summer of 1939 the administration conceded defeat. Neither house of Congress ever scheduled hearings, and the convention was officially withdrawn from consideration. The administration argued that this agreement would benefit both nations, but the cattlemen refused to listen and Roosevelt deferred to this domestic pressure.[32]

The administration tried another way to improve relations in April 1939 by accepting an Argentine bid to supply canned corned beef to the United States navy. The price was eight cents lower than the closest American competitor, but congressmen refused the cheaper offer. Raymond Springer, Republican from Indiana, argued in the House that by approving the Argentine contract, Roosevelt had violated the Buy American Act and reduced domestic livestock sales. As for inter-American cooperation, he held: "A good-neighbor policy is not one which materially helps the one and naturally hurts the other. That policy . . . is one of equality and of fairness, where due consideration is reasonably extended by each to the other. We have been the paymaster for the past 6 years, and our own people are suffering materially because of it. We have much to do within our own borders to rehabilitate our farmers, labor, business, and industry, and to save our own country."[33] This sentiment gained enough momentum to place an amendment on the naval appropriation providing that its foodstuffs must come from the mainland or its possessions.[34]

Congressional opposition to Argentine imports compelled the administration to seek other measures to improve bilateral economic ties. Late in 1940, for example, an Argentine mission came to Washington and signed two agreements; one was a 60 million dollar loan from the Export-Import Bank to increase trade, and the Treasury Department gave another 50 million dollars for currency stabilization. Neither measure passed the Argentine Congress, for by 1941 exports of wheat, beef, and tungsten had risen enough to make the loans unnecessary. Toward the end of the year the United States signed a reciprocal trade agreement with Argentina, giving the latter a distinct trading advantage; however, with enlarged purchases from the Allies, any possible United States political leverage was minimized. The Argentine government did not need its newly acquired market; the British one was more than adequate.[35]

The entrance of the United States into the war further complicated American-Argentine commercial policies. Secretary Morgenthau felt that the Buenos Aires administration's sympathies toward the Axis warranted economic sanctions, and in May 1942 he recommended freezing Argentine assets in the United States. Hull objected to economic sanctions at that moment, and he did not appreciate the Treasury Department's diplomatic interference. Roosevelt followed the State Department's counsel, but allowed Morgenthau to monitor Nazi trends in the Americas.[36] The president told the treasury secretary on May 14 not to do "anything to upset all the good work that has been done in South America." The following day Roosevelt added: "You know I am a juggler, and I never let my right hand know what my left hand does. . . . I may have one policy for Europe and one diametrically opposite for North and South America. I may be entirely inconsistent, and furthermore I am perfectly willing to mislead and tell untruths if it will help win the war. . . . If the thing gets worse *I* will send for all of the representatives of the South American Republics, and tell them what is going on in the Argentine."[37]

United States military leaders also were concerned about Argentine intentions. That South American state had the largest, best-equipped, and best-trained army, and its navy was more potent than the rest of the navies of the American republics combined. In July 1940 American and Argentine military representatives met secretly without coming to any conclusive agreement. Shortly after the Pearl Harbor attack, an Argentine military delegation came to Washington and applied for lend-lease aid. Welles declined to provide it until Argentina severed its bonds with the Axis. The Buenos Aires government refused and paid a stiff price for its decision. Without modern armaments, Argentina moved to second place, behind its rival Brazil, which became the leading military power in South America. Welles hoped that the awareness of this shifting power balance would make the Argentine military leaders apply pressure for the rupture, but this did not occur.[38] Neither country altered its course, and on April 10, 1942, Duggan summarized the situation: "We have been following a cool policy with the Argentines. We have given them no military or naval equipment and are scrutinizing every priority and export license request so as to give the minimum consistent with the maintenance of Argentina's economy. I think that this policy which is based upon the idea of helping those who help us, particularly when they have taken the risk, is beginning to bear some fruit in Argentina."[39]

Duggan's guarded optimism was misplaced. He waited for a change that did not come. Neutrality and pro-Axis sentiment had large followings. Although Castillo favored both of these policies, this did not guarantee him firm internal control. When he announced his handpicked successor in May 1943, a group of dissatisfied military officers who had organized a secret society known as the Grupo de Oficiales Unidos (GOU) earlier in the year planned a coup d'état rather than acquiesce to the president's choice. The decision by the war minister, General Pedro Ramírez, to challenge the administration candidate in the election precipitated a confrontation. To weaken Ramírez's presidential bid, Castillo called for the war minister's resignation of June 3. This did not strengthen the government's position, for on the following day the plotters used this firing as a pretext to lead a bloodless revolt that surprised Castillo and removed him from office. After a brief period of political jockeying, Ramírez became interim president. He privately promised the United States that he would break relations with the Axis, but the pledge was premature, since he did not have sufficient support to alter the existing policy. This predicament did not create immediate problems, for the new government easily won recognition.[40]

The political turmoil in Buenos Aires came at an inopportune time for both Argentina and the United States. Welles had resigned, and Felix Espil, Argentine ambassador to the United States for over a decade, had left his post. These men had directed their energies toward finding ways to accommodate the interests of both states in bilateral negotiations. Without their influence, inflexible and imprudent attitudes replaced the moderation that these diplomats had championed.

The new Argentine foreign minister, Admiral Segundo Storni, was not a trained diplomat. In August 1943 he showed his inexperience by writing Hull a poorly conceived letter, outlining his policies. Storni declared his personal allegiance to the inter-American system and the United Nations. To translate his wishes into concrete actions, the foreign minister needed time and implied that the United States could hasten this conversion by sending lend-lease aid to demonstrate the Roosevelt administration's support for his efforts. Storni did not understand the State Department's rigidity toward having Argentina sever its Axis connections before granting any military assistance. Despite his naiveté the foreign minister had outlined his pro-Allied goals and a willingness to work toward policies the United States desired.

Instead of using restraint in replying to Storni's communication, Hull answered with a scathing and intemperate indictment of Argentine transgressions. Lend-lease supplies, the secretary held, were solely for those fighting the Axis and not neutral nations who consorted with it. This response was just what the pro-Axis followers in Buenos Aires wished. They published the Storni-Hull exchange to illustrate United States antipathy. Nationalists claimed that the Roosevelt administration wanted them to compromise their honor for armaments. Rather than succumb to this intimidation, they demanded continued neutrality, which forced Storni's resignation and the appointment of a much more cautious successor. Hull had vented his anger against Argentine wartime conduct, but the result not only reinforced the strained bilateral relations, it also guaranteed an even firmer neutrality stand in Buenos Aires.[41]

The State Department carried its opposition to the Argentine government over to the issue of food supplies. Since the Ramírez administration exported its raw materials to the United Nations for profit and nothing else, Hull excluded her representation from international relief organization planning and also tried to reduce American-Argentine trade. These decisions proved counterproductive, for the Allies desperately needed Argentine exports. Even while the diplomatic corps publicly condemned the Buenos Aires government's Axis complicity, other United States agencies were expanding their food purchases. Hull ignored this agricultural dependence and acted only out of his slanted perspective. To disrupt the Argentine economy, for example, he reduced oil shipments—with disastrous consequences. Without fuel, Argentina burned wheat for energy, enough to feed two million people for a year. This effectively reduced Argentine wheat surpluses and decreased its availability for a war-torn world in need of this stable crop.[42]

Other Roosevelt spokesmen shared the blame for an unrealistic Argentine policy by pushing the State Department toward this militant position. Vice President Wallace openly denounced the fascists in Argentina during early 1944 and advocated strong economic sanctions. He predicted that the Nazis might use Buenos Aires in the postwar era as a base from which to launch their next war.[43] On January 28 he summarized his pessimistic outlook: "The South American situation still looks bad to me. My impression is that Argentina has not yet had a real change of heart and that the Nazi burrowing will continue. I feel there is great peril to the Democratic cause in Latin American through Argentina. The whole situation will stand a lot of watching. If we don't watch the Nazis with the utmost care in South America we shall be in for a very unpleasant awakening."[44]

Secretary Morgenthau echoed similar sentiments and applied constant pressure throughout 1944 for the State Department to freeze Argentine funds in the United States. Hull disagreed. He wanted to topple the Buenos Aires government, but freezing funds was not the answer. This dispute further embittered the relationship between the State and Treasury Departments, which served to heighten the distrust between the cabinet officials and led it to spread to their associates.[45]

The views expressed by Morgenthau and Wallace gained widespread public support. This fact plus the possible Argentine complicity in the Bolivian revolt placed additional pressure on the State Department to become more belligerent. Individuals like Berle worried that the Ramírez government was trying to foment revolutionary movements in Chile, Peru, and Paraguay. To halt this possibility, he wanted Hull "to get tough" with Argentina. Bonsal, offering a contrary view, called for patience. The United States would not gain anything by moving aggressively against Argentina. The secretary abandoned his usual cautious nature and chose to "to get tough."[46]

The Argentine foreign ministry quickly felt the change. The State Department assumed a more belligerent attitude. The United States also sent a powerful naval detachment to the River Plate as a symbol of Allied might in South America. Politicians in Buenos Aires furthermore appreciated the fact that Hitler's armies were retreating. Under these circumstances, Foreign Minister General Alberto Gilbert informed the United States embassy in early 1944 that his government would shortly sever its connections with Germany and Japan, and the official announcement came on January 26.

The belated action did not alter existing relations between Argentina and the United States. The State Department withheld the release of an exposé on Argentine assistance to the enemy, but Hull insisted on concrete anti-Nazi measures before providing any lend-lease supplies. While the embassy in Buenos Aires reported spy arrests and pro-Allied cabinet appointments, the United States did not understand that its refusal to establish friendlier bonds with the Ramírez administration weakened its internal control. Many GOU members, led by Colonel Juan D. Perón, held steadfastly to neutrality and deplored the Axis rupture as appeasement to the United States and an insult to national honor. Pushed by this local dissension in one direction and pulled by constant United States demands in the other, Ramírez resigned in late February and passed his powers to Vice President General Edelmiro Farrell.[47]

Instead of carefully analyzing the meaning of the shift in power, the State Department acted precipitously. After some superficial consultation with the other American republics, the United States announced its refusal to recog-

nize the new government on March 4. This nonrecognition policy was even
less effective than the one toward Bolivia. As a major hemispheric power,
Argentina exercised considerable influence. Chile, Bolivia, and Paraguay
acknowledged this fact by promptly recognizing the Farrell administration,
and others, like Brazil and Colombia, hesitantly followed Hull's lead. The
secretary also repeated another mistake that he made in the Bolivian case by
not announcing any guidelines for the resumption of relations. When Ambassador Norman Armour returned from Buenos Aires to confer at the State
Department in July, he suggested listing the requirements for recognition,
but Hull would not listen. Argentina knew its transgressions, according to the
secretary, and had to supply the remedy.

Hull's anti-Argentine crusade became a personal campaign to upset the
Farrell government. The secretary withdrew the United States ambassador
and demanded that other Allied nations follow his example; he applied
limited economic sanctions like freezing Argentine gold in the United States
and forbidding United States vessels from entering Argentine ports; and he
blasted the country for being the center of Axis espionage in the Americas.
While the secretary received widespread domestic applause for these measures, Latin Americans saw the Argentine-American embroilment as a conflict
between two traditional arch rivals.[48] Rather than seek some accommodation,
the secretary refused to compromise and told several Latin American representatives on September 12 that "the Argentine Government had fallen
into the hands of a bunch of desperados. Argentina not only deserted the
other Republics, it had gone over to the enemies." Nonrecognition stood.[49]

Welles contributed to Hull's obstinance by heading the public opposition
to the State Department's Argentine position. The former undersecretary
informed readers from his May 10 column in the New York *Herald Tribune*
that policy was seriously damaging hemispheric unity. Nonrecognition was
only useful as a prelude to hostilities: "The policy of non-recognition in order
to exert political pressure is always sterile." Welles correctly pointed out that
the United States had acted unilaterally instead of consulting the rest of the
American republics. As a result of these actions, the State Department upset
inter-American solidarity and allowed Farrell to assume the role of a martyr
against Yankee interference.[50]

Hull deeply resented his attack. Late in the summer he told Morgenthau
that his diplomatic subordinates had supplied the former undersecretary with
confidential information. These disloyal diplomats plotted against him
because rumors were circulating that once Roosevelt had won his fourth term
Welles would reenter the foreign service and end the nonrecognition policy.
Finally Hull dejectedly conceded that Roosevelt had done nothing to squelch
this gossip.[51]

The secretary was also distraught over his inability to gain British cooperation in applying economic sanctions against Argentina. The English bought
tremendous quantities of goods from that Latin American state, and Hull

asked Churchill to take part in a boycott.[52] On January 23 the prime minister appealed to the president against such a scheme: "We can always save up and pay them back when our hands are clean." Roosevelt understood: "I would feel the same way if I were a Britisher."[53] Hull fought for a hopeless cause, but still persisted in his futile struggle to persuade the English to join his crusade. He had the British ambassador from Buenos Aires withdrawn in June, an action Permanent Undersecretary of State Alexander Cadogan deplored.[54] That, for Cadogan, was the limit: "A row with the Argentine means a fairly heavy cut in our meat ration." He would go no further to placate the State Department: "We had already asked about as much as we were entitled to of the inhabitants of these islands. Why should we do more for a purely ideological election whim of old Hull—for it is nothing more."[55]

The secretary refused to concede defeat and continually lectured British officials on the evils of Argentine fascism. Hull even promised them that the United States would restrict businessmen from making postwar agreements with that nation to assure English markets in the region. The British response irritated the secretary. Its government officials either stalled or tried to mollify Hull with statements against Argentina's political system. He knew that Churchill's financial ministers were expanding their commerical ties with the administration in Buenos Aires. The secretary was not fooled by this hedging, but he had no recourse.[56]

Faced with Hull's opposition to the Argentine government and his own antipathy toward the Nazis, Roosevelt occasionally spoke out when the issues commingled. On October 15, 1943, he announced that the suspension of Jewish publications in Argentina was an internal affair, but that he personally abhorred this anti-Semitism patterned on Hitler's model. A few hours after Roosevelt released this statement, Jewish presses resumed operations. The president, in most cases, believed that Hull had exaggerated the situation. Roosevelt relegated the Argentine dispute to a secondary level; for instance, he wrote Getulio Vargas on February 19, 1944: ". . . I wish that Argentina would behave itself!" As the presidential election approached, Roosevelt declared his support for nonrecognition because of Argentina's Nazi activities. The president subscribed to an illogical argument that claimed that the Argentina people were democratic, while the small ruling clique followed the Nazi doctrine. The latter, Roosevelt warned, would be held accountable at the war's conclusion.[57]

Hull never understood his Argentine folly. He had little if any appreciation of that country's nationalism or the diplomatic rivalry for hemispheric supremacy. He ultimately convinced himself that Argentina was simply a "bad neighbor." "Our quarrel," he later reflected, "was not with the Argentine people but with the Government at Buenos Aires." He condemned its leaders and held the British responsible for their survival. Hull never realized that Perón thrived and rose to power because of the secretary's keeping Argentina in a state of flux through his inconsistent actions.[58]

Bilateral mistakes extended to multilateral considerations. Pan American conferences had played a major role in the Good Neighbor, and yet American foreign ministers had not gathered since 1942. By early 1944 pressure mounted for another meeting to discuss a wide range of subjects, and State Department personnel debated the merits of this idea throughout much of the year. Those who favored it, like Berle, Duggan, and Bonsal, had strong regional attachments and were closely identified with Welles, who publicly was already calling for a meeting. They argued that the United States needed to reinvigorate its sagging hemispheric prestige and offer new initiatives to regain inter-American leadership. Diplomats like James Dunn, Green Hackworth, and Harley Notter were in Hull's inner circle. They had a European outlook and opposed any hemispheric gathering until the major powers outlined general postwar guidelines.[59]

The secretary accepted the grand alliance argument and pushed regional considerations to a low priority. As a consequence, when Argentina called for a meeting in late October to answer charges made against its wartime record, the State Department was caught unprepared to deal with the situation. Hull had been hospitalized since the beginning of the month, which left Stettinius to shape a reply to the Argentine proposal. Before he responded, the undersecretary consulted the other American republics, and their reactions varied. Some felt that Argentina had scored a diplomatic victory; a few even wished to accept the initiative; and others desired a gathering of some kind to discuss wartime and postwar problems.[60]

While the State Department groped for an effective response, Mexican Foreign Minister Ezequiel Padilla, a firm backer of United States collaboration and hemispheric solidarity, took independent action. Since the beginning of 1944, he had discussed the possibility of a meeting with several Latin American ambassadors to include a wide range of hemispheric concerns. The State Department had been aware of his activities, but had paid scant attention and given no encouragement. Conditions had quickly changed and the United States began considering a Padilla-sponsored gathering as the alternative to the Farrell request.[61] Assistant Secretary Long understood the dilemma that Argentina had created: "It is considered impolitic to refuse and impractical to comply." When Stettinius presented Roosevelt with the issue, the president decided to back Padilla's conference; the Argentine proposal would, therefore, be postponed. Long did not quarrel with this approach, but wondered: "I am not sure now-a-days that things are properly and fully presented to the President and in such manner that he can pass on these matters with a full understanding of the consequences of decisions."[62] Long's doubts did not stop the State Department from asking Padilla to formulate an agenda for a possible conference. The foreign minister responded enthusiastically. He discussed his ideas with several Latin American diplomats in Mexico City, and they developed a broad agenda.[63]

One suggestion that the United States refused to consider was extending an invitation to the Farrell administration if the Buenos Aires government carried out the Rio resolutions and pledged to hold prompt national elections. Other American republics offered their suggestions, but all finally agreed to most of Padilla's original draft, with the United States' exclusion of Argentina. The United States did compromise slightly by agreeing to discuss the Argentine issue at the end of the meeting—after the official business was completed.[64] Even this modification did not hide the rigidity of the State Department, as one internal memorandum illustrated: "We would go into such a meeting 'loaded for bear' with the purpose of obtaining a final, irrevocable condemnation of the present Argentine regime. We have . . . made it clear that we are *not recommending* any discussion of the Argentine question at a meeting of foreign ministers, but we feel that it would play into the hands of the Argentines if *we* were to take the initiative in refusing them a hearing."[65]

In reality, the United States had agreed to the meeting as a maneuver to sidetrack the Argentine proposal rather than to shape some broad hemispheric consensus. The State Department focused on maintaining nonrecognition far more than on developing inter-American initiatives. To find a way to prevent Argentine attendance, this meeting deviated from earlier ones by admitting only those American nations that had cooperated in the war effort. In essence the State Department viewed the conference from an extremely narrow perspective—the Argentine proposal had be stopped and the status quo preserved. Enthusiasm for a meeting to strengthen inter-American solidarity was distinctly absent.

Hull did not take part in the preliminary discussions for the conference, but the State Department positions conformed to his views. Tired and ill, he was well aware that Roosevelt no longer sought his counsel. Pushed aside, he resigned just after the presidential election of 1944, and his departure received mixed reviews. Admirers praised him as an architect, while detractors labeled him inept. Neither of these characterizations was totally accurate; he was really somewhere in the middle. He won a national following for his advocacy of peace and reduced tariffs. Unfortunately for him, he had difficulty translating his lofty principles into specific plans. For that he heavily relied on Welles. After Welles's ouster, Hull's poor health and managerial inexperience became onerous burdens. Roosevelt compounded his problems by ignoring or rejecting his advice. The secretary took personal command of inter-American diplomacy with tragic consequences after Welles's departure. By the time of the secretary's resignation, hemispheric cooperation was seriously impaired on both the bilateral and multilateral levels. He blamed others for his shortsightedness and left the cabinet a frustrated, disappointed man, in large part by his own design.[66]

15 ★ THE REGION BEFORE THE WORLD

T
HE DISINTEGRATION of Pan American solidarity upset Vice President Wallace, who perceived that Latin Americans felt ignored—and worse, exploited. Writing in mid-December 1943, he observed: "It is a rather disturbing thought that we in the United States can maintain a deep interest in Latin America only so long as we think we have something to gain by it. I hope . . . during the next few years that Latin America will feel that we are really her friend and not merely a friend for expedient purposes in time of great need."[1]

Hemispheric leaders noted this deterioration, but they optimistically believed that as long as Roosevelt continued in the presidency the situation could easily be reversed. Although regional affairs did not play a role in the presidential election of 1944, Latin Americans applauded Roosevelt's victory. Indeed, some greeted his reelection with greater fervor than some domestic followers. Throughout the Americas, he had come to personify and symbolize friendship and understanding.[2]

Shortly after the ballots from the November election had been counted, Roosevelt promoted Edward Stettinius to the secretaryship. He had an agreeable personality but was incapable of directing the nation's foreign affairs. This fact did not trouble the White House, for in reality, Roosevelt conducted the country's diplomacy. He used Stettinius to relay instructions, or as Secretary Morgenthau sarcastically remarked, the new appointee was a "good clerk."[3]

Although Stettinius chose most of his principal advisers, by the spring of 1944 Roosevelt had decided to make Nelson Rockefeller assistant secretary of state for Latin American affairs. The chief executive liked the youthful coordinator of the Office for Inter-American Affairs and believed that he had handled his assignment with considerable skill. Rockefeller, after four years in Washington, was no stranger to bureaucratic intrigue and the importance of presidential support. He promptly learned that he owed his position to the president, not Stettinius. Rockefeller accepted that arrangement and relished his direct White House links.[4] He later recalled: "I don't believe in working from the bottom up. I believe in working from the top down."[5]

During his tenure as OIAA director, his relationship with Hull had been cordial until he began attacking the secretary's Argentine policies at the end of 1943. Rockefeller opposed the nonrecognition policy and vigorously supported the Argentine proposal for an inter-American gathering. He reasoned that the Farrell government had asked for the meeting and would have to abide by its results. If it refused, this would conclusively prove the Buenos Aires administration's unwillingness to conform with hemispheric wishes. Hull rejected this argument and began to look upon Rockefeller as an adversary.[6]

The new assistant secretary added to his problems by selecting his staff from individuals who had close connections with Welles. Avra Warren, experienced in hemispheric matters and departmental politics, became director of the American Republics Division. Besides these qualifications, Warren also had Rockefeller's trust, for he had cooperated with the OIAA when many foreign service officers had refused. One other appointment caused friction. Stettinius had unceremoniously fired Berle as an assistant secretary of state. Rockefeller valued his counsel and prevailed upon Roosevelt to make Berle ambassador to Brazil.[7]

These personnel matters were minor when compared to Rockefeller's inexperience in his dealings with the foreign service and its lack of consistent hemispheric policies. Welles viewed the OIAA as encroaching on his domain and treated the coordinator in like fashion. Thus the undersecretary confined any discussions with Rockefeller to matters directly affecting the OIAA and tacitly approved of State Department officials following that obstructionist course. Whatever knowledge Rockefeller had about inter-American policies had basically been acquired outside of the foreign service, which denied him valuable information concerning diplomatic matters.

After Welles's departure, hemispheric continuity fragmented. Hull viewed the former undersecretary's staff with suspicion and therefore ignored its opinions. Stettinius, furthermore, was unable to provide leadership in hemispheric matters. As a result Hull acted precipitously and often illogically. The inconsistent nonrecognition policies toward Argentina and Bolivia added to the confusion; Hull's intransigence toward a regional conference impeded any movement to formulate a hemispheric consensus on topics of mutual concern. This situation shocked Rockefeller when he entered office. He had the onerous task of solving immediate problems and restoring consistency. In both cases he did not have the benefit of having shaped earlier bilateral or multilateral hemispheric strategies. Without previous diplomatic experience or thorough briefing, he had to develop his own ideas.[8]

Since Rockefeller's authority flowed directly from Roosevelt, the assistant secretary presented the chief executive with his recommendations on January 3, 1945. Stettinius attended this meeting to discuss his own business, but did not participate in the hemispheric dialogue. Thus, by design or default, after this first encounter, Rockefeller met privately with the president to shape Pan American policy.

During the interview Rockefeller outlined and won presidential backing for ambitious programs. He called for cultural and economic collaboration, which included projects for public health, food supply, transportation, industrialization, agricultural diversification, and educational exchanges. Rockefeller emphasized: "Only in this way can we hope to have economic, social and political stability among the nations of this Hemisphere—without which we can never realize the permanent unity of the Americas."[9]

The assistant secretary also outlined his Argentine strategy. After he reviewed the State Department's position toward that nation, Rockefeller rejected Hull's dogmatic approach in favor of more flexible proposals. The United States had several options. It could guarantee Argentina's neighbors against any military threat or financial coercion. In addition, the Roosevelt administration could further isolate the Farrell government by cooperating with the British in the application of economic sanctions. Rockefeller presented another plan. The State Department had earlier suggested that the Argentine rulers turn over the government apparatus to the supreme court president, who would then declare war on Germany and Japan, eliminate subversive elements, and supervise prompt national elections. If the military leaders followed those recommendations, the United States would grant recognition. Without Stettinius's knowledge, Rockefeller decided to revive this idea and received presidential permission to send a personal emissary, a close friend and former Costa Rican ambassador to the United States, Rafeal Oreamuno, to see Perón.[10]

Before Oreamuno undertook his mission, Ambassador Berle had an opportunity to discuss this very subject with Perón from his post in Rio. On February 7 Berle traveled to Buenos Aires and spoke with the military strongman. After the conversation the ambassador concluded that Perón was in total command, refused to surrender his powers, and intended to conduct free, honest elections before the end of 1945.[11] Berle's impression was that this Argentine leader had "completely fascized the life of the country; there is no tangible opposition in sight. The bulk of the country is against him, but as they are silenced and cowed, nothing is going to happen." According to the ambassador the United States had "to build a high wall around Argentina, trying to make it clear that a military policy of this kind is going nowhere." The Roosevelt administration had to thwart Perón's aggressive designs by forcing him to follow a pacific path.[12]

Berle's position clearly paralleled the one that Hull had initiated and maintained. When several Latin American countries that supported this position expressed their concern over possible Argentine retaliation, Stettinius went so far as to discuss the likelihood of sending Allied troops to southern Latin America. Thus in early 1945 the State Department had two Argentine policies: Stettinius's publicly adhering to Hull's course, and Rockefeller's private diplomacy, leaning toward greater flexibility.[13]

While the State Department worked at cross purposes on Argentine nonrecognition, the diplomatic corps struggled with the Farrell government's request for an inter-American meeting. Many Latin American nations wanted Argentine attendance, but Stettinius refused. By mid-December the participants agreed to a meeting that was limited to those American republics collaborating in the war effort against the Axis. The Argentine proposal before the Pan American Union, which traditionally organized hemispheric conferences, was disposed of by a parliamentary table when the foreign ministers decided to make the arrangements through normal diplomatic channels.[14]

Rockefeller took charge of his duties after this decision had been made. He was not party to the discussions within the State Department leading up to the meeting. Those talks had centered more on how to reverse the momentum of the Argentine initiative—this approach was essentially negative. Rockefeller, unaware of this background, moved positively to make the gathering a major hemispheric event. He consulted several Latin American ambassadors in Washington, and working together, they divided the agenda under four headings: (1) prosecution of the war; (2) the future international organization and its relationship to the inter-American system; (3) economic and social conditions; and (4) Argentina. Rockefeller got this agenda accepted, and by early January 1945 the involved American republics had agreed to hold the meeting in Mexico City during mid-February.[15]

Invitations for the Inter-American Conference on Problems of War and Peace, better known as the Chapultepec conference, went out on January 10. The State Department on the following day announced that Stettinius would lead the United States delegation with Rockefeller serving as his alternate. Other foreign service officers, politicians, businessmen, and labor and agricultural leaders also attended, but the primary negotiators came from the diplomatic corps and Congress.[16]

The delegation's broadbased composition was not reflected in the method of preparation. Stettinius organized a committee within the State Department and chaired by Rockefeller to develop United States policies. Assistant Secretary of State for Economic Affairs William Clayton handled matters under his jurisdiction. Rockefeller, with Warren's aid, studied hemispheric subjects, especially the regional system and its place in the world organization. Rockefeller kept the president informed of the progress made in the preliminary planning sessions, for Roosevelt was particularly interested in Pan American social and economic problems along with their connection to regional and global associations' proposals.

Stettinuis personally followed this latter issue by assuming responsibility for the world organization topic. Two principal assistants in the International Organization Division helped the secretary. Alger Hiss had come from a prominent family in Baltimore, won his Phi Beta Kappa key from Johns

Hopkins University, and finished his university training with a Harvard law degree. He entered the New Deal as an attorney in the Agriculture Department and moved over to the diplomatic corps in the late 1930s. By early 1945 he was deeply involved and committed to building a global structure. Leo Pasvolsky was even more dogmatic in his support for a powerful world association. Born in Russia in the late nineteenth century, he had immigrated to the United States and became a citizen in 1911. He followed an academic career and joined the Brookings Institute in Washington, D.C., where he focused on international relations with a special emphasis on Europe and the Soviet Union. In 1936 he began working in the State Department as an adviser to Hull on trade matters. By the time of the preparations for the Mexican conference, this short, balding, mustachioed, bespectacled, and pipe-smoking scholar-turned-diplomat fully accepted the supremacy of a universal body to the exclusion of all others. Stettinius heavily depended on the views of these two men, but neither had any experience in hemispheric concerns.[17]

The division of responsibility for the conference within the diplomatic corps had one glaring flaw. Two different philosophies competed on how best to achieve a peaceful postwar world. Pasvolsky and Hiss, who had greatly influenced Hull, prevailed upon Stettinius to support a global body that would control the actions of any regional system. Rockefeller argued just as vehemently for the advancement of Pan American cooperation. Since each side directed its own committee, the inevitable clash of ideas was avoided during preparatory stages.[18]

Latin American diplomats were also active during this period. Many of them had distinguished records as experts on international law and played leading roles at the League of Nations, but they had been virtually ignored in the initial talks on the international organization. Suspicious of a global structure that did not reflect their views, they urged regional autonomy. This emphasis threatened to embarrass United States efforts in working with its major allies in behalf of the world organization, and Stettinius hoped that hemispheric attacks in this direction would be minimized at Mexico City.[19]

Economic considerations were featured as a preconference subject. Fearing repetition of the financial chaos following World War I, Latin American nations argued for a smooth transition from war to peace. The United States had already reduced its purchases of raw materials, and hemispheric leaders anticipated further decreases. After the war the prospects of unrestricted competition from other world markets and United States manufacturers turning their attention to domestic customers possibly meant disastrous economic consequences for the rest of the Americas. To eliminate this, Latin American commercial experts wanted some conference action to protect their interests through restrictive tariffs for infant industries, continued United States bilateral procurement contracts, and commodity agreements at wartime levels.

Many United States diplomats understood this anxiety. Rockefeller won presidential encouragement for the formulation of transitional programs from war to peace, using long-range development projects. Others, like Ambassador Messersmith in Mexico City, appealed for concrete proposals.[20] He warned on January 6, 1945, that the United States must make specific suggestions, for the "economic phase of the conference will be as important as the political and it will depend a good deal on the economic as to how the political will come out."[21]

These fears, in part, arose from worries about other foreign powers resuming their commercial contacts in the Western Hemisphere. Throughout 1944 and at the start of 1945, United States officials generally dismissed Soviet commercial expansionism in the Americas, but as the end of the war approached, there was a growing fear of Soviet interference. This feeling was qualified, for if the United States neglected regional economic growth, Latin Americans, faced with a depression, might look to a Marxist model for salvation. British competition was a far more immediate concern. The Churchill government not only had rejected financial sanctions against the Argentines, but concurrently, it had expanded commerical contacts. Some feared that British-Argentine ties were only the beginning of a major English drive to increase hemispheric markets, but Rockefeller, aware of the historic ties between these two nations, assured the English that the United States would not interfere with traditional trading patterns.[22]

The remaining conference topic focused on Argentina. The State Department hoped to relegate the question to a secondary level by insisting that the meeting's agenda not specifically mention that nation but use the broad heading of other matters for the conferees' consideration. The political, economic, and social problems, United States diplomats felt, were the center of attention. If the Argentine question gained too much publicity, this might detract from whatever positive accomplishments came out of the gathering. This tactic did not have the desired results. Leading up to the opening session, the policy of Argentine nonrecognition remained a central topic of the Latin American states.[23]

During the final stages of the Mexico City preparations, Roosevelt and Stettinius left for the Yalta meeting in the Crimea while Rockefeller completed the planning for the conference. He kept the secretary informed about the provisions of the United States resolutions, and when Stettinius was about to leave the Soviet Union, Rockefeller telegraphed: "Things are shaping up extremely well for the Conference in Mexico. There is a growing enthusiasm on all sides and I feel confident that the outcome will be of utmost importance to the future of our country."[24]

On his flight to Mexico City, the secretary stopped briefly in Brazil to confer with Getulio Vargas. Their one-and-a-half hour talk touched on vital issues: Soviet-Brazilian diplomatic relations, bilateral economic cooperation with the United States, the relationship of the inter-American system to the world order, and Vargas's hope for an Argentine invitiation to the upcoming gathering. Stettinius flatly rejected any participation by the Buenos Aires administration; as for the rest, he listened and made few substantive comments. The secretary did not realize that the Latin American representatives waiting for his arrival would highlight many of these same concerns.[25]

Rockefeller was far better prepared to discuss these matters. He frequently discussed hemispheric problems with Latin American diplomats in Washington with whom he had formed friendships since his days in the OIAA. As assistant secretary, he maintained these personal relationships to assure cooperation. To build a greater sense of unity, Rockefeller chartered a plane to fly to Mexico City and invited the Latin American diplomats selected to attend to accompany him, and most accepted. They departed on February 16 and arrived at their destination two days later. The assistant secretary believed that traveling together strengthened the spirit of comradeship, which contributed to Pan American solidarity and the prospects for a successful gathering.[26]

After Rockefeller arrived in Mexico City he coordinated the delegation's activities. One prominent United States member handled a major agenda item with assistance from others. Avra Warren was the single exception. He had no special assignment and was therefore able to act quickly if unexpected trouble arose. The delegation met each morning to talk over pressing issues. In the afternoon Stettinius held a press conference, which Rockefeller also attended in order to answer questions and coach the secretary.[27]

Avila Camacho, president of Mexico, opened the conference on February 21, and on that day Foreign Minister Padilla was elected the meeting's chairman. Both Mexican leaders addressed the assemblage, calling for hemispheric solidarity. Paraguay's request for an immediate debate on Argentine admission temporarily interrupted the harmonious spirit, but the motion was quickly set aside. Stettinius then spoke, pledging a continuation of the Good Neighbor in peacetime as well as during the war. Believing that he had helped to set a positive tone, the secretary optimistically predicted a successful outcome of the deliberations.[28]

The secretary ignored the fundamental political clash of ideas within the State Department before the conference opened. When issues that affected the regional and universal advocates arose at Chapultepec, one side fought for hemispheric exclusiveness and the other steadfastly held to a global frame of reference. Stettinius was unaccustomed to this kind of rigidity. He followed an organizational model where his advisers argued a question, a consensus was reached, and a decision finalized. During the Chapultepec debates, the two warring factions refused to work according to Stettinius's team concept.[29] Messersmith watched these events and commented: "Stettinius was . . . completely beyond his depth."[30]

When the delegation had no serious disagreements, the secretary's division of responsibility operated well. Adolf Berle, who had temporarily left his

Brazilian post to participate at the meeting, headed the United States staff at the deliberations before Committee I, called "Further Measures to Intensify Cooperation of the War Effort." Resolutions favoring continued wartime cooperation, armament controls, elimination of subversion, and punishment for war criminals easily won acceptance among the delegates, for these declarations did not raise any conflict between the regionalists and globalists.[31]

Discussions before Committee II, "World Organization," provided a quite different set of circumstances. Stettinius chaired the sessions, where Pasvolsky and Hiss prevented any serious discussion on proposals for a future world organization. To achieve this result, the secretary infrequently called meetings. This maneuver frustrated Latin American representatives; many of them had a great deal of experience at the League of Nations and wanted a thorough exchange of views to understand the new proposal in fuller detail. The United States tactics, which tried to prevent frank talks, did not stop hemispheric delegates from expressing their deep reservations over a potential world body. Latin Americans were concerned over the imbalance of powers made possible by the larger dominating the smaller nations, the lack of a strong international court, and a minimal commitment to worldwide intellectual and moral cooperation. Even though the committee passed several vague statements favoring some kind of world structure, hemispheric diplomats openly presented their dissatisfaction to some features of the future organization.[32]

Since Stettinius would not discuss the possible effects of a global umbrella covering their regional network, hemispheric strategists turned to Committee III, "Inter-American System," as their forum. Rockefeller and Senator Warren Austin, Republican from Vermont, led the United States representation before this committee. The Colombian Foreign Minister Alberto Lleras Camargo, who had actively displayed antagonism toward United States unilateral actions in establishing its nonrecognition criteria in Bolivia and Argentina and in setting up an international organization, chaired the sessions with every intention of discussing the relationship of the regional system to the world body.[33]

Major changes in the PAU also came up and were settled. Latin American delegates called for the enlargement of the PAU's scope, movement of its headquarters from Washington, removal of the secretary of state as permanent chairman of its governing board, and appointment of specially designated members to the union. The State Department objected to some of these recommendations, so Rockefeller and Lleras Camargo worked out a compromise. The PAU stayed in the United States, while the Latin Americans won on the other points. In addition, the conferees decided to schedule international conferences of American states at four-year intervals, annual meetings of foreign ministers except during the year of the international conference, and emergency gatherings at the recommendation of the governing board of the PAU. These actions brought the PAU's mandate into the political arena. Latin Americans had earlier rejected this. At Chapultepec, rather than fearing Pan American political activity, hemispheric leaders welcomed it.[34]

While these steps significantly enhanced the PAU's prestige, they did not hold center stage of the committee's debate. The main controversy centered on an initiative taken before the conference convened. On January 8, 1945, Rockefeller met with Eduardo Santos, a former Colombian president who had just returned from a Latin American tour. Santos's observations impressed the assistant secretary enough that he arranged an interview between the former chief executive, Roosevelt, and himself at the White House. Santos told Roosevelt that the lend-lease aid had fostered an armament race. Each American republic feared its neighbor's military potential, and therefore dramatically increased military budgets. The Colombian reasoned that dictators would use defense rhetoric to provide their armed forces with more sophisticated weaponry, which, in effect, would entrench their power. While these rulers increased their authority through military might, pressing social problems like illiteracy and malnutrition remained unanswered. As a result, totalitarianism gained and democracy lost. To reverse this trend, Santos suggested reviving the recommendation Woodrow Wilson made in 1915 to guarantee borders against invasion, thereby eliminating the rationale for massive armament races. Roosevelt liked the idea and promised his backing for a Colombian resolution of this nature at Chapultepec.[35]

The Colombians took this presidential encouragement seriously. Their delegation, with strong support from other American republics, introduced a resolution before Committee III for the guarantee of national boundaries. If any American nation committed an aggressive act, the others would consider it an attack against all and would consult to determine a response.[36]

Unfamiliar with the Roosevelt-Santos background, Senator Austin heard the Colombian proposal for the first time on February 27. Since he had not expected anything so far-reaching, he was unwilling to vote and stalled for time by asking to study an English translation and confer with Senator Tom Connally, whose arrival was delayed. After the session, he berated Rockefeller for not briefing him on the security measure. The assistant secretary then explained the events leading up to the resolution. The explanation satisfied Austin and that evening he revised the text to include sections on measures during wartime and during peace and conformity to the world organization charter. The senator deleted provisions giving power to mobilize armed forces by a majority vote of the American republics; he knew that his colleagues would never allow the Latin American nations to dictate the deployment of United States troops.[37]

The United States delegation held a hotly contested debate over Austin's textual changes on March 1. Pasvolsky strenuously objected to this scheme because it committed military forces without the world organization's permission. Berle rebutted for the inter-American system. If the world body had the privilege of deciding regional disputes, this decreed automatic foreign influence in the Americas. Europe, he stressed, had no intention of making similar concessions.[38] As for the opposition, Berle confided to his diary "that most of these world organization people regard the hemisphere as a positive enemy. It is interesting that they have no hemispheric experience and some of them very little experience with the United States."[39]

After both sides argued their points, the delegation agreed on a resolution, which was a clear victory for the regionalists: during wartime presidential prerogatives would meet aggression; after the war a treaty would formalize the commitment to guarantee borders in conformity to the charter of the universal organization. By March 3 the other delegates approved the revised draft. Promptly labeled the Act of Chapultepec, it leaked to the United States press, which, like the Latin Americans, enthusiastically hailed it as a symbol of solidarity and a guard against possible Argentine militarism.[40]

Although economic and social issues were widely discussed before the meeting, the deliberations before Committee IV, "Economic and Social Problems," and Committee V, "Economic Problems," were disappointing. Assistant Secretary Clayton directed United States efforts before those bodies and chose to disregard Latin American desires for concrete proposals on tariff protection, possible inflation, and transitional purchasing agreements from war to peace. He instead pledged to help Latin America during the postwar era without making special arrangements. Other nations, he observed, faced similar or even worse reconversion difficulties, and therefore the United States would not discriminate in behalf of the Americas. As some feared, in the place of specific action, lofty resolutions reaffirming the principles of low tariffs and equality of treatment passed.[41] As a consequence the economic and financial committees lost a valuable opportunity to shape postwar programs.

Argentina was the final agenda item. Unknown to the Latin American delegates, Rockefeller, upon leaving for Mexico City, received a report from his private envoy in Buenos Aires that Perón had categorically rejected any proposal to relinquish his authority. Without this knowledge, some hemispheric leaders before the conference hoped that Argentina would be invited if it made government personnel changes. Several Latin American diplomats even approached Rockefeller with a proposed similar to the one Perón had already refused. The assistant secretary, without telling the Latin Americans about this fact, consented to the initiative. He also informed Stettinius of this effort, and the secretary exploded. He knew that Hull would view this gesture as appeasement, but Rockefeller reassured Stettinius that the president had approved this action.[42]

The Latin Americans who had hoped for Argentina's return to the inter-American system were frustrated. Camacho had referred to Argentina as part of the family in his opening address, and its flag hung in the meeting rooms. Throughout the conferences the hemispheric representatives anticipated a positive reply from Buenos Aires to their suggestions. Stettinius, too, sensed this feeling, and began to minimize the role of subversive forces in Argentina. Late in the gathering, the delegates dejectedly learned the Perón had no intention of making any changes. Disappointed by this rebuff, they wrote a resolution calling for Argentina to declare war on the enemy, sign the Chapultepec resolutions, and adhere to the United Nations Declaration. Only after the Farrell government fulfilled these requirements would Argentina reenter the Pan American family. Padilla, as conference chairman, sent this resolution through the PAU to Buenos Aires. Thus, what had begun as an Argentine initiative to the PAU had returned there as an ultimatum.[43]

While most of the delegates wrestled with hemispheric questions during the closing stages of the meeting, Stettinius directed his energies toward the upcoming San Francisco gathering. On March 5 he announced that the United States was extending invitations to a conference that would create a world organization. In his statement he minimized any ideological conflict between regionalism and globalism. Privately, however, he ordered Rockefeller to prevent the formation of any Latin American bloc that opposed the objectives of the San Francisco meeting.[44]

The Chapultepec conference ended on March 8 to mixed reviews. Stettinius was delighted: the Act of Chapultepec reinforced hemispheric unity; Argentina did not disrupt the proceedings; and a direct attack on the world organization was avoided. Messersmith was also elated, for the United States had reasserted its predominance in the Americas. Others were less enthusiastic and saw little progress. Argentina was still unrecognized and banned from full membership in the inter-American system. More critical, the Act of Chapultepec had not settled the question of where the regional structure fit into the global one.[45] This did not trouble Senator Austin, who believed that the Mexico City resolution served as a model for multilateral cooperation. The establishment of the world body would relegate the regional one to a supportive role. If the parent organization failed, Austin foresaw: "The Inter-American arrangement would be a bulwark of security and peace, not merely for the Western Hemisphere, but through its influence, for all the world."[46]

Argentina also was looking to the future. The military rulers in Buenos Aires were concerned about declining prestige. The nation had been exluded from the Mexico City meeting and the same was likely to occur at San Francisco. To stop this from happening, on March 27, the Farrell government agreed to sign the Chapultepec resolutions and declare war on Germany and Japan. These steps did not signal any fundamental internal changes, for the present administration maintained control and the daily routine in the capital was unaffected. No question, the Argentine leaders took these measures as a purely opportunistic gesture.[47]

Despite the obvious insincerity, the hemispheric community welcomed these actions. Shortly after Rockefeller and several Latin American diplomats returned to Washington from the conference, they met with Roosevelt, and he told his guests that once the Buenos Aires rulers obtained recognition he would work for Argentina's admission to the San Francisco meeting.[48]

When the military leaders took their diplomatic actions, some, rightly suspicious of the Argentine motivation, wanted to proceed cautiously before granting recognition, but just the opposite occurred. By the end of March recognition momentum had accelerated, and at the start of April, Stettinius prepared to resume normal diplomatic relations and even selected Spruille Braden as ambassador for the Buenos Aires embassy. Roosevelt approved these decisions, and on April 9 the American republics formally extended recognition. Even in the midst of this activity, State Department officials differed in their understanding of the event. Stettinius and his close advisers did not consider the resumption of normal relations as an assurance of an invitation to San Francisco. Rockefeller did. Late in the month he decided that Argentina had fulfilled its obligations and recommended that it sign the United Nations Declaration as a formality for admission to the world conference. The assistant secretary, who regularly bypassed the secretary and worked through the White House, felt that the Argentine question was settled; others in the foreign service disagreed.[49]

As long as Roosevelt made foreign policy, Rockefeller was confident that his viewpoint would prevail, but the assistant secretary was unable to obtain a definitive decision on Argentine representation to the global meeting. The president was ill and had traveled to Warm Springs, Georgia, at the end of March to recuperate. His health appeared to improve; he was working better and sleeping more soundly. On April 12 just before lunch he complained of a headache, lapsed into a coma, and died of a massive cerebral hemorrhage in the early afternoon.[50]

An era had come to an end, but pressing questions remained unanswered. Shortly after Roosevelt's death, Germán Arciniegas expressed his sorrow and trepidation: "We, and our parents and grandparents, have had to rub our eyes to see and believe this man, simple and friendly, held to his chair by his immobile limbs, and his gaze taking in continents and oceans so that all people could recognize in it the gaze of man in love with freedom and justice." Roosevelt, to Arciniegas, personified the Good Neighbor, and he chose advisers who mirrored his attitude. "The question facing us now is knowing the fate in the immediate future of those ideals which Roosevelt and his Secretaries represented with respect to friendship between the Americas."[51]

The answer to Arciniegas's inquiry was that Roosevelt's death marked the end of Good Neighbor diplomacy. Latin Americans felt a profound sense of loss. More than a president of the United States, Roosevelt had become a citizen of the Americas. No one remained to assure continuity. Hull had retired and had neither the strength, disposition, or expertise to return and provide guidance. Welles and his close associates had been removed and discredited. Rockefeller and Berle lingered on, but they were not Stettinius's confidants. Without leadership, a void existed. What would a new, inexperienced chief executive, burdened by the enormous task of ending World War II and following a martyred president, do to carry on hemispheric programs that neither he nor his advisers comprehended?

16 ★ THE REGION AND THE WORLD

T HE ASCENSION of Harry Truman to the White House ended the Good Neighbor era. By chance, his last vice-presidential duty in the Senate was presiding over the passage of the Mexican Water Treaty, which guaranteed the development of common rivers for the two countries' mutual advantage. As president he signed this treaty as a symbol of the Good Neighbor's continuation, but this action and other statements in favor of Roosevelt's policies were mainly rhetorical. Truman simply lacked his predecessor's prestige, knowledge, and commitment concerning hemispheric affairs.[1]

Indecision within the State Department further contributed to this trend. Stettinius, with Roosevelt's death, moved from titular to actual secretary of state and next in line for the presidency. Since Truman wanted a regular Democrat to succeed him, the new president almost immediately began looking for a replacement, and rumors of this decision quickly spread throughout the capital.[2] Stettinius's own inadequacies compounded his ability to function. The day following Roosevelt's death, Secretary of War Stimson recorded in his diary: "Stettinius has not got a firm enough hand on his affairs and with all his pleasantness and briskness he does not make his machine go."[3] From inside the diplomatic corps, Rockefeller later recalled that the secretary "was a terrific hand-shaker, but he just simply could not make a big decision." He "was lost as soon as Roosevelt died." He "carried out Roosevelt's plans, Roosevelt's concepts, they were Roosevelt's emissaries and when Roosevelt wasn't there it's like pulling the plug out of the light, the light goes off."[4]

These leadership problems were temporarily hidden when Truman underscored his resolve to his predecessor's diplomacy. During his first evening in office, for example, the new chief executive assured the Allies that the San Francisco United Nations meeting would be held as scheduled. This announcement guaranteed the gathering's convocation, but neither the president nor his secretary of state realized that it also foreshadowed an acrimonious struggle between regional and global factions within the State Department.

Long before the crisis at Chapultepec, debate over the inter-American system's place in a world framework had been slowly evolving. Arthur

Sweetser, a League of Nations official, admitted in early February 1940: "There has always seemed to me to be something lacking in the relations between the League as a universal agency of international cooperation and the Pan-American movement as a regional effort for international cooperation." When the Germans conquered Europe, he feared global division—with the United States dominating Latin America. During the next two years, Sweetser talked to Roosevelt, Wallace, Hull, and Welles about a new universal body emerging from the League's origins, but he came away disillusioned by the responses. At a time when the nation needed careful planning and publicity for an effective international structure, the Democratic leadership refused to move boldly. On July 23, 1943, Sweetser implored Welles to act "if we are to avoid being completely lost in a forest of conflicting ideas and policies."[5]

Sweetser exaggerated the drift. The undersecretary, from the outbreak of the European war until his resignation, devoted considerable time to shaping a postwar international order that incorporated a major hemispheric thrust. Late in 1939 Welles established and chaired a State Department committee to examine postwar problems. While that body's deliberations proceeded slowly, the undersecretary started to speak publicly about a future world organization. In an address on July 22, 1941, he closely associated hemispheric and global peace under the same heading. Later in the year he warned an audience that the United States' failure to follow Woodrow Wilson's crusade after World War I must not be repeated.[6]

The undersecretary broadened the scope of his postwar committee's planning activities once the United States began fighting. His public declarations on a future international organization also became more frequent and explicit.[7] On May 30, 1942, he called for a worldwide police force and economic stability. Within his concept Pan Americanism occuped a key position in achieving these goals: "I cannot believe the peoples of the United States and of the Western Hemisphere will ever relinquish the inter-American system they have built up. Based as it is on sovereign equality, on liberty, on peace, and on joint resistance to aggression, it constitutes, the only example in the world today of a regional federation of free and independent peoples. It lightens the darkness of our anarchic world. It should constitute a cornerstone in the world structure of the future."[8]

During his last years in office, Welles reiterated and refined several themes: the hope for a lasting peace, a major United States role in postwar international relations, and a functional world organization that made provision for wide-ranging regional initiatives. Using these ideas as his base, he discouraged calls for an American League of Nations, for the world body would grant the Americas sufficient latitude to supervise their internal affairs.[9]

Vice President Wallace shared many of Welles's views. He urged a new League with strong United States participation to insure international economic cooperation. This was the only practical means to raise the world's standard of living, for if other areas prospered, the United States would benefit through the expansion of its overseas markets. The final result would be lasting peace. Wallace reasoned that the parent body would solve global disputes, while regions settled local ones.[10]

Hull remained silent on an international order until Welles's and Wallace's pronouncements prompted him to assert his position as the principal spokesman on foreign affairs. In the summer of 1942 the secretary gave a cautious address on a global structure, less dramatic than those of the other two men, embracing the largest conceivable consensus.[11] Shortly after the speech, Sweetser met with Hull, who recalled Wilson's humiliating defeat and the aftermath of disillusionment. Sweetser described Hull's mood as "very cautious, even discouraging, regarding the future, notably as regards post-war reaction, development of the United Nations. . . ." The secretary worried about a later administration repudiating his actions.[12]

Roosevelt only briefly considered this subject. He had vivid memories of his vice-presidential campaign in the 1920 election on the League platform, where the Democrats received a stunning rejection. During World War II his first objective was victory, then came postwar problems. When he discussed an international organization, he leaned toward Welles's opinions. The American public, the president knew, had accepted the Good Neighbor policy. Why not adapt that success to a world pattern? Roosevelt also saw the possibility of a worldwide police network with regional assignments controlled by the major powers: the United States in Latin America; United States and China in Asia; Britain and Russia in Europe; and Brazil, Britain, and others in Africa. These, however, were only visions; the president would let others speculate while he concentrated on defeating the enemy.[13]

Welles's resignation abruptly changed the State Department's emphasis on Latin Ameica in the world body. Hull placed Pasvolsky, an ardent advocate of universalism, to guide the postwar planning. This shift came through clearly after the secretary returned from the Moscow conference in late 1943 and announced plans for the formation of an international organization. When Hull reported to Congress, he promised to end special arrangements and spheres of influence.[14]

Latin Americans apprehensively studied Hull's statements. Did the secretary mean to abolish the special arrangement in the Americas? As the League's influence decined, the enthusiasm generated by the Good Neighbor increased. Hemispheric diplomats had promoted regionalism during the 1930s, reversing their earlier strategy of trying to turn the League into a counterbalance against United States might. In the area of postwar problems, the delegates at the Panama conference established the Inter-American Neutrality Committee (changed to the Inter-American Juridicial Committee in 1942). Although its deliberations had no appreciable effect on the future international organization, the committee showed hemispheric interest on this subject.[15]

Welles's departure and the subsequent cracks in Pan American solidarity created a greater demand within Latin America to strengthen the regional framework. Hemispheric diplomats pressed for talks on postwar issues, but Hull dismissed these overtures as premature. When the American republics took part in multilateral programs, these nations joined as Allies. The United Nations Relief and Rehabiliation Administration, for example, which was formed in the winter of 1943, grew out of worldwide considerations; Latin America had no distinctive assignments. Other steps within the State Department fit into this pattern of subordinating hemispheric desires to global priorities.[16]

Diplomats who specialized in regional questions warned against relegating the Americas to a secondary status. Duggan, on October 13, 1943, offered some cogent advice: "If we pay a little attention from this point forward to our friends in the other American republics we will have their support at the peace tables. If we ignore them, we will find them drifting into other camps."[17] Others reiterated this theme. Without collaboration, Latin Americans might form their own bloc to protect their interests. To prevent the disintegration of hemispheric solidarity, the United States had to handle Pan American questions with consummate skill. Unfortunately for these advocates, no one influential enough in hemispheric affairs remained in the diplomatic corps to have these recommendations accepted.[18]

Welles aggravated the situation within the State Department by lobbying for his regional approach from a public forum. Roosevelt, he argued, had to provide leadership in creating international stability by first negotiating an accord among the major Allies and then building a global structure with an executive committee where regional associations reported. Throughout 1944 he continued his press campaign. The State Department, he said, needed to solicit advice from nations like Brazil and Mexico. He refined his conceptualization of the world order. Using his rationale, hemispheric multilateralism formed the foundation for any world federation, and therefore the region should have autonomy to settle internal disputes. Welles's publications stimulated widespread discussion, but within the foreign service, they only served to reinforce Hull's antipathy toward whatever Welles promoted.[19]

The secretary's obsession against his former undersecretary's opinions had disastrous regional consequences. The announcement that the Dumbarton Oaks meetings, starting on August 21 and ending on October 7, 1944, and designed to draft international organization proposals, would be limited to the United States, Russia, Britain, and China surprised and infuriated Latin American diplomats. Hull had not consulted them or given them an opportunity to comment on the topics leading up to the gathering. Adding to the disenchantment, three days after the conference convened, Rockefeller suggested a dinner for the Latin American ambassadors and the British and

Soviet delegations, but the State Department hierarchy even rejected this social encounter.[20]

The Dumbarton Oaks talks briefly brushed on matters concerning the Americas. The delegates promptly disposed of the regional issue on September 7 by deciding to subordinate it to global concerns. Regional bodies only had power to settle local disagreements with security council approval. In regard to the security council, the participants agreed on eleven members with five permanent seats. On August 28 Roosevelt flirted with an idea of making Brazil the sixth member, but Stettinius dissuaded him. The secretary claimed that the British and Soviets objected; he neglected to mention his own reservations that if the Brazilians were represented, others would complain about Brazil's prestige and demand equality.[21]

Before the conference concluded, Hull realized his mistake is not consulting the hemispheric leaders. To repair the damage, he met twice with several Latin American ambassadors in mid-September, promising to defend their rights during the talks and continue the Good Neighbor commitment. He pleaded for trust and pledged thorough consultations on the world structure after the current sessions ended.[22]

Hull kept his word. After the conference adjourned, he advocated a presidential address before the Latin American ambassadors on Columbus Day.[23] Roosevelt accepted this advice and on October 12 he told his audience that the world must prevent future wars through understanding. The formation of the Grand Alliance, Roosevelt stressed, had not diminished Latin America's importance, for "the inter-American system can and must play a strong and vital role."[24]

Following the speech Stettinius hosted a reception for the Latin Americans across from the White House at Blair House, where he outlined the Dumbarton Oaks proposals. The undersecretary tried to reassure his guests that the United States had carefully considered Pan Americanism in the discussions and wanted their reactions to the proposals. These introductory statements marked the start of informal Blair House gatherings between the United States and Latin American representatives that lasted until the end of the year. Rockefeller, who attended the first session, offered suggestions to Stettinius, which he valued; he invited the coordinator to participate at subsequent meetings. Stettinius believed that these exchanges helped to restore hemispheric solidarity and optimistically predicted Pan American unity at San Francisco.[25]

The Latin Americans did not reach the same conclusions. Their representatives repeatedly asked questions about regional autonomy under the United Nations and the power of the larger over the smaller nations. As the Chapultepec meeting approached, Latin American opposition to the security council veto, the absence of a permanent Latin American council seat, and the destruction of regional independence grew more vocal. Speaking for the

State Department, Pasvolsky reiterated his central theme: regionalism decentralized authority and thus weakened the universal nature of the organization. To him, these exchanges were meaningless:[26] "The meetings continue to be slow and tedious, with lengthy speeches."[27] He did not perceive that many Latin Americans had arrived at the same conclusion.

While the State Department's inept handling of the Dumbarton Oaks talks crushed the multilateral consensus, the Roosevelt administration also mishandled the issue of the "associated nations." When the United States declared war, it wanted the other American republics to sever relations with the Axis—not declare war. The State Department reasoned that the Latin American war declarations would make those countries vulnerable to attack, and the United States did not have sufficient forces to defend them. Thus, when six Latin American nations ruptured Axis ties, they were designated "associated nations." This label allowed them to participate at Allied and Pan American conferences, and at the same time the United States did not have to worry about their military weakness. Problems arose in early January 1945, when Roosevelt secretly agreed to Stalin's proposal making admission to the San Francisco meeting dependent on United Nations membership. This decision forced the State Department to have the six nations declare war without providing the rationale.[28]

Rockefeller recognized the embarrassment of complying with this decision by the "associated nations." Why should Latin Americans make war on a nearly exhausted enemy for no apparent reason? To achieve the desired result, the assistant secretary decided to resolve this delicate issue by having Roosevelt address personal letters to the presidents of the involved countries; Rockefeller would concurrently explain the situation to their Latin American ambassadors in Washington. Before he had sufficient time to complete these steps, Roosevelt and Stalin arbitrarily set March 1 as the deadline for the "associated nations" declaration of war. All signed the United Nations Declaration by late February, but the need for this measure remained a mystery, adding to Latin American doubts concerning the great powers' intentions.[29]

Faced with attacks on regional autonomy, the Latin Americans pushed vigorously at Chapultepec for hemispheric exclusiveness. The Mexico City resolutions clearly envisioned a postwar treaty granting considerable inter-American independence, but this victory did not satisfy hemispheric representatives. Roosevelt's death created grave fears about United States motives, for he alone had guaranteed inter-American solidarity. Stettinius and his advisers favored a mighty United Nations with subservient satellites. Latin Americans knew that, if unchecked, these foreign service officials would destroy the inter-American system at San Francisco.

The membership of the United States delegation gave no comfort to the Latin Americas. Hull, too ill to attend, had the honorary title of senior

delegate. Stettinius led the delegation with powerful congressional participation from Tom Connally and Arthur Vandenberg, Republican senator
from Michigan. Harold Stassen, a midwestern Republican, also took part
in crucial negotiations. While the individuals came from varied backgrounds,
these men had one common deficiency—none had any significant Pan American experience.[30]

The United Nations conference opened on April 25 with a message from
Truman calling for a successful meeting. The next day's organizational proceedings quickly cast doubts on that outcome. British Foreign Minister
Anthony Eden was selected to nominate Stettinius as the conference's
permanent chairman. Eden, however, learned that the Russians wanted a
rotating chairman among the Big Four (the United States, Britain, China, and
Russia), and he unilaterally decided to introduce a compromise. Instead of
making the expected speech, he recommended a rotation of chairmen at
plenary sessions and Stettinius as permanent chairman of the executive and
steering committees.

Mexican Foreign Minister Padilla, whom Stettinius had asked to second his
nomination, was surprised by Eden's statement, but proceeded as if the
British foreign minister had made the expected nomination. As representative of the host nation, Padilla asserted, Stettinius was the logical and appropriate choice for the permanent chairman. Russian Commissar for Foreign
Affairs Vyacheslav Molotov vigorously objected to the Mexican's viewpoint
and accused Padilla of acting as a United States puppet. Already suspicious of
the international organization's prerogatives, the Latin American delegates
took the Soviet's assault on Padilla as an affront to the entire inter-American
system. Molotov's opposition did not muster enough votes for his cause,
and Stettinius became permanent chairman. This was a minor defeat for the
Russian. His major blunder was that he unified the Latin American representatives in their attempts to defend Pan Americansim from hostile Soviet
actions.[31]

The formation of the Latin American bloc was only one of Stettinius's
concerns as chairman. In the morning he chaired his delegation's meetings,
seeking a consensus on various issues; during the afternoon he held press
conferences, where, on many occasions, he allowed others to present and
interpret United States positions; in the evening he tried to find solutions to
a multitude of questions by meeting with an assortment of foreign diplomats. For assistance in his efforts he relied heavily on Hiss and Pasvolsky,
who were only two of approximately two hundred experts and technicians
attached to the American staff. Over forty-two different associations also
lobbied frantically to influence the delegation for a variety of causes. In the
midst of contradictory advice, the secretary frequently called his bedridden
predecessor at the Bethesda Naval Hospital for guidance.[32] Messersmith, who
happened to be with Hull on one occasion, recalled: "Stettinius was dealing

with matters in which he had no adequate preparation and in which he had no background nor experience, and by the very nature of his position was required to make decisions."[33]

Stettinius added to his predicament by excluding any Latin American expert from the delegation. Rockefeller, for instance, was not even listed as a staff adviser. Despite his exclusion he chartered a plane and flew most of the hemispheric representatives to the conference as his guests. Instead of taking rooms at the Fairmont Hotel with the United States members, he stayed at the St. Francis, which was the headquarters for the other American republics. Each morning over breakfast he met with a group of Latin American diplomats to plan strategy. Rockefeller kept this from Stettinius, for the assistant secretary distrusted many of the secretary's advisers—a feeling they reciprocated. This mutual suspicion did not diminish the United States reliance on Latin America. Those countries represented almost 40 percent of the voting nations, and the secretary forced Rockefeller into the difficult position of an intermediary between the United States and Latin American delegations. As a mediator he had to convince either or both sides to cooperate. Given the emotions raised by some of the issues, this task, at times, was a seemingly impossible and thankless one.[34]

The first major problem came over inviting Argentina to participate at the conference. Before the start of the meeting, the State Department queried its major allies on this subject. The British had no objections, but Stettinius expected Russian opposition. On two separate occasions at Yalta, the secretary listened to Stalin suggest punishment for Argentina's Axis sympathies. Both times Roosevelt excused these as reflection of the authoritarian rulers and not the majority's democratic spirit.[35]

Following the Chapultepec conference, the Farrell administration gained recognition from the other American republics in mid-April. It even asked to sign the United Nations Declaration, which assured a San Francisco invitation, and to establish diplomatic relations with the Soviet Union and China. Although the March 1 deadline set at Yalta for admission to the conference had expired, Roosevelt had told several Latin American diplomats along with Rockefeller that as president, he would support an Argentine invitation after it took those positive steps. Stettinius informed Truman of that pledge. Neither man liked it, but they both agreed to honor Roosevelt's word unless some maneuver could be found to forestall Argentine admission.

Any possible delay or rejection disappeared on the first day at San Francisco, when Molotov demanded the enforcement of a Yalta agreement seating White Russia and the Ukraine at the conference. The Latin Americans accepted this Soviet action on behalf of its two satellites as fulfilling a promise made by Roosevelt and extended the same rationale for Argentine admission.

The United States delegation never had an opportunity to discuss the merits of an Argentine invitation because of the Russian ultimatum. Until the two Soviet republics won seats, other activities ceased. The Latin Americans capitalized on this dispute. They considered Argentina a parallel case and took their own unequivocal stand. If the two satellites received membership, Argentina must. Unable to divide these issues, the United States considered its quandary. If the members supported the Russians and not the Latin Americans, Rockefeller warned that hemispheric solidarity would collapse. Molotov complicated the picture by offering his own solution. He would consent to Argentine admission if the Soviet-sponsored Lublin government in Poland was invited. Since its composition was the subject of Big Three (United States, Russian and British) negotiations, the American and British delegations flatly rejected bringing this emotional and politically charged question to the meeting.[36]

After an acrimonious debate within the United States delegation, it decided to support both the Soviet republics' and Argentine invitations. These measures passed on April 30, and afterwards Molotov held a press conference. He deplored the decision to invite a fascist nation while Poland was absent and quoted from statements by Roosevelt and Hull to lend greater credence to his charges. Molotov's attack did not bother the Latin Americans, for they had Argentina seated.

Argentina was not invited because it had met the admission criteria, but because of a dispute between the major powers. The invitation of the two Soviet republics started the debate, and Molotov's efforts to include the Lublin government further distorted the issues. The Big Four opened the breach and the Latin Americans widened it. Argentina's wartime activities never received a full airing to decide on a standard for its invitation.[37]

Stettinius added to the controversy over Argentine admission by publicly refusing to let Argentina sign the United Nations Declaration and announcing his own reservations toward the fascist nature of the Buenos Aires administration. He failed to mention that the Russians had precipitated the crisis. Rather than offend Molotov, he tarnished his own reputation by issuing inconsistent and damaging statements. From his vantage the resolution of the seating dispute preserved the conference and allowed the delegates to begin drafting the charter.[38]

Prominent Americans who advocated Soviet-American friendship worried about this incident. Henry Wallace, for example, feared that the American delegation sided with the Latin Americans against the Russians. Joseph Davies, a former ambassador to Russia, believed that Argentine admission would confirm Communist prophesies of a United Nations dominated by Western Europe, the United States, and Latin America. Stalin might consider this issue as a prelude to isolate or contain his nation.[39]

Avid regionalists maximized hemispheric unity over Allied harmony. They preferred autonomy to Russian subservience. Rockefeller applauded Argentine admission as a forward step for inter-American solidarity. Samuel Inman, who watched the events at San Francisco, believed that the Latin Americans worked for Argentina's participation to strengthen Pan Americanism. Padilla, for instance, ignored the internal fascist policies of the Buenos Aires government and reasoned that the United Nations would force its rulers to change.[40]

From his post in Rio, Berle offered a glimpse into his ambivalent thinking that troubled many United States diplomats. Equally opposed to fascism and communism, Berle felt that the actions taken in regard to Argentina and the Soviet Union tarnished the American image in the hemisphere. He opposed Perón and therefore Argentine admission, which increased the military leader's prestige. At the same time he deplored any Communist penetration in the hemisphere and felt that the debate over the Argentine seating gave the Soviets an opportunity to influence Pan American affairs as never before. The ambassador blamed these events on Rockefeller's inexperience. Yet, Berle volunteered no solutions, just observations.[41]

Hull reluctantly supported the Argentine invitation in order to preserve hemispheric solidarity, but he did not disguise his disdain for those who made it possible. Pasvolsky provided the former secretary with his prejudicial account of the delegation's debate centering on Rockefeller's activities.[42] During a phone conversation with Pasvolsky on May 10, Hull vented his anger against the assistant secretary and his chief adviser, Warren. The former secretary condemned the American membership for turning "over the leadership to those South American politicians and two or three third-raters in the State Department. They will grab the leadership and lead us into more sinkholes before we know it, just like the Argentine thing."[43]

The United States delegation simply was unprepared to act on major regional issues. At a preliminary meeting to the conference on April 10, the delegates merely reaffirmed support for the Dumbarton Oaks proposals giving the security council veto power over regional action. Pasvolsky reiterated his opinion that the universal body superseded all others. Distorting the events at Mexico City, he declared that the Act of Chapultepec solely applied to wartime; thereafter, the United Nations gained supremacy.

Rockefeller, speaking for the minority, vigorously dissented. The Chapultepec conference clearly anticipated a postwar treaty for a strong American association. The Latin Americans, the assistant secretary cautioned, would fight any measure aimed at reducing hemispheric autonomy. Hemispheric leaders feared Soviet agitation in the Americas, and the Russians veto right would effectively eliminate any Pan American response. Since none of Rockefeller's listeners understood the magnitude of the problem, his arguments were ignored. The Latin American fears about post-Roosevelt changes toward the hemisphere proved valid.[44]

Regionalists received unexpected support from Secretary Stimson. He did not influence the preparatory discussions for the global gathering, but had serious reservations about the universal framework and relayed these to the military advisers at San Francisco. To him, the Monroe Doctrine was a bulwark of American diplomacy. Even the League of Nations, Stimson pointed out, had accepted the doctrine in its charter, acknowledging United States hegemony in the Americas.[45] On April 29 he warned: "If this Administration consents to an overriding of the Doctrine, they are in for trouble. But it is pretty hard to handle such international problems indirectly and at a long distance when the protagonists are young, ignorant, and inexperienced."[46]

The regional question, surprisingly, did not spring from any Western Hemispheric plan. Instead, the French and Soviet delegations, with tacit English approval, offered an amendment to the Dumbarton Oaks proposals exempting the security council veto from Allies negotiating bilateral treaties that would prevent a German military resurgence. Pasvolsky, expressing United States consent, accepted this change for two reasons: (1) these arrangements would only last until the security council demonstrated its power, and (2) the treaties were directed against the Axis.[47]

The American delegation considered these alterations from the European perspective. Its members did not seriously envision any hostile Latin American reaction. No one asked the critical question: If the Europeans exempted their continent from the veto, why not apply the same standard to the Americas? Stettinius saw this inconsistency but quickly dismissed it. The Big Four had agreed on a formula for regional arrangements; the problem was solved.[48]

After Argentina's seating, Rockefeller flew to Washington, reported to the president, and testified before the House appropriations committee. Upon his return to San Francisco on May 5, he learned that the Allies had exempted their military alliances from the security council veto, but this did not similarly apply to the treaty promised at Chapultepec. Rockefeller realized that Stettinius did not comprehend the full significance of this position and sought an interview. He was told to see Pasvolsky.[49]

Rather than hold fruitless talks with his adversary, Rockefeller chose another approach. He arranged a dinner for himself, several Latin Americans, and the most powerful Republican member of the United States delegation, Senator Vandenberg. The hemispheric diplomats explained their position. They did not oppose European regional treaties but did ask for equal treatment. As the senator listened to these objections, he raised his own. If the Monroe Doctrine was eliminated, he knew that the Senate would never ratify the United Nations charter. To inform the delegation of these fears, Vandenberg, with assistance from Rockefeller and Colombian Foreign Minister Lleras Camargo, drafted a letter and sent it to Stettinius with copies to the rest of the membership. It raised three fundamental questions: (1) Did the denial of equal treatment for a regional alliance under the Act of Chapultepec mean that the United States was abandoning its Pan American pledges at Mexico City for an untested United Nations? (2) How would the unilateral aspects of the Monroe Doctrine be guaranteed if non-American nations had the power to veto regional initiatives? and (3) Would the Senate accept such radical changes in American diplomacy?

After the delegation received the Vandenberg letter, they held a heated debate on the morning of May 7. In many respects the opinions reflected the same philosophical differences expressed at the Mexico City meeting. Dividing into two groups, Vandenberg and his congressional colleagues supported by Rockefeller and the military advisers demanded a hemispheric exemption for regional alliances from the security council veto.[50] Pasvolsky, speaking for the other side, retorted: "If we open the way anywhere to regional action, the world organization is finished. . . . There will be four or five armed camps consisting of groups of nations . . . and another world war."[51]

The Latin Americans rejected this argument in their own caucus that evening and voiced displeasure over what they conceived to be United States favoritism toward Europe. To some the American diplomatic actions foreshadowed renunciation of the pledges made at Chapultepec and abandonment of Latin America in the postwar period. Others worried about a rising Soviet presence through Communist party gains in the wake of Pan American disintegration. Certain delegates were so disillusioned and exasperated that they threatened to leave San Francisco if the inter-American system lost its independence.[52]

At the height of the conflict, hemispheric leaders met at Stettinius's penthouse to discuss their grievances. The Latin Americans repeated their concern that the Truman administration was crushing Pan Americanism for an untried world order. If the United Nations replaced the inter-American system, each Latin American country would look to a permanent security council member for protection. Hemispheric representatives believed that this kind of maneuvering would destroy regional understanding. Stettinius saw the logic of these arguments and recalled the threat of Nazi penetration in the Americas to undermine United States security and wondered if the Soviets had similar intentions. This exchange had shaken the secretary's support toward globalism, and he promised to find a solution that would preserve the inter-American system and maintain a world order. Lleras Camargo pledged his cooperation in this effort and reminded his host that he chaired the committee that handled the regional question. He did not need to add that until this issue was resolved, the Latin Americans virtually halted other conference proceedings.[53]

Stettinius wrote in his diary on May 8 that the regional issue "was now wide open." Smaller nations like Australia asked for changes in the Dumbarton Oaks proposals, and rumors circulated that the Arab delegates wanted to combine forces with the Latin Americans to defeat the original regional resolution. The United States delegation was sharply split. Pasvolsky un-successfully appealed directly to Hull for his intervention. Stimson urged his advisers to back hemispheric autonomy—even at the expense of Russian antipathy. This division within the United States delegation disrupted unity among the larger nations, which added to the confusion and delay in reaching a viable solution.[54]

In the midst of the dispute, Rockefeller met privately with Stassen to see if they could find a solution. As a result of their discussion the Minnesotan introduced a new approach to his colleagues on May 10. The Latin Ameri-cans, he held, objected to the security council's authority halting regional initiatives to resolve hemispheric matters. To meet this objection, he argued that the charter should protect the signatories' rights of self-defense. Thus he wanted to add provisions declaring: (1) nothing would abrogate the right of self-defense against a nation that violated the charter; (2) the principles in the Act of Chapultepec and the Monroe Doctrine were recognized by the world organization; and (3) any nation had an automatic privilege to use pacific measures for settling disputes without prior security council permission.[55]

The United States delegation approved Stassen's suggestions and lobbied for their acceptance. On May 11 Eden reacted unfavorably, holding re-gionalism would destroy globalism. Vandenberg, Connally, and Stassen tried to change his views. The senators stressed the difficulty of ratifying the charter without protecting the Monroe Doctrine; they also mentioned their troubles with the Latin Americans, who were demanding an autonomous regional system. Eden became more conciliatory and rewrote the draft, accepting the concept of self-defense while deleting specific references to the Act of Chapultepec and the Monroe Doctrine. By evening the United States membership had approved the foreign minister's wording, and Truman gave his consent the following day.[56]

Stettinius met with Latin American leaders on May 14 to gain their concurrence for the new draft. Lleras Camargo objected to the deletion of specific hemispheric references. Without that clarification the United Nations might reinterpret the clauses at some future date to destroy Pan Americanism. Both Connally and Vandenberg pledged to prevent this by making these points clear in their report to the Senate foreign relations committee. The Latin Americans wanted more substantial assurances. If no mention was made of the Act of Chapultepec or the Monroe Doctrine, hemispheric leaders wanted a pledge to enact the regional postwar treaty promised at Mexico City in the near future. Since only Truman could provide this guarantee, Stettinius phoned him on May 15 and received support for an inter-American con-ference in the autumn to formalize the Act of Chapultepec in treaty form. The secretary informed the Latin Americans of this presidential pledge, and Connally reinforced it with his backing. These actions were sufficient; the Latin Americans agreed to vote for the existing draft.[57]

The major powers gave their qualified acceptance four days later. After several minor Soviet changes, on June 9 the conferees passed Article 51 providing for collective self-defense without security council permission; Article 52 allowed for regional arrangements that would try to achieve peaceful settlements of local problems; Article 53 guaranteed the Allied alliances against enemy states; and Article 54 reaffirmed the security council's interest in regional agencies and their role in the maintenance of world peace. The regionalists had won their point. Those favoring universality were able to maintain a semblance of the security council's advisory capacity, but regional independence laid the foundation for structures like the Organization of American States, the North Atlantic Treaty Organization, and the Warsaw Pact.[58]

The remainder of the conference proved anticlimactic for the inter-American system. Some Latin Americans tried to attack security council prerogatives, especially the absolute veto, by trying to enlarge that body, obtain a permanent Latin American seat, or enhance the general assembly's powers. None of these efforts budged the leadership from the Yalta formula. When hemispheric representatives realized this fact, they demurred, and the measure passed on June 13. Eleven days later the delegates signed the United Nations charter.[59]

Throughout the sessions the United States delegation demonstrated its inability to handle issues concerning Latin Americans. They did not hide their opposition to globalism or their hopes to preserve the regional network. The State Department, however, dismissed these anxieties at the Dumbarton Oaks talks and afterward at the Blair House meetings. Rockefeller's exclusion from the staff further personified the universalists' purposeful intent of minimizing regionalism. Somehow Pasvolsky and those with similar views believed that they had gained sufficient control to ignore inter-American hostility.

Once the conference began, Latin American representatives unified into a powerful force, and Molotov's attack on Padilla reinforced that spirit. The success that the hemispheric leaders achieved still relied on Big Four disunity. On both Argentine admission and regionalism, the Russians initiated the crises. Latin American diplomats merely commingled the Soviet demands with their own. In each instance the United States reacted instead of providing leadership. Its members were placed in positions that required compromise. Thus the hemispheric system built by Roosevelt, Hull, and Welles received its greatest boost at San Francisco from the Latin American benefactors with assistance from a sympathetic minority within the United States delegation. This combination worked because of the unique circumstances. It could not be sustained. To build a stronger inter-American system, the United States had to lead. Unfortunately for regionalists, Truman never provided that guidance.

EPILOGUE

AS WORLD WAR II reached its final stages, the United States turned its attention to the problems of European devastation, recognition of the Soviet Union as a super power, and the advent of the nuclear age with the atomic explosions over Japan. These critical themes saturated news coverage, while other, less dramatic, issues were relegated to secondary status. Inter-American questions fell under this latter category, and while the shift in priorities was understandable, that did not lesson Latin American complaints that the United States had abandoned hemispheric solidarity for Great Power collaboration.

This allegation found many supporters, but it was oversimplified. Two prime ingredients made the Good Neighbor possible, and they had started gradually to fade before the end of the fighting. The first was the depression, which severely inhibited international intercourse and encouraged the United States to expand its regional initiatives. The return to prosperity coupled with the American commitment to world order struck a heavy blow against hemispheric exclusiveness. The second factor was the change in the Democratic leadership. Roosevelt, Hull, Welles, Duggan, and Rockefeller—each for his own motives—worked energetically to make Pan American solidarity a foreign policy imperative. When these personalities had their opportunity to shape diplomacy, they acted aggressively to assure that inter-American programs would be taken into consideration.

Truman faced a new set of circumstances. He not only had to solve problems brought on by the war, but he also had to assemble a staff. Once the United Nations charter was signed, the president replaced Stettinius with James Byrnes, a staunch Democrat and popular figure with Congress who knew little about foreign affairs in general and the Americas in particular. By the end of the summer, the new secretary had fired Rockefeller and selected Spruille Braden to assume his duties. Finally, in 1946, Berle left his ambassadorship in Brazil. With his departure the last character who had played a leading part in directing the regional effort left the diplomatic service.[1]

The removal or retirement of those connected with Roosevelt's Latin American policies added to the Good Neighbor's demise, but even as early as

March 1945 Mexican historian Daniel Cosío Villegas asserted: "There are hundreds of causes that array the Latin Americans against the Yankees. In the present circumstance of the war, this dislike is hidden or curbed; but once the war is over, it will break loose like an irresponsible wave."[2] Events like the Great Depression, the Roosevelt presidency, and the worldwide confrontation, which had united the Western Hemisphere, had disappeared.

During 1945 United States diplomats discussed the inter-American scene. Several individuals were overly optimistic about maintaining the Good Neighbor momentum. Others saw the transitional nature of the postwar era. In this critical time the United States would have to meet domestic Latin American challenges as well as external threats. The slogans and stereotypes flung at the Nazi menace started to be transferred to the Communists. To combat this potential infiltration, many experts urged social, economic, and military assistance, but they did not realize that other international concerns had pushed regional ones to inferior standing.[3]

Braden took office in the midst of these crosscurrents. Although he had served well under the Roosevelt administration in several hemispheric assignments, he did not participate in the formulation of broad diplomatic strategy, nor was he suited temperamentally to direct the entire regional effort. Besides these limitations Braden was unfamiliar with Truman's pledge at the San Francisco meeting to convene an inter-American gathering that autumn to turn the Act of Chapultepec into a treaty. Without this background Braden chose to cancel the expected conference and in doing so reneged on a presidential promise.[4]

While Braden's decisions contributed to hemispheric disenchantment, they were symptomatic of a larger malady. The Good Neighbor had grown as the result of a reduced global commitment, for the economic havoc created by the depression diminished interaction with European and Asian states. Just as this situation opened Latin America for a major diplomatic thrust, the postwar emphasis on globalism pushed Latin America to lesser importance.

The reasons for Pan American retrenchment were not understood; frustration and recrimination surfaced; critics alleged that the United States had deserted its hemispheric emphasis. Henry Wallace by the summer of 1948 accused Truman of financing Latin American dictators while social conditions in the region worsened. Samuel Inman, who had carefully watched the Good Neighbor's rise and fall, wrote to Secretary of State Dean Acheson in early 1949 to suggest several steps toward a hemispheric reorientation. Inman's recommendations were, in effect, a call for the return of those practices that made the Good Neighbor operational: the selection of an experienced individual to become assistant secretary of state in charge of inter-American matters, restoration of close consultation, stronger cultural programs, and increased economic aid to raise regional living standards. Acheson answered this letter and promised action wherever necessary, but Inman was dubious. The Truman administration focused on other areas at Latin America's expense. Few publicly were willing to concede the obvious—concerns elsewhere preempted Pan Americanism.[5]

By the early 1950s Welles lamented: "If President Roosevelt had lived and had been in good health during the years immediately after the end of the war we would face a very different world today."[6] Within this nostalgic context was the realization that Roosevelt had died before making the transition from war to peace in his regional programs. Writers have minutely dissected his role in the victory over the Axis but have virtually ignored the far more subtle struggle to maintain hemispheric allegiance. Here the president displayed sophistication seldom demonstrated by the White House. He won public acceptance for the Good Neighbor by establishing broad guidelines, ending military intervention, and molding actions like the security zone and the no-transfer declaration to fit into his anti-Hitler crusade. While he skillfully carried out these political objectives, his economic understanding was limited. His bilateral solutions for Cuban financial difficulties in 1933 and the Mexican oil expropriation were naive. His multilateral proposals for airport beacon lights at the Montevideo conference as well as his suggestion for a marketing cartel after the collapse of France were inappropriate. This hazy conceptualization of inter-American economic affairs was the president's principal weakness, and this issue also plagued the Truman years. Yet economic miscalculations were minimized when compared to the overall achievement. Roosevelt brought Latin America to the limelight as no chief executive before him had. If any period can be labeled the golden age of Pan American cooperation, the Roosevelt presidency deserves to be so labeled.

Hull never understood the Good Neighbor's scope. His massive memoirs are a testament to his lack of comprehension, but he was writing a defense of his tenure—not history. His reconstruction of hemispheric happenings placed him the center, while in fact he normally deferred to Welles's judgment. The secretary overemphasized the importance of the reciprocal trade agreements program and neglected the complex economic measures like the Export-Import Bank and the commodity agreements that laid the basis for wartime trade. Hull discussed his Argentine antipathy but was incapable of unraveling the basic causes for these strained bilateral relations. Lastly, the secretary deliberately dismissed Welles's vital position. As a result of slanted views, Hull's reflections distorted reality. His main purpose was not leading, but mirroring the public's cautious mood, moderating overly ambitious presidential schemes, and standing before his countrymen as the diplomatic representative who reassured them of the Good Neighbor's value.[7]

Welles occupied a different place within the State Department. His main attribute was finding answers to complicated questions, and he fit solutions into a broad political framework established by Roosevelt or the reciprocity project preached by Hull. The undersecretary's deficiencies were professional as well as personal. His bisexuality was the direct cause for dismissal, but his egocentrism had a far more lasting impact. He generally did not confide in others and refused to share responsibility—only *he* had the answers. Because of this attitude, Welles did not even attempt to win widespread approval for the Good Neighbor within the diplomatic corps to guarantee continuity.[8]

Duggan was Welles's closest associate. He shared many similar views but had a slightly different perspective. Duggan felt that only a few foreign service officers embraced hemispheric cooperation, and that the public lacked a deep understanding. Despite these factors he took pride in laying the foundations for wider regional contacts and assisting Latin American countries in making notable advances in human rights. He hoped that the United States would recognize the desirability of continuing to aid developing American states, and he urged patience in reaching that goal. Pan Americanism, after all, was still in its infancy and needed nourishment to mature. A pessimistic note also crept into Duggan's thinking. Progressive measures needed continual reinforcement, but the United States was not willing to pay the necessary price. Because large sums to expand hemispheric programs were not being allocated, collaboration was vanishing and so was the hope for the future.[9]

Toward the end of the 1960s Rockefeller confirmed Duggan's fears. "With the present United States government structure," Rockefeller asserted, "Western Hemispheric policy can neither be soundly formulated nor effectively carried out."[10] Inter-American projects were too decentralized; the State Department, for example, controlled less than half of them. The former assistant secretary wanted to establish clear national objectives for the region, create a secretary for Western Hemispheric affairs, and place a staff director inside of the executive offices to handle economic and social development. These recommendations were not enacted, but even if they had been, they would not be effective without strong presidential leadership.

Those who had shaped the Good Neighbor described many of the specific reasons for its rise and subsequent decline. Yet those experts like Welles, Duggan, and Rockefeller, who were so closely associated with the policy, ignored the fundamental causes for its success. First, the unique setting created by the depression gave the United States a chance to pursue an aggressive hemispheric program. Second, the president established the general approach and encouraged his regional assistants, who had direct access to the White House, to carry out the broad commitment. The Good Neighbor emerged as the result of the merger of both forces. Since 1945 American presidents have reached around the globe to influence world events, but in large part, they have neglected the Western Hemisphere, with tragic consequences. The lessons of the Good Neighbor have been forgotten.

ABBREVIATIONS USED IN THE NOTES

Some abbreviations need further explanation. Colonel John Child provided me with material from the files of the Inter-American Defense Board (IADB) in Washington, D.C. While the *Washington-Merry-Go-Round* was published in many newspapers, Jack Anderson's office in Washington, D.C., allowed me to use an extensive index. Footnotes for the Standing Liaison Committee (SLC), Harley Notter (HN), and the War Branch History Study (WBHS) are located in the Diplomatic Division, Record Group 59, at the National Archives in Washington, D.C. At present, I believe that Columbia University has not opened Nelson Rockefeller's oral history; my permission came directly from Mr. Rockefeller. Finally, I gained permission to use Sumner Welles's Federal Bureau of Investigation file from the Justice Department after years of negotiations.

   AB Adolf Berle (Franklin D. Roosevelt Library, Hyde Park, New York—FDRL)

 ABnr *Navigating the Rapids*, ed. Beatrice Berle and Travis Jacobs (New York: Harcourt Brace Jovanovich, 1973).

  AES A. Eric Sevareid (Manuscript Division, Library of Congress, Washington, D.C.—LC)

   AL Arthur Lane (Manuscript Division, Yale University, New Haven, Connecticut—YU)

   AM Archibald MacLeish (LC)

  AML Alfred M. Landon (Manuscript Division, Kansas Historical Society, Topeka, Kansas—KHS)

   AS Arthur Sweetser (LC)

  ASB Albert S. Burleson (LC)

  ASp *The Papers of Adlai E. Stevenson*, ed. Walter Johnson, 2 vols. (Boston: Little, Brown, 1972, 1973).

  AVd *The Private Papers of Senator Vandenberg*, ed. Arthur Vandenberg, Jr. (Boston: Houghton Mifflin, 1952).

   B. Book, Box, or Container

   BB Bernard Baruch (Manuscript Division, Princeton University, Princeton, New Jersey—PU)

   BL Breckinridge Long (LC)

 BLwd *The War Diary of Breckinridge Long*, ed. Fred Israel (Lincoln: University of Nebraska Press, 1966).

    CA Carl Ackerman (LC)
    CB Claude Bowers (Manuscript Division, Indiana University, Blooming-
        ton, Indiana—IU)
   CCB Claude C. Bloch (LC)
    CH Cordell Hull (LC)
   CHm Cordell Hull, *The Memoirs of Cordell Hull* 2 vols. (New York:
        Macmillan, 1948).
    CR *Congressional Record*
    CT Charles Taussig (FDRL)
  DGFP U.S. Department of State, *Documents on German Foreign Policy*
        (Washington, D.C., G.P.O., 1953-1966).
    DR Donald Richberg (LC)
    EK Ernest King (LC)
    EP Endicott Peabody (Manuscript Division, The Houghton Library,
        Harvard University, Cambridge, Mass.—HU)
    ER Eleanor Roosevelt (FDRL)
    ES Edward Stettinius, Jr.—(Manuscript Division, University of Virginia,
        Charlottesville, Virginia—UV)
   ESd *The Diaries of Edward R. Stettinius, Jr.*, ed. Thomas Campbell and
        George Herring (New York: New Viewpoints, 1975).
    EW Edwin Watson (UV)
    FA *Franklin D. Roosevelt and Foreign Affairs*, ed. Edgar Nixon, 3
        vols. (Cambridge, Mass., Belknap Press, 1969).
    FC Frank Corrigan (FDRL)
   FDR Franklin D. Roosevelt (FDRL)
        O.F. Official File
        PPF President's Personal File
        PSF President's Secretary File
    FF Felix Frankfurter (LC)
   FFd *From the Diaries of Felix Frankfurter*, ed. Joseph Lash (New
        York: W. W. Norton, 1975).
  FFrf *Roosevelt and Frankfurter*, annotated by Max Freedman (Boston:
        Little, Brown, 1967).
    FK Frank Knox (LC)
    FM Frank McNaughton (Harry S Truman Library, Independence,
        Missouri —HTL)
    FN Fred Nielson (LC)
    FR U.S. Department of State, *Foreign Relations of the United States,
        1933-1945* (Washington, D.C., G.P.O., 1950-1967).
    FS Francis Sayre (LC)
    FW Francis White (Manuscript Division, The Johns Hopkins University,
        Baltimore, Maryland—JHU)
   GFM George F. Milton (LC)
    GM George Messersmith (Special Collections, University of Delaware,
        Newark, Delaware—UD)
  G.P.O. Government Printing Office
    HA Henry Arnold (LC)

HAgm   Henry Arnold, *Global Mission* (New York: Harper and Brothers, 1949).
HDW   Harry D. White (PU)
HE   Howard Eaton (LC)
HF   Herbert Feis (LC)
HG   Hugh Gibson (Hoover Institution of War, Revolution and Peace, Stanford University, Palo Alto, California—HI)
HI   Harold Ickes (LC)
HIsd   Harold Ickes, *The Secret Diary of Harold L. Ickes*, 3 vols. (New York: Simon and Schuster, 1953-1954).
HM   Henry Morgenthau, Jr. (FDRL)
HMd   *From the Morgenthau Diaries*, ed. John Blum, 3 vols. (Boston: Houghton Mifflin, 1959, 1965, 1967).
HN   Harley Notter (National Archives, Washington, D.C.—NA)
HP   Herbert Pell (FDRL)
HPF   Henry P. Fletcher (LC)
HRW   Hugh Wilson (Herbert Hoover Presidential Library, West Branch, Iowa—HHPL)
HS   Henry Stimson (YU)
HSas   Henry Stimson and McGeorge Bundy, *On Active Service in Peace and War* (New York: Harper and Brothers, 1947, 1948).
HTm   Harry Truman, *Year of Decisions* (New York: Signet Books, 1965).
HW   Henry Wallace (LC, FDRL, and Manuscript Division, The University of Iowa Libraries, University of Iowa, Iowa City, Iowa—Ia)
HWpv   *The Price of Vision*, ed. John Blum (Boston: Houghton Mifflin, 1973).
IAA   *Inter-American Affairs*, ed. Arthur Whitaker, 5 vols. (New York: Columbia University Press, 1942-1946).
IADB   Inter-American Defense Board (Washington, D.C.)
JB   John Barrett (LC)
JD   Josephus Daniels (LC)
JDrd   *Roosevelt and Daniels*, ed. Carroll Kilpatrick (Chapel Hill: University of North Carolina Press, 1952).
JED   Joseph E. Davies (LC)
JEDmm   Joseph E. Davies, *Mission to Moscow* (New York: Simon and Schuster, 1941).
JF   James Forrestal (PU)
JFd   *The Forrestal Diaries*, ed. Walter Millis (New York: Viking Press, 1951).
JJ   Jesse Jones (LC)
JM   John Moore (LC)
JPM   Jay P. Moffat (HU)
JPMmp   *The Moffat Papers*, ed. Nancy Hooker (Cambridge: Harvard University Press, 1956).
JR   James Robertson (LC)
JW   John Wiley (FDRL)
LH   Leland Harrison (LC)

   LP Leo Pasvolsky (LC)
   LR Leo Rowe (Columbus Memorial Library, Pan American Union, Washington, D.C.—PAU)
   LS Laurence Steinhardt (LC)
NAACP National Association for the Advancement of Colored People (LC)
   NB Newton Baker (LC)
   ND Norman Davis (LC)
   NR Nelson Rockefeller (Rockefeller Family Archives, Pocantico, New York—NY)
  OHP Oral History Project (Columbia University, New York, New York—CU)
   PC Presidential Press Conferences of Franklin D. Roosevelt (FDRL)
   PJ Philip Jessup (LC)
   PL *F.D.R.: His Personal Letters*, ed. Elliott Roosevelt, 2 vols. (New York: Duell, Sloan and Pearce, 1950).
  PPA *The Public Papers and Addresses of Franklin D. Roosevelt*, ed. Samuel Rosenman, 13 vols. (New York: Harper and Brothers, Random House, and Macmillan, 1938-1950).
   RC Raymond Clapper (LC)
 RCww Raymond Clapper, *Watching the World* (New York: McGraw-Hill, 1944).
   RL Robert LaFollette (LC)
   RM R. Walton Moore (FDRL)
   RP Robert Patterson (LC)
   SB Sophonisba Breckinridge (LC)
   SE Stephen Early (FDRL)
   SH Stanley Hornbeck (HI)
   SI Samuel Inman (LC)
  SLC Standing Liaison Committee (NA)
   SW Sumner Welles file (Federal Bureau of Investigation, Washington, D.C.—F.B.I.)
 SW-1 _____. *Naboth's Vineyard*, 2 vols. (New York: Payson and Clarke, 1928).
 SW-2 _____. *Seven Decisions That Shaped History* (New York: Harper and Brothers, 1950, 1951).
 SW-3 _____. *The Time for Decision* (New York: Harper and Brothers, 1944).
 SW-4 _____. *The World of the Four Freedoms* (New York: Columbia University Press, 1943).
 SW-5 _____. *Where Are We Headed?* (New York: Harper and Brothers, 1946).
   WA Warren Austin (Manuscript Division, University of Vermont, Burlington, Vermont—UVe)
   WB William Borah (LC)
 WBHS War Branch History Study (NA)
   WC William Culbertson (LC)
   WD William Dodd (LC)

WDd   William Dodd and Martha Dodd, eds., *Ambassador Dodd's Diary* (New York: Harcourt, Brace, 1941).

WJC   Wilbur J. Carr (LC)

WL   William Leahy (LC)

WMR   *Washington-Merry-Go-Round*

WP   William Phillips (HU)

WRC   William R. Castle, Jr. (HHPL)

WW   William White (LC)

WWsl   *Selected Letters of William Allen White*, ed. Walter Johnson (New York: Henry Holt, 1947).

NOTES

CHAPTER 1

1. L. Ethan Ellis, *Republican Foreign Policy, 1921-1933* (New Brunswick, N.J.: Rutgers University Press, 1968), pp. 39-57; Elting Morison, *Turmoil and Tradition* (New York: Atheneum, 1964), pp. 258-59.

2. Edward Mishler, "Francis White and the Shaping of United States Latin American Policy, 1921-1933" (Ph.D. diss., University of Maryland, 1975), pp. 5-338.

3. Ellis, *Republican Foreign Policy*, pp. 229-32, 263-64, 289-90; Wilfred Callcott, *The Western Hemisphere* (Austin: University of Texas Press, 1968), p. 215; Joseph Tulchin, *The Aftermath of War* (New York: New York University Press, 1971), pp. 61-78, 234-53; Kenneth Grieb, *The Latin American Policy of Warren G. Harding* (Fort Worth: Texas Christian University Press, 1976), pp. 1-13.

4. Chargé in Haiti to Stimson, Nov. 13, 1930, 710.G/6 (all citations with decimal numbers come from Department of State, Record Group 59, National Archives, Washington, D.C.); Ernest Gruening, "The Issue in Haiti," *Foreign Affairs* 11 (Janaury 1933): 285-89; Donald Cooper, "The Withdrawal of the United States from Haiti, 1928-1934," *Journal of Inter-American Studies* 5 (January 1963): 83-96; Dana Munro, "The American Withdrawal from Haiti, 1929-1934," *Hispanic American Historical Review* 49 (1969): 1-22; Grieb, *Latin American Policy*, pp. 85-102.

5. Hanna to Hull, July 18, 1933, 710.G/175; Dana Munro, "The Establishment of Peace in Nicaragua," *Foreign Affairs* 11 (July 1933): 704-5; Bryce Wood, *The Making of the Good Neighbor Policy* (New York: W. W. Norton, 1967), pp. 13-47; William Kamman, *A Search for Stability* (Notre Dame, Ind.: University of Notre Dame Press, 1968), pp. 219-36.

6. Lorenzo Meyer, *Mexico and the United States in the Oil Controversy*, trans. Muriel Vasconcellos (Austin: University of Texas Press, 1977), pp. 4-148; Grieb, *Latin American Policy*, pp. 125-48.

7. Ellis, *Republican Foreign Policy*, pp. 277-78; Kenneth Grieb, "The United States and the Rise of General Maximiliano Hernández Martínez," *Journal of Latin American Studies* 3 (November 1971): 151-72; Dana Munro, *The United States and the Caribbean Republics* (Princeton, N.J.: Princeton University Press, 1974), pp. 287-90; Grieb, *Latin American Policy*, pp. 41-56; Richard Salisbury, "Domestic Politics and Foreign Policy: Costa Rica's Stand in Recognition, 1923-1934," *Hispanic American Historical Review* 54 (August 1974): 453-74.

8. Mishler, "Francis White," pp. 268-74; Ellis, *Republican Foreign Policy*, pp. 269-70.

9. Memo by White, Aug. 19, 1948, FW.

10. White to Bemis, Nov. 18, 1946, FW.

11. Ellis, *Republican Foreign Policy*, pp. 279-83; Grieb, *Latin American Policy*, pp. 157-70.

12. Faust to Stimson, May 12, 1931, 710.G/28, Wheeler to Stimson, Jan. 1,/118, Feely to Hull, Aug. 31, 1933,/223; Leslie Rout, Jr., *Politics of the Chaco Peace Conference* (Austin: University of Texas Press, 1970), pp. 3-39, 53-58; Bryce Wood, *The United States and Latin American Wars* (New York: Columbia University Press, 1966), pp. 19-41; David Zook, Jr., *The Conduct of the Chaco War* (New York: Bookman Associates, 1960), pp. 24-28, 43-58, 62-79, 84-116, 125-49.

13. Caffery to Stimson, Mar. 11, 710.G/18, Dawson to Stimson, March 20,/19, Dearing to Stimson, Sept. 9, 1931,/43, Caffery to Hull, Mar. 27, 1933,/38; FA, 1:182-83; PPA, 3:251-52; Dearing to Moore, Mar. 1, Nov. 2, 1933, B. 65, Feb. 21, 1934, B. 67, JM; Dearing to White, Oct. 27, 1935, FW; James Carey, *Peru and the United States* (Notre Dame, Ind.: University of Notre Dame Press, 1964), pp. 94-98; CHm, 1:310-12; Wood, *Latin American Wars*, pp. 169-251.

14. IAA, 5:16.

15. Ibid.; Tulchin, *Aftermath of War*, pp. 38-46, 79-117, 155-205; Callcott, *Western Hemisphere*, pp. 186-89; J. F. Normano, "Changes in Latin American Attitudes," *Foreign Affairs* 11 (October 1932): 170-72.

16. Callcott, *Western Hemisphere*, pp. 282-83, 289; Joan Wilson, *American Business and Foreign Policy* (Lexington: University Press of Kentucky, 1971), pp. 120-22, 181-83; Joan Wilson, *Herbert Hoover* (Boston: Little, Brown, 1975), pp. 180-82; Donald Giffin, "The Normal Years: Brazilian-American Relations, 1930-1939" (Ph.D. diss., Vanderbilt University, 1962), pp. 28-33.

17. F. W. Taussig, *The Tariff History of the United States* (New York: Capicorn Books, 1964), pp. 489-500; SW-3, pp. 189-91; Wilson, *Hoover*, pp. 175-79; Wilson, *American Business*, pp. 65-100.

18. Manuel Ugarte, *Destiny of a Continent*, trans. Catherine Phillips, intro. by J. Fred Rippy (New York: Alfred A. Knopf, 1925), p. 178.

19. Hoover to Stimson, Feb. 14, 1933, Reel 84, HS; Ellis, *Republican Foreign Policy*, pp. 259-61, 274-76; J. Manuel Espinosa, *Inter-American Beginnings of U.S. Cultural Diplomacy* (Washington, D.C.; G.P.O., 1976), pp. 18-27.

20. Ellis, *Republican Foreign Policy*, p. 278; Wilson, *American Business*, pp. 167, 169.

CHAPTER 2

1. Rowe to Stimson, Mar. 1, Lane to Stimson, Apr. 10, diary, Mar. 28, 1933, HS; Frank Freidel, *Franklin D. Roosevelt: Launching the New Deal* (Boston: Little, Brown, 1973), pp. 102-36.

2. Frank Freidel, *Franklin D. Roosevelt: The Apprenticeship* (Boston: Little, Brown, 1952), pp. 70, 139-40.

3. Ibid., pp. 227-32, 270-85, 333.

4. Frank Freidel, *Franklin D. Roosevelt: The Ordeal* (Boston: Little, Brown, 1954), pp. 135-37, 236-41; Foster Duller and Gerald Ridinger, "The Anti-Colonial Policies of Franklin D. Roosevelt," *Political Science Quarterly* 70 (March 1955): 1-4; Franklin D. Roosevelt, "Our Foreign Policy: A Democratic View," *Foreign Affairs* 6 (July 1928): 573-86.

5. Frank Freidel, *Franklin D. Roosevelt: The Triumph* (Boston: Little, Brown, 1956), pp. 3-371; Raymond Moley, *The First New Deal* (New York: Harcourt, Brace and World, 1966), p. 22; ABnr, p. 71; SW-3, pp. 191-92; Selig Adler, *The Uncertain Giant* (New York: Macmillan, 1965), pp. 109-11.

6. FA, 1:20.

7. Welles to Davis, Nov. 2, 1931, B. 63, ND; Nerval to FDR, Mar. 15, Wilson to Nerval, Apr. 6, 1933, 710.11/1780.

8. Moffat to Wilson, Apr. 22; also see Moffat to White, Apr. 7, 1933, JPM.

9. PPA, 2:129-33; SW-3, pp. 192-93.

10. Freidel, *Launching*, pp. 369-407; FA, 1:126-28, 155-58; PAA, 2:185-91; FR, 1933, 1:143-45.

11. Milton to Hull, Jan. 24, Milton to Rogers, Feb. 6, 1933, B. 12, GFM; Castle to Wilson, Feb. 10, 1933, B. 1, HW; Dodd to Hull, Feb. 11, 1933, B. 41, WD; diary, June 15, 1933, B. 6, JD; Stimson to Chambliss, Oct. 19, 1933, R. 85, HS; FA, 1:17; CHm, 1:3-163; Freidel, *Launching*, pp. 137-47; Daniel Roper, *Fifty Years of Public Life* (North Carolina: Duke University Press, 1941), pp. 290-91.

12. Diaries, Feb. 25, 26, Oct. 18, 1932, HS; Herbert Feis, *1933: Characters in Crisis* (Boston: Little, Brown, 1966), p. 80; Dean Acheson, *Present at the Creation* (New York:

W. W. Norton, 1969), pp. 9-10; FFrf, pp. 108-9; Louis Wehle, *Hidden Threads of History* (New York: Macmillan, 1953), pp. 129-31; James Roosevelt, *My Parents* (Chicago: Playboy Press, 1976), pp. 183-84.

13. OHP, WP; Moffat to Montgomery, Sept. 30, 1933, JPM; Feis, *1933*, p. 308; Harold Hinton, *Cordell Hull* (New York: Doubleday, Doran, 1942), p. 240; Wehle, *Hidden Threads*, p. 130; Joseph Lash, *Eleanor and Franklin* (New York: W. W. Norton, 1971), p. 571; Louise Overaker, "Campaign Funds in a Depression Year," *American Political Science Review* 27 (October 1933): 782.

14. Welles to Davis, Aug. 6, 29, Davis to Welles, Aug. 19, 1921, B. 63, ND; Welles to Peabody, Jan. 4, Nov. 19, Dec. 7, no year given, EP; Irwin Gellman, *Roosevelt and Batista* (Albuquerque: University of New Mexico Press, 1973), pp. 12-14; Lash, *Eleanor and Franklin*, p. 571; Elliott Roosevelt and James Brough, *A Rendezvous with Destiny* (New York: G. P. Putman's Sons, 1975), pp. 157-58; Frank Graff, "The Strategy of Involvement: A Diplomatic Biography of Sumner Welles, 1933-1943" (Ph.D. diss., University of Michigan, 1971), pp. 1-28.

15. Welles to Rollins, Feb. 10, 1953, PPF 2961; SW-1, pp. 1-11, 900-936.

16. SW-1, p. 937.

17. Welles to Davis, Feb. 17, Davis to Welles, Feb. 19, Welles to Davis, Feb. 21, Davis to Welles, Feb. 24, 25, Apr. 3, Welles to Davis, Apr. 6, 1931, Welles to Davis, Oct. 22, Nov. 19, 1932, B. 63, ND; Welles to FDR, Feb. 17, 1931, B. 177, FDR: Papers as governor, Welles to FDR, Dec. 19, 1932, OF 470, Welles to FDR, Jan. 23, 1933, PPF 2961; FA, 1:18-19; Frankfurter to Gruening, June 21, 1933, B. 60, FF; Graff, "Strategy of Involvement," pp. 37-39; Overaker, "Campaign Funds," p. 782.

18. Welles to Davis, Mar. 20, 1933, B. 63, ND; diary, Dec. 15, 1933, JMP; Dearing to Moore, Mar. 1, 1933, B. 65, JM; Dearing to Culbertson, Aug. 16, 1933, B. 14, WC; Freidel, *Launching*, p. 355.

19. Mishler, "Francis White," pp. 34, 36, 339-49.

20. Ibid., pp. 349-55.

21. White to Dodds, June 16, 1933, FW.

22. Moore to Moe, Jan. 8, 1934, B. 67, JM; US Department of State, *Register* (July 1, 1936), p. 165; Duggan, Report of South American visit, June-October 1929, pp. 1-31, Herbert Hoover Institution on War, Revolution and Peace, Sanford, Calif.; memo by Duggan, Jan. 17, 1933, 710.11/1776½; Anna Rothe, ed., *Current Biography, 1947* (New York: H. W. Wilson, 1948), pp. 181-82.

23. Green to Moffat, Nov. 25, 1935, JPM.

24. Caffery to Stimson, Mar. 11, 1931, 710.G/18, radio address by Caffery, Sept. 5, 1933, 710.11/1837; Caffery to White, July 29, 1933, FW; Messersmith to Long, Apr. 11, 1940, no. 1341, GM; FA, 1:468; Gellman, *Roosevelt and Batista*, p. 77; E. Wilder Spaulding, *Ambassadors Ordinary and Extraordinary* (Washington, D.C.: Public Affairs Press, 1961), pp. 261-65.

25. FA, 2:435-37.

26. Diary, Apr. 17, 1933, JPM; Dearing to Davis, Jan. 19, B. 10, Davis to Gibson, Apr. 27, 1933, B. 26, ND; Gibson to Lane, Apr. 24, Aug. 12, 1933, B. 7, AL; diary, Nov. 10, 1933, WP; Hull to FDR, Nov. 8, 1933, B. 35, CH; Freidel, *Launching*, p. 360.

27. Gibson to Lane, Feb. 1, 1934, B. 8, AL.

28. Lane to Hull, Apr. 16, 1933, 710.G/139; Baker to Daniels, Mar. 16, Daniels to Baker, Mar. 18, 1933, B. 84, NB; Daniels to Dodd, June 12, 1933, B. 40, Jan. 12, 1934, B. 44, WD; Dearing to Davis, Apr. 10, 1933, B. 12, ND; Daniels to Hull, Apr. 19, 1933, B. 34, Daniels to Hull, Aug. 17, 1934, CH; Daniels to FDR, May 25, B. 18, diary, July 19, 1933, B. 6, JD; JDrd, p. 193; E. David Cronon, *Josephus Daniels in Mexico* (Madison: University of Wisconsin Press, 1960), pp. 3-29.

29. Welles to Daniels, July 25, 1933, B. 703, JD.

. 30. Sack to Lane, Dec. 11, 1933, B. 8, AL; US Department of State, *Register* (July 1934), pp. 151-52, (July 1935), pp. 182-83, 252-53, (July 1936), p. 158, (October 1937), pp. 190, 223, 269, (October 1938), p. 100, (October 1939), pp. 158, 201, 209, (September 1944), p. 56, (October 1945), pp. 9, 44, 167-68, 258, 281.

31. Guggenheim to Stimson, June 29, 1931, 710.G/33; Robertson to FDR, Jan. 21, 1933, B. 45, JR; Bender to Denny, Feb. 13, 1933, B. 8, RC; Guggenheim to Jessup, Mar. 15, 1933, B. 14, PJ.

32. Diaries, Jan. 9, 1933, HS; Gellman, *Roosevelt and Batista*, p. 11.

33. Gellman, *Roosevelt and Batista*, pp. 12-14.

34. Reed to White, May 12, 1933, FW; Gellman, *Roosevelt and Batista*, pp. 15-17.

35. Gellman, *Roosevelt and Batista*, pp. 17-24.

36. Ibid., pp. 24-32.

37. Wilson to White, Aug. 18, 1933, FW; also see Welles to Barrett, Aug. 17, 1933, B. 2, JB; FFrf, p. 150.

38. Diary, Aug. 28, 1933, B. 8, WL; Gellman, *Roosevelt and Batista*, pp. 34-42.

39. Gellman, *Roosevelt and Batista*, pp. 43-52.

40. Diary, Sept. 5, 1933, B. 8, WL; Howe to Barrett, Sept. 26, 1933, B. 2, JB; FFrf, pp. 155.

41. PC, Sept. 6, 1933, R. 1.

42. Inman to Caffery, Sept. 9, Caffery to Inman, Sept. 16, 1933, 710.11/1834; Woolsey to White, Oct. 4, 1933, FW; FA, 1:390-92; Gellman, *Roosevelt and Batista*, pp. 55-61.

43. Stimson to White, Nov. 14, 1933, memo by White, Aug. 19, 1948, FW; Welles to Barrett, Oct. 4, 1933, B. 2, JB; Rublee to Stimson, Oct. 13, Stimson to White, Nov. 14, 1933, R. 85, HS; PL, 2:1445-46; Gellman, *Roosevelt and Batista*, pp. 62-70.

44. Welles to Gibson, Oct. 10, 1933, B. 48, HG.

45. Gellman, *Roosevelt and Batista*, pp. 70-74.

46. Wright to Hull, June 6, 710.G/151, Wright to Hull, June 22, /162, Dearing to Hull, Aug. 1,/196, Norweb to Hull, Sept. 3, 1933,/254; FR, 1933, 4:9-10; CHm, 1:317; Hubert Herring, "Will Montevideo Make History?" *Christain Century* 50 (December 1933): 1571-73.

47. Dearing to Hull, Oct. 1, 710.G/252, memo by Matthews, Oct. 13,/276, Weddell to Hull, Oct. 28,/307, Weddell to Hull, Oct. 30,/350, memo by Caffery, Oct. 31, 1933,/334; FR, 1933, 4:20, 28-30, 33-36, 38-39, 232-33; diary, Oct. 31, 1933, WP; Rowe to White, Nov. 9, 1933, FW; diary, Oct. 28, 31, 1933, HS.

48. Memo by Hull, Sept. 2, 710.G/210, memo of phone conversation, Sept. 22,1A/187, memo by Hull, Oct. 19, Personnel/122, Gibson to Hull, Oct. 24, Personnel/134, Hull to Gibson, Oct. 24, Personnel/140, memo by Hull, Oct. 26, 1933,/303; Hull to Krock, Sept. 5, Hull to Cox, Sept. 15, Hull to Gonzales, Oct. 25, 1933, B. 35, CH; Hull to Daniels, May 18, Aug. 9, Hull to Daniels, Oct. 24, 1933, B. 750, JD; Carr to Hull, Apr. 19, 1933, B. 10, WJC; PC, Oct. 25, 1933, R. 1; FA, 1:345-48; FR, 1933, 4:11, 14.

49. Hull to Braden, Oct. 14, 710.G Personnel/103, Hull to Weddell, Nov. 8, Personnel/216, Logan to FDR, Oct. 20, Applications-Breckinridge, S.P./7, Wallis to FDR, Oct. 26, Applications-Breckinridge, S.P./14, Chapman to FDR, Nov. 19, 1933, Applications-Breckinridge, S.P./18; Welles to Inman, Oct. 30, 1933, B. 13, SI; Welles to Davis, Sept. 4, 1933, B. 12, ND; McClure to Hull, Sept. 30, B. 34, Hull to Clark, Oct. 2, 1933, B. 35, CH; Rowe to Moore, Oct. 10, Nov. 7, 1933, B. 66, JM; diary, Nov. 6, 7, 1933, WP; FR, 1933, 4:43; PC, Nov. 8, 1933, R. 1; FA, 1:330, 363-64, 432-33, 459-60, 469; Laurence Duggan, *The Americas* (New York: Henry Holt, 1949), p. 63; Hinton, *Hull*, p. 244; Spruille Braden, *Diplomats and Demagogues* (New York: Arlington House, 1971), pp. 114-25.

50. Eberhardt to Hull, July 6, 710.G/169, Dawson to Hull, Oct. 4, 1933, Personnel/80, Sack to Hull, Oct. 24,/310, Harris, G-2 report, Nov. 8, Personnel/323, Welles to Phillips, Nov. 15, 1933, Personnel/294; Seventh International Conference of American States, *Final Act* (Uruguay: J. Florensa, 1934), pp. 9-16; US Department of State, *Report of the Delegates of the United States of America to the Seventh International Conference of American States, Montevideo, Uruguay, December 3-26, 1933* (Washington, D.C.: G.P.O., 1934), p. 2; Fredrick Pike, *Chile and the United States* (Notre Dame, Ind.: University of Notre Dame Press, 1963), pp. 134-35, 401.

51. White to Stimson, Feb. 19, 1932, 835.00/613, Dearing to Phillips, Dec. 4, 710.G Personnel/344, memo by Matthews, Oct. 17, 1933, 710.1012 Anti-War/36; Braden, *Diplomats and Demagogues*, p. 152; Hinton, *Hull*, pp. 246-48; Harold Peterson, *Argentina and the United States* (New York: State University of New York Press, 1964), pp. 380-82, 384-85; Pike, *Chile and the United States*, p. 412.

52. Brown to Hull, Nov. 15, 710.G Press/16, Weddell to Phillips, Nov. 24, Press/20, Wright to Phillips, Nov. 17, 1933, Press/17; Inman to Welles, Nov. 10, 1933, B. 13, SI; PPA, 2:459-64; CHm, 1:318-19; FA, 1:475-79.

53. Memo of press conference, Nov. 10, 1933, 710.G/362; Moffat to Davis, Nov. 11, 1933, B. 12, ND; Phillips to Dodd, Nov. 14, 1933, B. 42, WD; FR, 1933, 4:44-46; US Department of State, *Addresses and Statements by the Honorable Cordell Hull: In Connection with His Trip to South America, 1933-1934* (Washington, D.C.: G.P.O., 1935), pp. 7-8.

54. Gibson to Phillips, Dec. 1, 033.1110 Hull, Cordell/46, Barsloe to Phillips, Nov. 27, 1933,/48; Inman to wife, Nov. 23, 1933, B. 13, SI; US Department of State, *Addresses and Statements, 1933-1934*, pp. 11-12, 98; idem, *Report of the Delegates*, pp. 1-2.

55. Hull to FDR, Phillips, and Caffery, Nov. 24, 1933, Montevideo Conference, B. 633, RG 43; diary, Nov. 25, 1933, WP; diary, Nov. 26, Inman to Committee on Cooperation in Latin America, Dec. 5, 1933, B. 13, SI; FR, 1933, 4:40-42; Gellman, *Roosevelt and Batista*, pp. 74-76; US Department of State, *Addresses and Statements, 1933-1934*, pp. 13-16; Rowe to Berding, Aug. 29, 1946, B. 56, CH; CHm, 1:318-22, 325-26; Hinton, *Hull*, pp. 1-2, 240, 245-46; Duggan, *Americas*, pp. 63-65.

56. Diary, Nov. 28, 1933, WP; Hull to Phillips, Dec. 2, 1933, Montevideo Conference, 633, RG 43; FR, 1933, 4:42-43, 85-86, 157; Greene to Phillips, Dec. 2, 1933, 710.G Personnel/346; Breckinridge to Hull, Jan. 27, 1934, SB; George Coleman, "The Good Neighbor Policy of Franklin D. Roosevelt with Special Reference to Three Inter-American Conferences, 1933-1938" (Ph.D.: diss., State University of Iowa, 1951), p. 91; Albert Conil Paz and Gustavo Ferrari, *Argentina's Foreign Policy*, trans. John Kennedy (Notre Dame, Ind.: University of Notre Dame Press, 1966), pp. 33-35; CHm, 1:322-24, 326-30.

57. Memo by McClure, Feb. 24, 1934, 710.G/430; diary, Dec. 2, 1933, WP; US Department of State, *Report of The Delegates*, pp. 98-103.

58. Seventh International Conference of American States, *Minutes and Antecedents, with General Index* (Montevideo: Imprenta Nacional, 1935), pp. 7-23.

59. Ibid., p. 24.

60. Memo by Feis, Dec. 4, 710.G 1A/299, memo by Phillips, Dec. 6, 1A/300, and Hull to Phillips, Dec. 9, 1933, 1A/304; FR, 1933, 4:157-63, 168; Seventh International Conference of American States, *Minutes and Antecedents*, pp. 7-81, 87-140; Rowe to Hull, Dec. 13, 1933, B. 35, CH.

61. FA, 1:525; also see FR, 1933, 4:186-87; diary, Dec. 13, 1933, WP.

62. FR, 1933, 4:201.

63. Daniels to Hull, Dec. 4, 1933, 710.11/1900, Hawks to Hull, Mar. 16, 1934, 710.G/435; Seventh International Conference of American States, *Minutes and Antecedents*, pp. 103-20.

64. Seventh International Conference of American States, *Minutes and Antecedents*, p. 121.

65. Dunn to Welles, July 13, 1934, 710.G/490½, memo by Kelchner, Aug. 5, 1938, 710.G Rights and Duties of States/55; diary, Apr. 3, 1934, WP; FR, 1933, 4:214-18.

66. Memo by Phillips, Dec. 19, 1933, 710. G. Women's Rights/47; FR, 1933, 4:201, 211-14; FA, 1:524-25, 530-31; PC, Dec. 20, 1933, R.1; Seventh International Conference of American States, *Minutes and Antecedents*, pp. 7-46; Hinton, *Hull*, pp. 253-54; diary, Dec. 13, 14, 18, 19, 20, 1933, Jan. 6, 1934, WP; Lutz to Breckinridge, Jan. 1, *Chicago Daily News*, Jan. 9, Breckinridge to Sherwin, Jan. 9, Breckinridge to Hull, Jan. 10, Breckinridge to Ernest, Jan. 11, Shipley to Breckinridge, Jan. 13, Breckinridge to Weddell, Jan. 16, Breckinridge to Sherwin, Jan. 31, 1934, B. 25, SB.

67. FR, 1933, 4:187-88, 198-200, 205-6, 210-11; Seventh International Conference of American States, *Minutes and Antecedents*, pp. 143-65; CHm, 1:331-32.

68. Hull to Phillips, Dec. 12, 1933, 710.G/385, memo by Wright, Mar. 2, 1934, 724.3415/3425½; PPA, 2:521-23; FR, 1933, 4:207; US Department of State, *Report of the Delegates*, pp. 59-61, 119-31; Hinton, *Hull*, pp. 248-49, 254-55; CHm, 1:336-41; US Department of State, *Addresses and Statements, 1933-1934*, pp. 43, 46, 52-103; FA, 1:552-53; Pike, *Chile and the United States*, pp. 238-42; Braden, *Diplomats*

and Demagogues, pp. 126-35; Ernest Gruening, "Pan Americanism Reborn," *Current History* 39 (February 1934): 529-34; Gregory Wolfe, "The Seventh International Conference of American States: A Case Study in Inter-American Relations with Special Attention to Public Opinion" (Ph.D. diss., Fletcher School of Law and Diplomacy, 1961), pp. 136-45; Coleman, "Good Neighbor," pp. 108-10.
   69. Memo by Milton, Apr. 12, 1934, B. 15, GFM.
   70. PPA, 2:545; also see Daniels to FDR, Dec. 29, 1933, B. 16, JD; Moore to Hull, Dec. 29, 1933, B. 35. CH.
   71. FA, 1:573.
   72. Franklin Roosevelt, *On Our Way* (New York: John Day, 1934), pp. 108-9.
   73. Feis to Frankfurter, Jan. 29, 1934, B. 116, FF.

CHAPTER 3

   1. Sumner Welles, "Intervention and Interventions," *Foreign Affairs* 26 (October 1947): 119-22.
   2. Daniels to Dodd, Oct. 16, 1934, B. 44, WD; Daniels to Hull, Sept. 23, 1935, B. 38, CH; Daniels to Bowers, Dec. 19, 1935, B. 711, Daniels to FDR, Aug. 31, 1936, B. JD.
   3. FA, 2:242-44, 257-58, 361-63, 3:329-30; PPA, 4:450-52; E. David Cronon, "American Catholics and Mexican Anticlericalism, 1933-1936," *Mississippi Valley Historical Review* 45 (1958): 202-30.
   4. Niday to Borah, Jan. 5, Frantz to Borah, Feb. 3, Inman to Borah, Feb. 4, B. 384, Hawley to Borah, Feb. 18, Borah to Simmerman, Mar. 13, McLaughlin to Borah, May 7, 1935, B. 385, WB; Borchard to Borah, Feb. 5, Borah to Borchard, Feb. 6, 1935, B. 69, JM; Daniels to Dodd, Mar. 7, 1935, B. 712, JD.
   5. Duggan to White, Oct. 20, White to Duggan, Oct. 26, 1936, B. C-108, Marshall to Hull, Jan. 4, 1939, memo by Pickens, Jan. 3, 1941, B. C-231, Smith to Hull, Smith to Cárdenas, Oct. 16, Reed to Smith, Oct. 21, Tanis to Smith, Nov. 16, 1936, Quinones to NAACP, Mar. 17, 1939, B. C-283, NAACP.
   6. FR, 1937, 5:699-700; Maurice Halperin, "Mexico Shifts Her Foreign Policy," *Foreign Affairs* 19 (October 1940): 207-21; Karl Schmitt, *Mexico and the United States* (New York: John Wiley and Sons, 1974), pp. 80-85; Duggan, *Americas*, p. 67.
   7. Welles to Lane, Jan. 23, 1934, B. 8, AL.
   8. Welles to Lane, Apr. 12, 1934, B. 8, AL.
   9. Neill MacCaulay, *The Sandino Affair* (Chicago: Quadrangle Books, 1967), pp. 48-256; Munro, *Caribbean Republics*, pp. 277-79.
   10. Vladimir Petrov, *A Study in Diplomacy* (Chicago: Henry Regnery, 1971), pp. 1-40.
   11. Welles to Lane, Feb. 19, 1934, B. 8, AL; memo from Hackworth, Feb. 21, 1934, R. 88, HS; Daniels to Hull, Aug. 27, 1934, B. 37, CH; Petrov, *Study in Diplomacy*, pp. 24-63.
   12. Lane to Daniels, Mar. 4, 1934, B. 707, JD.
   13. Duggan to Lane, Dec. 4, 1936, B. 14, AL; Petrov, *Study in Diplomacy*, pp. 64-82.
   14. Welles to Lane, Oct. 27, 1936, B. 14, AL.
   15. Welles to Daniels, Nov. 8, 1937, B. 752, JD; Graff, "Strategy of Involvement," pp. 124-26.
   16. Davis to Hull, Sept. 7, 1933, 710.G/228; Lester Langley, "Negotiating New Treaties with Panama: 1936," *Hispanic American Historical Review* 48 (May 1968): 220-22.
   17. Hull to Gonzalez, June 18, 811.001 Roosevelt Visit file, Welles to FDR, June 27, 1934,/60A, Pittman to Hull, July 7, 1936, 411.00/134; Borchard to Moore, Apr. 3, Moore to Borchard, Apr. 4, 1936, B. 70, Borchard to Moore, Sept. 17, 1938, B. 74, JM; memo by Hull, Feb. 14, B. 36, Welles to Hull, Oct. 31, 1934, B. 37, CH; PC, Oct. 11, 1933, R. 1; PAA, 2:407-10, 3:348-49; FA, 2:351-52; PL, 1:409; Langley, "Negotiating New Treaties," pp. 224-33; SW-3, pp. 201-2; Duggan, *Americas*, p. 66; CHm, 1:344-

45; Sheldon Liss, *The Canal* (Notre Dame, Ind.: University of Notre Dame Press, 1967), pp. 35-69.

18. Duggan to Armour, Aug. 27, 1938, 710. H-Agenda/93½.

19. Corrigan to Welles, June 2, 1939, B. 10, FC; diary, Oct. 9, 1941, HS; diary, Oct. 10, 1941, B. 213, AB; McNaughton to McComaighy, Dec. 3, 1942, McNaughton Reports, FM; Borchard to Moore, Dec. 8, 1942, B. 82, JM; diary, Apr. 20, 1943, B. 5, BL; Duggan to Wallace, Apr. 27, 1943, B. 30, HW (FDRL); Liss, *Canal*, pp. 39-42; William Langer and S. Everett Gleason. *The Undeclared War* (New York: Harper and Brothers, 1953), pp. 147-50, 610-15.

20. Diary, Jan. 9, 1933, HS; White to Cutting, Feb. 27, ACLU to FDR, Sept. 29, 1933, B. C-329, NAACP; FA, 1:313-14.

21. PC, Aug. 4, 1933, R. 1; Cooper, "Withdrawal of the United States from Haiti," pp. 96-98; Munro, "American Withdrawal from Haiti," pp. 22-23; FA, 1:343-45; CHm, 1:312.

22. White to Detzer, Nov. 11, Buell to White, Dec. 7, White to Phillips, Dec. 8, 1933, B. C-329, Hull to White, Feb. 14, 1934, B. C-330, NAACP; diary, Mar. 29, 1934, WP; Ernest Gruening, "The Withdrawal from Haiti," *Foreign Affairs* 12 (July 1934): 678-79; Cooper, "Withdrawal of the United States from Haiti," pp. 98-101; PPA, 2:505-7; CHm, 1:345-46.

23. Hull to Armour, June 5, 811.001 Roosevelt Visit file, Armour to Hull, June 6,/14, FDR to Hull, July 5,/57, Armour to Hull, July 6,/58, Hull to Armour, July 18, 1934,/27B CF; White to Price-Mars, Apr. 4, 1934, B. C-330, NAACP; diary, Apr. 16, July 5, Aug. 17, 1934, WP; Armour to Foster, July 7, 1934, PPF 1710; Munro, "American Withdrawal from Haiti," pp. 23-26; PL, 1:404-5; PPA, 3:184-85, 341-42.

24. Duggan to White, Nov. 26, 1934, B. C-105, White to Vincent, Mar. 12, Gruening to White, Sept. 6, 1935, Duggan to Villard, Mar. 19, 1938, B. C-330, NAACP; Mayer to Wilson, June 1939, B. 3, HW; report on Haiti, Feb. 22, 1941, B. 136, PJ; PPA, 12:429-32; Duggan, *Americas*, pp. 65-66.

25. Stafford to Stimson, Aug. 13, 1931, 710.G/41, Brown to Hull, Oct. 4, 1933,/250; memo by FDR, Mar. 3, 1934, B. 36, CH; G. Pope Atkins and Larman Wilson, *The United States and the Trujillo Regime* (New Brunswick, N.J.: Rutgers University Press, 1972), pp. 28-52.

26. Daniels to Norweb, Nov. 16, 1937, B. 729, JD; Duggan to White, Dec. 28, Welles to White, Dec. 31, 1937, B. C-330, NAACP; Atkins and Wilson, *Trujillo Regime*, pp. 53-56.

27. Diary, Oct. 24, 1940, B. 4, HW; McKennis to George, Nov. 26, 1940, Committee on Foreign Relations Dominican Bonds, Hearings (Correspondence), Sen 76A-F 9, RG 46, NA; Duggan, *Americas*, p. 67.

28. Diary, Jan. 14, 16, 17, 1934, WP; Gellman, *Roosevelt and Batista*, pp. 77-79, 83.

29. Davis to Welles, Feb. 23, 1934, B. 63, ND; diary, Apr. 2, B. 6, Apr. 19, 1935, B. 9, JD; FA, 1:593; Gellman, *Roosevelt and Batista*, pp. 84-137.

30. Diary, May 29, 1934, WP; diary, July 22, 1934, B. 9, JD; FA, 2:124-25, 138-39; CHm, 1: 342-44; Duggan, *Americas*, p. 66; Gellman, *Roosevelt and Batista*, pp. 104-11.

31. Gellman, *Roosevelt and Batista*, pp. 138-58.

32. Duggan to Welles, Jan. 4, 1937, 710.Peace/907-26/27.

33. Early to Hull, May 21, 811.001 Roosevelt Visit file/65, Hull to Whitehouse, June 6,/14A CF, Whitehouse to Hull, June 7, 15, Hull to Whitehouse, June 18,/27A CF, Whitehouse to Hull, June 16, 1934,/80; FA, 2:156-57; PC, June 15, 1934, R. 2: PL, 1:407.

CHAPTER 4

1. FA, 1:116-17; Feis, *1933*, pp. 266-67.

2. PC, Dec. 6, 1933, R. 1.

3. Phone conversation between Hull and Daniels, Sept. 22, 1933, 710.G 1A/187; Inman to wife, Dec. 19, 1936, B. 14, SI; CHm, 1:355, 348-49.

4. Welles to Davis, June 26, Davis to Welles, June 29, Welles to Davis, July 1, 11, 1931, B. 63, ND; Cornelius to Nielson, Sept. 24, Nielson to Cornelius, Oct. 24, 1934, B. 15, FN.

5. Memorandum by White, June 24, 1935, White to Wright, Oct. 28, Clark to Hull, Nov. 25, 1936, White to Dearing, Mar. 16, 1937, FW; Mishler, "Francis White," pp. 361-68.

6. Hull to Harrison, June 18, 1934, 810.5151-Williams Mission/1; FR, 1934, 4:390-422.

7. Wright to Hull, Mar. 28, 1934, 560.AD iC/1, Hull to Wallace, Mar. 15, 1935,/99; US Department of State, *Report of the Delegates of the United States of America to the Pan American Commercial Conference held at Buenos Aires, Argentina, May 26-June 19, 1935* (Washington, D.C.: G.P.O., 1936), pp. 3-22; Braden, *Diplomats and Demagogues*, pp. 136-43.

8. Momorandum on Inter-American Highway, Dec. 1, 1933, 810.154/475, Philip to FDR, Dec. 7, 1938, 710.Peace Pan American Highway/100; diary, Mar. 3, 1934, WP; FR, 1931, 1:709-14; PC, Mar. 3, 1934, R. 2; PPA, 3:133-36; CHm, 1:348.

9. Diary, Sept. 30, 1938, Jan. 3, 5, 1939, B. 5, South American-Goodwill Mission-1938, B. 177, BL; Steinhardt to Untermeyer, Mar. 31, 1939, B. 78, LS.

10. PPA, 2:206; Allan Everest, *Morgenthau, the New Deal and Silver* (New York: King's Crown Press, 1950), pp. 45-46.

11. Diary, July 18, 1935, WP; Duggan to Inman, Mar. 8, 1938, B. 14, SI; presidential diary, memorandum of conversation, July 10, 1939, B. 1, HM; Pittman to Daniels, Aug. 14, 1939, B. 738, JD; Messersmith to Feis, July 21, 1942, B. 17, HF; FA, 3:275-76; Everest, *Morgenthau*, pp. 66-67, 79-100, 177-78; HMd, 1:199-204.

12. Diary, Taylor to Morgenthau, Feb. 9, B. 54, conversation with Welles, May 12, B. 68, joint statement, July 16, 1937, B. 78, HM; Duggan to Inman, Mar, 8, 1938, B. 14, SI; HMd, 1:493.

13. Welles to Bowers, Jan. 20, 1939, Bowers mss II, CB.

14. PC, Feb. 17, Mar. 10, 1939, R. 7.

15. Memorandum by Briggs, Jan. 18, 033.3211 Aranha, Oswaldo/36, Bogdan to Duggan, Apr. 24, 1939,/71; Welles to Daniels, Apr. 11, 1938, B. 752, JD; Giffin, "Normal Years," pp. 4-5; FA, 2:205-6; PPA, 8:69; Stanley Hilton, *Brazil and the Great Powers* (Austin: University of Texas Press, 1975), pp. 191-206.

16. Giffin, "Normal Years," pp. 160-64; HMd, 2:52-55.

17. Diary, memorandum to Klotz, Dec. 11, 1937, B. 101, HM; HMd, 1:524-27.

18. White to Morgenthau, Mar. 30, 31, memorandum by White, June 6, 1939, B. 6, HDW.

19. Wallace to Farley, Oct. 19, 1933, B. 35, CH; address by Wallace, Dec. 9, 1938, press release, US Department of Agriculture; Sam Walker, "Henry A. Wallace and American Foreign Policy" (Ph.D. diss., University of Maryland, 1974), pp. 117-18; CR, vol. 84, pt. 13, pp. 2740-41; FA, 2:163-64; Gellman, *Roosevelt and Batista*, pp. 102-3, 140-45, 160-61, 170-71; Duggan, *Americas*, p. 75.

20. Diary, memorandum of conversation, June 6, 1938, B. 127, HM; Hull to Jones, Feb. 20, 1939, B. 29, JJ; Feis to Hull, Dec. 15, 1938, B. 1, RG 43; FA, 1:663-64, 2:21; PPA, 3:76-81; Frederick Adams, "The Export-Import Bank and American Foreign Policy, 1934-1939" (Ph.D. diss., Cornell University, 1968), pp. 124-26; Gellman, *Roosevelt and Batista*, pp. 101-2.

21. McBride to Hull, June 5, 1933, B. 34, HC; FA, 1:28, 162-65, 214-20; PC, Apr. 5, June 9, 1933, R. 1, Freidel, *Triumph*, p. 251; CHm, 1:347-48; Robert Ferrell, ed., *The American Secretaries of State and Their Diplomacy*, Julius Pratt, "Cordell Hull" (New York: Cooper Square Publishers, 1964), 12:107-8; Hinton, *Hull*, pp. 7-8; Acheson, *Present at the Creation*, p. 55.

22. Phillips to Burleson, July 31, 1933, B. 29, ASB; FA, 1:301-5.

23. Irwin F. Gellman, "Prelude to Reciprocity: The Abortive United States-Colombian Treaty of 1933," *Historian* 32 (November 1969): 52-68.

24. Diary, Dec. 19, 28, 1933, WP; FA, 2:1-3, 257.

25. Moore to Hull, Nov. 27, 1933, B. 35, Welles to Hull, Oct. 31, 1934, Hull to

Daniels, Feb. 19, 1935, B. 37, CH; Feis to Stimson, May 17, June 7, 1934, R. 87, HS; Feis to Frankfurter, May 29, 1934, B. 116, FF; Frankfurter to Feis, Dec. 1933, B. 34, HF; ABnr, p. 103.

26. Roper to Dodd, July 31, 1933, B. 42, June 6, Oct. 2, 1934, B. 45, WD; Roper to Daniels, Mar. 9, 1934, B. 753, JD; Daniels to Burleson, Aug. 28, Burleson to Roper, Nov. 30, 1933, Roper to Burleson, Sept. 6, 1934, B. 29, Burleson to Roper, Dec. 9, 1935, B. 30, ASB; Sack to FDR, Oct. 16, 1933, Official Files 632; Tomlinson to Hull, Mar. 8, 1934, B. 36, CH; Baker to Daniels, May 3, 1936, B. 84, NB.

27. Burleson to Roper, July 28, 1933, B. 29, ASB.

28. Buell to Stimson, Apr. 30, 1934, R. 86, Stimson to Hoover, Dec. 9, 1935, R. 90, Stimson to Landon, Aug. 6, 1936, R. 91, Stimson to Moffat, Nov. 17, 1936, R. 92, HS; US-LA, July 1938, B. 21, WRC; Culbertson to McClure, May 3, 1933, B. 12, ND; diary, May 1, 1934, WP; HSas, pp. 298-300; WWsl, p. 341.

29. Diary, Jan. 22, 1935, V. 27, Hoover to Stimson, Dec. 2, 1935, R. 90, HS; diary, Dec. 11, 12, 1933, WP; Phillips to Hull, Dec. 13, 1934, B. 37, CH; HIsd, 1:360; Herbert Hoover, *The Memoirs of Herbert Hoover: The Great Depression* (New York: Macmillan, 1952), pp. 405-6; Dick Stewart, *Trade and Hemisphere* (Columbia: University of Missouri Press, 1975), pp. 31-61

30. Feis to Milton, Oct. 14, 1937, B. 22, Milton to Clayton, May 20, Clayton to Milton, May 23, 1938, B. 25, Milton to Garrett, Apr. 29, 1938, B. 82, GFM; Bullitt to Hull, Apr. 7, 1936, B. unnumbered, Hull to Knox, Oct. 28, 1938, B. 43, Bowers to Hull, Apr. 10, 1940, B. 46, CH; Jessup to Shanely, Jan. 10, 1940, B. 347, WW; memorandum by Kelchner, Apr. 28, 1939, 710. H-Inter-American Commerce/3; FA, 3:328-29; BLwd, pp. 38, 51.

31. Welles to Berle, July 25, Aug. 12, 1934, B. 12, AB; Caffery to Taussig, Apr. 30, 1934, B. 37, CT; diary, Oct. 29, 1934, V. 27, HS; Sayre to O'Mahoney, Aug. 2, 1939, B. 45, CH; FA, 1:178, 624, 2:177, 220-21; PL, 1:350; Gellman, *Roosevelt and Batista*, pp. 113-17, 128-30, 170-72, 174-75, 190-91.

32. Diary, Oct. 31, 1933, Oct. 11, 1934, WP; Welles to Gibson, Oct. 19, 1934, B. 48, HG; Sayre to Burleson, July 15, 1935, B. 29, ASB; Gibson to Hull, Sept. 13, 1935, Caffery to Hull, Apr. 20, 1943, B. 51, CH; Thurston to Hull, July 31, 1933, 710.G/197; FA, 2:244-48, 287-89, 410-15; PPA, 2:211-12; Giffin, "Normal Years," pp. 69-72, 255-56, 429-36; Hilton, *Great Powers*, pp. 48-84, 139-47, 154-59, 227-28.

33. Armour to Culbertson, Oct. 20, Culbertson to Armour, Nov. 6, 1941, B. 21, WC; Hull to Saavedra Lamas, Nov. 18, 1941, B. 49, CH; Wood to Jessup, Feb. 12, 1940, B. 31, PJ; Edith Blendon, "Venezuela and the United States: The Impact of Venezuelan Nationalism" (Ph.D. diss., University of Maryland, 1971), pp. 55-58; Kenneth Grieb, "Negotiating a Reciprocal Trade Agreement with an Underdeveloped Country: Guatemala as a Case Study," *Prologue* 5 (Spring 1973): 23-29; Gellman, "Prelude to Reciprocity," pp. 60-68; Peterson, *Argentina and the United States*, pp. 412-13; Conil Paz and Ferrari, *Argentina's Foreign Policy*, pp. 60-62; CHm, 2:1140.

34. Coleman, "Good Neighbor," pp. 212-14; Duggan, *Americas*, pp. 74, 76-78; Adler, *Uncertain Giant*, pp. 118-24; Edward Guerrant, *Roosevelt's Good Neighbor Policy* (Albuquerque: University of New Mexico Press, 1950), pp. 96-99.

35. SW-3, p. 55.

36. SW-2, p. 12-13.

37. Rout, *Chaco Peace Conference*, pp. 46-52.

38. Jenkins to Hull, July 11, 1940, 710.Consultation (2)/375; ABnr, pp. 260-61; Herbert Klein, "American Oil Companies in Latin America: The Bolivian Experience," *Inter-American Economic Affairs* 18 (Autumn 1964); 47-72; Wood, *Good Neighbor Policy*, pp. 168-202; Harold Davis, John Finan, and F. Taylor Peck, *Latin American Diplomatic History* (Baton Rouge: Louisiana State University Press, 1977), pp. 206-10.

39. Wynne to Nielson, May 21, 1934, B. 14, FN; Cronon, *Daniels*, pp. 130-53; Schmitt, *Mexico and the United States*, pp. 169-75.

40. FA, 3:589.

41. Daniels to Dodd, Dec. 10, 1936, B. 48, Daniels to Dodd, Nov. 25, 1938, B. 56, WD; Daniels to White, Jan. 10, 1938, B. 735, JD; Daniels to Inman, Nov. 18, 1938, B.

14, SI; Chapper to Landon, Nov. 3, 1938, B. 89, AML; PC, Apr. 1, 1938, R. 6.

42. Welles to Castillo Nájera, Nov. 4; also see Welles to Daniels, Nov. 8, 1937, B. 790, JD.

43. Howard Cline, *The United States and Mexico* (New York: Atheneum, 1963), pp. 229-38; Cronon, *Daniels*, pp. 154-84; Schmitt, *Mexico and the United States*, pp. 175-88.

44. Daniels to FDR, Sept. 14, 1937, B. 16, JD; Cronon, *Daniels*, pp. 185-229; Meyer, *Mexico and the United States*, pp. 149-72.

45. Daniels to FDR, May 27, June 4, Aug. 31, Sept. 15, 1938, B. 16, Daniels to Hull, Aug. 22, 1938, B. unnumbered, Daniels to Bowers, Sept. 6, 19, B. 732, Mar. 3, 1939, B. 736, JD; Daniels to Inman, June 30, 1938, B. 14, SI; Daniels to Baruch, Apr. 18, 1938, V. 1938, BB.

46. Daniels to FDR, Mar. 22, 1938, B. 16, JD.

47. HMd, 1:493-97.

48. Diary, Jan. 31, 1939, B. 210, AB.

49. Diary, Dec. 14, 1939, B. 211; ABnr, pp. 177, 185, 212, 234; HIsd, 2:352-53; Charles A. Lindbergh, *The Wartime Journals of Charles A. Lindbergh* (New York: Harcourt Brace Jovanovich, 1970), pp. 380-81.

50. Memo by Moore, Mar. 30, 1938, B. 10, RM.

51. Messersmith to Heineman, Nov. 7, 1938, no. 1067, GM.

52. Baruch to Hull, Mar. 29, Baruch to Daniels, Apr. 11, June 28, 1938, V. 1938, BB.

53. Borchard to Moore, Mar. 26, Apr. 21, Aug. 2, 6, Sept. 12, 17, Moore to Borchard, Sept. 5, 16, 1938, B. 74, Borchard to Moore, Apr. 17, July 2, Nov. 2, Dec. 15, 1939, B. 76, Moore to Cory, Jan. 26, Moore to Borchard, Feb. 24, Aug. 3, Borchard to Moore, Mar. 27, Apr. 18, 1940, B. 78, Borchard to Moore, Jan. 24, May 7, Moore to Armstrong, Aug. 24, 1941, B. 80, JM; McAdoo to Daniels, Sept. 12, 1938, B. 734, Creel to Daniels, Dec. 13, 1939, B. 736, Corrigan to Daniels, Apr. 21, 1940, B. 740, JD; diary, Oct. 18, 1938, B. 9, WL.

54. Hadley Cantril, *Public Opinion, 1935-1946* (Princeton, N.J.: Princeton University Press, 1951), p. 549.

55. JDrd, pp. 185-86.

56. Diary, May 19, 1938, B. 8, RC; *The Mexican Oil Seizure, 1939*, B. 11, address by Richberg, Apr. 14, 1939, B. 22, DR; Richberg to Castillo Nájera, Mar. 22, B. 44, Preston to Hull, June 20, 1939, B. unnumbered, CH; JDrd, pp. 189-90; HIsd, 2:604, 626-27.

57. Richberg to Teagle, Feb. 17, 1941, B. 2, DR.

58. Meeting of the LC, Apr. 23, 1940, SLC; memo by Gosnell, Feb. 2, 1948, Welles file, WBHS; Welles to Daniels, Apr. 11, Duggan to Daniels, Sept. 28, 1938, B. 752, Boal to Daniels, Aug. 21, Sept. 21, 1938, B. 754, JD; Hull to Daniels, Sept. 16, 1938, B. 43, Hull to Welles, Jan. 2, 1939, B. 44, Farish to Hull, Feb. 13, Blocker to Duggan, Feb. 14, 1940, B. 46, CH; diary, Sept. 13, 1938, JPM; Harrison to Long, Nov. 9, 1938, B. 124, BL; diary, Mar. 24, 1938, V. 28, HS; OHP-HW; ABnr, pp. 169-70; Lloyd Gardner, *Economic Aspects of New Deal Diplomacy* (Madison: University of Wisconsin Press, 1964), pp. 112-23.

59. Daniels to Creel, Jan. 29, 1941, B. J. Daniels, 1940s I, JD; Cronon, *Daniels*, pp. 230-71; Meyer, *Oil Controversy*, pp. 173-216.

60. Daniels to Bowers, Oct. 25, 1940, Bowers mss II, CB; Daniels to Baruch, Nov. 18, 1940, B. 740, JD; Wallace to Inman, Nov. 18, 1940, B. 14, SI; Wallace to Oswaldo, Dec. 9, B. 43, Messersmith to Wallace, Nov. 22, Wallace speech, Dec. 4, 1940, B. 44, HW (LC); Boal to Wallace, Jan. 4, 1941, R. 22, HW(Ia); Walker, "Wallace," pp. 142-45; Langer and Gleason, *Undeclared War*, pp. 158-62.

61. Wallace to Hull, Dec. 19, 1940, FDR to Wallace, Wallace to Camacho, Jan. 10, 1941, R. 22, HW(Ia).

62. JDrd, pp. 204-5.

63. Ibid., pp. 205-6; PL, 2:1228-29; PC, Oct. 31, 1941, R. 9.

64. Duggan to Daniels, McGurk to Daniels, Nov. 25, 1941, B. 749, JD; Cline, *The United States and Mexico*, pp. 239-51; Duggan, *Americas*, pp. 67-70; CHm, 2:140-43; Meyer, *Oil Controversy*, pp. 217-24.

65. Diary, Feb. 8, June 28, 1942, Feb. 7, Mar. 14, Aug. 29, 1943, B. 10, Jan. 23, 1944, B. 11, HI; FDR to Hull, Dec. 7, 1942, B. 31, JJ; Messersmith to Hull, July 21, 1944, B. 53, CH; oil expropriation, vol. 2, no. 17, Hull, Ickes and oil, vol. 3, no. 22, B. LX, GM; Gardner, *Economic Aspects*, pp. 205-9; HIsd, 3:628-29; Harry Stegmaier, "From Confrontation to Cooperation: The United States and Mexico, 1938-1945" (Ph.D. diss., University of Michigan, 1970), pp. 288-90.

66. Braden to Taussig, May 23, 1939, B. 33, CT; David Bushnell, *Eduardo Santos and the Good Neighbor* (Gainesville: University of Florida Press, 1967), pp. 95-102; Stephen Randall, "The International Corporation and American Foreign Policy: The United States and Colombian Petroleum, 1920-1940," *Canadian Journal of History* 9 (August 1974): 179-96; Braden, *Diplomats and Demagogues*, pp. 218-24.

67. Wilson to Stimson, Jan. 7, 1931, 710.G/57; report on Ven., Feb. 27, 1941, B. 136, PJ; diary, Oct. 10, 1942, B. 9, HI; Blendon, "Venezuela and the United States," pp. 50, 93-94.

68. Corrigan to Hull, Dec. 30, 1939, 740.00111 A-Neutrality Patrol/57.

69. Wood, *Good Neighbor Policy*, pp. 260-82.

70. CR, vol. 83, pt. 9, pp. 937-38; Milton to Scotten, Aug. 11, 1937, B. 81, GFM.

71. CR, vol. 85, pt. 2, p. 1368.

72. Watson to Hull, Mar. 6, 1939, B. 44, CH; Culbertson speech, Mar. 11, B. 19, memo by meeting, Oct. 31, 1939, B. 18, WC.

73. Memo on Brazil, Nov. 1, 1939, B. 18, WC.

74. White to Feis, Dec. 20, 1939, B. 16, HF.

75. IAA, 1:178-81.

CHAPTER 5

1. Division of current information, Aug. 28, 1934, 710.11/1937; FA, 3:326-29, 336-37; Coleman, "Good Neighbor," pp. 149-52; Gruening, "Withdrawal from Haiti," p. 679; C. H. Haring, "Recent Pan American Achievements," *Bulletin of the Pan American Union* 70 (February 1936): 78-84; Hinton, *Hull*, p. 282.

2. Rowe to Hull, Dec. 17, 1934, B. 37, CH; Borah to Hartley, Jan. 15, 1935, B. 378, WB; Daniels to FDR, Apr. 1, B. 16, Daniels to Dodd, Apr. 9, 1935, B. 712, Gruening to Daniels, Apr. 22, B. 720, Daniels to Meyer, Apr. 20, Lambeth to Daniels, May 9, B. 721, Rippy to Daniels, Mar. 13, 1936, B. 722, JD.

3. Barrett to Lewis, May 5, 1936, B. 30, JB.

4. Stabler to White, Feb. 28, 1936, FW; Borchard to Johnson, Apr. 17, 1936, B. 70, JM; Krock speech, May 29, 1935, B. 38, CH.

5. William Castle speech, "Uncle Sam and Latin America," Aug. 27, 1933, B. 20, WRC; Castle to Moore, June 14, 1934, B. 67, JM; Marshall to Fletcher, Dec. 2, Fletcher to Marshall, Dec. 6, 1936, B. 16, HPF; ASp, 1:306-11.

6. William Castle speech, "Intervention and the Policy of the Good Neighbor," July 6, 1934, B. 37, CH.

7. Cumming to Castle, July 23, 1934, B. 20, WRC.

8. Butler to Culbertson, Feb. 6, Nicholson to Culbertson, Mar. 24, Butler to Culbertson, Apr. 8, Aug. 17, 1934, B. 14, Feb. 20, 1935, B. 15, WC; Weddell to Hull, Aug. 3, Welles to Hull, Oct. 31, 1934, B. 37, Hull to Hudson, Apr. 9, 1935, B. 38, CH; Haden to Milton, May 13, 1937, B. 81, GFM; Braden to Feis, July 29, 1938, B. 11, HF; FA, 2:112-13, 294-98, 3:66-67; PPA, 3:268-78, 8:351-54; PC, May 18, 1934, R. 2, Oct. 11, 1938, R. 6; CHm, 1:346-47; Anthony Eden, *The Memoirs of Anthony Eden: Facing the Dictators* (Boston: Houghton Mifflin, 1962), pp. 100-101; Rout, *Chaco Peace Conference*, pp. 58-217; Zook, *Chaco War*, pp. 158-256; Wood, *Latin American Wars*, pp. 40-166; William Garner, *The Chaco Dispute* (Washington, D.C.: Public Affairs Press, 1966), pp. 1, 108-22; Peterson, *Argentina and the United States*, p. 389; Conil Paz and Ferrari, *Argentina's Foreign Policy*, pp. 28-33.

9. Dearing to Hull, Aug. 13, 710.Peace/7, Daniels to Hull, Oct. 3, 1935, 811.001 Roosevelt Visit/139; FR, 1935, 4:1-6; PPA, 4:405-12; CHM, 1:493; Braden, *Diplomats and Demagogues*, p. 145.

10. Weddell to Hull, Feb. 10, 710.Peace/39, Justo to FDR; Feb. 22, 1936,/12; diary, Feb. 13, 1936, WP; Arjona to Dodd, Feb. 15, 1936, B. 49, WD; Moore to Rowe, Feb. 28, 1936, B. 71, JM; FR, 1936, 4:3-5, 9; PC, Mar. 17, 1936, R. 4; PPA, 5:72-74; CHM, 1:493.

11. Phillips to Moffat, Apr. 16, 1936, JPM-1936, JPM; FR, 1936, 5:10-12, 23-24; press release, Apr. 14, 710. Peace/408, press conference, Apr. 17,/461, memo by Duggan, June 29, Agenda/75, Pittman to Hull, July 7, 411.00/134, press release, July 10, 1936, 710.Peace/678; Inman to Welles, June 10, 1936, B. 14, SI; FR, 1936, 5:15-17; FA, 3:328; PPA, 5:124-25; Inter-American Conference for the Maintenance of Peace, *Special Handbook for the Use of Delegates* (Washington, D.C.: Pan American Union, 1936), pp. 1-3.

12. Gibson to Hull, Mar. 4, 710.Peace/227, Hull to Gibson, Oct. 21, Agenda/120, Welles to Scotten, Oct. 31, 1936, Agenda/129; Welles to Gibson, Aug. 8, Sept. 25, 1936, B. 48, HG; FR, 1936, 5:13-16.

13. Press conference, Apr. 14, 710.Peace/443, Oct. 2, Agenda/116, memo by Welles, Oct. 8, Agenda/156, Duggan to Welles, Nov. 29, 1936, 907-12/27; Moore to Rowe, Apr. 12, 1936, B. 71, JM; Moore to Davis, Nov. 20, 1936, B. 40, ND; Jessup to Hackworth, Nov. 24, 1936, B. 14, PJ.

14. Weddell to Hull, May 28, 1935, 710.11/2887½, O'Donoghue to Hull, May 8, 710.Peace/497, Daniels to Hull, Aug. 7,/705, Gilbert to Moore, Nov. 10, Personnel/256, Dawson to Hull, Oct. 30, 1936, Agenda/132; Moore to Rowe, Mar. 25, B. 71, Moore to Borchard, May 25, 1936, B. 70, JM; Daniels to Dodd, Apr. 20, 1936, B. 719, JD; Hull to Wilson, May 15, 1936, B. 39, CH; Welles to Inman, June 12, 1936, B. 14, SI; diary, Aug. 29, 1936, B. 8, RC; FR, 1936, 5:17-21, 25-27, 31-32; Phelps Phelps, "League of American Nations," *Port of New York Journal* (September 1936): 13-17.

15. Memo by Welles, Mar. 23, 710.Peace/331½, memo by Stinebower, Aug. 11,/716½, Hawkins to Sayre, Oct. 9, Agenda/118½, McClure to Sayre, Oct. 11, Agenda/118½, memo by Duggan, Nov. 13, Agenda/168, 169, 170, Duggan to Welles, Nov. 14,/907-5/27, Welles to Duggan, Nov. 20, 1936,/907-9/27; Roper to Hull, Nov. 12, 1936, B. 16, HF; Feis to Frankfurter, Nov. 6, 1936, B. 54, FF; FA, 3:258-59; FR, 1936, 5:27-29, 31.

16. Memo by Studebaker, June 17, 1936, 710.Peace-Agenda/49, 50, 51.

17. Fenwick to FDR, Apr. 11, 710.Peace-Personnel/4, Welling to Hull, Aug. 18, Applicants/137, Duggan to Welles, Nov. 8, 1936, /907-1/27; Milton to Hull, Apr. 20, 1936, B. 19, GFM; Welles to Gibson, May 12, 1936. B. 48, HG; Welles to Barrett, Oct. 30, 1936, B. 30, JB; US-BA conf., Nov. 19, 1936, B. 21, WRC; Braden to Taussig, Jan. 8, 1937, B. 33, CT; FA, 3:315; PL, 1:579; HIsd, 1:693; CHm, 1:494-95.

18. Hull to Phillips, Oct. 24, 26, 1936, B. 39, CH; Milton to Brown, Nov. 2, 1936, B. 80, GFM; Messersmith to Hull, Nov. 6, 1936, B. 49, WD; Inman to wife, Nov. 18, 1936, B. 14, SI; US Department of State, *Addresses and Statements by the Honorable Cordell Hull in Connection with His Trip to South America to Attend the Inter-American Conference for the Maintenance of Peace Held at Buenos Aires, Argentina, December 1-23, 1936* (Washington, D.C.: G.P.O., 1937), pp. 47-63.

19. US Department of State, *Addresses and Statements, December 1-23, 1936*, p. 53.

20. Inman to wife, Nov. 25, 1936, B. 14, SI; Milton to Dehlgren, Nov. 27, Milton to Lamm, Nov. 28, 1936, B. 27, GFM; Hull to Davis, Nov. 28, B. 27, ND; Hull to Davis, Dec. 1, 1936, B. 40, CH; US Department of State, *Addresses and Statements, December 1-23, 1936*, pp. 3-4, 64-69; CHm, 1:495; Hinton, *Hull*, p. 310.

21. Daniels to FDR, Nov. 2, 1936, B. 16, JD; Weddell to Hull, Oct. 2, 710.Peace/805, Weddell to Moore, Nov. 10, 1936, 811. 001 Roosevelt Visit/209; Moore to Dodd, Nov. 11, 1936, B. 49, WD; PC, Nov. 6, 1936, R. 4; PPA, 5:583-84; FA, 3:433, 477; PL, 1:626-27; Inter-American Conference for the Maintainance of Peace, *Proceedings* (Buenos Aires: Imprenta Del Congreso Nacinal, 1937), p. 4; ABnr, p. 119; HIsd, 1:704; Donald Dozer, *Are We Good Neighbors?* (Gainesville: University of Florida Press, 1959), pp. 16-23, 26-33; Roosevelt and Brough, *Rendezvous with Destiny*, pp. 146-48; Eleanor Roosevelt, *The Autobiography of Eleanor Roosevelt* (New York: Harper and Brothers, 1961), p. 187.

22. Moore to Hull, Nov. 16, 811.001 Roosevelt Visit/222A, Moore to Weddell, Nov. 16, 1936,/228A, Duggan to Armour, Aug. 30, 1938, 710.H/99½; Roper to Daniels, Nov. 23, 1936, B. 752, JD; PC, Nov. 17, 1936, R. 4; PL, 1:631; FA, 3:469-71, 490-91.

23. Mitchell to Moore, Nov. 30, 811.001 Roosevelt Visit/261½, Scotten to Moore, Dec. 9, 1936,/280,281; James Roosevelt to Barrett, Nov. 28, 1936, B. JB; PPA, 5: 597-603; FA, 3:513-14; PL, 1:632-35; James Roosevelt and Sidney Shalett, *Affectionately F.D.R.* (New York: Harcourt Brace, 1959), pp. 284-86.

24. Weddell to Moore, Jan. 7, 1937, 811.001 Roosevelt Visit/302; US-BA conf., Dec. 1936, B. 2, SI; FA, 3:515-16; Hinton, *Hull*, pp. 310-12; CHm, 1:497.

25. Lane to Daniels, Feb. 8, 1935, B. 713, JD; PPA, 3:498-99, 4:121, 5:604-10; FA, 2:431-32, 3:72, 152-56, 238-45, 259-60, 313, 372, 377-84, 516-23; HIsd, 1:533; US Department of State, *Report of the Delegation of the United States of America to the Inter-American Conference for the Maintenance of Peace, Buenos Aires, Argentina, December 1-23, 1936* (Washington, D.C.: G.P.O., 1937), p. 10; *Proceedings*, p. 650; ABnr, pp. 119-20.

26. Diary, Mar. 20, 1935, WP; FDR to Dodd, Dec. 2, 1935, B. 47, WD; PC, Mar. 20, 1935, R. 3; PL, 1:487; HIsd, 1:312.

27. Dodd to Arjona, Feb. 13, Moore to Dodd, Aug. 31, 1936, B. 49, WD; FA, 3:170-71; HIsd, 1:479, 494, 514, 2:7; Arthur Krock, *Memoirs* (New York: Funk and Wagnalls, 1968), p. 183.

28. PL, 1:625.

29. Davis to Hull, Nov. 17, 1936, B. 40, CH; Davis to Sweetser, Nov. 18, 1936, B. 31, AS; Roper to Dodd, Dec. 2, 1936, B. 49, WD; Messersmith to Moore, Dec. 5, 1936, No. 790, GM; FA, 3:525-26; SW-2, p. 67.

30. Berle to Taussig, Dec. 1, 1936, B. 21, CT.

31. PPA, 5:606.

32. Johnson to Hull, Aug. 22, 710.Peace/740, Armour to Moore, Dec. 3,/1054, Gilbert to Moore, Dec. 4,/1049, Bullitt to Moore, Nov. 13,/910, Dec. 2,/1024, Kirk to Hull, Apr. 23, 1936,/493, Phillips to Moore, Jan. 8, 1937,/1257, Mayer to Hull, May 11,/549, Dodd to Moore, Dec. 4, 1936,/1039; Dodd to Hull, Oct. 7, 1936, B. 39, CH; Dodd to Hull, Oct. 7, Dodd to FDR, Dec. 7, Dodd to Moore, Dec. 19, 1936, B. 49, FDR to Dodd, Jan. 9, 1937, B. 51, WD; FR, 1936, 3:32; FA, 3:533; WDd, pp. 362-64, 367, 368-69, 377; Robert Dallek, *Democrat and Diplomat* (New York: Oxford University Press, 1968), pp. 293-95, 297.

33. Hull to Moore, Dec. 2, 811.001 Roosevelt Visit/262, 263, Lay to Moore, Dec. 3,10,/266,288, Weddell to Moore, Dec. 11, 1936, Jan. 7, 1937,/302; FA, 3:523-25, 531-32, 534, 539, 549-50, 553-54, 556, 558-59; PL, 1:538, 636-38; PPA, 5:612-17, 6:157-60; Sack to Moore, Dec. 4, 710.Peace/1080, Duggan to Welles, Dec. 5, 1936,/ 907-16/27; Dearing to FDR, Dec. 19, 1936, PPF 1210; FFrf, pp. 365, 404; HIsd, 2:14-15; Roosevelt, *Autobiography of Eleanor Roosevelt*, pp. 187-88.

34. FDR to Sweetser, Dec. 9, 1936, B. 34, AS; FA, 3:534.

35. Sweetser to FDR, Jan. 30, FDR to Sweetser, Feb. 18, 1937, B. 34, AS; Moore to Dodd, Mar. 20, 1937, B. 51, WD; PL, 1:617-72.

36. Philip to Hull, Oct. 14, 1936, 710.Peace-Personnel/80; diary, Oct. 17, 1936, B. 7, JD; Inter-American Conference for the Maintenance of Peace, *Proceedings*, pp. 9-15; Conferencia Internacional de Consolidacion de la Paz, *Informe de la delegacion de Mexico a la Conferencia Interamericana* (Mexico: D.A.P.P., 1938), pp. 14-15; CHm, 1:499.

37. Weddell to Hull, Oct. 12, 1935, 710.Peace/10.

38. Dearing to Hull, Feb. 12, 710.Peace/96, Weddell to Hull, Feb. 16,/1327, Weddell to Hull, Feb. 16,/75, Weddell to Hull, Mar. 30,/322, Weddell to Hull, Apr. 1,/331, Weddell to Hull, June 2,/602, Weddell to Hull, Sept. 25,/791, Bullitt to Hull, Oct. 19, 1936, Agenda/118; Saavedra Lamas to Hull, Oct. 19, B. 39, Hull to Saavedra Lamas, Nov. 26, 1936, B. 40, CH; FR, 1936, 5:5-9, 12; Coleman, "Good Neighbor," pp. 285-86; Peterson, *Argentina and the United States*, p. 390; CHm, 1:497.

39. Hull to Moore, Dec. 4, 1936, 710.Peace/1041; Inter-American Conference for the Maintenance of Peace, *Proceedings*, pp. 666-67; US Department of State, *Addresses and Statements, December 1-23, 1936*, pp. 5-21; CHm, 1:498-99.

40. Memo by Inman, Nov. 29, Inman to wife, Dec. 1936, B. 14, SI; Braden to Taussig, Dec. 3, 1936, B. 33, CT; Moore to Hull, Dec. 9, 1936, B. 40, CH; Inter-American Conference for the Maintenance of Peace, *Proceedings*, pp. 19-22, 30, 651-60; ABnr, p. 120; Hull to Moore, Dec. 8,710.Peace-Neutrality/13, Dec. 10, /17, Dec. 11, Agenda/ 180,181, Dec. 12, Neutrality/24, Dec. 15, 1936/28; Inter-American Conference for the Maintenance of Peace, *Proceedings*, pp. 44-187, 677-98; Conferencia Internacional de Consolidation de la Paz, *Informe de la delegacion de Mexico*, pp. 31-40; Publicaciones del ministerio de relaciones exteriores, *Conferencia delegacion de El Salvador* (San Salvador: Imprenta Nacional, 1937), pp. 17-50; US Department of State, *Report of the Delegation, December 1-23, 1936*, pp. 16-23; US Department of State, *Addresses and Statements, December 1-23, 1936*, pp. 25-29; Conil Paz and Ferrari, *Argentina's Foreign Policy*, pp. 35-43; CHm, 1:500-501.

41. Inman to wife, Dec. 15, 1936, B. 14, SI.

42. Hull to Moore, Dec. 22, 1936, 710. Peace-Economic Problems/7, memo by Butler, Jan. 11, 710.Peace/1262½, Dawson to Hull, Feb. 1,/1294, memo by Kelchner, Feb. 16, 1937,/1323; Moore to Bullitt, Jan. 22, 1937, B. 3, RM; Welles to Inman, undated in 1938, B. 14, SI; Inter-American Conference for the Maintenance of Peace, *Proceedings*, pp. 136-50, 252-72, 280-327, 332-415, 440-501, 520-97; US Department of State, *Report of the Delegation, December 1-23, 1936*, pp. 23-40; Conferencia Internacional de Consolidacion de la Paz, *Informe de la delegacion de Mexico*, pp. 66, 69-73, 77-86, 89-100, 103-17; Publicaciones del ministerio de relaciones exteriores, *Conferencia delegacion de El Salvador*, pp. 26-32, 53-56, 59-62, 65-76, 79-99, 103-8, 143-45; US Department of State, *Addresses and Statements, December 1-23, 1936*, pp. 30-33.

43. US Department of State, *Report of the Delegation, December 1-23, 1936*, p. 15; idem, *Addresses and Statements, December 1-23, 1936*, pp. 34-43; Inter-American Conference for the Maintenance of Peace, *Proceedings*, pp. 780-800.

44. FDR to Hull, Dec. 24, 1936, 710.Peace/1158, Moore to *Democratic Digest*, Jan. 9, 1937,/1229; Milton to Faymonville, Milton to Dominick, Jan. 8, Milton to Corcoran, Milton to Nordvall, Jan. 9, Milton to Haden, Feb. 10, Milton to Moe, Feb. 22, Milton to Geist, Mar. 11, 1937, B. 81, GFM; PPA, 5:6-7; FA, 3:559-60; US Department of State, *Addresses and Statements, Dec. 1-23, 1936*, pp. 73-91; Adler, *Uncertain Giant*, pp. 112-16; CHm, 1:501-3.

45. Weddell to Hull, Braden to Hull, Jan. 8, 1937, B. unnumbered, Inman to Hull, Nov. 12, 1945, B. 55, CH; Milton to Buell, Jan. 26, B. 20, Haden to Milton, Feb. 1, Milton to Haden, Feb. 10, 1937, B. 81, GFM; Samuel Inman, "An Inside View of the Inter-American Conference," *South and World Affairs* 7 (April-May 1945): 31; Peterson, *Argentina and the United States*, pp. 392-93; Braden, *Diplomats and Demagogues*, pp. 174-81; SW-2, pp. 104-5; SW-3, pp. 204-8; CHm, 1:499.

46. Duggan to Welles, Dec. 23, 1936, 710.Peace/907-25/27, press release, Jan. 9,/ 1252, press release, Feb. 2,/1304, press release, Mar. 20, 1937,/1383; Welles to Hull, Jan. 19, 1937, B. 40, CH; Welles to Barrett, Jan. 25, 1937, B. 31, JB; Welles to Corrigan, Feb. 10, 1937, B. 10, FC; Sumner Welles, "The New Era in Pan American Relations," *Foreign Affairs* 15 (April 1937): 443-54; SW-3, pp. 60-61; SW-2, pp. 103-5, 180; Duggan, *Americas*, pp. 70-72.

47. Carlos de Macedo Soares to Hull, Dec. 24, Fenwick to Hull, Dec. 26, 1936, Bingham to Hull, Jan. 4, Barrett to Hull, Jan. 19, Castro Ramires to Hull, Jan. 21, 1937, B. 40, CH; Norweb to Daniels, Dec. 22, 1936, Daniels to Norweb, Jan. 1, Norweb to Daniels, Feb. 24, 1937, B. 728, JD; Borchard to Moore, Jan. 14, B. 72, Moore to Rowe, Mar. 26, 1937, B. 73, JM; Feis to Hull, Jan. 19, B. 22, Feis to Dearing, Jan. 23, 1937, B. 10, HF; Messersmith to Hull, Jan. 30, 1937, No. 838, GM; Davies to Hull, Feb. 4, 1937, B. 3, JED; Monroe Doctrine, PAU statements, etc., early 1937, LR; Coleman, "Good Neighbor," pp. 275-80; US Department of State, *Report of the Delegation, December 1-23, 1936*, pp. 12-15; Conferencia Internacional de Consolidacion de la Paz, *Informe de la delegacion de Mexico*, pp. 119-20; Hinton, *Hull*, p. 313; Hubert Herring, "Exit the Monroe Doctrine," *Harper's Magazine* 174 (April 1937): 449-58.

48. Inter-American Conference for the Maintenance of Peace, *Proceedings*, p. 730.

49. Vernon, Aug. 4, 710.Peace-Peoples Mandate/1, Welles to Vernon, Aug. 11,/2, Woolley to FDR, Sept. 29,/6, Nicholson to Hull, Nov. 6,/43, Scotten to Hull, Nov. 11,/

45, Reed to Hull, Nov. 16,/51, Wilson to Hull, Nov. 24,/55, Frost to Hull, Nov. 22,/54; Weddell to Inman, Nov. 9, 1937, B. 14, SI; Welles to Berle, Dec. 18, 1937, B. 216, AB; Inter-American Conference for the Maintenance of Peace, *Proceedings*, pp. 657-60.

50. Rowe to Hull, Sept. 15, B. 34, Hull to Moore, Dec. 19, 1933, B. 35, Hull to Gruening, Feb. 7, CH; diary, Feb. 5, B. 6, Hull to Daniels, Oct. 2, 1934, B. 750, JD; Stimson to Hoover, June 26, 1934, R. 87, HS; Frances Hull to Breckinridge, Apr. 28, 1934, B. 18, SB; Green to Moffat, Phillips to Moffat, Oct. 12, 1935, J.P.M.-1935, JPM; Peabody to Milton, Apr. 23, 1936, B. 19, Frances Hull to Milton, May 14, 1937, B. 20, GFM; Moore to Bullitt, Mar. 31, 1936, B. 3, RM; OHP-WP; FA, 3:557-78; CHm, 1:346, 349-51; HIsd, 2:3.

51. Moore to Hull, Nov. 27, 1933, B. 35, CH; diary, Jan. 3, 1935, WP; JPMmp, p. 108.

52. Hull to Gardenhire, Aug. 21, 31, Sept. 4, 8, 10, 18, Oct. 7, Dec. 30, Gardenhire to Hull, Aug. 28, 30, 1935, Jan. 3, 1936, B. unnumbered, CH; memo by Hull, Jan. 21, 1936, B. 18, SB.

53. White to Stimson, Nov. 26, 1933, Wright to White, Jan. 9, Castle to White, May 23, Cintas to White, Dec. 7, 1934, FW; Moore to Hull, Nov. 27, 1933, Barrett to Hull, Jan. 18, 1934, B. 35, CH; White to Stimson, Nov. 26, 1933, R. 85, HS; Green to Moffat, Apr. 22, 1936, J.P.M.-1936, JPM; Davis to Gibson, Jan. 8, 1938, B. 26, ND; FDR, Hull, Welles, B. IX, Vol. 3, no. 22, GM; OHP-WP; WDd, p. 94.

54. Memo by Welles, Mar. 17, 26, 1936, 710.11/2026; diary, Jan. 14, 1935, WP; Welles to Hull, Jan. 25, 1935, B. 37, CH; Welles to Davis, Apr. 5, 1935, B. 63, ND; Green to Moffat, Oct. 12, 1935, J.P.M.-1935, JPM; OHP-WP.

55. Green to Moffat, Oct. 12, 1935-36, Green to Moffat, Apr. 22, Davis to Moffat, July 26, Hickerson to Moffat, Aug. 25, Wynn to Moffat, Sept. 11, Green to Moffat, Sept. 12, 1936, J.P.M.-1936, JPM; Pratt, "Hull," pp. 270-300, Moore to Daniels, Nov. 13, 1936, B. 752, JD; Moore to Dodd, Nov. 19, 1936, B. 49, Moore to Dodd, Feb. 20, 27, Mar. 29, 1937, B. 51, WD; Moore to Bullitt, Jan. 22, 1937, B. 3, RM; WMR, July 10, 1936; Beatrice Farnsworth, *William C. Bullitt and the Soviet Union* (Bloomington: Indiana University Press, 1967), p. 154; diary, Dec. 15, 1936, B. 3, ND; WMR, Mar. 3, 17, 26, 1937; Moore to Dodd, Mar. 20, 1937, B. 51, WD; ABnr, pp. 110-18, JEDmm, pp. 147-48, 373.

56. Moore to Bullitt, Oct. 3, 1936, B. 3, RM; Moore to Dodd, Apr. 17, 27, July 14, Nov. 12, Dec. 14, Dodd to FDR, Dec. 23, 1937, B. 51, Moore to Dodd, Sept. 19, 1938, B. 56, WD; WDd, pp. ix-x, 421-22, 427, 434, 443, 445; Dunn to Moffat, Dec. 19, 1936, J.P.M.-1936, JPM; Berle to Welles, Apr. 21, 1937, B. 26, AB; WBfp, pp. 211, 214; SW-2, p. 8; Acheson, *Present at the Creation*, pp. 11-12.

57. Welles to Hull, Sept. 7, 1937, B. unnumbered, CH; Frances Hull to Milton, Apr. 14, Hull to Milton, May 11, 1938, B. 25, GFM; diary, Mar. 24, 1939, vol. 28, HS; Hull to Baruch, Oct. 18, 1938, vol. 1938, BB; Bowers to Daniels, Mar. 22, 1937, B. 790, JD; Davis to Gibson, June 10, 1937, B. 67, ND; diary, June 1, 1938, B. 127, HM; Welles to Wilson, July 26, 1937, B. 4, HW; Moffat to Doyle, Apr. 25, 1938, J.P.M.-1938, diary, May 12, 1938, JPM; Schoenfeld, July 21, Aug. 4, 1937, B. 77, LS; Hull to Inman, Dec. 14, 21, 1937, B. 14, SI; Return to the Department, vol. 1, no. 45, B. VIII, Cordell Hull, vol. 3, no. 22, B. IX, GM; WMR, June 3, Sept. 13, 1937; HIsd, 2:221-22, 351, 388, 419; Duggan, *Americas*, pp. 74-75; Anthony Eden, *The Reckoning* (Boston: Houghton Mifflin, 1965), p. 48; Spaulding, *Ambassadors*, p. 252.

58. Chapter 3, Under Secretary Welles, WBHS.

59. Welles to Corrigan, May 29, 1937, B. 10, FC.

60. Chapter 3, Under Secretary Welles, WBHS; Schoenfeld to Steinhardt, Dec. 15, 1937, B. 19, LS.

61. Messersmith to Moffat, May 29, Messersmith to Frankfurter, May 31, 1940, B. 85, FF; Messersmith to Harrison, Feb. 12, May 31, 1940, B. 29, LH; diary, Nov. 8, 1939, B. 5, Messersmith to Long, Mar. 21, 1940, B. 133, BL; Messersmith to Moore, Mar. 12, 1940, B. 79, Moore to Borchard, Nov. 3, 1942, B. 82, JM; Jonathan Daniels to Josephus Daniels, Jan. 26, 1944, B. 836, JD; memo by Hull, Jan. 25, 1938, B. 42, CH; Burlingham to Davis, Feb. 8, 1942, B. 3, ND; diary, Feb. 6, 1940, B. 4, HW; CHm, 1:495; George Kennan, *Memoirs* (New York: Bantam Books, 1969), pp. 68-69; FFrf, p. 209.

62. Memo by Duggan, Mar. 21, 1936, 710.11/2058; Moore to Daniels, Nov. 14, 1935, B. 787, JD; Robert Sherwood, *Roosevelt and Hopkins* (New York: Harper and Brothers, 1950), p. 63.

63. Armour to Moffat, June 3, 1935, J.P.M.-1933, JPM.

64. Briggs to Moffat, Apr. 12, 1934, J.P.M.-1934, JPM.

65. Dearing to Gibson, Apr. 26, 1936, B. 45, HG; also see Dearing to Moore, Nov. 29, 1936, B. 71, JM; Dearing to Steinhardt, May 1, 1937, B. 19, LS.

66. Diary, Sept. 18, Nov. 8, 1934, Jan. 17, May 15, Sept. 21, 1935, WP; Phillips to FDR, Nov. 28, 1934, B. 37, Hull to McKellar, Mar. 20, 1937, B. 40, memo by FDR, undated, B. 56, CH; diary, Nov. 6, 1937, JD; Castle to Moffat, Mar. 28, 1936, J.P.M.-1936, JPM; Butler to Culbertson, Feb. 20, 1935, B. 15, WRC; Carr to Stimson, Sept. 3, 1935, R. 89, HS.

67. Sevier to Hull, Aug. 6, 18, 1934, B. unnumbered, CH; US Department of State, *Register* (July 1, 1935), pp. 252-53; Braden, *Diplomats and Demagogues*, pp. 97, 135.

68. Scotten to Hull, Sept. 5, 1934, B. unnumbered, CH.

69. Scotten to Hull, Sept. 11, Oct. 3, Nov. 7, 1934, Sevier to Hull, Jan. 16, Aug. 9, 1935, B. unnumbered, CH; Flexer to Lane, Mar. 24, 1935, B. 10, AL.

CHAPTER 6

1. Daniels to Hull, Sept. 27, 812.52/3345, memo by Duggan, Sept. 27, 1938, 718.1915/1019, Daniels to Hull, Nov. 22, 1938, 710.H/210; Armour to Welles, Aug. 1, 1938, B. 43, CH; Coleman, "Good Neighbor," pp. 317-18; HIsd, 2:521-22; CHm, 1:610; Duggan, *Americas*, p. 70.

2. Dearing to Hull, Aug. 8, 1935, 710.H/2, Steinhardt to Hull, Mar. 25, 1938,/53, Welles to Steinhardt, Apr. 15, 1938,/62; FR, 1936, 5:1; FR, 1938, 5:1-8.

3. Press release, Nov. 12, 1938, 710.H/183, memo by Welles, Nov. 15, 1938, Agenda/184, press release, Nov. 19, 1938, 710. H/196½; Herring to Robertson, Aug. 26, 1938, B. 58, JR; Jessup to Davis, Oct. 26, 1938, B. 32, ND; FR, 1938, 5:3, 8-10, 37-38; CHm, 1:602.

4. Press release, Nov. 5, 1938, 710.H-Continental Solidarity/1.

5. Tuck to Hull, Nov. 8, 710.H-Continental Solidarity/3, Reed to Hull, Nov. 12,/18, Welles to Hornibrook, Dec. 13, 1938, 711.18/45, Welles to Tomlinson, Oct. 14, 1938, 710.H/128, Steinhardt to Welles, Nov. 18, 710.H-Continental Solidarity/28, Tuck to Hull, Nov. 18,/29, Frost to Welles, Nov. 19,/30, Green to Welles, Nov. 23, 1938,/46; Milton to Welles, Nov. 10, 1938, B. 84, GFM; Landon to Clapper, Oct. 25, 1941, B. 49, RC; FR, 1938, 5:38-43.

6. FR, 1938, 5:43-44.

7. Hull to Steinhardt, Nov. 12, 710.H-Personnel/123, memo by Hull, Nov. 23, 111.018/97, press release, Nov. 29, 710.H-Personnel/308, memo by Gosnell, Feb. 2, 1948, Welles file, WBHS; Mrs. Hull to Daniels, Oct. 18, 1938, B. 750, JD; Armour to Culbertson, Nov. 15, 1938, B. 78, WC; diary, Jan. 10, 1939, B. 210, AB; FR, 1938, 5:10-12; ABnr, p. 193; CHm, 1:603; Hinton, *Hull*, p. 334.

8. Landon to Mussman, Landon to Mayberry, Nov. 12, B. 90, Castle to Landon, Hull to Landon, Nov. 14, Landon to Jackson, Nov. 15, Buell to Landon, Nov. 16, Landon to Johnson, Nov. 19, Clark to Landon, Nov. 21, 1938, B. 89, AML; Landon to White, Nov. 18, 1938, Series C, B. 288, WW; Milton to White, Nov., 30, 1938, B. 84, GFM; Hinton, *Hull*, p. 333.

9. Landon to Johnson, Nov. 19, 1938, B. 89, AML.

10. Memo by Hull, Feb. 23, 710.H-Agenda/28, memo by Welles, Mar. 4,/34, Welles to FDR, Nov. 17, 1938, 818.24/8A; Ricardo Alfaro, "Toward an American Association of Nations," *Quarterly Journal of Inter-American Relations* 1 (January 1939): 25-36; FR, 1938, 5:12-19, 27-30, 57-80; Cantril, *Public Opinion*, pp. 548-49; Frank McCann, *The Brazilian-American Alliance* (Princeton, N.J.: Princeton University Press, 1973), pp. 117-22.

11. Weddell to Hull, Aug. 17, 710.H-Personnel/27, Weddell to Hull, Aug. 29, 1938, 710.H/97, memo by Duggan, Sept. 22, 1938, 800.8830/703; diary, Jan. 5, 1939, B. 5,

BL; FR, 1938, 5:31-37, 44-46.

12. Weddell to Hull, Sept. 28, 710.H-Personnel/57, Tuck to Hull, Nov. 18, 710.H/211, Baker, G-2 Report, Nov. 25, 1938, 710.H-Personnel/343, Tuck to Welles, Dec. 6, 1938, 710.H/280; FR, 1938, 5:51-52; Hinton, *Hull*, pp. 334-36; CHm, 1:603-5; Conil Paz and Ferrari, *Argentina's Foreign Policy*, pp. 43-49; Peterson, *Argentina and the United States*, p. 395.

13. Culbertson to wife, Dec. 10, 16, 1938, B. 18, WC; US-Lima conf., Dec. 1938, B. 2, Hull, Cordell, B. 36, SI; Duggan to Steinhardt, Oct. 2, 1937, B. 19, Apr. 6, 1938, B. 23, LS; ABnr, pp. 191-92.

14. Welles to Hull, Dec. 1, 710.H-Continental Solidarity/50, press release, Dec. 8, 710.H/293, Welles to Hull, Dec. 9, 1938, 710.H-Continental Solidarity/65; FR, 1938, 5:47-50.

15. Hull to Welles, Dec. 17, 1938, 710.H/301; *New York Times*, Dec. 19, 1938.

16. Welles to Hull, Dec. 19, 710.H/313, press release, Dec. 19, 1938,/335; Gillespie to Landon, Dec. 20, 1938, B. 89, AML; Rowe to Pittman, Dec. 20, 1938, Committee on Foreign Relations, Lima Conference, Sen. 76A-F9, RG 46; *Washington Post*, Dec. 19, 1938.

17. Davis to Hull, Nov. 22, 1937, 710.H/22, Duggan to Kirk, June 1, 1938,/77, memo by Kelchner, Jan. 23, 1939,/448½; Patterson to Steinhardt, Nov. 18, 1938, B. 23, LS; Ester Crooks, "Women at the Lima Conference," *Goucher Alumnae Quarterly* 17 (February 1939): 9-12; Eighth International Conference of American States, *Report on the Results of the Conference* (Washington, D.C.: Pan American Union, 1939), pp. 1-6, 21-23; FR, 1938, 5:74-75.

18. Frost to Welles, Dec. 17, 710.H/325, Tuck to Welles, Dec. 20, 1938, 710.H-Continental Solidarity/107, Dec. 31, 1938, 710.H/372, Daniels to Hull, Feb. 13, 1939, 710.H-Continental Solidarity/149; US-Lima, Dec. 23, 1938, B. 2, SI; Messersmith to McReynolds, Dec. 23, 1938, No. 1108, GM; Culbertson to wife, Dec. 22, 1938, B. 18, WC; FR, 1938, 5:80-88; Eighth International Conference of American States, *Report on the Results*, pp. 7-10; idem, *Final Act, December 1938* (Lima: Torres Aguirre, 1938), pp. 115-18; JPMmp, pp. 222-23; SW-2, p. 105; HIsd, 2:528; CHm, 1:605-11.

19. Hinkle to Welles, Dec. 28, 710.H-Continental Solidarity/121, Corrigan to Welles, Dec. 30, 1938, 710.H/369, Greene to Welles, Jan. 3,/395, Reed to Welles, Jan. 10,/426, Boal to Hull, Jan. 15, 1939,/403; Daniels to Hull, Jan. 20, Diez de Medina to Hull, Jan. 27, 1939, B. 44, CH: Eighth International Conference of American States, *Final Act*, pp. 17-19, 46-47, 81; idem, *Report on the Results*, pp. 10-21, 23-24, 37-44; Peterson, *Argentina and the United States*, pp. 396-97.

20. Reed to Welles, Nov. 25, 710.H-Continental Solidarity/27, Bowers to Welles, Dec. 2,/39, memo by Briggs, Dec. 10, 710.H/296, Kirk to Welles, Dec. 13,/279, Dec. 16,/295, Callanan to Welles, Dec. 19,/396, Grew to Welles, Dec. 21,/378, Wilson to Welles, Dec. 28, 1938,/351, memo by Hull, Jan. 12, 1939, 611.94931/170.

21. Dreyfus to Hull, July 25, 800.20210/129, Gilbert to Welles, Nov. 22, 710.H-Continental Solidarity/219, Gilbert to Welles, Nov. 30, 710.H/288, Gilbert to Welles, Dec. 13, 710.H/293, Gilbert to Welles, Dec. 28, 1938, 710.H-Continental Solidarity/115; Moore to Borchard, Dec. 31, 1938, B. 74, JM; FR, 1938, 5:50-51.

22. DGFP, 5:885-86.

23. Hull to Welles, Dec. 23, 1938, 710.H/328; memo by Hull, Dec. 26, 1938, B. 43, CH; Henry to Landon, Dec. 24, Chester to Landon, Dec. 31, 1938, B. 89, address by Landon, Dec. 24, FDR to Landon, Dec. 29, 1938, Landon to FDR, Jan. 5, 1939, B. 90, AML; White to Landon, Jan. 7, 1939, Series C, B. 318, WW; Landon to Clapper, Dec. 22, 1938, B. 48, RC; Landon to Milton, Feb. 15, 1939, B. 84, GFM.

24. Landon to Chester, Jan. 26, 1939, B. 89, AML.

25. Borchard to Moore, Nov. 29, 1938, B. 74, JM.

26. Thomas to Hull, Dec. 6, 1938, 710.H/285.

27. Milton to Hawkins, Dec. 23, 1938, B. 84, GFM; Alton Frye, *Nazi Germany and the American Hemisphere* (New Haven: Yale University Press, 1967), pp. 112-13; Duggan, *Americas*, pp. 72-74; CHm, 1:600-602.

28. Welles to Hull, Dec. 26, 1938, 710.H/344, press release, Mar. 16, 1939,/714; Fenwick to Hull, Jan. 13, Hull to Brock, Jan. 16, 1939, B. 44, CH; Rowe speech, Mar.

10, 1939, LR; Taussig to Feis, Feb. 20, 1939, B. 16, HF; Hull to Steinhardt, Dec. 27, 1938, B. 23, LS; HIsd, 2:558; PPA, 7:650-51.
29. Memos from Kelchner, Butler, Briggs, Jan. 23, 24, 26, 1939, 710.H/458; diary, Jan. 17, 1939, BL; Coleman, "Good Neighbor," pp. 373-76; SW-3, pp. 208-9; ABnr, p. 193; Duggan, *Americas*, p. 73; William Langer and S. Everett Gleason, *The Challenge to Isolation* (New York: Harper and Brothers, 1952), pp. 41-42.
30. Inman to Eichelberger, Jan. 3, 1939, B. 14, SI.
31. Hoover speech, Feb. 1, 1939, R. 97, HS.
32. Castle speeches, Dec. 7, 1938, Jan. 1, Feb. 21, Nov. 21, 1939, B. 21, WRC; Ackerman to Castle, Mar. 21, 1939, B. 26, CA.
33. Castle speech, Apr. 1, 1939, B. 21, WRC.
34. Inman to Hull, Oct. 13, 1939, B. 14, SI; Norweb to Daniels, Oct. 24, 1938, B. 734, JD; Pabst to Ackerman, Dec. 5, 1938, B. 49, CA; Knox to Hull, Oct. 12, 1937, B. 42, Apr. 10, 1939, B. 44, CH; RCww, p. 256.
35. Press release, July 20, 1938, 710.11/2153, June 16, 1939,/2400; CR, vol. 84, pt. 2, pp. 420-23.
36. Press release, Apr. 2, 1938, 710.11/2222, see Sept. 12, 1938,/2278; Laurence Duggan, "Our Relations with the Other American Republics," *Annals* 199 (July 1938): 128-32.
37. Daniels to Inman, Aug. 17, 1938, B. 14, SI; Daniels to Hull, Oct. 18, 1938, B. 43, CH; press release, May 2, 1939, 710.11/2383.
38. Berle to Corrigan, May 8, 1939, B. 1, FC.
39. Press release, Mar. 15, 1938, 710.11/2221; CR, vol. 83, pt. 9, pp. 863-64.
40. Dozer, *Good Neighbors*?, pp. 36-37; PPA, 7:219-21, 411-13, 8:142-44, 563-66.
41. *PPA*, 8:195-99; ABnr, pp. 210-11.
42. PC, R. 7, Apr. 20, June 19, 1939.
43. ABnr, pp. 245, 253; PC, Apr. 10, Sept. 15, 1939, R. 7; FR, 1939, 5:40; PL, 2:936-37, 952.
44. Stark to Bloch, Sept. 4, 8, 14, Oct. 4, Bloch to Stark, Sept. 11, 1939, B. 4, CCB; FR, 1939, 5:32-33; Samuel Morison, *The Battle of the Atlantic* (Boston: Little, Brown, 1966), pp. 14-16; Stetson Conn and Byron Fairchild, *The Framework of Hemispheric Defense* (Washington, D.C.: G.P.O., 1960), pp. 23-25.
45. Stark to Bloch, Oct. 14, 1939, B. 4, CCB.
46. Ibid., Oct. 1939.
47. Memo by Notter, Aug. 24, 710.H-Continental Solidarity/102, memo by Flourney, Aug. 24,/162, Aug. 25,/163; FR, 1939, 5:15-26; Duggan to Corrigan, Aug. 25, 1939, B. 3, FC; ABnr, pp. 246, 248-49; CHm, 1:688-89; Joseph Alsop and Robert Kinter, *American White Paper* (New York: Simon and Schuster, 1940), pp. 72-73.
48. Armour to Hull, July 11, 710.11/2401, Armour to Hull, Sept. 8, 740.00111-A.R./90, Armour to Hull, Sept. 8,/240, Caffery to Hull, Aug. 25, 760C.62/1038, Bowers to Hull, Sept. 13,/203, Santos to FDR, Sept. 1,/8, memo by Briggs, Sept. 14,/264, Dawson to Hull, Sept. 8, 1939,/242; diary, Sept. 6, B. 9, Sept. 4, 12, B. 17, JD; FR, 1939, 5:17, 22-23, 26-27; JDrd, pp. 188-89; Conil Paz and Ferrari, *Argentina's Foreign Policy*, pp. 50-53; Peterson, *Argentina and the United States*, pp. 400-401; Welles to Armour, Sept. 25, 740.001111-A.R./350, Welles to Hull, Oct. 3, 1939,/425; Duggan, *Americas*, pp. 82-83; SW-2, p. 105; Peterson, *Argentina and the United States*, pp. 401-2.
49. Welles to FDR, Sept. 13, 740.00111-A.R./230, press release, Sept. 15,/290, Hull to Prieto, Sept. 16, 1939,/218; Welles file, WHBS; FR, 1939, 5:19-20, 22; ABnr, pp. 250, 252; Welles to Hull, Sept. 22, 740.00111-A.R./333, Bowers to Hull, Sept. 27,/419, Dawson to Hull, Sept. 27,/417, Burdett to Hull, Sept. 28, 1939,/451; SW-4, pp. 1-10.
50. Memo by Duggan, Sept. 12, 710.11/2417½, Welles to Hull, Sept. 25, 740.00111-A.R./351, Hull to Welles, Sept. 27,/351, 357, Welles to Hull, Sept. 30,/392, Thoms to McDermott, Oct. 3, 1939,/427.
51. White to Hull, Nov. 9, Series C, B. 318, FDR to White, Nov. 13, B. 320, Daniels to White, Nov. 17, 1939, Series C. B. 316, WW; White to Daniels, Nov. 13, Daniels to White, Nov. 17, White to Daniels, Nov. 23, 1939, B. 739, JD; diary, Nov. 8, 1939, B. 5, BL; Borchard to Moore, Nov. 8, 16, Moore to Borchard, Nov. 20, 1939, B. 76, JM;

PC, Nov. 7, 10, 14, 1939, R. 7; FR, 1939, 5:79, 82; ABnr, pp. 261-62, 268-69; James Farley, *Jim Farley's Story* (New York: McGraw Hill, 1948), p. 210.

52. Daniels to Hull, Sept. 5, memo by Welles, Sept. 7, 1939, 740.00111-A.R./39; Borchard to Moore, Dec. 21, 1940, B. 80, JM; diary, Oct. 1, 19, 1939, B. 5, BL; PC, Nov. 3, 1939, R. 7; FR, 1939, 5:28, 30-32, 54-58, 64-65, 67-78, 80-84; BLwd, pp. 191-95; HIsd, 3:393-95; PL, 2:917-18; H. L. Trefousse, *Germany and American Neutrality* (New York: Octagon Books, 1969), pp. 85-89; IAA, 1:89, 202, 203, 206, 207, 217, 227.

53. Hull to Daniels, Sept. 13, 740.00111-A.R./211, Mayer to Hull, Sept. 14,/219, Welles to Hull, Sept. 19,/292, Hull to Welles, Sept. 21,/292, press release, Nov. 13, 1939,/754; FR, 1939, 5:25, 26, 33-37; CHm, 1:688-90; Alsop and Kinter, *White Paper*, pp. 60-62, 68-69; Langer and Gleason, *Challenge to Isolation*, pp. 206-8; J. Lloyd Mecham, *The United States and Inter-American Security* (Austin: University of Texas Press, 1961), pp. 77-78.

54. Press release, Oct. 11, 740.00111-A.R./628, Hull to Welles, Oct. 4,/447A, Welles to Coster, Oct. 20, 1939,/586.

55. WMR, Oct. 14, 1939.

56. Armour to Hull, Oct. 4, 740.00111-A.R./435, Armour to Hull, Nov. 7,/721, Bowers to Hull, Oct. 11, 825.51/1154, Caffery to Hull, Oct. 4, 740.00111-A.R./432, Corrigan to Hull, Oct. 9, 1939,/518; diary, Nov. 6, 1939, B. 7, Daniels to FDR, Nov. 4, 1939, B. 17, JD; FR, 1939, 5:37-38.

57. Frost to Hull, Sept. 7, 740.00111-A.R./68, Daniels to Hull, Sept. 9,/135, Desportes to Hull, Sept. 12,/274, Kirk to Hull, Sept. 15,/231, Hull to Welles, Sept. 16,/277B, Dawson to Hull, Sept. 19, 701.6214/33, Hull to Welles, Sept. 21, 740.00111-A.R./322A, memo by Bonsal, Sept. 22,/324, Dawson to Hull, Sept. 23, 1939,/367; FR, 1939, 5: 28-29; DGFP, 8:68-88, 157-58; Saul Friedlander, *Prelude to Downfall*, trans. Aline and Alexander Werth (New York: Alfred A. Knopf, 1967), pp. 45-46.

58. Kirk to Hull, Oct. 4, 740.00111-A.R./443, Oct. 5, 1939,/455.

59. DGFP, 8:304.

60. Wilson to Hull, Dec. 14, 740.00111-A.R./854, Dec. 15, 740.0011 EW 1939/ 1172, 1175, Dec. 20, 1939,/1341,/1344; Willi Frischauer and Robert Jackson, *The Altmark Affair* (New York: Macmillan, 1955), pp. 11-45, 119-34; Dudley Pope, *Graf Spee* (Philadelphia: J. B. Lippincott, 1957), pp. 19-118; Friedlander, *Prelude to Downfall*, p. 63.

61. Wilson to Hull, Dec. 14, 740.00111-A.R./853, Dec. 15,/855, Dec. 15, 740.0011 EW 1939/1176, Dec. 16,/1183,/1208, Dec. 17,/1196, Dec. 19, 1939,/1346; FR, 1939, 5:93-94, 102.

62. Wilson to Hull, Dec. 17, 740.0011 EW 1939/1220, Kirk to Hull, Dec. 18,/1228, /1229, Armour to Hull, Dec. 22, 1939,/1346; FR, 1939, 5:105-6; DGFP, 8:541-45, 547-48; BLwd, p. 41.

63. Wilson to Hull, Dec. 20, 740.0011 EW 1939/1340, Armour to Hull, Dec. 21,/ 1363, Wilson to Hull, Dec. 21,/1345, Armour to Hull, Dec. 21,/1360, Dec. 29, 1939,/ 1427.

64. DGFP, 8:562.

65. FR, 1939, 5:91-96.

66. Memo by Welles, Dec. 14, 1939, 740.0011 EW 1939/1280.

67. Armour to Hull, Dec. 16, 740.0011 EW 1939/1190, Cabot to Hull, Dec. 16, 1939/1201; FR, 1939, 5:96-101.

68. Burdett to Hull, Dec. 18, 1939, 740.0011 EW 1939/1328; diary, Dec. 19, 1939, B. 211, AB; FR, 1939, 5:105.

69. Diary, Dec. 19, B. 211, AB.

70. Caffery to Hull, Dec. 18, memo by Hull, Dec. 19, 740.0011 EW 1939/1225, Armour to Hull, Dec. 20,/1361, Armour to Hull, Dec. 26,/1320,1386, Dreyfus to Hull, Dec. 26,/1383, Wilson to Hull, Dec. 26,/1418, Briggs to Cabot, Dec. 28,/1389, Armour to Hull, Dec. 29, 1939,/1426, Wilson to Hull, Jan. 3, 1940,/1459; FR, 1939, 5:107-17, 120-21; Bowers to Welles, Dec. 27, 1939, Bowers mss II 1939, CB; *New York Times*, Dec. 24, 1939, Peterson, *Argentina and the United States*, p. 402.

71. Feis to Wilson, Feb. 19, 1941, B. 16, HF; CHm, 1:690-92; Langer and Gleason, *Challenge to Isolation*, pp. 210-18; Dozer, *Good Neighbors?*, pp. 56-58; Bushnell, *Santos and the Good Neighbor*, pp. 30-32.

72. Memo by Hull, Oct. 4, 740.00111-A.R./538, press release, Nov. 3,/689, memo by Welles, Nov. 29, 1939, 740.00111 A-Neutrality Patrol/42; diary, Dec. 20, 1939, B. 211, AB; diary, Nov. 2, 1939, B. 5, BL; ABnr, pp. 260, 262-64; BLwd, pp. 78-79.

73. Walsh to Hull, Oct. 2, 1939, 740.00111-A.R./414; Borchard to Moore, Oct. 23, 1939, B. 76, Jan. 3, 1940, B. 78, Moore to Borchard, Jan. 5, July 11, 1940, B. 78, JM.

74. Landon speech, Nov. 1, 1939, Series C, B. 318, WW; Clapper to Landon, Nov. 1, 1939, B. 94, AML.

75. Hull to Welles, Sept. 27, 740.00111-A.R./375B, memo by Duggan, Nov. 1, 1939,/445, Johnson to Hull, Dec. 21, 740.0011 EW 1939/1291, memo by Welles, Dec. 22, 1939,/1396, Wilson to Welles, Dec. 8, 1940,/7029; FR, 1939, 5:29, 30, 39, 85-91, 115, 117-23, 126-27; IAA, 1:198, 200; Joseph Lash, *Roosevelt and Churchill* (New York: W. W. Norton, 1976), pp. 64-72.

76. Kirk to Hull, Nov. 7, 1939, 740.00111-A.R./677; DGFP, 8:348, 9:616; FR, 1939, 5:40-41; Friedlander, *Prelude to Downfall*, pp. 46-47; Frye, *Nazi Germany and the American Hemisphere*, pp. 123-24; James Compton, *The Swastika and the Eagle* (Boston: Houghton Mifflin, 1967), pp. 137-141; Douglas Anglin, *The St. Pierre and Miquelon Affaire of 1941* (Toronto: University of Toronto Press, 1966), p. 130.

77. Kirk to Hull, Nov. 24, 740.00111 A-Neutrality Patrol/22, Dec. 30, 1939, 740.0011 EW 1939/1367; diary, Dec. 19, 1939, B. 211, AB; FR, 1939, 5:97-98, 103, 107, 109-12, 123-25; Morison, *Battle of the Atlantic*, p. 35, Friedlander, *Prelude to Downfall*, pp. 62-64; Trefousse, *Germany and American Neutrality*, pp. 40-42, 61-63.

78. PL, 2:1040; memo by Bonsal, Mar. 24, 1941, 710. Consultation (3)/9-2/7.

79. HSas, pp. 368-69; HIsd, 3:491, 492, 503; HMd, 2:252; Conn and Fairchild, *Framework*, pp. 107-10; Lash, *Roosevelt and Churchill*, pp. 306-8.

80. PC, Apr. 25, 1941, R. 9, also see PPA, 10:132-38.

81. PL, 2:1148-50, 1154-55.

82. PC, July 8, 1941, R. 9.

83. PL, 2:1213-14; Morison, *Turmoil and Tradition*, 428-32; Lash, *Roosevelt and Churchill*, pp. 316, 317, 320-30, 371-73, 415-28.

84. Memo by Bonsal, June 25, 1940, 710.Consultation (2)/130½; F. H. Hinsley, *Hitler's Strategy* (Cambridge: At the University Press, 1951), pp. 169-75, 204-10; Trefousse, *Germany and American Neutrality*, pp. 115-22, 150-51; Conn and Fairchild, *Framework*, pp. 68-74; Sherwood, *Roosevelt and Hopkins*, p. 373.

CHAPTER 7

1. Diary, June 10, 1940, B. 9, WL; Borchard to Moore, May 12, July 8, 1940, B. 78, JM; White to FDR, June 10, 1940, B. 347, WW; Stimson to FDR, May 18, 1940, R. 101, HS; Jessup to Wood, Apr. 16, 1940, B. 31, PJ; PC, Feb. 9, 1940, R. 8; PPA, 9:158-62, 184-87; ABnr, p. 305.

2. PC, Apr. 18, June 5, 14, 1940, R. 8.

3. PC, May 30, June 21, 1940, R. 8; PPA, 9:273-74; HIsd, 3:204.

4. Diary, July 1, 1940, B. 212, AB; diary, memo of conversation, June 27, 1940, B. 276, HM; ABnr, pp. 292-93, 319, 324-26; Langer and Gleason, *Challenge to Isolation*, pp. 629-35; HMd, 2:320-21.

5. Memo by Collado, July 10, 1940, 710.Consultation (2)/428; Memo by Culbertson, "Current proposals for regulating and controlling inter-American trade," June 7, Culbertson to Evans, June 8, 1940, B. 20, WC; Borchard to Moore, June 18, July 26, 1940, B. 78, JM; PC, June 28, 1940 R. 8; DGFP, 9:689, 10:145-47.

6. White to Knox, May 24, 31, 1940, Series C. B. 344, WW.

7. Knox to Stimson, May 22, 1940, R. 101, HS.

8. Knox to White, May 28, 1940, Series C, B. 344, WW; Stimson to Salter, May 18, Stimson to Knox, May 25, 1940, R. 101, HS; Fadley to Bowers, July 3, 1940, Bowers mss II, CB; HSas, pp. 318-20.

9. Caffery to Welles, June 11, 740.0011 EW 1939/3712, memo by Walmsley, June 12,/3712 CF, Welles to FDR, June 12,/3721, Caffery to Welles, June 22, 1940, 710.Consultation (2)/51; Messersmith to Hull, June 15, 1940, no. 1381, GM; Welles to Bowers, June 27, 1940, Bowers mss II, CB; McCann, *Brazilian-American Alliance*, pp. 176-86.

10. Phillips to Hull, June 23, 1940, 710.Consultation (2)/59; CR, vol. 86, pt. 16, pp. 4147-48; WDd, p. 19; SW-3, pp. 95-97.

11. Hull to Biddle, June 17, 1940, 710.Consultation (2)/204B; diary, June 17, 1940, B. 5, BL; John Logan, *No Transfer* (New Haven: Yale University Press, 1961), pp. 326-30; BLwd, p. 107; FR, 1940, 5:180-81.

12. Hull to Berlin embassy, June 17, 1940, 710.Consultation (2)/2A.

13. Heath to Hull, July 2, 1940, 710.Consultation (2)/144; Friedlander, *Prelude to Downfall*, p. 108.

14. Press release, July 5, 1940, 710.Consultation (2)/297; Dexter Perkins, "Bringing the Monroe Doctrine Up to Date," *Foreign Affairs* 20 (January 1942); 253-65; Dexter Perkins, *A History of the Monroe Doctrine* (Boston: Little, Brown, 1963), pp. 384-87.

15. Logan, *No Transfer*, pp. 296-98, 317-26.

16. Memo by Duggan, Feb. 13, 1936, 710.Peace/230, Welles to Duggan, May 18, 710.11/2492, memo by National Policy Committee, June 24, 740.0011 EW 1939/5459, memo by Duggan, Aug. 6, 1940, 710.Consultation (2)/553; Pittman to Hull, Jan. 2, 1936, B. 38, Statements regarding the Monroe Doctrine, April 1933 to April 1941, B. 49, CH; memo by Moore, Oct. 23, 1933, B. 10, RM; Daniels to Norweb, Mar. 12, 1937, B. 728, JD; Messersmith to Frankfurter, May 31, 1940, B. 83, FF; FA, 1:470-75; Coleman, "Good Neighbor," pp. 396-97; A. Lawrence Cowell, "The Frontiers of the United States," *Foreign Affairs* 17 (July 1939): 663-69.

17. Duggan to Witzl, June 7, 1940, 710.11/2484.

18. Welles to Armour, Mar. 27, 1937, Bowers mss II, CB; memo by Chapin, Dec. 9, 1938, SLC; FA, 2:390, 3:403-4; PL, 1:607-8, 2:871-72, 909; HIsd, 2:704-5; Logan, *No Transfer*, pp. 330-40.

19. PL, 2:1023.

20. Memo by Duggan, June 18, 710.Consultation (2)/5½, memo by Bonsal, June 25,/130½, Duggan to Welles, June 26, 1940,/114½, Messersmith to Long, June 26, 1940, B. 133, BL; FR, 1940, 5:181-89. 193-94, 198, 205-8, 213-14; Logan, *No Transfer*, pp. 284, 287-88, CHm, 1:816; HIsd, 3:213.

21. Davis to Hull, June 21, 710.Consultation (2)/98, memo by Collado, July 10,/428, Armour to Hull, July 5, 1940, 835.001 Ortiz, R.M./103; FR, 1940, 5:192-93, 196-97, 199, 216-17; Peterson, *Argentina and the United States*, p. 404.

22. Messersmith to Hull, June 19, 1940, 710.Consultation (2)/117½, memo by Ray, July 5,/308, Hornibrook to Hull, July 7,/303, Muccio to Hull, July 8,/218, Hornibrook to Hull, July 12,/366, Armour to Hull, July 13,/292, Messersmith to Welles, June 20, 837.00-N/144, memo by Ray, June 27, 1940, 740.0011 EW 1939/4524; Messersmith to Hull, June 26, July 3, 13, 1940, B. 47, CH; Wallace to Messersmith, July 11, 1940, R. 22, HW; DGFP, 9:632-33, 660, 10:229-30; Friedlander, *Prelude to Downfall*, pp. 108-11; Frye, *Nazi Germany and the American Hemisphere*, pp. 127-30; CHm, 1:813, 821.

23. Press release, July 18, 1940, 710.Consultation (2)/403; Messersmith to Hull, June 25, Hull to Messersmith, July 3, 1940, B. 47, CH; FR, 1940, 5:206-7, 210, 212-13; Hinton, *Hull*, pp. 72, 345-46; CHm, 1:822.

24. Diary, July 21, 1940, B. 9, WL; ABnr, pp. 328-29; Langer and Gleason, *Challenge to Isolation*, pp. 688-701.

25. Press release, July 22, 710.Consultation (2)/461, Armour to Welles, July 23,/491, Armour to Hull, July 23,/492, Armour to Welles, July 25,/540, Notter to Duggan, July 26, 1940, 710.11/7-2640; FR, 1940, 5:239-41; CHm, 1:822-26.

26. FR, 1940, 5:237-38, 241-50; PPA, 9:421-26; Cordell Hull, *Achievements of the Second Meeting for the Foreign Ministers of the American Republics* (Washington, D.C.: G.P.O., 1940), pp. 7-8; Kenneth Grieb, "Jorge Ubico and the Belice Boundary Dispute," *Americas* 30 (April 1974): 448-74; ABnr, pp. 329-30; Conil Paz and Ferrari, *Argentina's Foreign Policy*, pp. 53-59; Peterson, *Argentina and the United States*, p. 405; SW-3, pp. 214-16; CHm, 1:826-30.

27. Duggan, *Americas*, pp. 83-84; J. Lloyd Mecham, *A Survey of United States-Latin American Relations* (Boston: Houghton Mifflin, 1965), p. 135.

28. PC, Aug. 6, 1940, R. 8.

29. Wilson to Welles, Aug. 2, 710.Consultation (2)/569, Messersmith to Welles, Aug. 2,/549, press release, Aug. 4,/552, Braden to Hull, Aug. 13,/621, Hornibrook to Hull, Aug. 15,/615, press release, Aug. 24,/631, press release, Aug. 29, 1940,A/3; Messersmith to Hull, Aug. 1, Berle to Hull, Aug. 2, memo by Hull, Aug. 4, 1940, B. 47, CH; diary, Aug. 2, 1940, B. 212, AB; FR, 1940, 5:252-56; ABnr, p. 330; HIsd, 3:289; Bushnell, *Santos and the Good Neighbor*, pp. 34-38.

30. Diary, memo to Morgenthau, Aug. 2, 1940, B. 288, HM; FR, 1940, 5:238-39, 242; HMd, 2:321.

31. Kirk to Welles, July 23, 710.Consultation (2)/417, July 25,/445, July 26, 1940,/456; Baruch to Forrestal, July 26, Forrestal to Baruch, July 30, Baruch to Hull, Sept. 11, 1940, V. 1940, BB; ABnr, pp. 330-31; DGFP, 10:448-50; Friedlander, *Prelude to Downfall*, pp. 111-12.

32. PC, Aug. 16, 1940, R. 8; Winston Churchill, *Their Finest Hour* (New York: Bantam Books, 1962), pp, 342-56; Conn and Fairchild, *Framework*, pp. 51-62.

33. PL, 2:1162.

34. Welles to Corrigan, Apr. 18, 740.0011 EW 1939/2349A, Pendelton to Hull, June 27, Briggs to Pendleton, July 6, 710.Consultation (2)/115, memo by Hull, July 8, 1940, 856B.01/44; diary, May 11, 1940, B. 5, BL; FR, 1940, 5:210-11; JPMmp, pp. 321-22; PL, 2:1281; Logan, *No Transfer*, pp. 309-13.

35. PC, Apr. 12, 1940, R. 8, Apr. 11, 15, 1941, R. 9; PPA, 10:110; FR, 1940, 5: 251-52; ABnr, pp. 305-6, 356-57; PL, 2:1142-43; Logan, *No Transfer*, pp. 298-307.

36. Memo by Berle, July 12, 1940, 710.11/2551, memo by Welles, Feb. 19, 1941,/2679; HSas, p. 373; Logan, *No Transfer*, pp. 307-9.

37. Lindbergh, *Wartime Journals*, pp. 515-16.

38. Memo by Welles, July 30, 710.Consultation (2)/513, Muccio to Hull, Aug. 28,/630, Hull to de Saint-Quentin, Aug. 30,/632, memo by Duggan, Oct. 28, 1940, 740.0011 EW 1939/6770; diary, Dec. 14, 19, 1941, Feb. 11, 21, 24, 25, 28, Mar. 4, 5, 10, 12, 23, 27, 1942, B. 10, July 2, 5, 1943, B. 11, WL; Wallace to Welles, May 26, Welles to Wallace, June 12, 1941, B. 108, HW(FDRL); diary, Oct. 26, 1940, V. 31, HS; diary, Dec. 14-21, 1941, B. 8, HI; ABnr, pp. 334, 402, 403, 414; Logan, *No Transfer*, pp. 341-45; Morison, *Battle of the Atlantic*, pp. 30-33.

39. Diary, Dec. 21-27, 1941, B. 8, HI; PL, 2:1268; BLwd, pp. 239-41, 247; ABnr, pp. 388-91, 393, 395; JPMmp, pp. 358-70; Anglin, *St. Pierre and Miquelon*, pp. 3-138; Sherwood, *Roosevelt and Hopkins*, pp. 479-89; Krock, *Memoirs*, pp. 203-5; Conn and Fairchild, *Framework*, p. 163.

CHAPTER 8

1. Memo by Ray, June 22, 1940, 710.Consultation (2)/613, Caffery to Hull, June 23, 740.0011 EW 1939/12369, Welles statement, June 23, 1941,/12385a; Messersmith to Long, Nov. 12, 1940, B. 133, BL; Stimson to FDR, June 23, 1941, R. 104, HS; Bowers to FDR, June 23, 1941, Bowers mss II, CB; Private report by Dean, "Impressions of South America," summer 1941, B. 135, PJ; BLwd, pp. 208-9; JEDmm, pp. 453-57; Callcott, *Western Hemisphere*, pp. 346-48; Ernest May, *"Lessons" of the Past* (New York: Oxford University Press, 1973), pp. 23-27.

2. Memo by Ray, June 22, 1940, 710.Consultation (2)/613; Dean, "Impressions of South America," summer 1941, B. 135, PJ; Norweb to Bowers, Mar. 25, 1941, Bowers mss II, CB; Dozer, *Good Neighbors?*, pp. 40-45; IAA, 1:180-81.

3. Feis to Norweb, May 7, 1941, B. 17, HF.

4. Norweb to Bowers, Mar. 25, 1941, Bowers mss II, CB; Butler to Hull, May 6, 1942, 710.Consultation (3)/771; Dawson to Feis, June 16, Feis to Boal, July 28, 1941, B. 11, HF; Conn and Fairchild, *Framework*, pp. 186-91; Stegmaier, "From Confrontation to Cooperation," pp. 117-20.

5. DGFP, 6:700-707; Compton, *Swastika and the Eagle*, pp. 3-23; Frye, *Nazi Germany and the American Hemisphere*, pp. 31, 64-72, 152-62; Friedlander, *Prelude to Downfall*, pp. 27, 28, 30, 225-27; US Department of State, *The Cultural-Cooperation Program, 1938-1943* (Washington, D.C.: G.P.O., 1944), p. 28; Ronald Newton, *German Buenos Aires* (Austin: University of Texas Press, 1977), pp. 3-183.

6. DGFP, 3:74-75, 930-33, 5:863-67, 1081-82, 9:614-16, 10:102-3, 529-31; Carleton Beals, "Totalitarian Inroads in Latin America," *Foreign Affairs* 17 (October 1938): 89; Friedlander, *Prelude to Downfall*, pp. 26-27; Frye, *Nazi Germany and the American Hemisphere*, pp. 72-79; Hilton, *Great Powers*, 40-48, 53-70; IAA, 1:180-81.

7. Feis to Stimson, May 17, 1934, R. 87, HS; Sayre to Dodd, May 3, 1935, B. 47, Sayre to Dodd, Feb. 8, 1937, B. 51, WD; Percy Bidwell, "Latin America, Germany and the Hull Program," *Foreign Affairs* 17 (January 1939): 374-90.

8. Sayre to Dodd, May 3, 1935, B. 47, WD.

9. Duggan to Wilson, July 16, 1938, B. 1, HW.

10. Lutz to Breckinridge, May 4, 1934, B. 25, SB; Messersmith to Moore, Dec. 22, 1936, No. 807, Messersmith to Hull, Feb. 17, 1938, no. 947, GM; Schoonmaker to Stimson, Oct. 6, 1939, R. 99, HS; Verissimo to Jessup, Mar. 27, 1942, B. 133, PJ; CR, Vol. 83, pt. 4, p. 3986; DGFP, 5:824-27,, 832-34, 880-85, 9:598-99, 630-31, 659, 10:41-42, 100-101, 131-32, 177-78, 426; Giffin, "Normal Years," pp. 72-75, 258-324; HIsd, 2:353; WDd, pp. 410, 424, 431; Frye, *Nazi Germany and the American Hemisphere*, pp. 101-17, 166-67; Hilton, *Great Powers*, pp. 84-109, 147-54, 159-63, 168-82; McCann, *Brazilian-American Alliance*, pp. 7-9, 48-51, 77, 105, 148-75.

11. Dodd to Sayre, Jan. 22, Dodd to Hull, May 27, B. 51, Dodd to FDR, Nov. 12, 1937, B. 49, WD; WDd, pp. 381, 388, 432-33.

12. LaGuardia to Baruch, Apr. 17, 1938, V. 1938, BB.

13. Diary, memo to Morgenthau, Jan. 31, B. 107, presidential diary, Morgenthau to FDR, Oct. 17, 1938, B. 1, HM; Baruch to Hull, Oct. 16, Baruch to Byrnes, Oct. 17, 18, 1939, V. 1939, Baruch to Welles, Mar. 18, 1939, V. 1939, Baruch to Hooker, Sept. 25, 1940, V. 1940, Baruch to Daniels, Nov. 29, 1940, V. 1940, BB; HMd, 2:43-44, 50.

14. Memo by Ray, June 22, 1940, 710.Consultation (2)/613; Feis to Stimson, Oct. 16, 1939, R. 99, HS; diary, Mar. 1940, B. 7, HW; diary, June 9, 1940, B. 212, AB; Wood to Jessup, July 5, 1940, B. 31, PJ; Frost to Taft, June 3, 1941, B. 21, WC, ABnr, pp. 299-300.

15. Memorandum, "What This Country Faces If Germany Wins," Dec. 30, 1940, 740.0011 EW 1939/7354½.

16. Hull to Welles, Sept. 20, 740.00111-A.R./314A, meeting of the Liaison Committee, Feb. 8, Apr. 25, 1939, SLC; Gibson to James, Mar. 13, 1935, B. 2, HG; diary, Sept. 22, 1939, B. 211, AB; Brady to Long, June 26, 1940, B. 130, BL; diary, July 25, 1940, V. 30, HS; FDR to Jones, Oct. 10, 1940, B. 29, Jones to FDR, June 26, Jones to Husbands, Aug. 1, Hull to Jones, Oct. 29, 1941, B. 30, JJ; memo to Hull, Welles and Marshall, Feb. 25, memo of conversation, June 4, 1941, B. 21, WC; radio broadcast, Dec. 20, 1941, B. D-1, AES; Lane to FDR, Jan. 15, 1943, O.F. 617; CR, Vol. 86, pt. 13, p. 837; PL, 2:1511-12; ABnr, pp. 301, 336-37, 392; Melvin Hall and Walter Peck, "Wings for the Trojan Horse," *Foreign Affairs* 19 (January 1941): 347-69; Stephen Randall, "Colombia, the United States, and Inter-American Aviation Rivalry, 1927-1940," *Journal of Inter-American and World Affairs* 14 (August 1972): 298-321; HAgm, pp. 201-2; McCann, *Brazilian-American Alliance*, pp. 213-39; Conn and Fairchild, *Framework*, pp. 238-49; Friedlander, *Prelude to Downfall*, pp. 225-26; William Burden, *The Struggle for Airways in Latin America* (New York: Council on Foreign Relations, 1943), pp. 13-15, 32-35, 46-51, 67-69, 70-72, 128; Duggan, *Americas*, p. 85; Bushnell, *Santos and the Good Neighbor*, pp. 18-23.

17. Gilbert to Moffat, Sept. 23, 1937, V. 1937, JPM.

18. Moore to Rowe, Dec. 18, 1937, B. 73, JM; Duggan to Inman, Mar. 8, 1938, B. 14, SI; Welles to FDR, Dec. 6, 1938, O.F. 621; memo of conversation, Dec. 13, 1938, B. 29, JED; Braden to Taussig, Dec. 27, 1937, B. 33, CT; Rippy to Dodd, Dec. 29, 1937, B. 52, WD; Duggan to Steinhardt, Apr. 30, 1938, B. 23, Steinhardt to Trygger, May 20, 1937, B. 78, LS; Ulloa to Scott, Dec. 30, 1940, Dean, "Impressions of South

America," summner 1941, B. 135, PJ; Wallace to Welles, Mar. 10, 1942, B. 108, HW (FDRL); Clarence Haring, "Is There a Fascist Danger in South America?" *Quarterly Journal of Inter-American Relations* 1 (January 1939): 7-17; Richard Behrendt, "Foreign Influences in Latin America," *Annals* 204 (July 1939): 1-8.

19. Daniels to Dodd, Jan. 25, 1938, B. 732, Daniels to Corrigan, May 8, B. 740, Daniels to Pearson, June 24, 1940, B. 794, JD; Daniels to Baker, Apr. 28, 1937, B. 84, NB; Daniels to Dodd, Jan. 25, 1938, B. 52, WD; Daniels to Corrigan, June 25, 1940, B. 3, FC.

20. Daniels to Bowers, Apr. 20, 1940, B. 740, JD.

21. Wallace to Riley, late Apr. 1939, R. 21, HW(Ia).

22. Fenwick to Welles, June 24, 1940, 710.Consultation (2)/225; Stimson statement, Apr. 5, Stimson to Eden, July 17, 1939, R. 98, HS; Wallace to Foster, Aug. 5, 1940, R. 22, HW (Ia); Knox to Ebert, Nov. 29, 1940, B. 1, FK; HIsd, 2:352, 497.

23. Keeley to Welles, Aug. 14, 1940, 740.0011 EW 1939/5209; Boas to Stimson, Oct. 29, 1938, R. 96, Coudert to Stimson, Aug. 26, 1940, R. 102, diary, Aug. 27, 1940, V. 30, HS; Stearns speech, Sept. 1, 1939, B. 22, PJ; Richberg to Lilienthal, Nov. 22, 1940, B. 2, DR; White to Landon, Feb. 19, 1941, Series C, B.376, WW; ASp, 1:493-501.

24. Memo, Feb. 26, 1941, B. 21, SE; Welles to Gunther, Feb. 3, 1942, B. 24, AM; Carleton Beals, "Swastika over the Andes," *Harper's Magazine* 177 (July 1938): 176-86; Samuel Bemis, "The New Holy Alliance Crosses the Ocean," *Quarterly Journal of Inter-American Relations* 1 (January 1939): 18-24; William Hessler, "Is South America Hedging on the War?" *Inter-American Quarterly* 3 (July 1941): 5-12; RCww, pp. 250-54, 263-65; Kenneth Grieb, "The Fascist Mirage in Central America: Guatemalan-United States Relations and the Yankee Fear of Fascism, 1936-1944" in *Perspectives in American Diplomacy*, ed. Jules Davids (New York: Arno Press, 1976), p. 25.

25. John Gunther, *Inside Latin America* (New York: Harper and Brothers, 1941), pp. x, 30, 478.

26. Memorandum, "America Faces the War," Dec. 30, 1940, 740.0011 EW 1939/8035, Casey to Hornbeck, Apr. 17,/10488, Rockefeller to Hull, Mar. 12, 1941, 710.11/2686; "The Fortune Survey: 32–The War," *Fortune* 22 (July 1940): supplement; George Gallup, *The Gallup Poll* (New York: Random House, 1972), pp. 184, 265, 279.

27. Press release, Nov. 5, 1938, 710.11/2297; Feis to Stimson, Nov. 22, 1937, Jan. 21, 1938, R. 94, Berle to Stimson, Mar. 20, 1940, R. 100, HS; Moore to Dodd, Nov. 8, 1938, B. 56, Feb. 27, Mar. 23, 1939, B. 57, WD; Messersmith to Hull, Feb. 16, no. 946, Messersmith to Heineman, Nov. 7, 1938, no. 1067, Messersmith to Jackson, Feb. 1, 1939, no. 1149, Messersmith to Welles, June 5, 1940, no. 1374, GM; Long to Messersmith, Oct. 8, Messersmith to Long, Oct. 15, 1940, B. 133, BL; diary, Feb. 20, 1939, B. 210, June 2, 1941, B. 212, AB; Messersmith to Harrison, Dec. 23, 1938, B. 29, LH; Messersmith to Milton, Apr. 27, 1939, B. 84, GFM; Messersmith to Corrigan, Mar. 6, 1941, B. 7, FC; Welles to Bowers, May 29, 1940, Bowers mss II, CB; ABnr, pp. 186, 200, 206-10, 230, 267-68, 318, 320, 322; BLwd, pp. 166-67; Feis, *1933*, p. 137.

28. Mayer to Davis, Oct. 6, 1938 and Oct. 14, 1939, B. 40, ND.

29. Davis to Early, Sept. 11, 1939, B. 40, ND.

30. Diary, memo of conversation, Apr. 24, 1939, B. 181, HM; Daniels to Bowers, Aug. 7, 1939, B. 736, Bowers to Daniels, May 30, 1940, B. 794, JD; Bowers to Dodd, July 21, 1940, B. 57, WD; Bowers to Long, Nov. 28, 1940, B. 130, BL; Bowers to Hull, Jan. 1, 1941, B. 48, CH.

31. Bowers to FDR, June 26, 1940, O.F. 303.

32. FDR to Bowers, July 12, 1940, O.F. 303.

33. White to Mathon, Jan. 8, Mathon to White, Jan. 13, O'Mahoney to White, Jan. 21, Mathon to White, Jan. 22, White to Mathon, Feb. 3, 1941, B. 228, NAACP; *New York Herald Tribune*, Jan. 8, 1941; *New York Times*, Jan. 18, p. 2, 19, p. 14, 1941.

34. *New York Times*, July 30, 1941, p. 8.

35. PC, July 29, 1941, R. 9; PL, 2:1194-95.

36. PPA, 6:406-11; PC, Apr. 15, 1939, R. 7.

37. FDR to White, Dec. 14, 1939, B. 320, WW; PPA, 9:1-10; PC, Nov. 15, 1938, R. 6; HIsd, 2:317, 568; ABnr, pp. 223-24; Conn and Fairchild, *Framework*, pp. 3-5, 421-22; Sherwood, *Roosevelt and Hopkins*, pp. 125-26.

38. FDR to Bowers, May 24, 1940, Bowers mss II, CB; PPA, 9:460-67.
39. PPA, 10:40-42.
40. FDR to Stimson, May 21, 1940, R. 101, HS.
41. FDR to Churchill, May 14, 1941, 740.0011 EW 1939/10944½.
42. PPA, 10:181.
43. Bonsal to Welles, June 9, 1941, 740.0011 EW 1939/11509; diary, May 28, 1941, B. 10, WL; Federalist Papers, May 28, 1941, Miscellaneous Manuscripts, HE; ABnr, p. 370; Friedlander, *Prelude to Downfall*, pp. 227-28; HIsd, 3:526-27; Sherwood, *Roosevelt and Hopkins*, pp. 292-99; WWsl, pp. 430-31.
44. Diary, June 14, 1941, B. 10, WL; PPA, 10:274.
45. Diary, Sept. 12, 1941, B. 10, WL; PPA, 10:384-92; Bushnell, *Santos and the Good Neighbor*, pp. 57-62; Braden, *Diplomats and Demagogues*, pp. 240-41.
46. *New York Daily Mirror*, Aug. 25, 1941, B. 44, Personal Secretary File, Diplomatic Germany, 1940-1941, FDRL; diary, Oct. 29, 1941, B. 10, WL; PC, Oct. 28, 1941, R. 9; PPA, 10:438-44; Compton, *Swastika and the Eagle*, pp. 88, 251; Callcott, *Western Hemisphere*, p. 348; William Shirer, *The Rise and Fall of the Third Reich* (Greenwich, Connecticut: Fawcett Publications, 1960), pp. 1149-55; John Toland, *Adolf Hitler* (New York: Doubleday, 1976), pp. 691-93.

CHAPTER 9

1. Knox to Bingham, Oct. 7, 1940, B. 1, FK.
2. Gollan to Ackerman, Nov. 6, 1940, B. 50, CA; Daniels to Bowers, Nov. 8, 1940, B. 740, JD; Robert Divine, *Foreign Policy and U.S. Presidential Elections, 1940-1948* (New York: New Viewpoints, 1974), pp. 3-89; Frye, *Nazi Germany and the American Hemisphere*, p. 151; Dozer, *Good Neighbors?*, pp. 84-99.
3. Introduction, B. 1, WHBS.
4. Acheson, *Present at the Creation*, p. 38.
5. Daniels to Dodd, Sept. 19, 1935, B. 712, Bowers to Daniels, Aug. 16, B. 732, Bowers to Daniels, Oct. 25, 1938, B. 791, JD; Baruch to Welles, June 18, 1940, V. 1940, BB; HMd, 1:452.
6. Daniels to Bowers, Sept. 6, 1938, B. 732, JD.
7. Hull to Watson, Feb. 16, 1940, B. 46, CH; memo for record, Apr. 8, 1953, B. 17, HF; Buell to Milton, Mar. 29, Milton to Buell, Mar. 30, 1939, B. 26, GFM; WMR, Mar. 24, Oct. 14, 1939; BLwd, pp. 1-2, 37; ABnr, p. 242; HIsd, 3:68.
8. Sayre to Hull, Apr. 10, B. 46, memo by Hull, July 3, 1940, B. unnumbered, CH; Farley to Sayre, Feb. 8, Sayre to Farley, Apr. 8, 1940, B. 4, FS; White to Milton, Aug. 16, 1939, B. 85, GFM; Landon to Inman, Aug. 26, 1939, B. 14, SI; Messersmith to Burlingham, July 13, 1939, no. 1259, GM; diary, Mar. 1940, B. 7, HW; Lash, *Eleanor and Franklin*, pp. 616-17; PL, 2:972-73; BLwd, p. 46, HIsd, 2:555; Claude Bowers, *My Life* (New York: Simon and Schuster, 1962), pp. 295-96.
9. Calendar 1940, 1941, R. 39, CH; Sayre to Hull, Aug. 22, 1941, B. 4, FS; diary, May 27, 1941, V. 34, HS; presidential diary, memo of conversation, June 4, 1941, B. 4, HM; JPMmp, pp. 332-33; WMR, May 28, 1941; Sherwood, *Roosevelt and Hopkins*, p. 185; HIsd, 3:286, 389; BLwd, pp. 175-76; HMd, 2:58, 261; Bowers, *My Life*, pp. 286-87.
10. Diary, Aug. 19, 1941, V. 35, HS; Hull to Davis, July 17, 1941, B. 27, ND; memo by Gosnell, Jan. 23, 1947, Feb. 2, 1948, Welles file, WBHS; WMR, Dec. 28, 1940; HIsd, 3:401; BLwd, pp. 179, 201, 210, 212, 214-15; Hinton, *Hull*, p. 8; Alsop and Kinter, *White Paper*, p. 83; Farley, *Jim Farley's Story*, pp. 341, 343.
11. Davies to Welles, Mar. 22, 1939, B. 9, JED; Duggan to Daniels, Nov. 25, 1939, B. 736, JD; diary, Apr. 3, 1940, B. 7, HW; CR, vol. 86, pt. 16, p. 3613; BLwd, p. 36; Orville Bullitt, ed., *For the President: Personal and Secret* (Boston: Houghton Mifflin, 1972), p. 410; HIsd, 3:273; Stanley Hilton, "The Welles Mission to Europe, February-March 1940: Illusion or Realism?" *Journal of American History* 58 (June 1971): 93-120; Graff, "Strategy of Involvement," pp. 217-22, 260-307.

12. Diary, Feb. 17, 1940, B. 211, AB; diary, May 16-June 11, 1940, B. 7, JD; diary, May 8, 1940, V. 29, HS; BLwd, p. 67; ABnr, pp. 205-6, 323-24; HIsd, 3:138, 216-19; Farley, *Jim Farley's Story*, p. 233.

13. Wilson to Hull, Mar. 13, B. 44, Braden to Hull, Dec. 22, 1939, B. 45, Howard to Farley, Hull to Howard, Nov. 12, 1940, B. unnumbered, CH; Culbertson to Armour, May 31, Armour to Culbertson, June 8, 1939, B. 18, Braden to Culbertson, Jan. 8, 1940, B. 20, WC; Milton to Hull, July 21, 1937, B. 21, GFM; Armour to Inman, Dec. 29, 1944, B. 15, SI; Erwin to McIntyre, no. 7, 1939, O.F. 2824; CHm, 2:1378; memo by Bonsal, Feb. 19, memo by Welles, Feb. 22, 1941, 740.00 EW 1939/8419, Gordon to Berle, Sept. 3, 710.11/2797, memo by Wright, Nov. 10,/2820, FDR to Murphy, Nov. 26, 1941,/2821½; Milton to Hull, May 27, Hull to Milton, June 2, 1937, B. 21, GFM; Messersmith to Daniels, Nov. 22, 1940, B. 755, JD; Messersmith to Frankfurter, Dec. 2, 1941, B. 83, FF; Braden to Inman, May 29, Daniels to Inman, June 2, 1941, B. 15, SI; Bushnell, *Santos and the Good Neighbor*, p. 14.

14. Bowers to Inman, June 10, 1941, SI.

15. Cantril, *Public Opinion*, pp. 95, 210, 549; Geoffrey Perrett, *Days of Sadness, Years of Triumph* (Baltimore: Penguin Books, 1974), pp. 162-65.

16. The Pan American League to Jessup, May 16, B. 22, Dean, "Impression of South America," summer 1941, B. 135, PJ.

17. Memo by Jessup, Sept. 8, 1941, B. 132, PJ.

18. Dawson to Stimson, Dec. 23, 1932, 710.G 1A/107, Sparks to Hull, Feb. 14, 1936, 710.Peace/193, Dreyfus to Hull, Oct. 13, 1938, 710.H/129, Welles to Lane, Dec. 16, 1941, 710. Consultation 3/47; Ulloa to Finch, Jan. 19, 1942, B. 135, PJ; memo of phone conversation, May 10, 1945, B. 4, LP; FR, 1941, 6:121, 123, 127, 129-31; FA, 3:348; PPA, 3:84-85; Wood, *Latin American Wars*, pp. 255-342; Langer and Gleason, *Undeclared War*, pp. 615-17; Carey, *Peru and the United States*, pp. 99-100.

19. Welles to Bowers, Jan. 7, 1942, Bowers mss II, CB; diary, Dec. 8, 10, 1941, B. 10, WL; FR, 1941, 6:124-25; PPA, 10:538; Blendon, "Venezuela and the United States," pp. 58-77; IAA, 2:8, 171-73; Langer and Gleason, *Undeclared War*, p. 624; CHm, 2:1139; Cline, *The United States and Mexico*, pp. 261-71; Mecham, *United States and Inter-American Security*, pp. 80-87; Bushnell, *Santos and the Good Neighbor*, pp. 103-17; Peterson, *Argentina and the United States*, p. 414; Toland, *Hitler*, pp. 693-96.

20. ABnr, pp. 384, 387.

21. Duggan to Welles, Dec. 9, 710.Consultation 3/40, Lane to Hull, Dec. 15, 1941,/ 48; FR, 1941, 6:118-26; SW-3, pp. 219-32; SW-2, pp. 97-100; Claude Bowers, *Chile* (New York: Simon and Schuster, 1958), pp. 74-80.

22. BLwd, p. 237.

23. Memo by Duggan, Dec. 17, 710.Consultation 3/82, memo by Halle, Dec. 18,/ 112, 2/11, Hull to Wilson, Dec. 19,/68, memo by Collado, Dec. 20,/141, Welles to Caffery, Dec. 30, 1941,/142D; FR, 1942, 5:23-24; CHm, 2:1143-44.

24. FR, 1942, 5:13.

25. Welles to FDR, Jan. 8, 710.Consultation 3/281A, Welles to Hull, Jan. 13,/304, Simmons to Hull, Jan. 14, 1942,/409; Welles, B. 1, WHBS; FR, 1941, 6:131-32; FR, 1942, 5:9-12, 14-15; SW-2, pp. 94-97.

26. FR, 1942, 5:26.

27. Welles to Caffery, Dec. 26, 710.Consultation 3/125A, Caffery to Welles, Dec. 29,/132, Bowers to Welles, Dec. 30, /138, Caffery to Welles, Dec. 31, 1941,/148, Welles to Caffery, Jan. 4, /218A, Bowers to Hull, Jan. 5, /276, Armour to Hull, Jan. 7, 1942, 740.0011 EW 1939/18259; FR, 1941, 6:120, 127-28; FR, 1942, 5:7-9, 15-16, 22; Bowers, *Chile*, p. 59; SW-3, pp. 415-17.

28. Memo by Welles, May 14, 15, 1941, 740.0011 EW 1939/11290.

29. Armour to Bowers, May 28, 1942, Bowers mss II, CB.

30. Armour to Hull, Dec. 12, 710.Consultation 3/37, Caffery to Hull, Dec. 22, 1941, /87, Armour to Hull, Jan. 5,/135, Jan. 12, 1942,/297, Armour to Hull, Dec. 24, 1941, 740.0011 PW/1512, Jan. 7, 1942, 740.0011 EW 1939/18260; FR, 1942,

5:6, 16-22, 24, 27; Peterson, *Argentina and the United States*, pp. 415-16; CHm, 2:1144-45; SW-2, pp. 100-107; Conil Paz and Ferrari, *Argentina's Foreign Policy*, pp. 62-72.

31. Berle to Welles, Jan. 15, 1942, 710.Consultation 3/330B.

32. Caffery to Hull, Jan. 6, 710/Consultation 3/220, Welles to Caffery, Jan. 7,/254A, Caffery to Hull, Jan. 16,/341, Dawson to Hull, Jan. 29, 1942,/587; radio broadcast, Jan. 16, 1942, B. D-1, AES; Duggan, *Americas*, pp. 86-88; SW-4, pp. 34-54.

33. Welles to Hull, Jan. 16, 710.Consultation 3/344, Welles to Bowers, Jan. 19,/598, Welles to Armour, Jan. 20,/598, Bowers to Hull, Jan. 21,/423, memo by Hull, Jan. 21,/453, Bowers to Welles, Jan. 22,/598, Hull to Dawson, Jan. 27, 1942,/489; radio broadcasts, Jan. 19-22, 1942, B. D-1, AES; FR, 1942, 5:27-28, 30-32, 34, 39-42; Duggan, *Americas*, pp. 88-89.

34. Armour to Welles, Jan. 21, 710.Consultation 3/576, memo of conversation, Jan. 22,/450, Armour to Welles, Jan. 22,/576, Hull to Welles, Jan. 22, 1942,/450; FR, 1942, 5:33-34.

35. FR, 1942, 5:33.

36. Welles to Hull, Jan. 23, 1942, 710.Consultation 3/458; diary, Jan. 24, 1942, B. 10, WL; diary, Jan. 25, 1942, V. 37, HS; OHP, pp. 308-11, NR; WMR, Aug. 29, 1944; FR, 1942, 5:34-39; ABnr, pp. 389-99; CHm, 2:1145-48; SW-2, pp. 108-9, 115-17.

37. Caffery to Hull, Jan. 24, 710.Consultation 3/468; press release, Jan. 24,/582, Welles to Hull, Jan. 28,/514, Cross to Hull, Jan. 28, 1942,/598; radio broadcasts, Jan. 24, 26, 27, 1942, B. D-1, AES; FR, 1942, 5:36, 43; BLwd, p. 245; SW-2, pp. 110-15, 119-22; SW-3, pp. 233-35; McCann, *Brazilian-American Alliance*, pp. 250-58.

38. Mac To Inman, Feb. 1, 1942, B. 15, SI.

39. *Time*, Feb. 9, 1942, pp. 28-29.

40. Daniels to Butler, Feb. 3, 710.Consultation 3/612, Corrigan to Hull, Feb. 11, 1942,/639, memo by Berle, Mar. 4, 1944,/855A; meeting of LC, June 22, 1942, Liaison Minutes 4, SLC; FR, 1942, 5:40-41; Karl Loewenstein, "Pan Americanism in Action," *Current History* 5 (November 1943): 229-36; CHm, 2:1149-50; SW-2, pp. xv-xvi, 117-19; Duggan, *Americas*, pp. 93-94, 97-101.

41. Hull to Welles, Jan. 29, 710.Consultation 3/536A, Caffery to Hull, Jan. 30,/541, press release, Feb. 2, 1942,/616; diary, Feb. 1-7, 8-15, 1942, B. 8, HI; Corrigan to Welles, Feb. 19, 1942, B. 10, FC; diary, Apr. 12, 1942, B. 214, AB; PPA, 2:193-95; SW-4, pp. 55-65.

42. Hull to FDR, Jan. 10, B. unnumbered, CH; ABnr, p. 400; BLwd, pp. 242-43; JPMmp, pg. 378-79.

CHAPTER 10

1. Memo by Butler, May 13, 1938, meeting of LC, Sept. 13, 1939, SLC.

2. Memo by Briggs, Jan. 9, 1938, 810.24/5½; John Child, "Latin America: Military-Strategic Concepts," *Air University Review* 27 (Sept.-Oct. 1976): 28-34; Gerald Haines, "Under the Eagle's Wing: The Franklin Roosevelt Administration Forges an American Hemisphere," *Diplomatic History* 1 (Fall 1977): 376.

3. Conn and Fairchild, *Framework*, pp. 265-68; Hilton, *Great Powers*, pp. 110-31; McCann, *Brazilian-American Alliance*, pp. 108-16; Giffin, "Normal Years," pp. 425-26.

4. Welles to Gibson, Jan. 14, B. 48, Hull to Gibson, Jan. 15., 1936, B. 46, HG; Weddell to Hull, Mar. 20, memo by Welles, Mar. 31, 1936, B. 38, CH; Green to Moffat, Apr. 22, 1936, JPM. 1936, JPM; FA, 3:273-75.

5. Diary, Jan. 27, Apr. 20, Aug. 11, 1937, B., WL; diary, Aug. 13, 1937, JPM; PC, Aug. 10, 1937, R. 5; CR, vol. 81, pt. 8, pp. 8482-83; Bryce Wood, "External Restraints on the Good Neighbor Policy," *Inter-American Economic Affairs* 16 (Autumn 1962): 3-24; HIsd, 2:85-86.

6. Inman to Hull, Aug. 13, Hull to Inman, Aug. 16, 1937, B. 14, SI.

7. Welles to FDR, Nov. 17, 1938, 810.24/8A, Welles to Pittman, Mar. 25, 1939,/23B; meeting of LC, Jan. 21, Feb. 8, 1939, SLC; diary, June 26, 1937, B. 8, July 6, 11, 1938,

Feb. 15, 1939, B. 9, WL; McCann, *Brazilian-American Alliance*, pp. 123-47; Forrest Pogue, *George C. Marshall: Education of a General* (New York: Viking Press, 1963), pp. 338-42.

8. Burdett to Hull, Dec. 13, 1939, 740.00111 A-Neutrality Patrol/50.

9. Welles to FDR, May 10, 1938, meeting of LC, Apr. 1, 1939, SLC; diary, July 16, 1938, JD; Conn and Fairchild, *Framework*, pp. 173-75.

10. Memo by Chapin, Dec. 15, Welles to FDR, Dec. 20, 1938, meeting of LC, SLC.

11. Leahy to Bloch, Apr. 28, 1938, B. 2, CCB; diary, Apr. 18, 1938, B. 9, WL; Messersmith to Layton, Feb. 25, 1938, No. 955, GM; Swanson to Daniels, Aug. 20, 1938, B. 754, JD; PC, Apr. 20, 1938, R. 6; Bushnell, *Santos and the Good Neighbor*, pp. 8-13.

12. Bloch to Leahy, Apr. 12, July 28, 1938, B. 2, CCB.

13. Meeting of LC, Oct. 16, Dec. 7, 1939, June 10, 1940, SLC; Chapin to Corrigan, Sept. 27, 1940, B. 2, FC; King to Knox, Jan. 17, 1941, B. 8, EK; *Pearl Harbor Attack: Hearings before the Joint Committee on the Investigation of the Pearl Harbor Attack* (Washington, D.C.: G.P.O., 1946), pt. 14, p. 944, pt. 15, pp. 1506-10; BLwd, p. 202; CHm, 2:1139.

14. Memo by Green, Nov. 3, 821.796 SCA 2/401½ CF, memo by Hunt, Dec. 5, 1939, 740.00111-A.R./880; diary, Aug. 1, 1944, V. 48, HS; Conn and Fairchild, *Framework*, pp. 249, 264.

15. Philip Taylor, "Hemispheric Defense in World War II," *Current History* 56 (June 1969): 333-39; Louis Morton, "Germany First: Basic Concept of Allied Strategy in World War II," in *Command Decisions*, ed. Kent Greenfield, (New York: Harcourt Brace, 1959), pp. 3-20; Conn and Fairchild, *Framework*, pp. 7-22, 413-14; Pogue, *Marshall: Education*, pp. 336-37.

16. Diary, Sept. 13, 1934, WP; Welles to Hull, Sept. 5, 7, Inman to Hull, Dec. 8, 1934, B. 37, CH; U.S., Congress, Senate, *Hearings before the Special Committee Investigating the Munitions Industry, 1934-1946* (1936), pt. 1, pp. 57-62, pt. 2, pp. 586-92, pt. 10, pp. 2344-65; Gellman, *Roosevelt and Batista*, pp. 117-18.

17. Memo by Wilson, Feb. 10, 1933, 810.24/1, memo by Green, Dec. 27, 1935/4, memo by Briggs, Jan. 9, 1938,/5½, memo by Gantenbein, Dec. 27, 1937, 825.5151/ 452½; diary, Oct. 20, 1938, B. 9, WL; HIsd, 2:110-11.

18. Meeting of LC, Nov. 6, 1939, SLC.

19. Walsh to Welles, Jan. 18, Welles to Walsh, Jan. 25, 810. 24/8, memo by Welles, Feb. 1, 1939,/26; meeting of LC, Jan. 21, Feb. 8, 1939, SLC; diary, Feb. 3, 1939, B. 9, WL.

20. Welles to Pittman, Mar. 11, 1939, 810.24/12A.

21. Welles to Pittman, Mar. 25, 810.24/23B, Hull to AR missions, June 27, 1939,/ 24, memo by Welles, Feb. 15, 1940,/85, 1940,/85, Hull to Braden, July 5, 1939, 810.50/50; meeting of LC, Apr. 25, July 26, Aug. 3, 11, Sept. 13, 1939, SLC; diary, Mar. 15, 22, 1939, B. 9; WL; Welles to Bowers, May 23, 1940, Bowers mss II, CB; Braden to Feis, Apr. 25, 1939, B. 11, HF; Hull to American Republics, Jan. 16, 740.0011 EW 1939/7695A, memo by Bonsal, Jan. 28, 710.Consultation 3/7, Feb. 17, 1941,/8; Landon broadcast, Mar. 10, 1941, Series C, B. 376, WW; Stimston to Moore, Mar. 12, 1941, R. 103, HS; Roper to Daniels, Mar. 24, 1941, B. 747, JD; CR, vol. 86, pt. 7, pp. 7615-16; FR, 1939, 5:1-14; FR, 1940, 5:1-9; Langer and Gleason, *Challenge to Isolation*, p. 619; Conn and Fairchild, *Framework*, pp. 207-14, 217-24; Langer and Gleason, *Undeclared War*, pp. 162-64; Churchill, *Their Finest Hour*, pp. 470-89; Edward Stettinius, *Lead-Lease* (New York: Macmillan, 1944), pp. 37-42, 78-85.

22. Hull to FDR, Mar. 28, Welles to Hull, Mar. 28, Welles to Hull, Apr. 8, Swanson to Hull, Apr. 9, Woodring to Hull, Apr. 11, Welles to Craig, Apr. 12, 1939, memo by Duggan, Aug. 18, memo by Notter, Sept. 1, memo by Hull, Nov. 3, Log of U-L, Nov. 29, 1939, SLC; memo by Chapin, Mar. 20, 1940, 740.0011 EW 1939/1882½; Langer and Gleason, *Challenge to Isolation*, pp. 40-41, 273.

23. Memo by Gosnell, Feb. 2, 1948, Welles file, WBHS; diary, Nov. 25, Dec. 23, 1940, Jan. 4, 7, 1941, V. 31, HS; Stimson to White, Jan. 2, 1940, B. 347, WW; HSas, pp. 318-20, 325-26; Morison, *Turmoil and Tradition*, pp. 399, 421.

24. Logan, *No Transfer*, pp. 290-95, 315-17; Conn and Fairchild, *Framework*, p. 30.

25. Diary, May 20, 1940, B. 4, HW.

26. Welles to Bowers, June 10, 18, 28, FDR to Bowers, July 1, 1940, Bowers mss II, CB; diary, June 4, 1940, B. 212, AB; Friedlander, *Prelude to Downfall*, p. 225; Conn and Fairchild, *Framework*, pp. 31-44, 62-67, 175-83; Bushnell, *Santos and the Good Neighbor*, pp. 50-54.

27. Messersmith to Long, June 17, 1940, B. 133, BL.

28. Morton, "Germany First," pp. 21-38; Sherwood, *Roosevelt and Hopkins*, pp. 410-18; Conn and Fairchild, *Framework*, pp. 74-76, 88-96; Langer and Gleason, *Undeclared War*, pp. 151-58; Forrest Pogue, *George C. Marshall: Ordeal and Hope* (New York: Viking Press, 1965), pp. 52-55.

29. Memo by Notter and King, Jan. 24, 1941, 740.0011 EW 1939/7874½.

30. Conn and Fairchild, *Framework*, pp. 96-100, 183-86; *Pearl Harbor Attack*, pt. 14, p. 1379.

31. Memo by Bonsal, Dec. 27, 1941, 710.Consultation 3/112 4/11; memo for the Chief of Staff, Dec. 31, 1941, Stimson to Hull, Jan. 2, Analysis of State Department Proposal, Jan. 2, Johnson to Embick, May 21, 1942, 341.187, IADB; diary, Dec. 30, 1941, V. 36, Jan. 12, 1942, V. 37, HS; Knox address, Mar. 30, 1942, B. 8, FK; Conn and Fairchild, *Framework*, pp. 191-99; Mecham, *United States and Inter-American Security*, pp. 222-25.

32. Meeting of LC, Jan. 21, June 16, July 26, Oct. 18, 1939, Feb. 15, 1941, SLC; Gruening to White, Mar. 30, 1937, B. C-108, NAACP; diary, Mar. 7, 1938, May 12, 1940, B. 9, WL; PC, Feb. 19, 1940, R. 8; memo of cabinet meeting, Sept. 13, 1940, B. 6, RP; report of Panama, Mar. 3, 1941, B. 136, PJ; memo for FDR, Mar. 14, Wilson to Stimson, Mar. 21, diary, Mar. 11, 1942, V. 38, HS; diary, Mar. 8-15, 1942, B. 8, HI; Stetson Conn, Rose Engelman, and Byron Fairchild, *Guarding the United States and Its Outposts* (Washington, D.C.: G.P.O., 1964), pp. 301-22, 327, 333-37, 344-50, 408-15, 424-29; Ladislas Farago, *Game of Foxes* (New York: Bantam Books, 1973), pp. 63-67; *Pearl Harbor Attack*, pt. 20, p. 4277; Louis Johnson, "Hemisphere Defense," *Atlantic Monthly* 166 (July 1940): 1-7; HSas, pp. 406-7; Morison, *Battle of the Atlantic*, pp. 149-54; U.S. Congress, House, Committee on Military Affairs, Aviation Subcommittee, *Special Mission by Aviation Subcommittee of the Committee on Military Affairs,* House Report no. 950 *(Merritt Report)* 78th Cong., 1st sess., 1943, p. 4.

33. Conn et al., *Guard the United States*, pp. 322-26, 329-35, 337-39, 351-52.

34. BLwd, p. 252.

35. Memo by Patterson, Apr. 8, 1942, B. 61, RP; diary, Mar. 2, 1944, B. 11, WL; memo for Stimson, Apr. 8, 1942, R. 105, HS; Morison, *Battle of the Atlantic*, pp. 126-48, 257-59, 346-52; Conn and Fairchild, *Framework*, pp. 423-24; Conn et al., *Guarding the United States*, pp. 416-24, 429-41; Pogue, *Marshall: Ordeal*, p. 273; House, *Merritt Report*, p. 5.

36. Hull to Culbertson, Apr. 10, 1941, B. 21, WC; diary, Mar. 13, 1941, B. 7, JD; JDrd, p. 201; Langer and Gleason, *Undeclared War*, pp. 605-10; Conn and Fairchild, *Framework*, pp. 333-38; Stegmaier, "From Confrontation to Cooperation," pp. 102-5, 126-83.

37. Meeting of LC, Nov. 26, 1942, SLC; memoirs, vol. 2, no. 12, vol. 3, no. 18, B. IX, GM; Messersmith to Hull, May 6, 20, June 25, July 10, Messersmith to Shaw, Aug. 7, 1942, B. 50, CH; Messersmith to Daniels, Aug. 20, 1943, B. 820, JD; PPA, 11:256; Conn and Fairchild, *Framework*, pp. 338-63; House, *Merritt Report*, p. 2; Stegmaier, "From Confrontation to Cooperation," pp. 229-63.

38. Hull to Welles, Oct. 3, 1939, 740.00111-A.R./427B; Stimson to FDR, June 19, R. 104, diary, June 19, V. 34, Dec. 17, 1941, V. 36, HS; HIsd, 3:435; *Pearl Harbor Attack*, pt. 14, pp. 1378-79, pt. 15, p. 1642; Morison, *Battle of the Atlantic*, pp. 83-84, 376-91; McCann, *Brazilian-American Alliance*, pp. 187-212; Langer and Gleason, *Undeclared War*, pp. 600-605; Conn and Fairchild, *Framework*, pp. 76-81, 83-88, 113-21, 125-30, 268-312.

39. Welles to FDR, Jan. 18, 1942, 710.Consultation 3/598.

40. Welles to Hull, Jan. 29, 1942, 710.Consultation 3/527; meeting of LC, Jan. 11, Feb. 8, 1942, SLC; diary, June 30, 1942, V. 39, HS; Duggan to MacLeish, Aug. 15, 1942, B. 6, AM; diary, Aug. 22, 1942, B. 11, WL, PPA, 11:339-40; Conn and Fairchild, *Framework*, pp. 313-30; HAgm, p. 288; McCann, *Brazilian-American Alliance*, pp. 259-90, 343-77, 403-42.

41. Stimson to Hull, Apr. 7, 1941, B. 49, CH.

42. Caffery to Hull, Mar. 11, 740.0011 EW 1939/8949, memo by Bonsal, Mar. 14, 710.Consultation 3/9, Mar. 24, 1941,/9-2/7; Duggan to Bowers, Dec. 22, 1941, Bowers mss II, CB; Conn and Fairchild, *Framework*, pp. 228-32; Langer and Gleason, *Undeclared War*, pp. 596-600; Bushnell, *Santos and the Good Neighbor*, pp. 54-56; IAA, 1:102-3.

43. Braden to Welles, Jan. 15, 1942, 710.Consultation 3/598, memo by Duggan, June 28, 710.11/6-2844, Berle to Bursley, Nov. 1, 1944,/11-144; meeting of LC, June 14, Aug. 6, 1943, SLC; Welles to FDR, Mar. 11, FDR to Welles, Mar. 24, 1942, B. 184, Stettinius to Braden, June 27, 1944, B. 719, ES; Conn and Fairchild, *Framework*, pp. 232-37; Mecham, *A Survey of United States-Latin American Relations*, p. 152.

44. Knox address, Mar. 30, 1942, B. 8, FK; meeting of LC, July 13, 1942, SLC; memo for Embick, Mar. 4, 1943, 341.187, IADB.

45. Meeting of LC, Feb. 24, 1943, SLC; memo on Inter-American Military Agency, Oct. 30, 1945, B. 294, Harley Notter File, RG 59; Johnson to Embick, Mar. 30, memo for Whiship and Embick, May 3, memo for secretary general, Oct. 19, memo for the Chief of Staff, Nov. 30, Knox and Stimson to IADB, Dec. 1, 1943, memo for Porter, mid-1944, memo for the record, Aug. 18, 1945, 341.187, IADB; Stettinius to King, Dec. 8, 1943, B. 15, EK; memo by Patterson, Dec. 19, 1946, B. 23, RP; meeting of LC, Aug. 10, 1942, SLC; Stimson to Hull, Dec. 10, 1943, 710.11/3199; diary, Nov. 8, 28, 1944, V. 49, June 26-30, 1945, V. 51, HS; Mecham, *United States and Inter-American Security*, pp. 225, 293-99.

46. Memo on aircraft, Jan. 30, 1945, 710.Conference W-PW/1-3045; diary, Feb. 22, 1944, B. 215, AB; diary, Aug. 9, 1944, B. 241, ES; Conn and Fairchild, *Framework*, pp. 225-28; IAA, 3:42-43.

47. Diary, May 2, 1945, Journals, HA; HAgm, pp. 553-54, 556-59.

48. Arnold to Salgado, May 13, 1945, B. 243, HA.

49. Memo on state department, undated, B. 225, HA.

50. Welles to Hull, Jan. 28, 1942, 710.Consultation 3/598; memo for Johnson, Mar. 13, 1943, 341.187, IADB; meeting of LC, Aug. 31, 1942, SLC; PL, 2:30-46; HWpv, p. 86; Corrigan to King, Oct. 13, 1943, B. 10, EK; ASp, 2:57; Conn et al., *Guarding the United States*, pp. 340-43.

51. Meeting of LC, Aug. 31, 1942, SLC; Child, "Military-Strategic Concept," pp. 34-36; Mecham, *United States and Inter-American Security*, pp. 335-41.

52. ASp, 2:67-68, 107.

53. Memo for Forrestal, Oct. 30, 1945, B. 11, EK.

54. JFd, p. 115.

55. Memo by Dreier, Mar. 20, 1944, 710.11/3294; Hull to Stimson, Aug. 17, 1944, 341.187, IADB; Messersmith to Hull, Sept. 6, 1945, B. 55, CH; IAA, 3:12.

56. Memo by Dreier, July 5, 1945, 710.11/7-545; Duggan, *Americas*, pp. 94-96, 177-89.

CHAPTER 11

1. Espinosa, *Inter-American Beginnings*, pp. 30-44, 255-58; US Department of State, *Cultural Cooperation Program*, pp. 28-30.

2. Welles to Rowe, Aug. 30, 1945, VIP. Autographs, LR; Hull to Rowe, Dec. 22, 1942, B. 50, CH; Espinosa, *Inter-American Beginnings*, pp. 9-24; US Department of State, *Cultural-Cooperation Program*, pp. 41-44; IAA, 1:130-34, 2:100-102, 4:189, 190, 196, 197; CHm, 1:351; Duggan, *Americas*, pp. 115, 159, 192-95.

3. Butler to Wallace, Apr. 21, 1941, B. 135, memo by Jessup, Sept. 8, 1941, B. 132, PJ; Institute of Latin American Studies, *Inter-American Intellectual Interchange* (Austin:

The University of Texas Press, 1943), pp. 3-11; Guerrant, *Good Neighbor Policy*, pp. 128-34; IAA, 1:152-58.

4. The Pan American League to Jessup, June 7, July 17, 1940, Wallace to Harrison, Sept. 3, 1941, B. 22, PJ; Espinosa, *Inter-American Beginnings*, pp. 45-49; US Department of State, *Cultural-Cooperation Program*, pp. 8-9; IAA, 1:126-28, 134-36.

5. Ackerman to Freeman, July 7, 1936, B. 8, RM; Ackerman typescript, 1937, B. 117, CA.

6. Ackerman to Cabot, Sept. 9, 1937, B. 118, CA.

7. Ackerman speech, Nov. 10, 1939, B. 49, Ackerman remarks, Nov. 6, 1940, B. 50, CA; Jane Clapper, *International Dictionary of Literary Awards* (New York: Scarecrow Press, 1963), p. 67.

8. Butler speech, Nov. 6, 1940, B. 50, CA.

9. Coudert to Butler, Jan. 28, Conference of the Inter-American Bar Association, Mar. 24-28, Ryan speech, Mar. 25, 1941, B. 135, PJ; Borchard to Moore, Apr. 1, 1941, B. 80, JM; Enrique Gil, "The Long View of Hemispheric Solidarity," *American Bar Association Journal* 27 (November 1941): 679-81; IAA 1:136-39; Espinosa, *Inter-American Beginnings*, pp. 92-101.

10. Welles to Butler, May 4, Welles to Davis, May 11, Davis to Welles, May 13, 1935, B. 63, ND; Espinosa, *Inter-American Beginnings*, pp. 68-76.

11. Welles to Daniels, Mar. 18, 1937, B. 752, JD; Welles to Kelchner, Mar. 24, 1937, B. 656, RG 43; US Department of State, *Cultural-Cooperation Program*, p. 10; Espinosa, *Inter-American Beginnings*, pp. 80-86, 89-92, 96-100.

12. Espinosa, *Inter-American Beginnings*, pp. 118-22; Charles Thomson, *Overseas Information Service* (Washington, D.C.: Brookings Institution, 1948), pp. 161-64.

13. Inman to Pickett, Jan. 8, Hull to Inman, June 2, Welles to Inman, Jan. 10, 1938, B. 14, SI; Espinosa, *Inter-American Beginnings*, pp. 101-2.

14. Welles to Inman, Jan. 10, 1938, B. 14, SI.

15. FR, 1945, 1:462-63; Espinosa, *Inter-American Beginnings*, pp. 111-13.

16. Press release, June 12, 1940, 710.11/2515; MacLeish to Bloom, Apr. 30, 1945, B. 3, AM; diary, Feb. 20, 1939, B. 7, JD; Daniels to Hull, Feb. 24, 1939, B. 44, CH; FR, 1938, 5:75-78; Espinosa, *Inter-American Beginnings*, pp. 114-18, 124-28, 130-32, 139-55, 159-81; Callcott, *Western Hemisphere*, pp. 345-46; IAA, 1:117-22; Guerrant, *Good Neighbor Policy*, pp. 115-20; US Department of State *Cultural-Cooperation Program*, pp. 10-12.

17. Welles to Wallace, July 9, 1941, B. 108, HW(FDRL); Messersmith to Hull, Dec. 11, 1943, B. 53, CH; Espinosa, *Inter-American Beginnings*, pp. 129, 187-204, 225-34, 241-47; US Department of State, *Cultural-Cooperation Program*, pp. 25-28, 32-35, 51-54, 57-58; IAA, 1:139-41, 4:188-89.

18. Espinosa, *Inter-American Beginnings*, pp. 250-55; US Department of State, *Cultural-Cooperation Program*, pp. 23-25.

19. Messersmith to Jessup, Apr. 1, 1941, B. 134, PJ.

20. Espinosa, *Inter-American Beginnings*, pp. 248-50, 263-75, 281-98; US Department of State, *Cultural-Cooperation Program*, pp. 9-10, 14-17, 55-57.

21. Wallace to Rockefeller and Wallace to Welles, Dec. 26, 1940, R. 22, HW; US Department of State, *Cultural-Cooperation Program*, pp. 25-28, 32-35, 51-54, 57-58; IAA, 1:139-41, 4:188-89.

22. Interview, NR; US Office of Inter-American Affairs, *History of the Office of the Coordinator of Inter-American Affairs* (Washington, D.C.: G.P.O., 1947), pp. 3-8, 279-80; Joe Morris, *Nelson Rockefeller* (New York: Harper and Brothers, 1960), pp. 128-53; Peter Collier and David Horowitz, *The Rockefellers* (New York: Holt, Rinehart and Winston, 1976), pp. 213-14.

23. Interview, NR; OHP, pp. 8-10, NR; PAA, 1939, pp. 335-38; Michael Kramer and Sam Roberts, "*I Never Wanted to be Vice-President of Anything!*" (New York: Basic Books, 1976), pp. 50-51; Collier and Horowitz, *Rockefellers*, pp. 206-7.

24. Interview, NR; Collier and Horowitz, *Rockefellers*, pp. 228-33; Frank Ninkovich, "The Currents of Cultural Diplomacy: Art and the State Department, 1938-1947" *Diplomatic History* 1 (Summer 1977): 218.

25. Draft article by Nelson Rockefeller on dyslexia, Oct. 1976, office of the vice-president, Washington, D.C.; Collier and Horowitz, *Rockefellers*, pp. 208-12.

26. Draft article by Rockefeller; Morris, *Rockefeller*, pp. 111-27; James Desmond, *Nelson Rockefeller* (New York: Macmillan, 1964), p. 52; HIsd, 2:204.

27. Diary, Sept. 21, 1940, B. 212, AB.

28. Duggan to Welles, Sept. 30, 1940, 710.11/2599½.

29. Interview, NR; PPA, 10:297-306; memo by Duggan and Welles to Rockefeller, Feb. 24, 710.Consultation 3/112 10/11, memo by Bonsal, Feb. 25, 1942,/689; Tomlinson to Hull, Oct. 5, 1940, B. 48, CH; OHP-CB; Daniels to Duggan, Apr. 26, 1944, B. 824, JD; *US Office of Inter-American Affairs, History*, pp. 9-10, 181-90, 280-81; Morris, *Rockefeller*, pp. 154-69; Duggan, *Americas*, p. 161; Braden, *Demagogues and Diplomats*, pp. 263-64, 274-75, 452; Carey, *Peru and the United States*, p. 102; McCann, *Brazilian-American Alliance*, pp. 249-50.

30. Interview, NR.

31. Gibson to James, Sept. 24, Gibson to FDR, Oct. 11, FDR to Gibson, Oct. 26, 1933, B. 2, HG; diary, May 23, 1934, JPM; Sack to Hull, Apr. 15, 1936, B. 38, CH; Brown to Ackerman, Oct. 18, 1938, B. 49, CA; FA, 1:348, 444-49, 464-65; PC, Mar. 16, 1934, R. 2; IAA, 1:128-30.

32. Diary, July 31, 1941, B. 213, AB; Welles to Early, June 23, 1942, B. 21, SE; Sorells to Clapper, Sept. 17, 1942, B. 50, RC; *US Office of Inter-American Affairs, History*, pp. 41-56, 83-89.

33. Chavez to Daniels, Mar. 9, B. 732, Welles to Daniels, Apr. 11, 1938, B. 752, JD; Carson address, July 5, 1938, B. 118, CA; PL, 2:779-80; HIsd, 2:606; US Department of State, *Cultural-Cooperation Program*, pp. 49-50.

34. *US Office of Inter-American Affairs, History*, pp. 57-66, 195-205; Haines, "Under the Eagle's Wing," pp. 381-82.

35. Fairbanks to MacLeish, Aug. 21, 1941, B. 7, AM; CR, vol. 86, pt. 14, p. 1787; US Department of State, *Cultural-Cooperation Program*, pp. 45-48; *US Office of Inter-American Affairs, History*, pp. 67-82; Haines, "Under the Eagle's Wing," pp. 382-84.

36. US Department of State, *Cultural-Cooperation Program*, pp. 39-41, 49; IAA, 4:194-96.

37. "Consul Claims Good Neighbor Policy Failure," *Tampa Daily Times*, Mar. 28, 1941; Ackerman speech, Mar. 31, 1941, B. 162, CA; Manuel Seone, "If I Were Nelson Rockefeller," *Harper's Magazine* 186 (February 1943): 312-18; Inman to Wallace, May 29, 1943, B. 15, SI.

38. *US Office of Inter-American Affairs, History*, pp. 271-78.

39. Welles to MacLeish, Dec. 5, Inman to MacLeish, Dec. 17, MacLeish to Inman, Dec. 26, 1944, B. 10, AM; FDRrf, p. 494; William Hassett, *Off the Record with F.D.R.* (New Brunswick, N.J.: Rutgers University Press, 1958), pp. 303-4.

40. Bowers to MacLeish, Dec. 6, 1944, B. 3, AM.

41. MacLeish to Bloom, Apr. 30, B. 3, Hanson to Byam, May 14, B. 2, MacLeish to Messersmith, June 26, B. 13, Welles to MacLeish, Aug. 20, 1945, B. 20, AM.

42. MacLeish to Bloom, June 9, 1945, B. 3, AM.

43. Duggan, *Americas*, p. 161.

CHAPTER 12

1. Simon Hanson, "Problems of an Inter-American Economy," *Quarterly Journal of Inter-American Relations* 1 (January 1939): 58-68; Hubert Herring, "Making Friends with Latin America," *Harper's Magazine* 179 (September 1939): 360-75; SW-3, pp. 209-10; Langer and Gleason, *Challenge to Isolation*, pp. 276-78.

2. Hull to Welles, Oct. 4, 740.00111-A.R./446½, Hull to Morgenthau, Nov. 2, 710.FEAC/9A, memo by Duggan, Nov. 4,/39, memo by Grady, Nov. 14,/25½, memo by Collado, Dec. 8,/106, Briggs to Duggan, Nov. 17, 1939, 710.H-Economics and Finance/130; diary, Sept. 18, 1939, B. 211, AB; FR, 1939, 5:43-44; CHm, 1:692.

3. Press release, Nov. 15, 710. FEAC/59, address by Castro, Nov. 15, 1939,/65; Borchard to Moore, Nov. 16, Moore to Borchard, Nov. 20, 1939, B. 76, JM; CR, vol. 86, pt. 13, p. 152.

4. PC, Jan. 12, 1940, R. 8.

5. Diary, June 6, 1940, B. 7, HW; Walker, "Wallace," pp. 132-34; US Department of Agriculture, *Report of the Secretary of Agriculture, 1940* (Washington, D.C.:G.P.O., 1940), p. 22; US Department of Agriculture, press releases, "Pan America–The Road of Our Destiny," Oct. 27, 1939, "Toward New World Solidarity," June 30, 1940; Wayne Rasmussen, "The United States Department of Agriculture and Inter-American Relations during the First Year of War" (Washington, D.C: US Department of Agriculture, Bureau of Agriculture Economics, War Records Project, February 1943), p. 1.

6. Wallace to Murphy, May 24, 1940, R. 21, HW; US Department of Agriculture press release, Aug. 6, 1940, pp. 2-3; Rasmussen, "United States Department of Agriculture and Inter-American Relations," pp. 4, 6; *US Department of Agriculture, Report, 1940*, pp. 21-26.

7. Wallace to Dan Wallace, Jan. 16, "Toward Pan-American Solidarity," Apr. 11, 1940, R. 21, HW; Wallace to Messersmith, Mar. 9, 1940, no. 1322, GM; Wallace to Rockefeller, Dec. 31, 1943, B. 87, HW(FDRL); US Department of Agriculture press release, "The Vital Role of Agriculture in Inter-American Relations," May 11, 1940; Rasmussen, "United States Department of Agriculture and Inter-American Relations," pp. 1-2, 7-9; *US Department of Agriculture, Report, 1940*, pp. 24-25; Duggan, *Americas*, pp. 141-42.

8. Memo by Bonsal, July 3, Leonard to Veatch, July 7, Leonard to Jessup, Sept. 20, 1943, B. 192, PJ; James George, Jr., "United States Postwar Relief Planning: The First Phase, 1940-1943" (Ph.D. diss., The University of Wisconsin, 1970), pp. 193-94, 212-13, 222, 276-79, 282-83; SW-4, pp. 89-94.

9. Wallace to Dickson, Nov. 14, 1941, R. 23, HW.

10. Presidential diary, memo of conversation, Sept. 12, Oct. 14, B. 2, diary, memo of conversation, Oct. 18, 1939, B. 218, HM; Walker, "Wallace," pp. 120-26; Langer and Gleason, *Challenge to Isolation*, p. 278.

11. Rowe to Hull, Mar. 10, 710.Peace-Monetary/1, memo by Feis, Mar. 25,/4, memo by Kelchner, Dec. 2, 1937,/11, Morgenthau to Hull, Nov. 1, 710.H-Agenda/151, memo by Livesey, Dec. 13, 1938, 710.H-Economics and Finance/6, memo by Feis, June 6, 710.H-Economics and Finance/26, Duggan to Berle, Nov. 21,/156, Duggan to Berle, Nov. 19,/155, Gaston address, Nov. 21,/166, Gaston to Hull, Dec. 12, 1939,/166; diary, memo of conversaton, Dec. 13, 1938, B. 156, memo of meeting, Feb. 7, B. 163, memo by White, May 10, B. 188, Gaston to Morgenthau, Nov. 28, 1939, B. 224, HM; FR, 1939, 5:42; HMd, 2:50-51.

12. Memo by Berle, Nov. 17, 710.FEAC/78 1/5, Nov. 28,/71, White to Berle, Dec. 4,/12-439, memo by Collado, Dec. 13,/85, Suarez to Welles, Dec. 13,/710.Bank/1½, FEAC resolution, Dec. 18, 1939,/2; Braden to Welles, Feb. 18, 1936, B. 11, HF; Edward Villaseñor, "Inter-American Bank: Prospects and Dangers," *Foreign Affairs* 20 (October 1941): 165-74; CR, vol. 86, pt. 2, pp. 2069-70; ABnr, pp. 271-78, 284, 291, 300-301; HMd, 2:57-58; David Green, *The Containment of Latin America*, (Chicago: Quadraugle Books, 1971), pp. 60-74.

13. Fitzgerald to Davis, June 2, Nov. 7, 1938, B. 25, ND; presidential diary, memorandum of conversation, July 14, 1939, HM; Russman to Berle, June 26, 1939, B. 44, CH; Braden to Feis, Mar. 18, Feis to Braden, Apr. 8, 1937, B. 11, Feis to Steinhardt, Feb. 10, 1939, B. 16, Feis to Caffery, Feb. 23, 1940, B. 11, HF; Dearing to Phillips, Feb. 6, 1934, B. 67, JM; Dearing to White, May 8, 1940, Mar. 19, 1941, FW; Duggan to Steinhardt, Dec. 4, 10, 1937, B. 19, Cochran to Steinhardt, June 15, Dreyfus to Steinhardt, July 6, 1939, B. 27, LS; Memorandum by Welles, July 25, 1938, 710.H-Agenda/81; PC, Feb. 13, 1940, R. 8; Giffin, "Normal Years," pp. 172-229, 423-24, 436-41; Gellman, *Roosevelt and Batista*, pp. 165-68, 187; Bushnell, *Santos and the Good Neighbor*, pp. 67-81; IAA, 1:107-9.

14. Steinhardt to Cochran, June 23, 1939, B. 78, LS.

15. HIsd, 2:209.

16. Presidential diary, memorandum of conversation, June 19, 1939, B. 1, HM.

17. Memo by Gosnell, Feb. 2, 1948, Welles file, WBHS; diary, June 23, 1939, B. 210, AB; Livesey to Feis, July 27, 1939, B. 17, HF; diary, memorandum to Morgenthau,

July 21, memorandum for the secretary, July 24, 1939, B. 204, memorandum of conversation, July 26, 1939, B. 205, HM; Moore to Borchard, Nov. 4, 1939, B. 76, JM; Lane to White, Dec. 15, 1941, FW; PC, Oct. 27, Dec. 19, 1939, R. 7; HMd, 2:55-57.

18. Henlich to Hull, July 22, 1940, 710.Consultation (2)/421; Convoy to Pittman, Jan. 8, 1940, Committee on Foreign Relations, Cuba, Sen. 76A-F 9, RG 46; "Loan to Latin America," Mar., "What About the Monroe Doctrine Now?" July 27, 1940, B. 22, WRC; Baruch to FDR, June 26, Baruch to Forrestal, July 24, 1940, BB; address by Farrell, July 29, 1940, B. 79, JM; Wood to Jessup, July 5, 1940, B. 31, PJ; CR, vol. 86, pt. 14, pp. 2240-42; BLwd, p. 111; Percy Bidwell, "El Dorado Beckons," *Foreign Affairs* 18 (January 1940): 324-36.

19. Stearns to Jessup, June 11, 1941, B. 22, PJ; diary, June 6, 1940, HW; Rasmussen, "United States Department of Agriculture and Inter-American Relations," pp. 2-7; HMd, 2:321-23; IAA, 1:98-100; SW-4, pp. 16-27; Pablo Minelli, "Are the Americas Ready?" *Virginia Quarterly Review* 16 (Winter 1940): 35-44; Alvin Hansen, "Hemispheric Solidarity," *Foreign Affairs* 19 (October 1940): 12-21; Percy Bidwell and Arthur Upgren, "A Trade Policy for Defense," *Foreign Affairs* 19 (January 1941): 282-96.

20. Memo by Notter, Apr. 11, 821.7962/428, Apr. 14, 821.796 SCA 2/429 CF, Hull to Welles, Sept. 15, 740.00111-A.R./277A, Sept. 18,/290A, Sept. 19,/292A, Sept. 22, 1939,/343A; Jones to FDR, Feb. 24, Mar. 4, May 10, 1939, B. 29, JJ; Braden to Taussig, July 19, 1939, B. 33, CT; Culbertson to Teagle, Sept. 29, 1939, B. 19, WC; Feis to Braden, May 15, 1939, B. 11, HF; Adams, "Export-Import Bank," pp. 173-74, 198-200; HIsd, 2:592; IAA, 1:98; Duggan, *Americas*, pp. 78-80.

21. Jones to FDR, Mar. 7, 1940, B. 29, JJ; PPA, 9:303-5; PC, July 23, 1940, R. 8; CR, vol. 86, pt. 10, pp. 10614-22, pt. 11, pp. 11833-48, 11897-918, pt. 16, pp. 4635-36, 4650, pt. 17, pp. 5028-33, 5189-90, 5382-83; IAA, 1:100-101.

22. ABnr, p. 335.

23. Memo of conversation, Apr. 10, 1940, B. 29, JJ.

24. Forrestal to Baruch, July 26, 1940, V. 1940, BB.

25. Baruch to Forrestal, Aug. 1, 1940, V. 1940, BB.

26. Feis to Souza Costa, July 13, 1940, B. 16, HF; Culbertson to Farish, Aug. 14, 1940, B. 20, WC; Baruch to Jones, Sept. 30, Jones to Baruch, Oct. 2, 1940, V. 1940, BB; Guinle to Jones, Sept. 25, 26, Jones to Eximbank, Sept. 26, 1940, B. 29, Jones to Eximbank, May 1, Dec. 8, 1941, JJ; Hilton, *Great Powers*, pp. 217-21.

27. Jones to Eximbank, Nov. 13, Dec. 9, 1940, B. 29, Feb. 26, Mar. 3, Apr. 30, May 1, June 6, July 1, 28, Aug. 12, Sept. 3, Oct. 16, Dec. 8, 1941, B. 30, JJ; Pierson to Bowers, June 11, 1942, Bowers mss II, CB; Hoover, *Memoirs*, pp. 459-60.

28. Speech, Nov. 12, 1940, B. 20, WC.

29. The Advisory Commission to the Council of National Defense to FDR, Nov. 27, FDR to Jones, Sept. 27, 1940, B. 29, Jones to FDR, June 12, 26, 1941, B. 30, JJ; Dean, "Impressions of South America," summer 1941, B. 135, PJ; IAA, 1:80-81, 87-88, 101-2; HIsd, 3:575-76; Guerrant, *Good Neighbor Policy*, pp. 160-70; Bushnell, *Santos and the Good Neighbor*, pp. 65-66.

30. Spaeth to Collado, Dec. 26, 710.Consultation 3/280, memo by Stinebower, Dec. 30, 1941,/281.

31. OHP-NR.

32. Ibid.

33. Welles to Land, Jan. 18, 710.Consultation 3/598, Welles to Hull, Jan. 19, 1942,/598; FDR to Jones, Jan. 20, Jones to FDR, Jan. 22, 1942, B. 30, JJ; diary, minutes of meeting, June 4, 1942, B. 537, Feb. 25, 1943, B. 612, HM; Welles to Wallace, May 12, 1943, B. 108, HW(FDR).

34. Jones to Rockefeller, June 27, 1941, Jones to Mulligan, Sept. 17, 1942, B. 42, JJ; *US Office of Inter-American Affairs, History*, pp. 25-31, 127-43; IAA, 2:61-62; Duggan, *Americas*, pp. 140-41; Morris, *Rockefeller*, pp. 175-79.

35. Interview, NR; IAA, 1:103-7; Morris, *Rockefeller*, pp. 172-74; Taylor to Bowers, Sept. 28, 1940, Bowers mss II, CB.

36. Interview, NR; Rockefeller to Clayton, July 9, 1945, 710.Conference P-PW/7-945; Messersmith to Acheson, Aug. 7, 1942, B. 50, CH; Messersmith to Feis, June 27, 30, 1941, B. 17, HF; FR, 1942, 5:7; PPA, 10:267-71; ABnr, p. 376; Tulchin, *Aftermath of*

War, p. 26; Duggan, *Americas*, pp. 85-86, 92-93; Bushnell, *Santos and the Good Neighbor*, pp. 62-65; *US Office of Inter-American Affairs, History*, pp. 16-17; Grieb, "Fascist Mirage," pp. 219-20.

37. IAA, 1:91-92; Callcott, *Western Hemisphere*, p. 370; Green, *Containment of Latin America*, pp. 74-79; Bushnell, *Santos and the Good Neighbor*, pp. 82-87.

38. *US Office of Inter-American Affairs, History*, pp. 115-26; Duggan, *Americas*, pp. 103-4.

39. *US Office of Inter-American Affairs, History*, pp. 98-103, 105-14; US Department of State, *Cultural Cooperation Program*, p. 54; IAA, 4:186-88.

40. OHP-NR; Bowers, *Chile*, pp. 316-17.

41. IAA, 1:76-80, 89-90; Dozer, *Good Neighbors?*, pp. 70-83.

42. LaVerre to Welles, Oct. 26, 1942, 710.11/2906; IAA, 3:64-86; Dozer, *Good Neighbors?*, pp. 112-36; John Campbell, "Nationalism and Regionalism in South America," *Foreign Affairs* 21 (October 1942): 132-48; Percy Bidwell, "Good Neighbors in the War and After," *Foreign Affairs* 21 (April 1943): 524-34; Edgar Brossard, "The Effect of the War on Trade in the Americas," *Bulletin of the Pan American Union* 76 (December 1942): 661-67.

43. LaVerre to Welles, Nov. 9, 1942, 710.11/2905½.

44. PPA, 10:290-99; ASp, 2:12-14, 16-18; HWpv, pp. 26-28.

45. Spaeth to Finletter, Mar. 19, 1942, 710.Consultation 3A; diary, Dec. 26, 1941, V.36, HS; diary, Apr. 14, 1942, B. 214, AB; Wallace to Bressman, Oct. 1, 1942, HW(LC); diary, minutes of meeting, Dec. 31, 1942, B. 600, HM; memo by Snow, June 16, 1943, B. 23, WC.

46. Memo by Duggan, Mar. 5, 1942, 710.11/2849½; Wallace to FDR, Mar. 26, 1942, R. 23, Wallace to Sullivan, May 20, 1943, R. 24, HW; diary, May 14, 1942, B. 214, AB; PC, May 1, 1942, R. 10; HWpv. pp. 58, 79; *US Office of Inter-American Affairs, History*, pp. 207-10; Braden, *Diplomats and Demagogues*, pp. 270-75.

47. Jones to FDR, Feb. 16, 1942, B. 30, JJ; IAA, 3:55-60.

48. Jones to Eximbank, Feb. 17, Mar. 4, Apr. 8, 20, May 16, July 1, B. 30, Oct. 12, Dec. 16, 1942, Feb. 2, 10, July 1, 1943, B. 31, JJ; FR, 1942, 5:45-47; IAA, 3:56-57.

49. Presidential diary, memo of conversation, July 6, 1943, B. 5, HM; Hoey to Daniels, Feb. 3, 1945, B. 838, JD; Jonathan Daniels, *White House Witness* (New York: Doubleday, 1975), pp. 162-63, 171-72, 175; Walker, "Wallace," pp. 164-65.

50. Messersmith to Stettinius, Mar. 26, 1945, B. 725, ES; Culbertson to Hull, Apr. 30, 1945, B. 26, WC; Messersmith to Hull, July 31, 1945, B. unnumbered, CH; Bowers, *Chile*, p. 289.

CHAPTER 13

1. Perrett, *Days of Sadness*, p. 239; Cantril, *Public Opinion*, pp. 95, 549-50; Jessup to Page, Jan. 5, 1942, B. 135, PJ.

2. The Pan American League to Jessup, Dec. 13, 1941, B. 22, PJ.

3. Galarza to Daniels, Jonathan Daniels to Daniels, Apr. 10, 1943, B. 818, JD; IAA, 3:39-40; Cantril, *Public Opinion*, p. 549.

4. Clapper to Bickel, Jan. 27, 1942, B. 50, RC.

5. Early to Wallace, May 19, 1942, R. 23, HW.

6. Luis Quintanilla, *A Latin American Speaks* (New York: Macmillan, 1943), p. 171.

7. PC, Nov. 24, 1942, R. 10.

8. Meeting of LC, Nov. 16, 1942, SLC; diary, Nov. 25, 27, 1942, B. 214, AB; PC, July 17, 1942, R. 10, May 7, 1943, R. 11; PPA, 11:250, 490-93, 12:201-2, 244-45, 13:45-48; IAA, 3:37-40; Hassett, *Off the Record*, pp. 132-33.

9. Memoris, vol. 2, nos, 9, 10, 18, B. IX, GM; PC, Feb. 2, 12, Apr. 19, 1943, R. 11; PL, 2:1138, 1412; PPA, 12:51-53, 59-60, 175-78, 181; McCann, *Brazilian-American Alliance*, pp. 307-8; Michael Reilly, *Reilly of the White House* (New York: Simon and Schuster, 1947), pp. 131-33.

10. LA trip, 1944, B. 2984, ER; Lash, *Eleanor and Franklin*, pp. 563, 637, 696-97, 747.

11. Diary, May 20, 1942, B. 14, HW; HWvp, pp. 77, 151.

12. Diary, Mar. 26, Duggan to Bowers, Mar. 13, 1943, Bowers mss II, CB; Wallace statement, Mar. 15, 1943, R. 24, HW; FR, 1943, 5:55-73.

13. FR, 1943, 5:63, 66.

14. Wallace to Alfonso Lopez, Wallace to Lane, Apr. 24, 1943, B. 51, HW(LC); Rockefeller to Wallace, May 19, B. 87, Wallace to Padilla, June 1, 1943, B. 79, HW (FDRL); press conference, Apr. 26, 1943, R. 24, Wallace to Hull, Mar. 24, 1944, R. 26, HW; Duggan to Daniels, Apr. 30, B. 818, Bowers to Daniels, May 4, 1943, B. 817, JD; Walker, "Wallace," pp. 174-79; Bowers, *Chile*, pp. 263-66.

15. Bowers to Hull, Oct. 18, 1939, 740.00111-A.R./612; Armour to Feis, July 29, Feis to Armour, Sept. 28, 1939, B. 11, HF; Wooten to Culbertson, Nov. 14, memo by Culbertson, Nov. 30, 1938, B. 18, WC; HIsd, 2:677-78.

16. Bowers to Hull, Jan. 31, 710.Consultation 3/552, Feb. 4,/605, Heath to Hull, Feb. 5,/611, Bowers to Hull, Feb. 17,/650, Mar. 6,/708, Heath to Duggan, Mar. 14, 1942,/737; Barros Jarpa to Jessup, Mar. 3, Jessup to Barros Jarpa, Mar. 16, 1942, B. 134, PJ; FR, 1942, 5:43:44; Pike, *Chile and the United States*, pp. 245, 247; Duggan, *Americas*, pp. 89-90.

17. Welles to Bowers, Feb. 7, 1942, Bowers mss II, CB.

18. Bowers to Hull, Mar. 14, 710.Consultation 3/722, Duggan to Heath, Mar. 21, 1942,/737; FDR to Bowers, Apr. 28, Welles to Bowers, Mar. 31, May 8, Armour to Bowers, May 28, Duggan to Bowers, July 16, 1942, Bowers mss II, CB; Jones to Eximbank, Mar. 4, 1942, B. 30, JJ; Bowers to Long, Apr. 28, 1942, B. 141, BL; Welles to Corrigan, Apr. 28, 1942, B. 10, FC; Robert Burr and Roland Hussey, eds., *Documents on Inter-American Cooperation*, 2 vols. (Philadelphia: University of Pennsylvania Press, 1955), 2:149-50.

19. Meeting of LC, June 22, 1942, SLC.

20. FDR to Bowers, Aug. 12, 1942, O.F. 303, FDRL.

21. SW-4, pp. 83-89.

22. Bowers to Hull, Nov. 25, 1942, 710.Consultation 3/833, memo by Heath, Feb. 13, 1943, 710.11/6-2244; meeting of LC, Jan. 11, 1943, SLC; diary, Oct. 9, 10, 11, Bowers to Welles, Oct. 10, Duggan to Bowers, Oct. 14, Welles to Bowers, Nov. 19, 1942, Bowers mss II, CB; Bowers to FDR, Jan. 19, 1943, O.F. 303, FDRL; Bowers to Frankfurter, Oct. 13, 1944, B. 25, FF; OHP-CB; CHm, 2:1383-84; Bowers, *Chile*, pp. 97-120; Davis et al., *Latin American Diplomatic History*, pp. 238-40.

23. Duggan to Bowers, Jan. 21, 1943, Bowers mss II, CB.

24. Spaeth to Duggan, Aug. 27, 1942, 710.Consultation 3/824; Jones to Eximbank, Mar. 2, B. 30, Jones to Jeffers, Dec. 16, 1942, Jones to Eximbank, Feb. 2, 1943, B. 31, JJ; Feis to Souza Costa, Mar. 18, 1942, Mar. 1, 1943, B. 16, HF; Welles to Wallace, Mar. 19, 1942, B. 108, HW(FDR); Jessup to Verissimo, June 3, 1942, B. 133, PJ; Caffery to Long, Mar. 30, 1943, B. 145, BL; BLwd, p. 386; IAA, 3:54-55; McCann, *Brazilian-American Alliance*, pp. 378-402.

25. Jones to Eximbank, Apr. 8, 1942, B. 20, JJ; memo of cabinet meeting, Mar. 12, 1943, B. 6, RP; memoirs, vol. 2, no. 11, B. IX, GM; IAA, 3:56; Stegmaier, "From Confrontation to Cooperation," pp. 292-95; House, *Merritt Report*, p. 3.

26. *US Office of Inter-American Affairs, History*, pp. 32-36, Stegmaier, "From Confrontation to Cooperation," pp. 285-88; memoirs, B. IX, GM.

27. Memoirs, B. IX, GM.

28. Memo by Welles, Aug. 6, 1942, Division of Latin American Affairs, B. 3, RG 59; Messersmith to Hull, Dec. 13, 1943, B. 53, CH; diary, Aug. 5, 1943, B. 215, AB; diary, Oct. 2, 1943, B. 14, JED; memoirs, vol. 3, no. 11, B. IX, GM; FR, 1942, 5:262-67; Cline, *United States and Mexico*, 292-98; Gellman, *Roosevelt and Batista*, pp. 199-200.

29. 1942 Calendar, R. 39, CH; Davis to Burlingham, Feb. 11, B. 3, Frances Hull to Davis, late Feb. 1942, Gray to Davis, Feb. 26, 1942, B. 27, ND; Wallace statement, Dec. 27, 1941, Wallace to Hull, Mar. 30, 1942, R. 23, HW; PC, Feb. 24, 1942, R. 10; BLwd, pp. 242-43, 258-59, 262; HWpv, pp. 67-68; Hassett, *Off the Record*, p. 42; ABnr, p. 400; JMPmd, pp. 378-79.

30. Memo by Hoover, Jan. 30, 1941, SW; O.F. 200–President's Trips (1940-1945), 200–TTTT–Jasper, Ala., September 16, 1940, FDRL; diary, Mar. 30, 1942, B. 13, HW; OHP-HW; HIsd, 3326-27; *New York Times*, Sept. 15, 1940; *Birmingham News*, Sept. 16, 17, 18, 1940.
31. Memo by Hoover, Jan. 3, memo for Hoover, Jan. 23, memo by Hoover, Jan. 30, 1941, SW.
32. Davis to Hull, Apr. 13, 1937, B. unnumbered, CH; diary, Feb. 9, B. 4, Mar. 1940, B. 7, HW; diary, June 18, 1937, AB; OHP-WP; *Baltimore Sun*, Feb. 19, 1940; ABnr, pp. 311, 828; BLwd, p. 58; Bullitt, *For the President*, pp. xi-xiii, 403-5, 497-98; Robert Murphy, *Diplomats Among Warriors* (New York: Doubleday, 1964), pp. 35-36; Marquis Childs, *Witness to Power* (New York: McGraw Hill, 1975), pp. 15-17; Farnsworth, *Bullitt*, pp. 155-69.
33. Memo for Hoover, Jan. 29, memo by Hoover, Jan. 30, 1941, SW; diary, Feb. 8, 1941, B. 212, AB; *New York Times*, Feb. 9, 1941; Bullitt, *For the President*, pp. 512-14.
34. Presidential diary, memorandum of conversation, Mar. 6, 1941, B. 4, HM; diary, Nov. 23-30, Dec. 1941, B. 8, HI; Bullitt, *For the President*, pp. 517-18, 528-29.
35. Memo by Hoover, Oct. 29, 1942, SW; diary, Mar. 31, B. 13, May 20, 1942, Aug. 24, 1943, B. 23, HW; diary, Mar. 30, 1942, B. 8, HI; Farnsworth, *Bullitt*, pp. 171-78, 233; BLwd, pp. 277, 281, 286.
36. Memo by Hoover, May 3, 1943, SW; diary, Feb. 14, Apr. 25, May 9, 1943, B. 10, HI; diary, Sept. 30, 1943, B. 23, HW; OHP-HW; BLwd, p. 311; Bullitt, *For the President*, pp. 514-16; FFd, p. 250.
37. Welles to FDR, Aug. 16, 1943, B. 96, Personal Secretary File, FDRL; diary, Aug. 21, 1943, B. 23, HW; diary, Aug. 15, 1943, B. 10, HI; Welles to Lane, Aug. 22, 1943, B. 21, ABL; Welles to Corrigan, Aug. 22, 1943, B. 10, FC; ABnr, pp. 443-45, 836; BLwd, p. 322; HWvp, pp. 237-41; Tyler Abell, ed., *Drew Pearson Diaries* (New York: Holt, Rinehart and Winston, 1974), pp. 136-37.
38. *New York Times*, Aug. 4, 27, 29, Sept. 27, 1943; *Washington Herald*, Aug. 24, 1943; *Washington Post*, Aug. 26, 1943; *New York Herald Tribune*, Aug. 26, 1943; *St. Louis Post Dispatch*, Sept. 5, 1943.
39. Diary, Oct. 12, 1943, B. 24, HW; PC, Aug. 31, 1943, R. 11; HWvp, p. 260.
40. Welles to FDR, Sept. 21, 1943, B. 96, P.S.F., FDRL.
41. *New York Times*, Sept. 26, 1943.
42. Bowers to Duggan, Nov. 4, 1943, Bowers mss II, CB.

CHAPTER 14

1. Diary, Oct. 12, 1943, B. 24, HW; diary, Jan. 6, 1944, B. 14, JED; Duggan to Hull, July 19, 1944, B. 53, CH; OHP, 351, NR.
2. Diary, Sept. 26, 1943, B. 11, WL; Messersmith to Watson, Sept. 27, 1943, B. 25, EW; Stettinius to Welles, Sept. 28, 1943, B. 716, ES; *New York Times*, Sept. 26, 1943; ESd, 9; Richard Walker, "E. R. Stettinius, Jr.," in *The American Secretaries of State and Their Diplomacy*, ed. Robert Ferrell (New York: Cooper Square Publishers, 1965), 14:1-10.
3. Bonsal to Stettinius, Oct. 19, 1943, 710.11/10-1943.
4. Braden to Hull, Dec. 14, 17, 1943, Scotten to Hull, Oct. 18, 1944, B. 54, CH; Boal to FDR, Jan. 21, 1942, O.F. 4746, FDRL; Lane to Harrison, Sept. 16, 1942, B. 31, CH; Dawson to Ackerman, May 11, 1942, B. 26, CA; HWpv, p. 442; Petrov, *Study in Diplomacy*, pp. 83-97; Acheson, *Present at the Creation*, p. 160.
5. Daniels to Wallace, May 20, 1943, B. 822, JD; WWsl, pp. 439-40; HWpv, pp. 77-78; Sherwood, *Roosevelt and Hopkins*, p. 757.
6. Diary, 1933, B. 8, RC; Stimson to Hoover, July 31, 1933, R. 85, HS; Adler, *Uncertain Giant*, p. 157; Fred Israel, *Nevada's Key Pittman* (Lincoln: University of Nebraska Press, 1963), pp. 131, 132, 144; Gellman, *Roosevelt and Batista*, p. 105.
7. HWpv, p. 488.
8. Diary, Jan. 18-25, 1942, B. 8, HI; memo by Hull, Jan. 22, 1942, B. unnumbered, CH; *Wall Street Journal*, Jan. 23, 1942; BLwd, p. 244.

9. Weddell to Hull, Aug. 17, 1938, Guffey to Hull, Apr. 4, 1939, B. unnumbered, CH; Stimson to Hornbeck, Mar. 7, Hornbeck to Stimson, Mar. 8, 1939, R. 97, HS.

10. Bailey to Hull, Dec. 10, 1940, 740.0011 EW 1939/7076; Vandenberg to Culbertson, Sept. 11, 1939, B. 19, WC; Winkler to Stimson, Oct. 7, 1939, R. 99, HS; Moore to Borchard, Feb. 27, B. 76, Johnson to Moore, July 7, 1940, B. 79, JM; CR, vol. 86, pt. 14, pp. 1409,10.

11. Ludlow to Daniels, July 2, 1940, B. 741, JD.

12. McNaughton to Hulburd, Oct. 16, 1941, McNaughton Reports, FM.

13. House, *Merritt Report*, pp. 1-11; IAA, 4:42-43.

14. Lawrence to Hull, Sept. 2, 710.11/2980¼, Norris to Hull, Sept. 7, /2980-2/4, memo by Duggan, Nov. 29,/3032, memo by Collado, Nov. 26,/3050, Erwin to Hull, Dec. 10,/3079, Boal to Duggan, Dec. 17,/3109, Muccio to Hull, Dec. 18,/3133, Rockefeller to Hull, Dec. 20,/3184, Warren to Hull, Dec. 24,/3138, Messersmith to Hull, Dec. 29, 1943,/3227, Hull to Messersmith, Jan. 8,/3228, memo by Duggan, Jan. 18, 1944,/ 3253; Hull to Bowers, Aug. 18, 1943, Bowers mss II, CB; Borchard to Moore, Nov. 29, 1943, B. 84, JM; McKellar to Stettinius, Dec. 16, 1943, B. 361, ES; Morris, *Rockefeller*, pp. 151-52; Wood, *Good Neighbor Policy*, pp. 316-26.

15. FR, 1943, 5:533-36.

16. Ibid., 536-43; ABnr, p. 449.

17. Cole Blasier, "The United States, Germany and the Bolivian Revolutionaries, 1941-1946," *Hispanic American Historical Review* 52 (February 1972): 44-49.

18. Memo by Duggan, June 12, 1941, 740.0011 EW 1939/11955 2/3, Dawson to Hull, Apr. 23, 1942, 710.Consultation 3/760; Boal to Hull, June 23, 1942, B. 50, CH; Boal to Wallace, Dec. 29, 1942, B. 10, HW (FDRL); HWpv, p. 158; Herbert Klein, *Parties and Political Change in Bolivia* (Cambridge: At the University Press, 1969), pp. 321-68; James Malloy, *Bolivia* (Pittsburgh: University of Pittsburgh Press, 1970), pp. 111-26, 323-26; Blasier, "United States, Germany and the Bolivian Revolutionaries," pp. 26-40.

19. FR, 1944, 7:427-46; diary, memo of conversation, Jan. 8, 1944, B. 692, HM; ABnr, pp. 451-52; ESd, pp. 23-24; Randall Woods, "United States' Policy toward Argentina from Pearl Harbor to San Francisco" (Ph.D. diss., The University of Texas, 1972), pp. 172-74, 199-200; Mecham, *United States and Inter-American Security*, pp. 228-33; Peterson, *Argentina and the United States*, p. 434; CHm, 2:1388-89; SW-5, p. 196.

20. FR, 1944, 7:447-51; Duggan, *Americas*, pp. 106-7.

21. Memo by Bonsal, Mar. 14, 1944, 710.11/3221.

22. FR, 1944, 7:452-55.

23. Ibid., 455-56, 458-59.

24. Ibid., 457-69; diary, May 23, 1944, B. 5, BL; Blasier, "United States, Germany and the Bolivian Revolutionaries," p. 43; Klein, *Parties and Political Change*, pp. 369-82; CHm, 2:1398-99.

25. McLaughlin to Bowers, July 14, 1944, Bowers mss II, CB; FR, 1944, 7:471-72; Blasier, "United States, Germany and the Bolivian Revolutionaries," p. 44.

26. Welles to Inman, Apr. 8, 1949, B. 16, SI; Duggan, *Americas*, pp. 199-200.

27. Welles, "Intervention and Interventions," pp. 122-27; SW-5, pp. 190-93.

28. Diary, Apr. 22, 1940, B. 221, AB; DGFP, 9:278-81, 344-45, 348-89, 355-56, 371-72, 419; Peterson, *Argentina and the United States*, pp. 402-3; Friedlander, *Prelude to Downfall*, pp. 105-6; Langer and Gleason, *Challenge to Isolation*, pp. 607-10; Joseph Tulchin, "The Argentine Proposal for Non-Belligerency, April 1940" *Journal of Inter-American Studies* 11 (October 1969): 571-604; Stanley Hilton, "Argentine Neutrality, September 1939-June 1940: A Re-Examination," *Americas* 22 (January 1966): 227-57.

29. Wood to Jessup, May 15, 1940, B. 31, PJ; DGFP, 5:1029-30; WDd, p. 230; Frye, *Nazi Germany and the American Hemisphere*, pp. 118-30, 163-65; Friedlander, *Prelude to Downfall*, pp. 29-30, 107, 227; Peterson, *Argentina and the United States*, pp. 393-94, 408-9; Robert Potash, *The Army and Politics in Argentina* (Stanford: Stanford University Press, 1969), pp. 117-19.

30. Reed to Hull, Feb. 19, 710.Consultation 3/711, Armour to Hull, June 10, 1942,/ 804; OHP, pp. 304-5, NR; Biddle to Hull, Aug. 17, 1942, B. 50, CH; BLwd, p. 284;

Woods, "United States' Policy toward Argentina," pp. 109-14; Peterson, *Argentina and the United States*, pp. 407, 409-10, 413-15, 422-23; Potash, *Army and Politics*, pp. 104-5, 141-66.

31. BLwd, p. 189; Peter Smith, *Politics and Beef in Argentina* (New York: Columbia University Press, 1969), pp. 119-21.

32. Memo by Hull, Mar. 23, 1933, Aug. 28, 1935, B. 57, Braden to Hull, Feb. 10, Weddell to Hull, Mar. 4, 1936, B. 38, Weddell to Hull, Feb. 6, 1937, B. 40, Weddell to Hull, Oct. 21, 1938, B. 43, CH; Campbell to Borah, June 9, Borah to Campell, June 12, Gray to Borah, June 15, Borah to Gray, June 17, 1935, B. 524, WB; diary, Jan. 26, 1936, B. 5, BL; speech, Nov. 20, 1936, B. 15, WC; PPA, 5:610-12; PC, Dec. 18, 1936, R. 4; CR, vol. 79, pp. 14043, 14044, vol. 81, pp. 147, 4525-4588, vol. 85, pp. 532, 538, 569, 610, 625, 955, 1054; Bryce Wood, "The Department of State and the Non-National Interest: The Case of Argentine Meat and Paraguayan Tea," *Inter-American Economic Affairs* 15 (Autumn 1961): 5-24.

33. CR, vol. 84, pt. 5, p. 5528.

34. PPA, 8:192-95; PC, May 12, 1939, R. 7; diary, White to Morgenthau, Apr. 24, 1939, B. 181, HM.

35. Peterson, *Argentina and the United States*, pp. 407-8, 410-12, 425.

36. Diary, May 14, 1942, B. 214, AB; memo by Hull, May 14, 1942, B. 50, CH; diary, May 21, 1942, V. 39, HS; HWpv, p. 80; HMd, 3:195-97.

37. Presidential diary, memo of conversations, May 14, 15, 1942, B. 5, HM.

38. Duggan to Bowers, Apr. 10, 1942, Bowers mss II, CB; meeting of LC, Aug. 10, 1942, Feb. 8, 1943, SLC; Peterson, *Argentina and the United States*, p. 410; Conil Paz and Ferrari, *Argentina's Foreign Policy*, pp. 73-101; Potash, *Army and Politics*, pp. 169-73.

39. Duggan to Bowers, Apr. 10, 1942, Bowers mss II, CB.

40. Armour to Bowers, Jan. 27, Apr. 7, Duggan to Bowers, July 20, Armour to Bowers, Aug. 7, 1943, Bowers mss II, CB; diary, June 12, 1943, B. 10, HI; OHP, pp. 312-15, NR; Woods, "United States' Policy toward Argentina," pp. 139-49; Duggan, *Americas*, pp. 90-91; CHm, 2:1384; Peterson, *Argentina and the United States*, pp. 428-29, 431; Potash, *Army and Politics*, pp. 178-220; Conil Paz and Ferrari, *Argentina's Foreign Policy*, pp. 102-7.

41. Peterson, *Argentina and the United States*, pp. 432-33; Conil Paz and Ferrari, *Argentina's Foreign Policy*, pp. 107-11; Potash, *Army and Politics*, pp. 221-22.

42. Armour to Bowers, Dec. 16, 1943, Bowers mss II, CB; Armour to Feis, May 2, 1941, B. 11, HF; diary, Oct. 3, 1943, B. 11, HI; memo by Collado, Jan. 5, 1944, B. 53, CH; Woods, "United States' Policy toward Argentina," pp. 87-100; George, "Postwar Relief Planning," pp. 194-96, 279-80; Peterson, *Argentina and the United States*, p. 410.

43. Diary, Jan. 29, 1944, B. 11, HI; Wallace to FDR, Jan. 6, 1944, R. 25, HW; HWpv, pp. 290, 294, 296-97, 318, 320.

44. Wallace to Daniels, Jan. 28, 1944, R. 25, HW.

45. Diary, memo of conversation, Nov. 1, memo by Randolph and Morgenthau to Hull, Nov. 2, B. 672, memo of conversation, Nov. 24, 1943, B. 679, Morgenthau to Hull, Jan. 8, B. 692, memo of conversation, Jan. 12, B. 693, memo for files, memo of conversation, Jan. 22, B. 696, Morgenthau to Hull, May 10, B. 739, memo for Morgenthau, Aug. 17, B. 763, Sept. 4, 1944, B. 768, presidential diary, memo of conversation, May 7, 1944, B. 5, HM; Stettinius to FDR, Oct. 25, Collado to Stettinius, Oct. 28, Morgenthau to Stettinius, Nov. 2, 1944, B. 719, ES; Woods, "United States' Policy toward Argentina," pp. 222-24, 230-38, 252-58; HMd, 3:162, 194-95, 197-206.

46. Patterson to Hull, Jan. 7, 710.11/3204, memo by Bonsal, Jan. 10, 1944,/3221; ABnr, pp. 449-50; Conil Paz and Ferrari, *Argentina's Foreign Policy*, pp. 112-17.

47. Diary, Feb. 12, 1944, B. 11, HI; OHP, pp. 330-32, NR; ESd, p. 23; Woods, "United States' Policy toward Argentina," p. 182; Peterson, *Argentina and the United States*, p. 434; Potash, *Army and Politics*, pp. 230-37.

48. Memo by Russell, Nov. 16, 1944, 710. Consultation W&PW/11-1644; memo, June 19, 21, 1944, B. 53, CH; diary, June 23, 1944, V. 47, HS; diary, June 26, July 3, 6, 1944, B. 215, AB; diary, July 5, 1944, B. 5, BL; US-Arg., July 26, 1944, B.8, WA; diary, July 29, 1944, B. 241, ES; diary, Nov. 16, 1944, B. 12, HI; OHP, pp. 332-35,

343-47, NR; BLwd, pp. 359-60; HWpv, p. 307; ESd, pp. 30, 75-76; ABnr, pp. 454-55; Cantril, *Public Opinion*, p. 550; McCann, *Brazilian-American Alliance*, pp. 320-42; Potash, *Army and Politics*, pp. 238-54; Peterson, *Argentina and the United States*, p. 435; Conil Paz and Ferrari, *Argentina's Foreign Policy*, pp. 117-27.

49. Memo by Cabot, Sept. 12, 1944, Harley Notter File, B. 290, RG 59.

50. Memo by Hackworth, July 15, 1944, B. 53, CH; Corrigan to Armour, July 19, 1944, B. 1, FC; New York *Herald Tribune*, May 10, Aug. 11, Oct. 13, 1944; SW-3, pp. 235-40; SW-5, pp. 196-203; Duggan, *Americas*, pp. 104-5.

51. Diary, memo of conversation, Aug. 18, B. 763, memo by Morgenthau, Sept. 8, 1944, B. 770.

52. Diary, Jan. 6, 1944, B. 215, AB; OHP, pp. 318-19, NR.

53. Francis Loewenheim et al., *Roosevelt and Churchill* (New York: Saturday Review Press, 1975), p. 418; FDR to Bowers, Apr. 25, 1944, Bowers mss II, CB; ESd, p. 24.

54. Diary, memo of conversation, Jan. 24, B.696, presidential diary, memo of conversation, May 17, 1944, B. 5, HM; David Dilks, ed., *The Diary of Sir Alexander Cadogan* (New York: G. P. Putnam's Sons, 1971), pp. 599, 643-44, 646; Loewenheim et al., *Roosevelt and Churchill*, pp. 418-20; ESd, p. 48; Eden, *Reckoning*, p. 542; Peterson, *Argentina and the United States*, pp. 439-40.

55. Dilks, *Diary of Six Alexander Cadogan*, p. 642.

56. Memo by Gray, Aug. 5, 1944, 710.Consultation 4/8-544; diary, Oct. 7, 1944, B. 15, JED; OHP, pp. 380-81, NR; Dilks, *Diary of Sir Alexander Cadogan*, p. 654; ESd, pp. 172, 174, 177; Peterson, *Argentina and the United States*, pp. 438-40.

57. Memo from Hull, Sept. 28, 1944, B. 54, CH; diary, Sept. 29, 1944, B. 5, BL; OHP, pp. 377-79, NR; PPA, 12:433-34, 13:298-300; PL, 2:1494-95; PC, July 11, 1944, R. 12.

58. CHm, 2:1377-78, 1400-1403, 1409-20.

59. Rowe to Hull, Jan. 5, 710.Consultation 4/8, Dunn to Hull, Jan. 8/8, Long to Hull, Jan. 8,/8, Berle to Hull, Jan. 10,/8, Hackworth to Hull, Jan. 21,/8, memo by Duggan, Feb. 12,/8, Duggan to Hull, Mar. 11,/8, Mar. 18,/3-1844, memo by Armour, Sept. 18, 1944,/9-1844; Notter to Pasvolsky, Jan. 22, 1944, B. 191 Harley Notter File, RG 59; PC, Oct. 13, 1944, R. 12; FR, 1944, 7:448-49; *New York Times*, June 23, 1944.

60. Memo by Armour, Oct. 28, 710.Consultation 4/10-2744, Braden to Hull, Oct. 29,/10-2944, memo by Armour, Nov. 1,/11-144, Braden to Hull, Nov. 1,/10-3144, Dawson to Hull, Nov. 4,/11-144, Bowers to Hull, Nov. 6,/11-644, Reed to Hull, Nov. 7, 1944,/11-744; OHP, pp. 381-86, NR; FR, 1944, 7:27-34, 36-38.

61. Wilson to Hull, Oct. 24, 710.Consultation 4/10-2444, Bursley to Hull, Oct. 25, 1944,/10-2544; diary, Oct. 3, 1943, B. 14, JED; Messersmith to Hull, Dec. 22, 1943, Jan. 8, June 8, 1944, B. 53, CH; OHP, pp. 347-48, NR; FR, 1944, 7:28-29, 433, 438.

62. Diary, Nov. 1, 1944, B. 5, BL.

63. Memo by Spaeth, Nov. 2, 710.Consultation 4/11-244, Messersmith to Spaeth, Messersmith to Hull, Messersmith to Armour, Nov. 7,/11-744, Messersmith to Armour, Nov. 8,/11-844, Messersmith to Hull, Messersmith to Armour, Nov. 9,/11-944, Messersmith to Hull, Nov. 10, 1944,/11-1044; diary, Nov. 10, 1944, B. 5, BL; FR, 1944, 7:42-56, 58-64; Duggan, *Americas*, pp. 105-6.

64. Memo by Wendelin, Nov. 20, 1944, 710.Consultation 4/11-2044.

65. Ibid.

66. Diary, Nov. 26, 1944, B. 15, JED; Sayre to Hull, Nov. 28, 1944, B. 4, FC; diary, Dec. 2, 1944, B. 12, HI; diary, Nov. 27, Dec. 12, 1944, V. 49, HS; Saavedra Lamas to Hull, Dec. 14, 1944, B. 54, CH; memo by Gray, Sept. 18, 1965, B. 208, SH; PC, Nov. 27, 1944, R. 12; BLwd, pp. 382-83, 386-87.

CHAPTER 15

1. Wallace to Rockefeller, Dec. 15, 1943, B. 87, HW(FDRL); also see Duggan, *Americas*, pp. 101-4.

2. Bowers to Frankfurter, Sept. 7, Nov. 13, 1944, B. 25, FF; Divine, *Foreign Policy*, pp. 91-164.

3. Diary, Nov. 7, 1944, Bowers mss II, CB; presidential diary, memo of conversation, Nov. 27, 1944, HM; diary, Nov. 26, 1944, B. 15, JED; diary, Dec. 2, 1944, B. 12, HI; Bowers to Daniels, Dec. 2, Daniels to Bowers, Dec. 9, 1944, B. 829, JD; OHP, pp. 457-58, NR; ESd, pp. 158-59; Thomas Campbell, *Masquerade Peace* (Tallahassee: Florida State University Press, 1973), p. 9.

4. Inman to wife, June 24, 1943, Inman to Rockefeller, Dec. 17, 1944, B. 15, SI; Stettinius to Banning, Apr. 9, 1941, B. 658, Stettinius to Rockefeller, Dec. 12, 1944, B. 707, ES; Lane to Corrigan, Dec. 2, 1944, B. 6, FC; presidential diary, memo of conversation, May 7, 1944, B. 5, HM; Rockefeller to Bowers, Dec. 15, 1944, Bowers mss II, CB; OHP, pp. 386-89, NR; Daniels, *White House Witness*, pp. 163-64; Morris, *Rockefeller*, pp. 184-89; Kramer and Roberts, *I Never Wanted*, p. 51; James Roosevelt, telephone conversation, Mar. 30, 1977.

5. Interview, NR.

6. Rockefeller to Stettinius, Oct. 31, 1944, 710.Consultation 4/10-3144 EG; Jonathan Daniels to Daniels, Dec. 4, 1943, B. 824, JD; OHP, pp. 301-4, 306-8, 315-16, 319-29, 350-54, 359-77, NR; interview, NR; Woods, "United States' Policy toward Argentina," pp. 85-87; HWpv, p. 309.

7. OHP, pp. 435-36, 468-69, NR.

8. OHP, pp. 389-95, 402-3, NR; ABnr, pp. 452, 458-59; Braden, *Diplomats and Demagogues*, pp. 298-300.

9. OHP, pp. 403-7, NR; memo for president, Jan. 3, 1945, PAMR, NR.

10. Memo for president, Jan. 2, 1945, 711.35/1-245; also see document with FDR's o.k. in PAMR, NR; OHP, pp. 407-10, NR; Frank Gervasi, *The Real Rockefeller* (New York: Atheneum, 1964), pp. 104-5; Morris, *Rockefeller*, pp. 188-94.

11. Diary, Feb. 7, 1945, B. 216, AB; ABnr, pp. 521-22.

12. Diary, Feb. 15, 1945, B. 216, AB.

13. Wiley to Stettinius, Dec. 23, 710.Consultation 4/12-2344, Stettinius to Wiley, Dec. 28, 1944, 710.Conference W-PW/12-2844, Beaulac to Stettinius, Jan. 3,/1-345, Bowers to Rockefeller, Jan. 4,/1-445, Wiley to Stettinius, Jan. 4, 1945,/1-445; diary, Dec. 22, 1944, Jan. 11, 1945, B. 1, JF; McKim to Inman, Dec. 20, 1944, Inman to Stettinius, Jan. 4, 1945, B. 15, SI; Stettinius to Rockefeller, Jan. 4, 1945, B. 220, ES; WMR, Feb. 20, 1945; ESd, p. 202.

14. Stettinius to Thurston, Dec. 2, 710.Consultation 4/11-2944, Stettinius to Scotten, Dec. 8,/12-844, Reed to Stettinius, Dec. 13,/12-1344, Spaeth to Dawson, Dec. 14,/11-2344, Stettinius to Daniels, Dec. 20, 1944,/12-2044; FR, 1944, 7:64-82.

15. Messersmith to Stettinius, Dec. 26, 1944, 710.Conference W-PW/12-2644, memo by Wendelin, Jan. 3,/1-345, Messersmith to Stettinius, Jan. 4, 1945,/1-445; OHP, pp. 395-402, 412-14, NR; FR, 1944, 7:82-86; FR, 1945, 9:5-6, 55-57.

16. PR, Jan. 8, 710.Conference W-PW/1-845, Messersmith to Clayton, Jan. 18,/1-1845, PR, Feb. 10,/2-1045, Bohan to McClintock, Feb. 13, 1945,/2-1345; Grew to Austin, Feb. 12, Austin to Messersmith, Feb. 15, 1945, B. 13, WA; OHP, p. 430, NR; FR, 1945, 9:3-5.

17. Agenda for conference, Feb. 21, 1945, PAMR, NR; OHP, pp. 420-22, 439-41, NR; FR, 1945, 9:43-47, 50-54; Anna Rothe, *Current Biography, 1945* (New York: H. W. Wilson, 1946), pp. 147-50; John C. Smith, *Alger Hiss* (New York: Penguin Books, 1973), pp. 10-134.

18. Memo for the record, Apr. 8, 1953, B. 17, HF; OHP, pp. 422-26, NR; FR, 1945, 9:62-63, 74-78, 100-101; ABnr, p. 520; Acheson, *Present at the Creation*, p. 251.

19. FR, 1945, 9:16-18, 20-21, 35-36, 57-62, 79-82, 85-87, 90-95, 116-20.

20. Messersmith to Stettinius, Jan. 8, 710.Conference W-PW/1-845, Clayton to Messersmith, Jan. 15,/1-945, memo of conversation, Jan. 17,/1-1745, memo by McClintock, Jan. 20,/1-2045, Messersmith to Rockefeller, Jan. 23,/1-2345, Feb. 7,/2-745, Bohan to McClintock, Feb. 7,/2-745, memo by McClintock, Feb. 14, 1945,/2-1445,/2-1445; Messersmith to Grew, Feb. 6, 1945, No. 1674, GM; OHP, pp. 426-30, NR; FR,

1945, 9:15, 47-50, 64-73, 83-84, 88-90, 102-5, 111-14; Rockefeller to Bowers, Jan. 18, 1945, Bowers mss II, CB; Wallace to Sweetser, Feb. 5, 1945, B. 35, AS; Patchin to Moore, Jan. 15, 1945, B. 86, JM.
    21. Messersmith to Rockefeller, Jan. 6, 1945, 710.Conference W-PW/1-645.
    22. Harriman to Stettinius, Dec. 13, 710.Conference W-PW/12-1344, memo by Rockefeller, Dec. 23, 1944,/12-2344, Messersmith to Stettinius, Jan. 8,/1-845, Messersmith to Rockefeller, Feb. 3, 1945/2-345, Braden to Stettinius, Dec. 15, 1944, 710.11/12-1544, report by Mecham, Oct. 14, 1944, B. 191, Harley Notter File; Messersmith to Hull, Jan. 4, 1944, B. 53, CH; diary, Jan. 7, 1945, B. 16, JED; memo, Feb. 7, 1945, B. 1, JF; OHP, pp. 441-44, 448-50, NR; ESd, p. 265.
    23. FR, 1945, 9:8, 11-12, 18-19.
    24. Rockefeller to Messersmith, Feb. 6, 710.Conference W-PW/1-2745, Rockefeller to Stettinius, Feb. 15, 1945/2-1545.
    25. Memo by Stettinius, Feb. 18, 1945, B. 279, ES; FR, 1945, 9:41-42; ESd, pp. 263-66; Edward Stettinius, Jr., *Roosevelt and the Russians* (Garden City, N.Y.: Doubleday, 1949), p. 291.
    26. OHP, pp. 450-53, 462-63, 472, NR; Morris, *Rockefeller*, pp. 194-95.
    27. OHP, pp. 459-68, 470-76, NR; Inman, "An Inside View," pp. 2-6; Campbell, *Masquerade Peace*, p. 112.
    28. Stettinius to Grew, Feb. 22, 1945, 710.Conference W-PW/2-2245; memo by Stettinius, Feb. 17, B. 279, diary, Feb. 21, 22, 1945, B. 285, ES; MacLeish to Acheson, Jan. 31, 1945, B. 1, AM; Daniels to Padilla, Mar. 6, 1945, B. 839, JD; Inman, "An Inside View," pp. 6-14; ABnr, p. 471; FR, 1945, 9:121-22.
    29. Chap. conf., Mar. 7, 1945, B. 68, WA; diary, Mar. 29, 1945, B. 12, WL; memo on state dept., undated, B. 225, HA; ABnr, p. 471.
    30. Chap. conf., 1945, B. IX, GM.
    31. OHP, pp. 464, 476-77, NR; Mecham, *United States and Inter-American Security*, p. 260.
    32. Summary of work of commission II, Chap. 1945, B. 287, Harley Notter File; Chap. conf., Mar. 4, 1945, B. 68, WA; OHP, pp. 464, 477-79, NR; FR, 1945, 9:124; ESd, pp. 271, 283-84; Campbell, *Masquerade Peace*, pp. 121-25; Ruth Russell, *A History of the United Nations Charter* (Washington, D.C.: Brookings Institution, 1958), pp. 557-58; Duggan, *Americas*, pp. 117-18.
    33. OHP, pp. 479-84, NR.
    34. Ibid.; Inman, "An Inside View," pp. 14-15, 28-29; Duggan, *Americas*, pp. 113-14.
    35. Memo by Rockefeller, Jan. 9, 1945, 710.11/1-945 CF; OHP, pp. 414-17, NR; Eduardo Santos, "Mis Conferencias con el Presidente Roosevelt y los Planes de Organización Militar Interamericana," *Revista de America* (April 1947), pp. 3-14; Bushnell, *Santos and the Good Neighbor*, pp. 6-23; Duggan, *Americas*, p. 112; Tulchin, *Aftermath of War*, p. 12.
    36. OHP, pp. 417-20, NR; Campbell, *Masquerade Peace*, pp. 114-15.
    37. Chap. conf., Feb. 26, 27, 28, 1945, B. 68, WA; OHP, pp. 484-91, NR; Inman, "An Inside View," pp. 25-26; ABnr, pp. 472-73; ESd, pp. 274-75.
    38. FR, 1945, 9:128-29; ABnr, pp. 470-72; ESd, p. 273.
    39. Diary, Feb. 27, 1945, B. 216, AB.
    40. Connally to Stettinius, Mar. 8, 710.Conference W-PW/3-845, memo by Johnson, Mar. 26, 1945,/3-2645; Chap. conf., Mar. 1, 2, 3, 5, 1945, B. 68, WA; diary, Mar. 1, 2, 1945, B. 285, ES; Blocker to Daniels, Mar. 6, 1945, B. 835, JD; Inman, "An Inside View," p. 30; FR, 1945, 9:139-40; ABnr, p. 472; ESd, pp. 276-77, 284; Russell, *United Nations Charter*, pp. 564-66.
    41. Diary, Feb. 25, 27, B. 285, Stettinius to Connally, Mar. 16, 1945, B. 729, ES; Chap. conf., Mar. 4, 6, 1945, B. 68, WA; OHP, pp. 465, 491-92, NR; Inman, "An Inside View," pp. 21-23, 35-37, ESd, pp. 277-78; FR, 1945, 9:122-23, 131-32, 135, 137, 148; Duggan, *Americas*, pp. 149, 155-56; Cline, *The United States and Mexico*, pp. 278-81; Blendon, "Venezuela and the United States," pp. 77-80; SW-5, pp. 237-41.
    42. Diary, Feb. 23, 24, 1945, B. 285, ES; diary, Mar. 13, 1945, V. 50, HS; San Fran. conf., June 4, 1945, B. 63, SI; WMR, Feb. 21, 1945; OHP, pp. 409-10, 453-59, 473, NR; Inman, "An Inside View," pp. 1, 24, 28; ESd, pp. 268-69; JFd, p. 35.

43. Diary, Mar. 5, 6, 7, 1945, B. 286, ES; Chap. conf., Mar. 7, 1945, B. 68, WA; Messersmith to Hull, July 31, 1945, B. unnumbered, CH; OHP, pp. 493-99, NR; ESd, pp. 286-88; ABnr, p. 474; SW-5, pp. 204-9.

44. Diary, Feb. 26, B. 285, Mar. 4, 8, 1945, B. 286, ES; FR, 1945, 9:142-44; Inman, "An Inside View," pp. 33-35; ESd, pp. 288, 290.

45. Messersmith to Stettinius, Mar. 12, 710.Conference W-PW/3-1245, Messersmith to FDR, Mar. 12,/3-1245, Lockett to Raynor, Mar. 22,/3-2245, Messersmith to Carrigan, Mar. 22,/3-2245, Rockefeller to King, Mar. 17, 1945,/3–1745; Messersmith to Austin, Mar. 13, Austin to Valentim Bouças, Mar.19, press by Mowrer, Mar. 8, 10, 1945, B. 13, WA; Aguirre to Daniels, Mar. 9, B. 835, Lockett to Daniels, Mar. 9, 1945, B. 838, JD; Inman, US-Chap., Feb.-March, 1945, B. 63, SI; FR, 1945, 9:149-50; ESd, p. 289; ABnr, p. 474, Stettinius, *FDR and the Russians*, p. 291; Duggan, *Americas*, pp. 116-17.

46. Comments by Austin, after conf., B. 13, WA.

47. Bursley to Daniels, Mar. 23, 1945, B. 835, JD; diary, Mar. 27, 1945, B. 12, WL; McKim to Hull, Mar. 28, 1945, B. 54, CH; FR, 1945, 9:150; Conil Paz and Ferrari, *Argentina's Foreign Policy*, pp. 127-31; Potash, *Army and Politics*, pp. 254-55; Duggan, *Americas*, pp. 115-16.

48. Stettinius to FDR, Mar. 27, 1945, B. 721, ES; Commentary by Walton, Mar. 29, 1945, B. 8, WA; ABnr, pp. 475-76, 525-26; Morris, *Rockefeller*, pp. 200-205.

49. Memo by Cabot, May 9, 1945, 500.CC/6-2145; memos by Hull, Apr. 2, 9, 1946, B. 55, CH; diary, Apr. 2, 1946, B. 12, WL; Woods, "United States' Policy toward Argentina," pp. 289-309; FR, 1945, 1:199-201; ESd, pp. 309-10; CHm, 2:1406-08.

50. Diary, Apr. 12, 1945, B. 12, WL; diary, Apr. 12, 1945, B. 16, JED; ABnr, pp. 526-28; Duggan, *Americas*, p. 60; Dozer, *Good Neighbors?*, pp. 147-51; Theodore Lippman, Jr., *The Squire of Warm Springs* (Chicago: Playboy Press, 1977), pp. 237-40.

51. *El Tiempo*, Apr. 17, 1945.

CHAPTER 16

1. Truman to Bowers, Apr. 26, 1945, Bowers mss II, CB; memo on Mexican Water Treaty, Mar. 13, CIO Latin American Affairs Committee, Mar. 14, 1945, B. 57, Series C, RL; McNaughton to Bermingham, Feb. 23, 1945, McNaughton Reports, FM; HTm, 1:75; Robert Donovan, *Conflict and Crisis* (New York: W. W. Norton, 1977), pp. x, xii-xiv, xvii, 3.

2. AVd, pp. 167-68; ASp, 2:233; HTm, 1:21, 310-11; Donovan, *Conflict and Crisis*, p. 17.

3. Diary, Apr. 16, 29, 1945, V. 51, HS.

4. Interview, NR.

5. Sweetser to Charron, Feb. 1, 1940, B. 16, Sweetser to Bonsal, July 28, B. 35, Sweetser to Welles, Aug. 5, B. 40, Sweetser to Grady, Aug. 7, 1941, memo by Sweetser, Aug. 6, 1942, B. 32, Sweetser to Welles, July 28, 1943, B. 40, AS, Mecham, *United States and Inter-American Security*, pp. 87-94.

6. Memo by Gosnell, Feb. 2, 1948, Welles file, WHBS; Graff, "Strategy of Involvement," pp. 382-94; SW-4, pp. 11-15, 28-33.

7. Graff, "Strategy of Involvement," pp. 395-403.

8. SW-4, pp. 66-75.

9. Welles to MacLeish, Aug. 13, 1942, B. 20, AM; Welles interview, Nov. 27, 1942, B. 40, AS; Welles to Inman, Mar. 1, 8, 1943, B. 15, SI; SW-4, pp. 76-82, 95-121; SW-5, p. 23.

10. Welles to Wallace, Dec. 30, 1942, R. 24, HW; Walker, "Wallace," pp. 154-71; *New York Times*, Dec. 29, 1942.

11. Diary, June 27, July 25, 1942, B. 214, AB; ABnr, p. 415; BLwd, p. 273; Russell, *United Nations Charter*, pp. 205-391.

12. Memo by Sweetser, Aug. 6, 1942, B. 32, AS.

13. PL, 2:1446-47; Forrest Davis, "Roosevelt's World Blueprint," *Saturday Evening Post* 215 (April 10, 1943): 20, 21, 109-10; SW-2, p. 189; Hassett, *Off the Record*, p. 166.

14. IAA, 4:45-46; Mecham, *United States and Inter-American Security*, pp. 252-53.
15. Caffery to Hull, Dec. 4, Welles to Caffery, Dec. 5, 740. 00111-AR/773, memo by Kelchner, Dec. 14, 20, 1939,/863, Fenwick to Welles, July 2, 1940, 710.Consultation 2/446, Aug. 29, 1941, 710.Consultation 3/15½, Fenwick to Duggan, Dec. 16, 1941, 740.0011 ARNC/219; Borchard to Moore, Nov. 24, Moore to Borchard, Nov. 25, 1939, B. 76, JM; FR, 1939, 5:45-47; Bonsal to Sweetser, Aug. 5, 1941, B. 35, AS; Permanent International Organization, Aug. 26, General International Organization, Dec. 11, 1943, B. 3, LP; Mecham, *United States and Inter-American Security*, pp. 234-35, 249-50; Callcott, *Western Hemisphere*, pp. 220-23; SW-3, pp. 212-13.
16. Hull to Scotten, Sept. 2, 710.11/2971, memo by Duggan, Dec. 18, 1943,/3161, June 14, 1944,/3328; Notter to Whitaker, Oct. 18, Commentary by Notter, Dec. 17, 1943, B. 191, HN; memo by Pasvolsky, July 11, 1944, B. 2, LP; OHP, pp. 348-50, NR; IAA, 4:46-47; Russell, *United Nations Charter*, pp. 59-75.
17. Duggan to Stettinius, Oct. 13, 1943, B. 191, HN.
18. Messersmith to Hull, Aug. 14, 710.11/8-1444, Aug. 22,/8-2244, Messersmith to McGurk, Sept. 5,/9-544, Berle to ARs, Sept. 13,/9-1344, Briggs to Hull, Nov. 16, 1944,/11-1644.
19. Sumner Welles, "The Shaping of Our Future," *Reader's Digest* 44 (July 1944): 41-44; *Newsweek*, Aug. 21, 1944; New York Times, Oct. 17, 1943, May 19, 30, June 24, 1944; SW-3, pp. 240-41, 368-70, 379-80, 403-5.
20. Stettinius diary, Aug. 24, 1944, B. 158, HN; memo by Stettinius, Sept. 27, 1944, B. 2, LP; Russell, *United Nations Charter*, pp. 392-408, 411-548; SW-5, pp. 34-35.
21. Diary, Aug. 28, 31, Sept. 1, 3, 4, 7, 1944, B. 158, HN; ESd, pp. 113, 118; AVd, pp. 115-18; Russell, *United Nations Charter*, pp. 442-44, 472-73; Mecham, *United States and Inter-American Security*, p. 247.
22. Memo by Cabot, Sept. 16, B. 290, Stettinius diary, Sept. 19, Oct. 5, 1944, B. 158, HN; Welles to MacLeish, Nov. 23, 1944, B. 20, AM; ESd, p. 141; *New York Times*, Oct. 5, 12, 1944; Russell, *United Nations Charter*, p. 551.
23. Stettinius diary, Oct. 6, 7, 1944, B. 158, HN.
24. PPA, 13:328-31.
25. Remarks by Stettinius, Oct. 12, meeting, Oct. 26, meeting, Nov. 9, memo for Stettinius, Dec. 28, meeting, Dec. 29, 1944, B. 2, LP; Rockefeller to Stettinius, Oct. 18, Stettinius to Rockefeller, Oct. 24, 1944, B. 707, ES; diary, Oct. 12, 1944, B. 5, BL; US Department of State, *Bulletin*, (Washington, D.C.: G.P.O., 1944), p. 525; ESd, pp. 160, 167; Russell, *United Nations Charter*, pp. 552-53.
26. Memo by Armour, Oct. 27, 710.Consultation 4/10-2744, Fenwick to Notter, Oct. 16, B. 291, HN, memo by Sandifer, Dec. 23, 1944, 710.Consultation 4/12-744, memo by Cabot, Jan. 2, 1945, 710.Conference W-PW/1-245; meeting, Jan. 26, 31, B. 2, memo of conversation, Jan. 8, 1945, B. 5, LP; Sweetser to Wallace, Jan. 30, 1945, B. 35, AS; FR, 1945, 1:10-11, 18, 27-35, 39, 46, 60-66; Abell, *Pearson*, 85.
27. Memo for Stettinius, Feb. 1, 1945, B. 5, LP.
28. Stettinius diary, Oct. 2, 1944, B. 158, HN, memo by Warren, Jan. 24, 1945, 710.Conference W-PW/1-2445; OHP, pp. 445-48, NR; FR, 1945, 1:12; Duggan, *Americas*, pp. 107-8; Bowers, *Chile*, pp. 128-30; Russell, *United Nations Charter*, pp. 506-9.
29. ESd, pp. 253-54; Stettinius, *FDR and the Russians*, pp. 199-200, 298; Russell, *United Nations Charter*, pp. 537-38, 556; Diane Clemens, *Yalta* (London: Oxford University Press, 1972), pp. 235-36.
30. Campbell, *Masquerade Peace*, p. 148; Russell, *United Nations Charter*, p. 543.
31. Rockefeller to Truman, Apr. 26, 1945, PPF 689 Nelson Rockefeller, HT; diary, May 21, 1945, B. 17, JED; OHP, pp. 531-33, 537-41, NR; AVd, p. 179; ESd, p. 337.
32. Stettinius diary, May 18, 1945, B. 282, HN; diary, May 25, June 4, 1945, B. 63, SI; OHP, pp. 410-12, NR.
33. Memoirs, vol. 3, no. 14, B. IX, GM.
34. Stettinius diary, Apr. 27, 1945, B. 282, HN; diary, May 29, June 4, 1945, B. 63, SI; OHP, pp. 528-29, 562-66, 570-73, 612-19, NR; interview, NR; Morris, *Rockefeller*, pp. 203-8; Duggan, *Americas*, pp. 118-19.

35. Rockefeller to Stettinius, Apr. 17, 1945, B. 721, ES; OHP, pp. 528-30, NR; FR, 1945, 1:328-29; ESd, pp. 324-25; Stettinius, *FDR and the Russians*, pp. 113, 199-200.

36. Stettinius diary, Apr. 27, B. 282, memo by Bohlen, Apr. 28, 1945, B. 278, HN; OHP, pp. 541-46, 550-62, 566-67, 573-81, NR; Oreamuno memos, Apr. 24, 1945, PAMR, NR; FR, 1945, 1:389, 394, 396-98, 400-401, 409, 411-13, 417-18, 483, 485, 486-88; ESd, pp. 340-44; AVd, pp. 177-78; Dilks, *Diary of Sir Alexander Cadogan*, pp. 735-37; Russell, *United Nations Charter*, pp. 631-33, 636-39; SW-5, pp. 41-42.

37. Stettinius diary, Apr. 30, 1945, B. 282, HN; diary, Apr. 30, 1945, B. 16, JED; FR, 1945, 1:501, 510; AVd, p. 182; ESd, pp. 344-45; HTm, 1:313-15; Morris, *Rockefeller*, pp. 209-14.

38. Stettinius diary, May 2, 29, 30, 1945, B. 282, HN; Grew to Braden, May 24, 1945, B. 18, AM; OHP, pp. 580-83, NR; Woods, "United States' Policy toward Argentina," pp. 326-32; ESd, p. 347.

39. Davies to a senator, diary, May, B. 16, diary, May 21, June 9, Davies to a friend, July 1945, B. 17, JED; diary, May 29, 1945, B. 63, SI; HWpv, pp. 439-40, 447.

40. Diary, May 29, 30, June 1, 9, 1945, B. 63, SI; HWpv, p. 444.

41. ABnr, pp. 530-33, 537, 538.

42. Memo by Savage, May 3, 1945, B. 4, LP; diary, May 12, 1945, B. 68, WA; diary, May 22, 1945, B. 17, JED; diary, June 4, 1945, V. 51, HS; presidential diary, memo of conversation, June 20, 1945, B. 7, HM; Messersmith to Hull, July 31, 1945, B. unnumbered, CH; FR, 1945, 1:531-32; WMR, July 31, 1945; HWpv, pp. 456-57; Krock, *Memoirs*, pp. 209-11; CHm, 2:1405-6.

43. Memo of phone conversation, May 10, 1945, B. 4, LP.

44. OHP, pp. 528, 530, NR; FR, 1945, 1:301-6; *New York Times*, Apr. 12, 1945.

45. Diary, Apr. 26, May 2, 10, 1945, V. 51, HS; FR, 1945, 1:591-97.

46. Diary, Apr. 29, 1945, V. 51, HS.

47. FR, 1945, 1:604-5, 607-12, 832-36; for another view of this issue, see: J. Tillapaugh, "Closed Hemisphere and Open World? The Dispute over Regional Security at the U.N. Conference, 1945," *Diplomatic History* 2 (Winter 1978): 25-42.

48. Stettinius diary, May 5, 1945, B. 282, HN; memo by Lockwood, May 5, 1945, B. 4, LP; FR, 1945, 1:613, 615, 630.

49. OHP, pp. 583-87, NR; Morris, *Rockefeller*, pp. 215-18.

50. Stettinius diary, May 7, 1945, B. 282, HN; OHP, pp. 587-93, NR; FR, 1945, 1:614, 617-28, 631-40; AVd, pp. 187-89; ESd, pp. 349-52.

51. ESd, p. 353.

52. Memo by Reed, May 7, 500.CC/6-2145, memo by Reed, memo by Cabot, May 8, 1945,/6-2145; Abnr, p. 536; Duggan, *Americas*, pp. 199-22.

53. Stettinius diary, May 8, 1945, B. 282, HN; ESd, pp. 353-55.

54. Memo by Cabot, May 9, 10, 1945, 500.CC/6-2145, Stettinius diary, May 8, 9, 10, 1945, B. 282, HN; memo of phone conversation, May 10, 1945, B. 4, LP; AVd, pp. 189-90; FR, 1945, 1:642-51.

55. Stettinius diary, May 11, 1945, B. 282, HN; OHP, pp. 593-606, NR; interview, NR; FR, 1945, 1:657-72.

56. Stettinius diary, May 12, 1945, B. 282, HN; diary, May 12, 1945, B. 68, WA; ESd, pp. 359-63; Dilks, *Diary of Sir Alexander Cadogan*, p. 741; AVd, pp. 191-92; FR, 1945, 1:674-86, 691, 707.

57. Memo by Reed, memo by Cabot, May 14, 500.CC/6-2145, memo by Cabot, May 15, 1945,/6-2145; memo by Sandifer, May 14, memo of meeting, May 15, 1945, B. 278, Stettinius diary, May 14, 15, 1945, B. 282, HN; AVd, pp. 192-93; ESd, pp. 364-71; FR, 1945, 1:707-10, 712-25, 730-39, 749; US Department of State, *Bulletin* (Washington, D.C.: G.P.O., 1945), p. 930.

58. Memo by Cabot, May 20, 1945, 500.CC/6-2145; memo of meeting, May 20, 1945, B. 278, Stettinius diary, May 16, 17, 19, 20, 24, 1945, B. 282, HN; memo of phone conversation, June 6, 1945, B. 4, LP; diary, June 14, 1945, B. 63, SI; interview, NR; FR, 1945, 1:758-61, 776, 780-82, 799-802, 812, 815-19, 823-26; AVd, pp. 197-98, 210, 366; ESd, p. 372; Dilks, *Diary of Sir Alexander Cadogan*, p. 744; ABnr, p. 475;

Morris, *Rockefeller*, pp. 218-22; Russell, *United Nations Charter*, pp. 688-712; *The Charter of the United Nations*; Ezequiel Padilla, "The American System and the World Organization," *Foreign Affairs* 24 (October 1945): 99-107.
  59. Memo by Cabot, May 3, 7, 19, 1945, 500.CC/6-2145; Stettinius diary, May 22, 26, B. 282, June 2, 4, 11, 15, 16, 1945, B. 283, HN; diary, May 28, June 15, 1945, B. 63, SI; memo of conversation, Apr. 21, 1945, B. 4, LP; memo on state dept., undated, B. 225, HA; Welles to Wallace, June 1, 1945, B. 35, HW; OHP, pp. 606-12, NR; interview, NR; FR, 1945, 1:356-60, 656, 843-44, 917; ESd, pp. 376-79, 381; Campbell, *Masquerade Peace*, pp. 177-87.

EPILOGUE

  1. Rockefeller to Byrnes, Aug. 15, 1945, 710.11/8-1545; Donovan, *Conflict and Crisis*, p. 17; Acheson, *Present at the Creation*, pp. 110, 199; Braden, *Demagogues and Diplomats*, p. 337; Collier and Horowitz, *Rockefellers*, p. 243.
  2. Daniel Cosio Villegas, "Sobre Estados Unidos" *Revista de América* (March 1945), p. 365.
  3. Francisco to Dreier, Jan. 6, 710.11/1-645, memo by Munro, Sept. 28,/9-2845, Messersmith to Byrnes, Oct. 16, 1945,/10-1645; memo on Latin America 1945, March 1945, B. 12, JW; MacLeish to Grew, July 17, 1945, B. 8, AM.
  4. Braden, *Demagogues and Diplomats*, pp. 316-37, 339, 356-70.
  5. Inman to Acheson, Feb. 15, Mar. 18, July 25, Acheson to Inman, Mar. 4, Sept. 12, 1949, B. 16, Wallace to Inman, Feb. 3, 1955, B. 17, SI; Walker, "Wallace," p. 61.
  6. Welles to Wallace, Sept. 15, 1952, R. 49, HW.
  7. CHm, 2:1422-26; Pratt, "Hull," 12:139-79, 13:677-717.
  8. Welles to Pell, Nov. 11, 1946, B. 15, HP; Welles to Inman, Feb. 21, 1949, B. 16, SI; SW-5, pp. 183, 388; SW-2, pp. 228-29.
  9. Duggan, *Americas*, pp. 61, 75-76, 82, 209-10, 214-17.
  10. Nelson Rockefeller, *The Rockefeller Report on the Americas* (Chicago: Quadrangle Books, 1969), p. 43.

INDEX

Acheson, Dean: diplomacy of, in 1940, 117; and low hemispheric priority, 226-27

Ackerman, Carl: comments on Nazi opposition by, 143-44; criticism of OIAA by, 153

Act of Chapultepec: assessment of, 208; importance of, at San Francisco conference, 223; Pasvolsky's opinion of, 220; postwar treaty issue and, 226; provisions of, 207; Vandenberg's interpretation of, 221-22

Act of Havana, 100-102

Admiral Graf Spee: Argentine protest against, 188; sea battle of, 88-90

Agricultural Adjustment Act, hemispheric impact of, 44

Agriculture, U.S. role in hemisphere, 157

Agriculture Department (U.S.), hemispheric interest of, 44

Air Corps: hemispheric, 138; Mexican squadron of, 136; and U.S. flights to Latin America, 130; and U.S. hemispheric position, 141

Airlines, German and U.S. influences on, in Latin America, 108-9

American League of Nations: Argentine opposition to, 74; discussion of, 62; Lima conference and, 75-76; Welles's opposition to, 212

"American Newsletter," 152

Antarctica, PAU trusteeship, 96-98

Anti-Comintern pact, 62

Anti-Semitism: Bolivian, 185; and persecution discussion, 78; FDR on Argentine, 195

Anti-War Pact, role of, at Montevideo conference, 24

Aranha, Oswaldo: Bolivian nonrecognition criticism of, 187, relations of, with Welles, 122, 174; Rio conference role of, 122-24; U.S. trip of, 42-43; and U.S. military talks, 128-29

Arciniegas, Germán, on FDR's death, 209

Argentina: alleged Nazi coup in, 114-15; Axis leanings of, 122-23, 188; and Berle-Perón meeting, 200; and Bolivian revolt in 1943, 185-87; bond sales of, 7; British interests in, 194-95, 203; Buenos Aires conference and, 61-67; Castillo's position, 98, 121; Chapultepec resolution and, 208; Chilean relations with, 124; cruiser deal objections of, 128; currency stabilization in, 190; Duggan's views of, 191; exclusion of, from Chapultepec, 197, 204, 207; Export-Import Bank loan, 190; German population in, 93; and Gilbert's diplomacy, 193; *Admiral Graf Spee* incident and, 89; Italian immigration to, 105; and League of Nations, 62; and Lima conference, 74, 77, 79; military strength of, 190; multilateralism and, 122; neutrality, 192; and no transfer, 98, 99, 100; nonbelligerency proposal of, 188; and Ortiz, 98, 121; Panama conference and, 83; proposal by, for 1944 meeting, 196-97, 199, 201; and Ramírez, 191, 193; Reciprocal trade agreement of, 48, 190; recognition of, in 1945, 218; Rio conference and, 124; Rockefeller's views on, 200; FDR's opinion of, 195; and Saavedra Lamas, 23; sale of canned corned beef by, 189-90; San Francisco conference and, 218-20; severance of Axis ties by, 125, 191-93; Stettinius's opposition to, 219; U.S. cattle dispute with, 189; U.S. freezing funds to, 193; U.S. nonrecognition of, 193-94; U.S. recognition of, 209; U.S. rivalry with, 187; war declaration by, 208; Welles's views on, 172, 173, 188, 191

Arias, Arnulfo, 33

Arias, Harmodio, 32-33

Armaments race: Brazilian cruiser deal and, 128; during WW II, 137-38; Santos-FDR visit and, 206; U.S.

Farrell, Edelmiro: as Argentine president, 193-94; and recognition issue, 218; role of, in proposed meeting, 199
Federal Reserve System, opposition of, to inter-American bank, 160
Feis, Herbert: antipathy of, toward Hitler, 111; on bond collections, 40; and Brazilian aid, 43; and diplomatic movement of 1933, 27; on Japanese expansion, 106; as Republican hold-over, 14
Fifth International Conference of American States, attack on U.S. at, 7, 8
First Meeting of Consultation of Ministers of Foreign Affairs of the American Republics. See Panama conference
First Meeting of Finance Ministers of the American Republics, importance of, 159
"Flying caravan." See People's Mandate to End War
Flying Fortress. See Air Corps
Food production, OIAA efforts at, 167
Foreign Bondholders Protective Council (FBPC), 40
Forrestal, James: appointment of, 148; on Brazilian steel mill, 162; friendship of, with Rockefeller, 149
France: colonies of, 102-3; fall of, 94-95; and Martinique issue, 102-3; reaction of, to Lima conference, 77; regionalism view of, 221; and St. Pierre affair, 103
Franco, Francisco, 105
Franklin, Benjamin, impact of, on Latin America, 142
Free French, St. Pierre affair and, 103
"Further Measures to Intensify Cooperation of the War Effort" (committee of Chapultepec conference), 205

Gadsden Purchase Treaty, importance of, to Mexico, 30
Galapagos Islands: hemispheric defense of, 184; U.S. purchase of, 96
Gandía, Enrique M., 147
Gaston, Herbert, 159
Gau Ausland, definition of, 106
General Motors: hemispheric economic role of, 164; Stettinius's position with, 181
Geneva Disarmament Conference, 12
Germany: and Admiral Graf Spee, 88-90; airline operations, 108-9; and alleged Bolivian coup, 50; and Argentine activities, 188-89; barter system of, 106-7; and Bismarck affair, 113-14; and Bolivian 1943 revolt, 185-86; cartel opposition of, 94; commercial

treaty of, with Brazil, 47-48; economic absorption of Latin America by, 106-9; fear of hemispheric invasion by, 64, 78-79, 114; financial penetration by, 43; and Havana conference, 99, 101; and immigration, 106; invasion of Russia by, 134; and Lima conference, 78-79; military resurgence of, 221; radio broadcasts by, 152; subversion and, 114-15; supporters in hemisphere, 106; and Panama conference activities, 85; Polish invasion by, 82; population in Argentina, 93; and security zone, 90-92; and FDR's Buenos Aires speech, 65; and FDR on economic penetration, 93; and FDR on hemispheric penetration, 82; and underestimate of U.S. policies, 104; and U.S. inaction, 188; and U.S. military plans, 130; and view of Monroe Doctrine, 94-95; war declaration on U.S. by, 123
Gibson, Hugh, 16
Gilbert, Alberto, 193
Gilbert, Prentiss, 109
Glass, Carter, 160
Globalism: Eden's support of, 223; Pasvolsky's support of, 220; postwar emphasis on, 226
Gómez, Juan, 55
Gómez, Miguel, 37-38
Good Neighbor policy: administration guidelines for, 72; and aid to British, 133; Berle's views on, 81, 121; and Bolivian oil dispute, 50; and Bowers's position, 119; and Hugh Butler's attack, 184; Nicholas Butler's view on, 144; Castle criticism of, 80; Commerce Department's comments on, 167; complexities of, 72; definition of, 1-2; Duggan's role in, 81; end of, 1933, 27-28; endorsement of, at Buenos Aires conference, 68; and extension of world involvement, 12, 25, 104; fragility of, 120; growth of, 226; lack of comprehension of, 170; Latin American rulers' stake in, 38; massive public relations for, 73; Montevideo conference impact on, 26; and non-intervention, 39; position of, in 1936, 60, 63; postwar hopes for, 226; FDR's role in, 11, 38, 68, 81-82, 170-71; reasons of, 225, 228; as solely applied to Latin America, 72; termination of, 209-11; Truman's role in, 224; Wallace's view of, 171; Welles's role in, 81
Graf Spee. See Admiral Graf Spee
Grau San Martín, Ramón, 20, 36
Great Britain: on Argentine admission

Rockefeller Foundation: as IIAA model, 166; Latin American role of, 143
Roosevelt, Eleanor, 171
Roosevelt, Franklin D.: and accusations of Nazi coups, 114-15; Allied hemispheric objectives of, 102-4; anti-Nazi crusade of, 112-13; Argentine activities of, 189-90, 195, 209, 218; as assistant secretary of navy, 10-11; and "associated nations" issue, 216; and Bankhead funeral, 176; BEW dismantling by, 169; and bondholders, 40, 161; and Brazilian issues, 43, 171, 215; and Buenos Aires conference, 61-65, 67; Bullitt visit to, 177-78; and Camacho meeting, 171; Caribbean visit of, 38; Chautuaqua address of, 64; on Chilean defense, 173; Colombian visit of, 38; on Cuban affairs, 10, 18, 21; and Daniels's friendship, 54; death of, 209, 216; and DeGaulle conflict, 103; and destroyer deal, 101; and Easter Islands purchase, 96; economic priorities of, 163; and Export-Import Bank, 99, 162; and fear of Nazi penetration, 10-11, 82, 93, 114-16; and foundation of OIAA, 148; Forrestal appointment by, 148; fourth term of, 198; Galapagos purchase by, 96; and Geneva Disarmament Conference, 12; and German map issue, 115; good neighbor policy of, 16-17, 65, 68, 81-82, 170-71; and Greenland, 102; and Haiti, 10, 34; and Havana conference, 100; and hemispheric cartel, 93; and hemispheric defense, 75, 93, 134, 238, 272; and hemispheric economics, 93; on Hoover and Latin America, 10; and Hull's role, 12-13, 118-19, 159, 179; and Iceland, 92; Knox appointment by, 94; Latin American views of, 10, 227; and Mexico, 10, 17, 29-30, 50; on military nonintervention, 21; and Monroe Doctrine, 11-12; Moore appointment by, 70; and Montevideo conference, 22-23, 25-27; and Munich, 113; and Nicaragua, 11; and no transfer resolutions, 101; on nonintervention, 27; and nonrecognition, 21; and "Our Foreign Policy," 11; and oil expropriation, 53; and Padilla proposal, 196; Pan American Address of, 11-12; and Pan American highway, 41; and Pan American trusteeship, 98; and Panama Treaty of 1936, 32-33; and Panamanian registration, 84; personality conflicts of, 44; Phillips's appointment by, 13; press coverage

of, in Latin America, 151; and reciprocal trade, 27, 45; and Rio conference, 125; and regionalism as a global pivot, 17, 63-64, 80; Rockefeller's relationship to, 149, 198-99; and St. Pierre affair, 103; and Santos meeting, 206; and security zone issue, 84-85, 91-92; and sergeants' revolt, 20; and Soviet aid, 175; and stab-in-the-back speech, 94; Stimson appointment by, 94; on tariff issue, 44-45; and U.S. business in Latin America, 157; on warships for Brazil, 128; Welles's relationship to, 13, 17, 19, 70, 118-19, 177-79, 227; and world organization, 213, 215
Roosevelt, Theodore, 32
Roosevelt Corollary, definition of, 5
Roper, Daniel, 46
Rossetti, Juan: as Chilean diplomat, 122; political ambitions of, 172; Rio conference role of, 124
Rubber, Latin American production of, 158
Rubber Reserve Corporation, 163
Ruiz Guiñazú, Enrique, 122-25

Saavedra Lamas, Carlos: background of, 23; and Anti-War Pact, 24; Buenos Aires conference role of, 65; Chaco War role of, 60-61, 187-88; European outlook of, 66; Montevideo conference role of, 187; opposition of, to consultation, 76; relationship of, to Hull, 24, 67
Sacasa, Juan, 31
St. Louis affair, Jewish refugees and, 185
St. Pierre, 103
Saludos Amigos, 153
Sandino, Augusto, 31
San Francisco conference: Articles 51 through 54, 224; meeting, 215-24; prelude to, 208, 211
Santos, Eduardo, 206
Sarmiento, Domingo, 142
Sayre, Francis: as assistant secretary, 46; opposition of, to German barter, 107
Scadta, 108-9
Schools, Protestant efforts at, in Latin America, 142
Scotten, Robert, 72
Second Meeting of Consultation of Ministers of Foreign Affairs of the American Republics. See Havana conference
Security zone: Argentine background of, 83; British use of, 115-16; criticism of, 89; Danish colonies in, 102; and diplomatic argument, 90; extension of size of, 91; German adherence to,

Library of Congress Cataloging in Publication Data

Gellman, Irwin F.
    Good neighbor diplomacy.

    (The Johns Hopkins University studies in historical
and political science; 97th ser., no. 2)
    Includes bibliographical references and index.
    1. Latin America–Relations (general) with the United
States. 2. United States–Relations (general) with
Latin America. 3. United States–Foreign relations–
1933-1945.   I.   Title.   II.   Series: Johns Hopkins
University. Studies in historical and political
science; 97th ser., no. 2.
F1418.G37   301.29'73'08   79-7561
ISBN 0-8018-2250-5